The Effects of Globalisation on Firm and Labour Performance

This book examines driving factors and the effects of globalisation on economic development through firm and product-level data.

The book is organised into four themes, i.e., productivity, innovation, wage and income gap, and within-firm reallocation of resources. The comprehensiveness and richness of firm and product-level data shed light upon the channels through which trade and investment affect firms' competitiveness and unveil factors shaping firms' heterogeneous responses towards globalisation. The book looks at Asian economies as well as Australia and how they have experienced substantial structural change and become more integrated into the global economy and will be a useful reference for those who are interested in learning more about the relationship between globalisation and firm performance.

This book will appeal to policy makers and researchers interested in the impact of globalisation on firm performance.

Chin Hee Hahn is Professor of Economics at Gachon University and the editor-in-chief of *The Korean Economic Forum* of Korean Economic Association.

Dionisius Narjoko is a senior economist at the Economic Research Institute for ASEAN and East Asia (ERIA).

Ha Thi Thanh Doan is an economist at the Economic Research Institute for ASEAN and East Asia (ERIA).

Shujiro Urata is Professor of Economics at Graduate School of Asia-Pacific Studies, Waseda University, Senior Research Advisor, Economic Research Institute for ASEAN and East Asia (ERIA).

Routledge-ERIA Studies in Development Economics

Production Networks in Southeast Asia
Edited by Lili Yan Ing and Fukunari Kimura

The Indonesian Economy
Trade and Industrial Policies
Edited by Lili Yan Ing, Gordon H. Hanson and Sri Mulyani Indrawati

Social Protection Goals in East Asia
Strategies and Methods to Generate Fiscal Space
Edited by Mukul G. Asher, Fauziah Zen and Astrid Dita

World Trade Evolution
Growth, Productivity and Employment
Edited by Lili Yan Ing and Miaojie Yu

Emerging Global Trade Governance
Mega Free Trade Agreements and Implications for ASEAN
Edited by Lurong Chen, Shujiro Urata, Junji Nakagawa and Masahito Ambashi

East Asian Integration
Goods, Services and Investment
Edited by Lili Yan Ing, Martin Richardson and Shujiro Urata

Developing the Digital Economy in ASEAN
Edited by Lurong Chen and Fukunari Kimura

The Effects of Globalisation on Firm and Labour Performance
Edited by Chin Hee Hahn, Dionisius Narjoko, Ha Thi Thanh Doan and Shujiro Urata

For more information about this series, please visit www.routledge.com/Routledge-ERIA-Studies-in-Development-Economics/book-series/ERIA

The Effects of Globalisation on Firm and Labour Performance

Edited by
Chin Hee Hahn,
Dionisius Narjoko,
Ha Thi Thanh Doan
and Shujiro Urata

Routledge
Taylor & Francis Group
LONDON AND NEW YORK

ERIA
Economic Research Institute
for ASEAN and East Asia

First published 2021
by Routledge
2 Park Square, Milton Park, Abingdon, Oxon OX14 4RN

and by Routledge
605 Third Avenue, New York, NY 10017

First issued in paperback 2022

Routledge is an imprint of the Taylor & Francis Group, an informa business

British Library Cataloguing-in-Publication Data
A catalogue record for this book is available from the British Library

Library of Congress Cataloging-in-Publication Data
A catalog record has been requested for this book

ISBN: 978-0-367-50710-7 (pbk)
ISBN: 978-0-367-50709-1 (hbk)
ISBN: 978-1-003-05090-2 (ebk)

DOI: 10.4324/9781003050902

Typeset in Galliard
by codeMantra

Contents

Figures

Tables

Contributors

Rafaelita M. Aldaba is Competitiveness and Innovation Undersecretary at the Philippine Department of Trade and Industry. She is formerly Senior Research Fellow and Vice President of the Philippine Institute for Development Studies.

Bo-Young Choi has been an Assistant Professor at the School of Economics and Trade, Kyungpook National University, South Korea since 2018.

Yong-Seok Choi is Professor of Economics at Kyung Hee University. Previously, he worked at the Bank of Korea and subsequently at the Korea Development Institute. As such, his research interests cover not only academic issues but also policy-oriented ones in the fields of international trade and economic growth.

Mi Dai is Associate Professor at the Business School, Beijing Normal University, China. He is also a non-resident fellow at Economic Development Center, Institute of World Economics and Politics at the Chinese Academy of Social Sciences.

Ha Thi Thanh Doan is an economist at the Economic Research Institute for ASEAN and East Asia (ERIA).

Chin Hee Hahn is Professor of Economics at Gachon University and the editor-in-chief of *The Korean Economic Forum* of the Korean Economic Association.

Kazunobu Hayakawa is Senior Research Fellow at the Development Studies Center, Institute of Developing Economies (IDE), Japan. He is also Editor for *Developing Economies* and Associate Editor for the *Asian Economic Journal*.

Kenta Ikeuchi is a Fellow at the Research Institute of Economy, Trade and Industry (RIETI), Japan. He is also Visiting Researcher at the National Institute of Science and Technology Policy (NISTEP) and Visiting Scholar at the SciREX Center, National Graduate Research Institute for Policy Studies (GRIPS), Japan.

Keiko Ito is Professor in the Faculty of Commerce, Chuo University. She is also Managing Editor of the *Asian Economic Journal*.

Juthathip Jongwanich is Associate Professor in the Faculty of Economics, Thammasat University. She works as an international consultant for various international organizations including the World Bank, the Asian Development Bank, and the Economic Research Institute of ASEAN and East Asia (ERIA). She currently serves as editor of *Thailand and the World Economy*.

Cassey Lee Hong Kim has been a Senior Fellow at the Institute of Southeast Asian Studies (ISEAS) – Yusof Ishak Institute in Singapore since 2014. He is also Coordinator for the Regional Economic Studies Programme at the Institute.

Archanun Kohpaiboon is an Associate Professor in the Faculty of Economics, Thammasat University. He works as an international consultant for international organizations including the World Bank, the Asian Development Bank, the Asian Development Bank Institute, and ERIA. He also serves as the associate editor of *Asian Economic Journal* and *Thailand and the World Economy*.

Qing Liu is Professor at the National Academy of Development and Strategy, Renmin University of China (RUC).

Toshiyuki Matsuura is Associate Professor at Keio Economic Observatory, Keio University.

Dionisius Narjoko is a Senior Economist at the Economic Research Institute for ASEAN and East Asia (ERIA).

Alfons Palangkaraya is Deputy Director, Centre for Transformative Innovation, Swinburne University of Technology, Australia, and Associate Professor in Economics, Centre for Transformative Innovation at the same university.

Chandra Tri Putra is a PhD Candidate in Economics at Arndt-Corden Department of Economics, Crawford School of Public Policy, Australian National University (ANU).

Ju Hyun Pyun has been Associate Professor at Korea University Business School (KUBS) since 2013. He is also Area Chair, International Business at KUBS, and Associate Editor for *Korean Economic Review*, *International Economic Journal*, and *Asian Economic Journal*.

Larry Dongxiao Qiu is the Sydney SW Leong Chair Professor of Economics, Head of Department of Economics, Lingnan University, Hong Kong

Sadayuki Takii is Professor in the Department of Economics, Seinan Gakuin University, Fukuoka, Japan.

Shandre Mugan Thangavelu is the Professor and Vice President of the Jeffrey Cheah Institute for Southeast Asia and Senior Fellow at Jeffrey Sachs Centre for Sustainable Development, Sunway University. He is also the Regional Director (Southeast Asia) of the Asia Growth Research Centre, Institute for International Trade at University of Adelaide.

Shujiro Urata is Professor of Economics at the Graduate School of Asia-Pacific Studies, Waseda University and Senior Research Advisor, Economic Research Institute for ASEAN and East Asia (ERIA).

Miaojie Yu is Deputy Dean at the National School of Development, Peking University. University Liberal Art Chair Professor & Chang-Jiang Scholar, and Deputy Editor for *China Economic Journal.*

Yifan Zhang is Associate Professor at Department of Economics, Chinese University of Hong Kong. He is also associate editor for China Economic Review.

Acknowledgements

We would like to thank Professor Hidetoshi Nishimura, President of the Economic Research Institute for ASEAN and East Asia (ERIA); Professor Fukunari Kimura, Chief Economist of ERIA; and other ERIA researchers and staff for their generous support of a series of Microdata Projects since 2010. We are also thankful to the participants of the Microdata Projects, who have contributed greatly to the successful outcome of the projects.

Materials from the following articles are reproduced with permission:

Choi, B.-Y., and J.-H. Pyun (2018), 'Does Real Exchange Rate Depreciation Increase Productivity? Analysis Using Korean Firm-Level Data', *The World Economy*, 41(2), pp. 604–33.

Hahn, C.-H., and Y.-S. Choi (2017), 'Trade Liberalisation and the Wage Skill Premium in Korean Manufacturing Plants: Do Plants' R&D and Investment Matter?', *The World Economy*, 40(6), pp. 1214–32.

Ito, K., and K. Ikeuchi (2017), 'Overseas Expansion and Domestic Business Restructuring in Japanese Firms', *The Developing Economies*, 55(2), pp. 75–104.

Jongwanich, J., and A. Kohpaiboon (2017), 'Trade Protection and Firm Productivity: Evidence from Thai Manufacturing', *The Developing Economies*, 55(2), pp. 130–57.

Liu, Q., L. Qiu, and M. Yu (2017), 'Worker Training, Firm Productivity, and Trade Liberalization: Evidence from Chinese firms', *The Developing Economies*, 55(3), pp. 189–209.

1 Introduction

Chin Hee Hahn, Dionisius Narjoko, Ha Thi Thanh Doan and Shujiro Urata

1.1 Background and objectives

This book consists of 13 selected country studies that were conducted in a series of ERIA (Economic Research Institute for ASEAN and East Asia) Microdata Projects in the 2010–2017 fiscal years. These projects aimed to clarify the effects of globalization on firms and the aggregate economy, as well as the globalization process itself, utilizing firm or firm product-level microdata, although the specific theme of each year's project varied.[1] Chapters in this book cover nine countries in the Asia-Pacific region: Australia, China, Indonesia, Japan, Korea, Malaysia, Philippines, Thailand, and Vietnam. The topics can be classified broadly into four categories: globalization, productivity and innovation (Ch.2–Ch.6), globalization and wage/income inequality (Ch.7–Ch.9), foreign direct investment (FDI) and domestic production structure/organization (Ch.10–Ch.12), and exchange rate, firm productivity and product choice (Ch.13–Ch.14).

During the past few decades, countries in the Asia-Pacific region, or East Asia in particular, have undergone tremendous changes in their economies and economic structures, which probably dwarf those in countries elsewhere. Above all, countries in this region have become more closely integrated through trade and foreign investment, not only among themselves but also with countries in other regions. At the same time, many of them have exhibited strong and sustained economic growth. Although most researchers and observers accept that globalization was at least one of the main driving forces behind the rapid growth of East Asian countries, exactly how and through what mechanism it promoted economic growth have not been satisfactorily understood. This provides the main motivation for many studies in this volume.

Rapid growth dramatically raised the living standards of the citizens but there were also some worrisome developments as well, such as rising within-country income inequality, as exemplified by the Chinese experience. In some countries, such as Japan, there was also a concern raised that the outbound FDI of firms may hurt the domestic economy by reducing domestic production and employment of multinationals as well as their supplier firms. Did globalization really contribute to rising wage/income inequality in East Asian countries? If so, exactly how and to what extent? Answering these questions provides another motivation for this volume.

During the past several decades, there has been a surge in empirical research that aims to understand the causes and effects of globalization utilizing firm- or firm-product-level microdata. This trend was triggered mainly by the appearance of monopolistic competition trade models with heterogenous firms, led by Melitz, which consider firm heterogeneity as the key building block, as well as by the increased availability of microdata to researchers. Melitz's model and its extensions show that trade induces a selection of more efficient firms into global activities (exporting and FDI) and makes less efficient firms contract and exit, leading to aggregate efficiency gains. Thus, the recent monopolistic trade model shows that the gains from trade are realized by increased product variety, the pro-competitive effect of lower prices, and selection-based between-firm resource reallocation, which go beyond the traditional gains from trade in comparative advantage trade models.

Most empirical studies along this line seem to have been guided by the theoretical models above and have certainly contributed a lot to understanding the causes and effects of globalization. However, whether recent trade models, as well as empirical studies guided by them, satisfactorily explain the causes and effects of globalization in the real world is, at the very least, arguable. For example, most, if not all, monopolistic competition trade models are based on the assumption that firm productivity is exogenously determined and not affected by their global engagements. However, whether this assumption adequately reflects reality may be questionable. In the real world, firms' global activities, such as exporting and FDI, may have beneficial effects on their own productivity and innovation as well as on the productivity of other firms through spillovers. Evidence of this possibility is provided by some of the chapters in this volume. To take another example, most recent trade models abstract away from inter-firm buyer-supplier linkages along the supply chain. Clarifying how the effects of globalization propagate through this linkage is likely to help us better understand the experiences of East Asian countries as well as the effects of globalization in general. Several chapters in this volume address this issue.

The chapters in this volume taken together give us the following several messages regarding the effects of globalization. First, globalization is likely to have positive effects, through various channels, on firm productivity and, hence, the aggregate economy, which may well go beyond those effects that are identified by standard monopolistic competition trade models. Firm productivity may rise in response to globalization through spillovers between foreign and domestic firms or from advanced foreign knowledge embodied in imported intermediate inputs. It may also rise as a result of the increased competition associated with output tariff reductions, which raise firms' incentive to conduct do R&D or to improve worker quality. Insofar as long-run economic growth of a country is driven by productivity improvement, the productivity-enhancing effects of globalization, as evidenced in this volume, suggest that globalization promotes long-run economic growth. If we take this effect into account, the gains from trade in the real world may be much larger than conventional estimates of the gains from trade based on standard theories.

Second, globalization may interact with skill-biased technical progress or within-firm changes in production structures to increase wage inequality between skilled and unskilled workers. We find some evidence of this effect in some countries (Japan, Korea, and Vietnam). However, it is not clear whether this conclusion can be generalized in other countries. Even when globalization affects wages of workers, it is not clear, either, whether it worsens *income* inequality across regions. Chapter 8 shows that, in the case of China, import tariff reductions lowered, rather than increased, income inequality across Chinese cities.

Third, some of the concerns casually expressed about the possible adverse effects of outbound FDI on domestic supplier firms may be exaggerated or even may not be supported by evidence. Chapter 11 shows evidence that Japanese firms' outbound FDI strengthens, rather than weakens, their existing transaction ties with domestic supplier firms. It shows further evidence that outbound FDI increases, rather than decreases, the employment of domestic supplier firms. More generally, the existence of inter-firm transaction linkages, which are mostly abstracted away in standard trade models, may play an important role in determining the effects of globalization in the real world. Further examination of this issue seems to be a profitable avenue for future research.

Below are the synopses of what follows.

1.2 Synopses

1.2.1 Globalization, productivity, and innovation

Liu, Qiu, and Yu's paper (Chapter 2), "Worker Training, Firm Productivity, and Trade Liberalization: Evidence from Chinese Firms", explores a novel mechanism, worker training, through which output tariff reduction affects firm productivity and its export market participation. The authors argue that one important question that has not received adequate attention in the literature is how exactly trade policy changes induce firms to improve productivity and, thereby, enter the export market. This paper argues that worker training is one important mechanism: the pro-competitive effect associated with tariff reduction on final goods is stronger for ex-ante low-productivity firms, so that the tariff reduction causes them to spend more on worker training, which boosts their productivity and enables them to enter export market more easily. In order to examine these mechanisms empirically, their paper employs disaggregated Chinese firm-level production data from 2004 to 2006. After controlling for firm's self-selection to invest in worker training, the authors obtain the following empirical results. First, with fiercer import competition, firms experience a decrease in profitability and hence are less likely to invest in worker training. Second, less productive firms are more likely to train their workers, as otherwise they would collapse and exit from the market. The lower the firm's productivity, the higher its worker training expenses. Finally, the effect of output trade liberalization on firm productivity is more pronounced for firms with more training investment.

Jongwanich and Kohpaiboon's paper (Chapter 3), "The Effect of Trade Policy on Firm Productivity in Thai Manufacturing", examines the effect of trade policy on firm productivity, using two recent industrial censuses of Thai manufacturing (2006 and 2011). As measures of trade policy, the authors consider effective rate of protection, as well as output and input tariffs. Generally, the authors find an important role of trade policy in promoting firms' productivity. Specifically, they find, first, that firms operating in a more liberal trade policy environment, measured by the lower effective rate of protection, generally have higher productivity. More importantly, they find that lowering input tariff negatively affects firms' productivity. The authors explain the latter results as follows. Lowering input tariffs would have at least two effects running in opposite. On one hand, it could enhance firms' productivity, as it allows firms to access higher-quality foreign inputs and benefit from increased input variety as well as advanced foreign technology embodied in them. Through these channels, input tariff reductions can positively affect firms' productivity, as found in most existing studies. On the other hand, however, lowering input tariffs could increase the effective rate of protection granted toward finished products, reduce competition pressure, and negatively affect firms' productivity. If the latter effect dominates the former, input tariff reductions can have an adverse effect on a firm's productivity. The authors argue that this result is what's new in this study. Based on these results, they argue that any trade policy reform process should consider both input and output tariffs so as to ensure that protection is actually reduced.

Takii and Narjoko's paper (Chapter 4), "FDI Forward Linkage Effect and Local Input Procurement: Evidence from Indonesian Manufacturing", examines FDI spillovers through forward linkages, using a dataset of Indonesian manufacturing plants over the period 2000–2008. Many Asian developing countries, including Indonesia, have liberalized their foreign investment regime and have used various "carrots" to induce inbound FDI. One key rationale for the provision of such carrots was that FDI has a positive spillover effect. While a large number of existing studies have found evidence of backward spillovers, the evidence in favor of forward spillovers is scarce. Under this context, this paper examines the latter. In particular, this paper examines whether the FDI forward spillover effects are stronger for firms in downstream industries that source inputs locally. Underlying this analysis is the presumption that foreign firms operating locally produce higher-quality, lower-cost inputs than imported inputs and/or increase the availability of inputs. Then, the downstream firms that source inputs locally are more likely to benefit from foreign firms in upstream industries. The authors find strong evidence to support their hypothesis, as well as evidence of backward spillover effects.

Palangkaraya's paper (Chapter 5), "The Link between Innovation and Export Performance of Australian SMEs", investigates the direction of causality between innovation and exporting by employing a propensity score matching methodology and a firm-level dataset of Australian industrial sectors. Unlike most existing studies on this issue, which focus on medium and large manufacturing firms, this paper covers all industrial sectors: primary (agriculture, fishery and forestry, and mining); secondary (manufacturing); and tertiary (services). For the all-industry sector sample, this paper finds a positive association between export and innovation, with causality running in both directions; innovation leads to exporting and, to a lesser extent, exporting leads to innovation. However, the results are somewhat different depending on the sector and type of innovation. The effect of innovation on exporting is strongest in the primary sector (agriculture and mining), while not very significant in manufacturing or services. The author interprets these results as reflecting the strength of Australia's primary sector in the international market. The effect of exporting on innovation is significantly positive only in services and when the innovation is process innovation. Based on these results, the author argues that trade liberalization should be complemented by innovation policy that addresses the bottlenecks faced by SMEs.

Aldaba's paper (Chapter 6), "Trade Reforms, Competition, and Innovation in the Philippines", addresses the effect of trade and investment liberalization on the innovation of Philippine manufacturing firms, utilizing a firm-level panel dataset over the period 1996–2006. She postulates that the effect of trade liberalization, which was implemented several times over the 1990s and 2000s, operates through the competition channel. She examines the effect through a two-stage regression approach. In the first stage regression, the tariffs are found to be positively related to price-cost margin, a measure of competition perceived by firms. In the second stage, she finds that higher competition stimulates R&D. Thus, overall, trade liberalization positively affects R&D through the product market competition channel. Based on the results, she argues that maintaining the contestability of markets or enhancing competition is important for the Philippines in order for it to appropriate potential gains from trade reforms. In this vein, she also argues that the gains from trade liberalization in the Philippines may have remained limited, leading to the country's slow economic growth, as the inadequate physical and institutional infrastructure of the country has kept market competition forces weak.

1.2.2 Globalization and wage/income inequality

Hahn and Choi's paper (Chapter 7), "Trade Liberalization and the Wage Skill Premium in Korean Manufacturing Plants: Do Plants' R&D and Investment Matter?", examines the effects of output and input tariff reductions on within-plant wage skill premium in Korean manufacturing plants. They find evidence that output tariff reductions interact differently with plants' R&D and investment behaviors, to affect wage skill premium. Specifically, output tariff reduction increases wage skill premium mostly in R&D-performing plants while reducing it mostly in plants making positive facility investments. While there is weak evidence that input tariff reductions increase wage skill premiums, no such interactive effects are found. One story behind these results is that, although both R&D and facility investments may respond to changes in profit opportunities due to output tariff reductions, R&D raises the relative demand for skilled workers, while facility investment, an activity of increasing production capacity, raises relative demand for the unskilled (production) workers. The results found in this study suggest that trade liberalization brings about not only benefits but also costs: increased disparity between skilled and unskilled workers in the labor market outcomes. The authors argue that a country liberalizing its trade should also consider strengthening its general social protection scheme in order to more equally share the benefits from liberalized trade among economic agents.

Dai and Zhang's paper (Chapter 8), "The Impacts of Import Tariff Reduction on Income Growth and Distribution in Urban China", examines the effect of import tariff reduction on urban income growth and income distribution utilizing the China Urban Household Survey from 2002 to 2007. As is well known, China has experienced explosive economic growth since its entry into the WTO in 2001 but has transformed itself into one of the most unequal countries in the world. The authors' empirical strategy is to utilize within-China city-level heterogeneity in exposure to tariff protection. They define a city's tariff reduction as the weighted average of the tariff cuts in all industries of a city, with the industry's employment share in 2001 as weights. Then they estimate the effect of city-level tariff reductions on local labor market outcome variables, such as individual income, unemployment rate, and inequality measures. They find that cities with larger tariff reductions after WTO entry experienced slower income growth for manufacturing workers, mainly through the decline in growth rates of wages and property incomes. However, they find no such effect for non-manufacturing workers. They did not find any evidence, either, that tariff reductions affected unemployment. Interestingly, they find that tariff reductions actually helped reduce, not increase, city-level income inequality.

Thangavelu's paper (Chapter 9), "Trade, Technology, Foreign Firms, and Wage Gap: Case of Vietnam Manufacturing Firms", examines the impact of trade and technology on the wage gap of skilled and unskilled workers, utilizing a firm-level dataset for Vietnamese manufacturing sector. It is found that trade tends to have skilled-biased effects by increasing the returns to skilled workers relative to unskilled workers. It is also found that firms that adopt new technologies and restructure their organization are likely to experience an increase in the wage gap between skilled and unskilled workers. He goes on to examine whether skill-biased technological changes are induced by globalization and finds some evidence consistent with this hypothesis. That is, he finds that firms that are part of international production networks are likely to undertake more restructuring. Based on the results, the author suggests that the government has an important role in managing the negative effects of globalization without sacrificing positive effects. In this regard, the author emphasizes general human capital development, as well as training and skill-upgrading programs, which are crucial to move unskilled workers displaced by technological changes and globalization to more productive sectors in the economy.

1.2.3 *Domestic production structure, organization, and supply chain*

Ito and Ikeuchi's paper (Chapter 10), "Overseas Expansion and Domestic Business Restructuring in Japanese Firms", examines the role of task tradability in determining the effects of expansion of overseas activities of multinational enterprises (MNEs) on their domestic plants, utilizing a large-scale firm-establishment-linked dataset. Specifically, they examine whether a domestic plant with a high task tradability measure is more likely to be shut down or reduce employment as an MNE expands its overseas operation. To do so, the authors measure routine-task intensity of each 3-digit industry to which an establishment belongs. The measured routine-task intensity captures task tradability or potential susceptibility of an occupation to displacement by computer technology and/or by low- or medium-skilled workers in low-wage countries. They find, as expected, that more routine-task intensive establishments are more likely to exit when a firm becomes multinational. They also find weak evidence that new entrants tend to be less routine-task intensive as a firm becomes multinational. Based on the results, the authors argue that it is important to ensure a non-disruptive and smooth job transfer, particularly for routine-task workers.

Hayakawa and Matsuura's paper (Chapter 11), "Overseas Production Expansion and Domestic Transaction Network", empirically examines how firms' FDI affects domestic transaction ties with the supplier firms as well as the latter's performance. In Japan, firms' outward FDI has raised concerns about a possible hollowing out of domestic industries, although many existing studies have shown that firms' outward FDI has a non-negative effect on the domestic performance of the firm itself. However, the effects of outward FDI are not limited to those firms which conduct outward FDI. Once firms start to invest abroad and expand their production abroad, they may reorganize sales and procurement strategies in the home country. Such a reorganization may lead to a termination of transaction relationships between FDI firms and their supplier firms (direct suppliers), resulting in worsening of the latter's performance, which may, again, indirectly affect the firms that supply to the supplier firms (indirect suppliers). Against this backdrop, the authors examine the effects of outward FDI on domestic supply chains as well as on supplier firms' employment. Foremost, this paper finds no evidence that customers' FDI tends to terminate their domestic transaction ties. To the contrary, direct suppliers' transaction ties with MNEs are found to be more persistent than those with other firms. In addition, this paper does not find any evidence that firms' outward FDI weakens the transaction relationship between direct and indirect suppliers. Finally, it finds that customers' FDI has a significantly positive effect on employment growth of both direct and indirect suppliers. These results provide, the authors argue, a strong support to the policy of encouraging firms to invest abroad.

Lee's paper (Chapter 12), "Exporting, Productivity, Innovation, and Organization: Evidence from Malaysian Manufacturing", examines the relationship between exporting, on one hand, and productivity, innovation, and firm organization on the other, utilizing firm-level data in the Malaysian manufacturing sector. One novelty of this paper probably lies in the fact that it examines the relationship between exporting and proxies of several aspects of firm organization, such as outsourcing/insourcing and decentralization of decision making. This paper first shows evidence of strong productivity premium of exporters—continuing exporters in particular— which is in line with most previous studies. Then it finds evidence that exporting causes innovation; process innovation, in particular. Finally, and most interestingly, the paper finds evidence that exporting is associated with more decentralized decision making, which the authors argue is consistent with the view that knowledge accumulation from exporting may cause routine-type decisions to be delegated to production workers.

1.2.4 Exchange rate, firm productivity, and product choice

Pyun and Choi's paper (Chapter 13), "Firm Productivity Response to Real Exchange Rate Depreciation Shocks: Analysis using Korean Firm-Level Data", examines effects of real exchange rate (RER) depreciation shocks on firm-level productivity in the Korean manufacturing industry during the period from 2006 to 2010 when Korean won depreciated sharply. This paper focuses on the three channels of exchange rate exposure pointed out by previous literature: export sales, foreign input share, and import penetration. A year-by-year analysis shows that RER depreciation shock has a positive effect on the productivity of firms with high net export exposure in foreign markets, where net exposure is export shares out of total sales less foreign input shares out of total cost. The authors interpret this result as reflecting price gains or scale economies associated with increased exports. However, this positive effect of RER depreciation shock on productivity of firms with high net exposure disappears when a sharp and persistent RER depreciation is identified by a difference-in-difference (DID) approach. This implies that although immediate RER depreciation leads to an increase in firm productivity, persistent RER depreciation may affect firm efficiency negatively, due to slack competition. Moreover, their DID analysis reveals that persistent RER depreciation decreases the productivity of domestic import-competing firms more in industries with higher import penetration. Based on these results, the authors conclude that while a low RER policy in Korea may help to increase firm productivity in the relatively short term, it is likely to worsen it when used for too long.

Putra and Narjoko's paper (Chapter 14), "The Exchange Rate in Exporting: Evidence from the Indonesian Manufacturing Sector", examines the impact of the exchange rate on export performance using plant- and product-level data from Indonesian manufacturing sector during the period 2008–2012. Specifically, this paper addresses the impacts of both the level and the volatility of exchange rate on the value, scope, and composition of exported products. First, the authors find that exchange rate depreciation leads to an increase in the value of exported products. They also find that the more volatile the exchange rate is, the lower the value of the export, similar to the conclusions of existing studies.

The authors argue that the latter findings may reflect the fact that Indonesian financial markets are not fully developed and that there are not enough hedging instruments available. Second, they find that exchange rate volatility is negatively and robustly related to a firm's export product scope, indicating that Indonesian manufacturing firms tend to reduce their exported-product scope if there is high uncertainty in exchange rate. Finally, the authors find some, although not very robust, evidence that an exchange rate appreciation encourages exporters to concentrate on exporting a smaller number of products, which presumably are their core-competence products. Based on these results, the authors argue that exchange rate fluctuation should be adequately managed, not only to increase export value but also to expand the scope of exported products.

Note

1 The themes of the annual project are: *Globalization and Innovation in East Asia* in fiscal year 2010, *Dynamics of Firm Selection Process in Globalization* in 2011, *Impact of Globalization on Labor Market* in 2012, *Globalization and Performance of Small and Large Firms* in 2013, *Trade Policy Changes and Firm Adjustment: A Search for the Underlying Mechanisms* in 2014, *Globalization, Structural Change, and Growth* in 2015, *Globalization, Interfirm Linkages, and Spillovers* in 2016, and *Export Dynamics and Export Industry Development* in 2017.

2 The link between innovation and export performance of Australian SMEs

Alfons Palangkaraya

2.1 Introduction

The objective of the study reported in this chapter is to empirically investigate the direction of causality between innovation and participation in the export market. A better understanding of the effects of globalisation on economic performance, particularly on the performance of firms, is important to ensure that relevant public policy draws out optimum benefits. One potential benefit of globalisation that could serve as the rationale of such policy comes in the form of productivity-improving knowledge (with its expected positive externalities) resulting from participation in the international (export) market. Existing empirical evidence and theoretical predictions suggest that instead of being a 'by-product' of (hypothesised) learning-by-exporting effects, the productivity advantage of exporting firms relative to non-exporting firms comes mostly from their pre-export differences in performance (Aw et al., 1997; Bernard and Jensen, 1999, 2004; Melitz, 2003). Hence, it is not clear whether there are any productivity-improving benefits from export market participation.

However, more recent studies that have looked at the intermediate role of innovation and investment in research and development (R&D) have found some evidence of possible learning effects from participating in the export market via that intermediate channel (Girma et al., 2003, 2008; MacGarvie, 2006; Crespi et al., 2008; Damijan et al., 2010; Fernandes and Paunov, 2010; Bustos, 2011). If the role of learning from exporting is as important as found by these studies, then failing to recognise it in policymaking could lead to suboptimal response to increased economic globalisation.

However, due to firm- and country-level heterogeneity, we still need further evidence on the importance of innovation in determining the direction of causality between globalisation and economic performance. In other words, we need more studies focusing on the role of the intermediate step, namely, innovation.

This study contributes to the existing literature by evaluating the link between exports and innovation in a similar fashion to recent literature, such as Damijan et al. (2010) and Crespi et al. (2008). Unlike these and many other existing studies that concentrate on medium and large manufacturing firms, the study in this chapter utilises data from a sample of small and medium-sized enterprises

(SMEs) from all industrial sectors: primary (agriculture, fishery and forestry, and mining); secondary (manufacturing); and tertiary (services). The more specific contribution for the relevant literature in the case of the Australian economy is that this study provides further insights to those established by existing work, such as those of Palangkaraya and Yong (2007, 2011), on the relationship between international trade and productivity by looking at innovation as the likely intermediate step.[1]

More generally, this paper contributes to the debate on the benefits of pro-globalisation policies for SMEs across different sectors. A confirmation of the learning-by-exporting hypothesis, for example, indicates that export market participation improves the performance of SMEs through the stimulation of innovative activities. Thus, the potential benefits from policies designed to improve global market activities (particularly in the export market) would be higher than in the case where there is no learning effect, and that such policies may be more effective if coordinated with innovation policy. Furthermore, the findings of this study could also demonstrate how learning effects are generated, given existing differences in the types of innovation involved. With a better understanding of these issues, governments would be in a better position to design policies that can address any market failure that may lead to suboptimal resource allocations in different types of innovative and export market activities.

In this study, I apply the propensity matching score (PSM) methodology on firm-level panel data obtained from the Australian Bureau of Statistics' Business Longitudinal Database (BLD) May 2004 to July 2006. The panel data cover approximately 3,000 firms with 200 employees or less. These SMEs operate in all sectors of the Australian economy except government administration, education, health, and utilities, which have been excluded from the database. To preview the results, I find a positive relationship between innovation and export, which runs in both directions of causality. I also find the relationship to depend on the sector (agriculture, mining, manufacturing, or services) and the type of innovation (product or process).

The rest of the chapter is structured as follows. Section 2.2 briefly discusses recent related studies and institutional backgrounds (export and innovation activities of Australian SMEs in general and case study-inspired illustrations of the link between export and innovation from SMEs in the Australian wine industry and the recipients of the Australian Exporter Awards in 2001–2010). Section 2.3 discusses the empirical framework and the data. Section 2.4 presents and discusses the results. Section 2.5 summarises the finding and discusses some policy implications.

2.2 Literature review

2.2.1 Export and innovation

The link between export and productivity has been the subject of manifold different studies for many years due to its important implications on the benefits of globalisation and the link between industrial and innovation policy and trade policy. As the availability of large, firm-level, longitudinal data has improved over the last 15 years, our ability to evaluate two major competing hypotheses (that are not necessarily mutually exclusive) behind the export-productivity relationship has also improved, in terms of details and sophistication.

The first hypothesis of interest is the 'self-selection' hypothesis. It is based on the idea that 'better' or more productive firms self-select into the export market because of its potentially high extra entry costs. These costs include (sunk) fixed costs and transaction costs of exporting, such as transportation costs, distribution or marketing costs, or costs to tailor the products for foreign consumers. Because of such entry barriers, firms may exhibit forward-looking behaviour by taking actions to improve their productivity before entering any foreign market. As a result, any cross-sectional performance difference between exporters and non-exporters can be explained by the ex-ante differences between the two types of firms.

The competing hypothesis, the 'learning-by-exporting' hypothesis, argues that export market participation provides the opportunity for exporters to improve their performance due to a higher level of market competition and the potential for knowledge flows from international consumers. Wagner (2007), for example, surveyed more than 40 studies based on firm-level data from more than 30 countries. He found that most studies support the self-selection hypothesis while participation in the export market does not appear to lead to improved productivity.

The lack of support for the learning-by-exporting hypothesis is further shown by several recent theoretical and empirical models, which emphasise the role of firm heterogeneity and R&D. For example, Constantini and Melitz (2008) 'endogenised' firms' decision to export and innovate and showed that the export–productivity link can be explained by the decision to innovate before entry into the export market. Recent empirical studies, such as Aw et al. (2008), looked into the relationship in more detail by incorporating R&D investment or the innovation decision and also found evidence for the self-selection hypothesis. Other recent studies that also support the self-selection hypothesis include Kirbach and Schmiedeberg (2008) and Chadha (2009). The latter is interesting because it found that innovation can act as a strategic tool to gain market share in world markets; thus, it is important for firms to innovate to enter the export market. Finally, Long et al. (2009) explored the effects of trade liberalisation on incentives for firms to innovate and on productivity. They found that trade liberalisation's impact is dominated by self-selection effects and the effects of trade on innovation or incentive to spend in R&D depend on the costs of trade.[2]

Other studies such as Crespi et al. (2008), Damijan et al. (2010), Girma et al. (2003, 2008), MacGarvie (2006), and Fernandes and Paunov (2010) provide evidence that globalisation may feed back into improved domestic performance through learning effects on innovation from global market participation. The last two studies mentioned above show that learning effects occur through imports while the other studies show they occur through export market participation. Furthermore, De Loecker (2007) and Ito (2012) found that firms that export more to higher-income and technologically more advanced regions exhibit stronger learning-by-exporting effects. This is consistent with the notion that export market participation provides benefits through better access to best practice technologies (Girma et al., 2003).

However, given the reliance of most of the studies cited above on data from medium and large enterprises and, particularly, from the manufacturing sector, we need further evidence based on SME data before we can generalise the findings. For example, due to the high costs of acquiring legal protections for innovation and their subsequent enforcement, SMEs may have a lower propensity to innovate than larger firms (Acs and Audretsch, 1988; Arundel and Kabla, 1998). Other examples include the tendency of SMEs lacking the necessary absorptive capacity to tap the world's best-practice technology in the global market, reducing learning-by-exporting effects (Ito and Lechevalier, 2010). Similarly, the export revenues of individual SMEs may not be large enough to induce the firm to invest in new technologies, an important channel for trade liberalisation to lead to growth, following their entrance into the export market, as argued by Bustos (2011). Furthermore, Jensen and Webster (2006) argued that the implication of under-investment in innovative activities by SMEs can potentially be more significant than realised, given that SMEs tend to hold a significant share of overall economic activity. In other words, a better understanding of the innovative patterns of SMEs is crucial for designing effective innovation policy that generates economic growth in the most optimal way.

In addition, we also need more evidence from firms in industrial sectors other than manufacturing as well as a better understanding of the role of different types of innovation. First, the extent of market failure in innovation activities vary by industrial sector; the effectiveness of instruments in combating such market failures, including the provision of intellectual property rights protection, also vary by sector (see, for example, Mansfield et al., 1981, as cited in Jensen and Webster, 2006). Second, the type of innovation activities may vary widely across industrial sectors because of the multifaceted nature of innovation. Also, Schumpeter (1934) discussed innovation in terms of product innovation, process innovation, organisation innovation, and market innovation. If we recognise that the variation in the types of innovation activities as classified above correlate with the characteristics of the products or markets in which a firm operates, then we may find certain firms in certain industries to be more concerned with product innovation while other firms in other industries are more concerned with process innovation. Consequently, we can expect the link between innovation and export to depend on the type of innovation activity. Furthermore, protection of intellectual property rights such as patents or trademarks may be more effective for product innovation than process innovation, leading to varying patterns of innovative activities and export-innovation relationships across industrial sectors as well.

2.2.2 Institutional background

2.2.2.1 Australian SMEs' export and innovative activities

Australian SMEs present an interesting case to study the determinants of firm-level innovative activities, including the link between exporting and innovation. As in most countries, SMEs are an important component of the Australian economy, accounting for slightly more than 60% of total employment and 50% of value added (ABS, 2001). Because of this, Australian SMEs have received a lot of government attention in terms of various policies and incentives targeted at them, to help them improve their productive and innovative performance.

Naturally, the importance of SMEs varies across industries (ABS, 2008). The highest share of value-added contribution can be found from SMEs in agriculture, forestry, and fishing (97% of the industry value added in 2006/2007); rental, hiring, and real estate services (90% of the industry value added); and accommodation, cafes, and restaurants (75% of value added). In contrast, the lowest share of value added can be found from SMEs in retail trade (56% of industry value added), manufacturing (45%), and information media and telecommunications (17%).

Similarly, the role of SMEs in Australia's export activities also varies by industry. Overall, in 2005–2006, they accounted for 90% of Australian businesses participating in the export market. However, as found in other countries, they accounted for less than 10% of the value of exported goods (ABS, 2006). Furthermore, a recent statistical report (ABS, 2010) shows that, based on the value of goods export, the share of SMEs in 2008–2009 was the highest in the following sectors: construction (37%), transport, postal, and warehousing (23%), and wholesale trade (16%). Thus, we probably will not learn much about the link between exports and innovation of Australian SMEs if we look only at the manufacturing industry.

On innovation, according to the latest ABS Innovation Survey conducted in 2005 (ABS, 2007), about 141,300 businesses[3] were operating in Australia and around 34% of them undertook innovation by introducing either a new product, an operational process, and/or organisational processes.[4] As expected, the extent of innovativeness varied by business size, with around 58% of very large businesses (250+ employees), 46%–48% of medium businesses (20–99 employees), and 25%–34% of small businesses (5–19 employees) reported as innovators. It also varies by industry – electricity, gas, and water supply (49% of businesses are innovators), wholesale trade (43%), and manufacturing (42%) were the leading industries. Also worth noting is that, according to the innovation survey, for Australian SMEs, operational process innovation is the most important type of innovation, compared to the other two. Thus, we may expect that if there is any link between SMEs' export and innovation activities, process innovation would be relatively more important.

Finally, in terms of the contribution to the degree of sales turnover, 65% of innovating businesses reported that their product innovation accounted for less than 10% of their turnover (ABS, 2007). In other words, in general, product innovation is not a significant revenue generator for Australian businesses. However, the contribution of production innovation on total revenues varies across industries, with businesses in most services industry reporting less than 10% share. This result is understandable, given the nature of the 'product' in the services sector. In contrast, for businesses in the mining and manufacturing industries, the share of product innovation on total revenue ranges from 10% to as high as 50%. Also, when we look at variations across business size, it is interesting to note that none of the large businesses (100+ employees) reported that product innovation contributes more than 50% of business turnover. In contrast, 12% of small businesses with 5–19 employees reported that more than 50% of their turnovers can be attributed to product innovation. In other words, innovation appears to be more important for the livelihood of smaller businesses, again highlighting the importance of a study on SMEs to complement those based on data from large enterprises.

2.2.2.2 Case studies

Given the anonymity of the firms in the BLD panel data used in this study, I discuss briefly the case of the Australian wine industry and SMEs, which received the annual Australian Exporter Award, to help interpret the estimation results.[5] The first, based on an in-depth study by Aylward (2004, 2006), illustrates the relationship between innovation and exports for Australian wine producers. The second case highlights some important characteristics of SMEs and how they relate to export performance, particularly for those in the services sector.

The most important lesson for these two case studies, which will be discussed below, is that export market participation appears to be driven by firms' ability to continuously come up with better processing technology via skill and technology updating to deliver their services.[6] Thus, export market participation appears to depend more on process innovation than on product innovation. Furthermore, how business owners or managers view the importance of innovation matters.

2.2.2.3 Australian wine industry

According to Aylward (2004, 2006), Australia was the fourth-largest exporter of wine in terms of value sharing – around 40% of global wine exports to the United States in 2004. The Australian wine industry consists of two major clusters (South Australia, and New South Wales and Victoria). However, while the South Australian cluster only accounted for around 25% of wineries, its shares of Australia's total wine production and exports were 50% and 60%, respectively. More interestingly, Aylward's studies found a close link between the South Australian wine cluster's higher productivity and propensity to export and also explained the differences between the two clusters in terms of the beliefs of business owners or managers regarding the importance of innovation.

For example, 66% of wine producers in South Australia who responded to Aylward's interview thought there was a strong link between their innovation and export performance. In contrast, only 42% of the respondents from the New South Wales and Victoria clusters believed the same. The interviewees also differed in terms of how they defined innovation, the extent of their firm's collaboration, and the use of the Australian wine industry's research and analytical services. One other finding to note from the study is that while there was negligible difference in how the firms in both clusters define *product* innovation, they differed significantly in defining what they thought *process* innovation entailed. This last finding points to the possibility that the latter is probably more important than the former in explaining the link between export and innovation in the industry.

2.2.2.4 Australian exporter award winners in the services sector

Over the last 48 years, the Australian government has awarded businesses deemed to have performed exceptionally in the export market every year. The awards are given to businesses belonging to various categories such as agribusiness, arts and entertainment, emerging exporter, and large and advanced manufacturer. For the purpose of this study, two categories of particular interest are the emerging exporter and small and medium-sized businesses in services categories. Between 2001 and 2010, 24 businesses received the former, 10 of which were from the services sector. In the same period, 16 businesses received the small and medium-sized exporters in services awards. In terms of their product characteristics, most of these award recipients in the services sector operated in information technology-related fields (10 businesses), highly specialised engineering design and prototype manufacturing operations (8 businesses), and specialised manufacturing and industrial consultancy services for the mining industry (4 businesses). For example, one of these businesses that operated in information technology services and employed around 50 people was considered the largest specialist provider of independent information security consulting services in the region. Its consumers were in more than 20 countries such as Singapore, Malaysia, South Korea, Japan, the United States, and France. Another Australian small business that excelled in the export market sold maritime simulation, training, and consultancy services to international maritime and defence industries. Unfortunately, no detailed case study similar to that of Aylward (2004, 2006) is available, to help us understand the importance of innovation to these services exporters.

2.3 Empirical model and data

2.3.1 Empirical model

To address my research questions, I need to make causal inferences as opposed to simply testing for the existence of correlation between innovation and exports. Thus, I adopt an empirical methodology that can produce unbiased estimates of the relevant treatment effects (from being an exporter or being an innovator) by assuming that the observables in the data can identify firms' propensity to either export or innovate to control for unobserved confounding factors. I follow the approach used in similar studies, such as Becker and Egger (2013) and Damijan et al. (2010), by adopting the propensity score matching (PSM) method.

As argued by an extensive literature on the PSM method, such as that of Dehejia and Wahba (2002), the estimation of causal effects based on a comparison of the treatment group with a 'non-experimental' comparison group may suffer from self-selection or other systematic biased relating to the sample selection. Under certain assumptions, the PSM method corrects sample selection bias by pairing treatment and comparison units according to observed characteristics. The method provides a natural weighting scheme that ensures unbiasedness of the estimated treatment effects.

In this study there are two treatment effects of interest: innovation effects and exporting effects. For the first, are innovators more likely to become exporters than non-innovators after we control for their propensity to innovate? Similarly, for the reverse direction of causality, are exporters more likely to be innovators than non-exporters who exhibit a similar propensity to become exporters? To answer, I identify non-innovators that exhibit a similar propensity to innovate and non-exporters that exhibit a similar propensity to export by estimating the following innovation and export propensity models (Damijan et al., 2010):

$$\Pr[I_{it}=1]=f(X_{it-1})+\varepsilon_{it} \tag{1}$$

and

$$\Pr[E_{it}=1]=f(Z_{it-1})+\eta_{it} \tag{2}$$

In both equations (1) and (2), each period t firm i's propensities to innovate $(\Pr[I_{it}=1])$ and to export $(\Pr[E_{it}=1])$ are expressed as a function of observed (exogenous or predetermined) previous period characteristics such as productivity, size of employment, capital intensity, and import status. Based on the estimated propensity to innovate (equation 1), I 'match' innovators and non-innovators at period t. Similarly, based on the estimated propensity to export (equation 2), I obtain a list of matched exporters and non-exporters. These two pairs represent the treatment and control groups.

I investigate the 'innovation effects' on export propensity using all kinds of innovation – product and process innovation – and for firms in three separate subsectors (primary, manufacturing, services). Specifically, using the list of matched innovators in period t, I estimate the average treatment effects of innovation (that is, the average treatment of the treated) on export market participation by comparing their probabilities to become exporters in period t and period

$t + 1$ separately. Period $t + 1$'s comparison may suffer less from the problem of unobserved contemporaneous shocks than the period t's comparison. Similarly, for the reverse case, using the resulting matched exporters in period t, I estimate the average treatment effects of export market participation on innovation by comparing their probabilities to become innovators (product and/or process) in period t and in period $t + 1$ separately.

The above analyses are also done on a subsample of the data consisting of only exporters (innovators) at period t who were *not* exporters (innovators) in period $t - 1$. This is a stronger test of the direction of causality. It asks if current period innovation (export market participation) leads firms to become 'new' exporters (innovators) in the current or next period. However, due to sample size limitation, there is no estimation at the sub-sector level.

2.3.2 Data

Model estimations are based on firm-level data from the first 'confidentialised' unit record file (CURF) edition of the BLD produced by the Australian Bureau of Statistics. The first CURF edition of the BLD contains data from two panels with a combined sample size of around 3,000 Australian SMEs employing 200 or less workers each year. The first panel in the data contains annual business-level data from the financial years 2004–2005 to 2006–2007. The second panel covers 2005–2006 and 2006–2007. Overall, the actual number of businesses covered by the BLD panel data with usable observations is 1,826 for 2004–2005; 3,486 for 2005–2006; and 3,314 for 2006–2007 – for a total of 8,626 firms across the years. The broad sectoral distribution of these firms by type of innovation and the firms' export status is provided in Table 2.1.

From Table 2.1, the services sector appears to have the largest sample size with 4,972 businesses. However, this may reflect more the sample design of the BLD at collection rather than the actual distribution of SMEs in the Australian economy. In terms of export market participation, of the 8,626 businesses in the full sample, 15% are exporters. As expected, the proportion of exporters in the sample varies by sector, with the manufacturing sector having the highest proportion at around 29% or double the rate of each of the other sectors. In terms of innovation, Table 2.1 also shows that overall around 30% of the sampled SMEs have either product or process innovation (7.8% product innovation only, 10.9% process innovation only, and 11.3% both product and process innovation). As in the case of export, the proportion of innovating SMEs also varies across sectors. For example, from Table 2.1 we can infer that businesses in the manufacturing sector have the highest proportion of innovators with around 40% of the businesses having either product or process innovation.

To ensure that each observation has non-missing values in the relevant variables, the cleaned estimating sample size is around 1,800 firms for each sample

Table 2.1 Distribution of Firms by Sector, Innovation, and Export Status (%)

Type of Innovation	*Export Status*	*Sector*			
		Primary (n = 2,330)	*Manufacturing (n = 1,324)*	*Services (n = 4,972)*	*Total (n = 8,626)*
Product innovation only (7.8)	Non-exporter	82.7	66.9	78.7	77.3
	Exporter	17.3	33.1	21.3	22.7
	Subtotal	100	100	100	
Process innovation only (10.9)	Non-exporter	83.8	66.1	84.1	80.7
	Exporter	16.2	33.9	15.9	19.3
	Subtotal	100	100	100	
Product and process innovation (11.3)	Non-exporter	76.2	54.5	76.7	71.4
	Exporter	23.8	45.5	23.3	28.6
	Subtotal	100	100	100	
No innovation (70.0)	Non-exporter	88.1	77.7	91.7	88.8
	Exporter	11.9	22.3	8.3	11.2
	Subtotal	100	100	100	
Total (100)	Non-exporter	86.7	71.1	88.0	85.0
	Exporter	13.3	28.9	12.0	15.0
	Subtotal	100	100	100	

Source: Processed from pooled panel data 2004/2005, 2005/2006 and 2006/2007 of the CURF Business Longitudinal Database (ABS, 2009) by the author.
Note: The primary sector includes agriculture, fishing and forestry, and mining. The services sector includes construction, wholesale trade, retail trade, accommodation, cafes and restaurants, transport and storage, communication services, property and business services, cultural and recreational services, and personal and other services.

year. A descriptive summary of the pooled clean sample for the 2005–2006 and 2006–2007 financial years is provided in Table 2.2.

From Table 2.2, in 2005–2006, approximately 20% of the sampled SMEs were product innovators and 26% process innovators. The proportion of those with either type of innovation was about 34%. These rates are comparable to the 30% innovation rate in the full sample described earlier. Also, including organisational processes innovation, the cleaned sample provides a similar rate of innovation produced by the Australian Innovation Survey data (discussed in Section 2.2).

From the same table, the proportion of manufacturing SMEs is approximately 15%. This is about double the proportion of manufacturing SMEs according to the overall figure for Australian SMEs (ABS, 2001), indicating that the estimating data oversample the sector. Finally, in terms of the propensity to export, about 15% of the SMEs in the data reported positive export income. This is significantly less than the overall proportion of exporting SMEs discussed earlier. Because of these sampling biases, particularly the underestimation of export propensity, the estimation results based on the export propensity equation need to be interpreted with caution.

Table 2.2 Descriptive Statistics

Variable	*Description*	t = 2005/06			t = 2006/07		
		N	*Mean*	*Standard Deviation*	N	*Mean*	*Standard Deviation*
$PRODINNOV_t$	= 1 if had goods/service innovation at period t	3670	0.203	0.402	3365	0.188	0.391
$PROCINNOV_t$	= 1 if had operational process innovation at period t	3688	0.263	0.440	3376	0.209	0.407
$INNOV_t$	= 1 if had product/process innovation at period t	3668	0.341	0.474	3365	0.290	0.454
$EXPORT_t$	= 1 if had any export income at period t	3440	0.156	0.363	3229	0.147	0.354
$EMPSIZE_{t-1}$	= number of employees at period t	1826	30.10	43.57	3764	31.49	44.74
$LLABPRODVA_{t-1}$	= log of value added (sales less non-capital purchases) per employee at period t	1594	10.25	1.354	3252	10.36	1.343
$LINVINT_{t-1}$	= log of capital purchase per employee in period t–1	1110	7.872	2.141	1559	10.70	1.534
$IMPORT_{t-1}$	= 1 if had any import purchase	1826	0.128	0.334	3476	0.169	0.374
MFG	= 1 if industry division is manufacturing	4123	0.152	0.359	3764	0.152	0.359
$SERVICE$	= 1 if industry division is services	4123	0.584	0.493	3764	0.579	0.494

Source: Processed from pooled panel data 2004/05, 2005/06, and 2006/07 of the CURF Business Longitudinal Database (ABS, 2009) by the author.

2.4 Results

2.4.1 Propensity to innovate and to export

Tables 2.3 and 2.4 present the estimated coefficients of the propensity to innovate and to export based on equations (1) and (2), respectively.[7] These estimates are based on a pooled sample across all industrial sectors as well as for each of the three major industrial divisions: manufacturing, services, and resources.[8] In general, the estimated coefficients are statistically significant and of the expected sign; in all cases, they are jointly statistically significant (Tables 2.3 and 2.4).

For innovation, Table 2.3 shows that the propensity to innovate in the current period is positively correlated with the immediately preceding period's levels of employment, labour productivity, and capital intensity and whether the businesses had any exposure to the import market. The positive relationships with size of employment and labour productivity appear to be nonlinear, with diminishing effects. For export propensity, Table 2.4 shows that only employment and import variables are statistically significant. It should be noted however that the variable constructed using employment size is limited in the sense that the employment size figure is only provided in three discrete intervals: 1–5, 5–19, and 20–99. This might contribute to a larger standard error of the estimates and the statistically non-significant coefficient estimates.

2.4.2 The effects of innovation on export market participation

Based on the estimated coefficients summarised in Tables 2.3, 2.4, and 2.A.1–2.A.3 and the resulting innovation propensity score, each SME that innovated in period t (the treated firm) is matched to one or more of the non-innovating firms (the untreated firms) using the nearest neighbour PSM methodologies.[9] The resulting matching estimators for the effects of innovation on export market participation are summarised in Table 2.5 below.[10]

In the first part of Table 2.5, under the '*Innovation*$_t$ →' heading, the estimated effects of current innovation on current export market participation are presented. While the estimated rate differentials in export market participation are based on matched innovators–non-innovators using previous period conditions, these estimates may not 'truly' indicate direction of causality because of their contemporaneous nature. There may still be some unobserved confounding factors that explain the positive correlation. The second part of Table 2.5 provides a clearer indication of whether innovation leads to export.

For example, from Table 2.5, if we lump all sectors together, current innovating firms have around 9–17 percentage points higher propensity to be in the export market. This effect is also significant in magnitude given that, as discussed earlier, the overall proportion of exporting SMEs in the sample is only around 15%. Furthermore, the variation in estimates across innovation type and sector suggests that the relationship between innovation and export differs across industrial sectors as well as types of innovation. For example, for the primary

Table 2.3 Propensity to Innovate – All Sectors

	Product or Process Innovation or Both $Pr[\text{INNOV}_t = 1]$		*Product Innovation* $Pr[\text{PRODINNOV}_t = 1]$		*Process Innovation* $Pr[\text{PROCINNOV}_t = 1]$	
	Coefficient	*dY/dX*	*Coefficient*	*dY/dX*	*Coefficient*	*dY/dX*
$EMPSIZE_{t-1}$	0.030***	0.011	0.027***	0.007	0.043***	0.013
	(0.009)		(0.001)		(0.010)	
$EMPSIZE^2_{t-1}$	-0.000***	-0.000	-0.000***	-0.000	-0.000***	-0.000
	(0.000)		(0.000)		(0.000)	
$LLABPRODVA_{t-1}$	0.357*	0.127	0.300	0.063	0.564**	0.170
	(0.195)		(0.226)		(0.276)	
$LLABPRODVA^2_{t-1}$	-0.019	-0.007	-0.018	-0.005	-0.029**	-0.009
	(0.010)		(0.011)		(0.014)	
$LINVINT_{t-1}$	0.064***	0.023	0.055*	0.015	0.072***	0.022
	(0.019)		(0.029)		(0.022)	
$IMPORT_{t-1}$	0.432***	0.162	0.625***	0.204	0.410***	0.136
	(0.087)		(0.106)		(0.104)	
$YEAR_{2006/07}$	-0.478***	-0.171	-0.396***	-0.113	-0.567***	-0.174
	(0.087)		(0.105)		(0.097)	
$CONST$	-3.089***		-2.363***		-4.391***	
	(0.997)		(1.144)		(0.339)	
Pr[Y=1]	0.329		0.224		0.251	
N. Obs.	1996		1501		1591	
Log pseudolikelihood	-1175.4		-720.6		-801.4	
Pseudo R^2	0.071		0.097		0.1067	

Source: Author's computation.

Note: (): standard errors. All probit regressions were estimated with 1-digit ANZSIC industry dummy variables when applicable and with robust standard error. ***,**,* indicate statistically significant at the 1%, 5%, and 10% level of significance.

Table 2.4 Propensity to Export

$Pr[\text{Export}_t = 1]$	*All Sectors*		*Primary*		*Manufacturing*		*Services*	
	Coefficient	*dY/dX*	*Coefficient*	*dY/dX*	*Coefficient*	*dY/dX*	*Coefficient*	*dY/dX*
$EMPSIZE_{t-1}$	0.004***	0.001	0.002	0.000	0.006	0.002	0.004***	0.001
	(0.002)		(0.001)		(0.017)		(0.001)	
$LLABPRODVA_{t-1}$	0.029	0.005	0.002	0.000	0.071	0.025	0.041	0.006
	(0.052)		(0.035)		(0.078)		(0.056)	
$LINVINT_{t-1}$	0.016	0.003	-0.036	-0.007	0.054	0.019	0.027	0.004
	(0.045)		(0.024)		(0.055)		(0.033)	
$IMPORT_{t-1}$	1.114***	0.309	0.886***	0.244	1.091***	0.398	1.178***	0.285
	(0.214)		(0.092)		(0.173)		(0.129)	
$YEAR_{2006/07}$	-0.121	-0.023	-0.040	-0.040	-0.106	-0.037	-0.206	-0.031
	(0.178)		(0.105)		(0.246)		(0.152)	
CONST	-1.857***		-0.994		-2.336***		-2.112***	
	(0.510)		(0.425)		(0.820)		(0.619)	
Pr[Y=1]	0.153		0.121		0.321		0.120	
N. Obs.	1993		502		324		1167	
Log-likelihood	-667.2		-174.6		-166.8		-321.9	
Pseudo R^2	0.2178		0.0596		0.1799		0.2480	

Source: Author's computation.

Note: (): standard errors. All probit regressions were estimated with 1-digit ANZSIC industry dummy variables when applicable and with robust standard error. ***,**,* indicate statistically significant at the 1%, 5%, and 10% level of significance.

Table 2.5 Does Innovating Lead to Exports?

Outcome: Export	*Average Treatment Effects on the Treated*					
Treatment: Innovation	Innovation$_t$→			Innovation$_t$→		
	ATT	*SE*	*N*	*ATT*	*SE*	*N*
All Sectors						
Innovation Type						
Product	0.168***	0.035	(334/334)	0.131**	0.061	(153/143)
Process	0.090***	0.034	(399/399)	0.114**	0.056	(201/200)
Product/process	0.104***	0.026	(655/655)	0.116***	0.043	(313/305)
Primary						
Innovation Type						
Product	0.222***	0.071	(45/45)	0.174**	0.810	(23/24)
Process	0.055	0.059	(73/73)	0.144*	0.079	(42/43)
Product/process	0.027	0.061	(110/110)	0.083	0.092	(60/60)
Manufacturing						
Innovation Type						
Product	0.123	0.098	(73/73)	0.156	0.273	(28/22)
Process	0.120	0.091	(100/100)	0.137	0.208	(46/37)
Product/process	0.140**	0.069	(143/143)	0.118	0.160	(61/54)
Services						
Innovation Type						
Product	0.070	0.048	(214/214)	0.022	0.081	(104/106)
Process	0.098**	0.040	(225/225)	0.133*	0.062	(112/111)
Product/process	0.108***	0.030	(397/397)	0.066	0.056	(190/186)

Source: Author's computation.

Note: *,**,*** denote statistically significant at 10%, 5%, and 1% respectively. The standard errors are computed based on Lechner's (2001) approximation. In the parentheses are the numbers of treated and matched control (possibly not unique) observations obtained using the nearest neighbour criterion.

sector, the contemporaneous relationship between product innovation and export market activities is the strongest (0.222). In contrast, for the services sector, the relationship between current innovation and export is slightly stronger in terms of process innovation (0.098) than product innovation (0.070).

To further investigate the direction of causality in the relationship between innovation and exports, I estimate the effects of current period innovation on the propensity to have any export income in the next period. The results of the estimation are provided in the second part of Table 2.5's columns under the heading '*Innovation*$_t$ →'. As can be seen from the table, when all sectors are pooled together, the innovative activities – either product or process – of Australian SMEs clearly lead to export. Unfortunately, the sample size is approximately halved when the analysis is performed at the sector level, possibly resulting in many of the sector estimates being statistically insignificant. The estimates for manufacturing, for example, show reasonable positive magnitude but none are statistically significant. Nevertheless, there is an indication that process innovation leads to services exports and that either product or process innovation leads to primary product export.

2.4.3 The effects of export market participation on innovation

Table 2.6 summarises PSM estimates of the possible reversed direction of causality running from export market participation to innovative activities. Using the estimated propensity to export in Table 2.4, I match current exporters ('treated' SMEs) to current non-exporters ('untreated' SMEs) and estimate the average

Table 2.6 Does Exporting Lead to Innovation

Outcome: Export	*Average Treatment Effects on the Treated*					
Treatment: Innovation	→			→		
	ATT	*SE*	*N*	*ATT*	*SE*	*N*
All Sectors						
Innovation Type						
Product	0.122**	0.058	(219/221)	0.077	0.317	(26/24)
Process	0.166***	0.054	(242/246)	0.178*	0.105	(104/106)
Product/process	0.129**	0.053	(299/303)	0.153	0.110	(131/128)
Primary						
Innovation Type						
Product	0.043	0.101	(46/46)	0.158	0.109	(25/24)
Process	0.055	0.091	(47/50)	−0.073	0.159	(25/24)
Product/process	0.251***	0.085	(54/58)	0.179	0.131	(28/28)
Manufacturing						
Innovation type						
Product	0.065	0.119	(70/69)	0.132	0.245	(39/36)
Process	0.264***	0.094	(91/91)	0.036	0.271	(39/36)
Product/process	0.062	0.102	(104/103)	−0.026	0.256	(39/36)
Services						
Innovation Type						
Product	0.225***	0.080	(102/102)	0.201	0.145	(46/47)
Process	0.279***	0.078	(104/104)	0.303**	0.123	(47/49)
Product/process	0.194**	0.077	(139/139)	0.167	0.147	(62/66)

Source: Authors' computation.

Note: *,**,*** denote statistically significant at 10%, 5%, and 1% respectively. The standard errors are computed based on Lechner's (2001) approximation. In the parentheses are the numbers of treated and matched control (possibly not unique) observations obtained using the nearest neighbour criterion.

treatment effects on the treated exporters on their propensity to have product innovation, process innovation, or a combination of both types of innovation.

From Table 2.6, it is visible that the estimated links from export to innovation also vary by industry and by type of innovation. SMEs in the services sector show the strongest and most robust positive relationship between export market participation and current innovation. More importantly, the second set of columns in Table 2.6 under the heading '→' provide clear evidence that exports lead to innovation, but only for process innovation and only in the services sector. For other types of innovation and other sectors, the evidence is not as clear. In other words, the benefits from exporting, such as technology-upgrading effects arising from the exposure to best-practice technology such as found by Girma et al. (2003), appear to be rather limited to SMEs in the services sector.

2.4.2 *New exporters and new innovators*

For a more definitive indication of the direction of causality between exports and innovation, I repeat the propensity matching analysis on a subsample of firms that can be identified as 'new' exporters or 'new' innovators. This allows for investigating how likely it is that innovation leads a business to switch from having been outside the export market before it innovates to participating in the export market in the next period; and, similarly, how likely it is that export market participation leads a business to switch from being a non-innovator before it participates in the current export market to becoming an innovator. Specifically, I define 'new exporters' as firms with no export income in period $t - 1$; similarly, 'new innovators' are firms without any innovation in period $t - 1$.[11]

The matching estimators of the average treatment effects on the treated are summarised in Table 2.7. However, due to the limitation of the resulting sample size, I only perform the analysis at the overall industry level. From the upper half of the table, it appears that current innovators, especially product innovators, *which are non-exporters in the previous period,* will more likely 'become' an exporter in the current period compared to current non-innovators. On the other hand, if I look at the probability of becoming a new exporter in period $t + 1$, the relationship is strongest for process innovators.[12] Thus, it appears that the processes that result in product innovation leading to a switch to becoming exporters work faster than processes associated with process innovation leading to exporting. To some extent, this finding is quite intuitive: when a firm has introduced a new product, then it might play as a market leader and enters the export market at around the same time. On the other hand, having innovated in production processes is not as strongly related to an immediate market leadership position.

The lower half of Table 2.7 provides the estimates relevant for addressing the second question: is current export participation associated with a higher probability of becoming a 'new' innovator in the current or the next period? The answer is that, unlike in the case when innovation is the treatment discussed above, none of the estimated relationships between current export and the propensity to become new innovator in period $t + 1$ are statistically significant. However,

Table 2.7 New Exporters and New Innovators

	Average Treatment Effects on the Treated					
Outcome: Export	Innovation$_t$ → Pr[NewEXPORTER$_t$]			Innovation$_t$ → Pr[NewEXPORTER$_{t+1}$]		
	ATT	*SE*	*N*	*ATT*	*SE*	*N*
Innovation Type						
Product	0.054***	0.020	(242/242)	0.007	0.039	(114/110)
Process	0.021	0.020	(288/288)	0.074***	0.025	(148/147)
Product/process	0.027*	0.014	(490/490)	0.027	0.027	(239/225)
Outcome: Innovation	Export$_t$ → Pr[NewINNOVATOR$_t$]			Export$_t$ → Pr[NewINNOVATOR$_{t+1}$]		
	ATT	*SE*	*N*	*ATT*	*SE*	*N*
Innovation Type						
Product	0.052	0.061	(129/132)	0.009	0.120	(57/59)
Process	0.176***	0.058	(143/144)	0.156	0.111	(68/71)
Product/process	0.155**	0.063	(157/162)	0.174	0.114	(76/77)

Source: Authors' computation.

Note: *,**,*** denote statistically significant at 10, 5 and 1% respectively. The standard errors are computed based on Lechner's (2001) approximation. In the parentheses are the numbers of treated and matched control (possibly not unique) observations obtained using the nearest neighbour criterion. 'New exporters' are defined by conditioning on $EXPORT_{t-1} = 0$. 'New innovators' are defined by conditioning on $INNOVATION_{t-1} = 0$.

current export appears to lead to a switch to becoming a process innovator in the same period.

Altogether, the nearest neighbour estimates provide a different characterisation of the link between innovation and exports for Australian SMEs. For example, for small firms like Australian SMEs – most of whose product innovation involves products that are not new to the world and that are more likely to be financially constrained, relative to large firms – the type of innovative activities that appears to matter the most as regards export market participation is process innovation. Also, consistent with the argument in Damijan et al. (2010), the results indicate that the positive effects of current product innovation on the probability of becoming an exporter in the current period (see upper half of Table 2.7) appear to support earlier findings that product innovation is crucial for entering the international market successfully (Cassiman and Golovko, 2007; Cassiman and Martinez-Ros, 2007, Becker and Egger, 2013). On the other hand, the strong positive relationship between current export market activity and the probability of becoming a 'new' process innovator in the current period see lower half of Table 2.7) appears to be consistent with the findings that once in the export market, firms need to conduct process innovation to stay competitive.

2.5 Conclusions and policy implications

In this study, I addressed the questions of whether exporting firms learned from their participation in the export markets – and thus, became more innovative than those that focused only on domestic markets (learning-by-exporting hypothesis) – and whether firms introduced innovation before they entered foreign markets (self-selection hypothesis). Based on data of Australian SMEs employing 200 or less workers, I assessed if existing evidence, mostly based on data from medium and large firms and firms in the manufacturing sector, could be generalised into the cases of small firms and firms from the primary and services sectors using the PSM methodology.

Depending on the sector and type of innovation, I found innovation leading to export and, with weaker evidence, export leading to innovation. For example, perhaps reflecting the strength of Australia's primary (mining and agriculture) sector in the international market, the primary sector exhibited the strongest statistical evidence that innovation leads export. For the services sector, I found that only process innovation leads to exporting and, only in this sector, evidence suggests that export leads to process innovation and is statistically significant.

I also found that current product innovators have a higher probability of becoming new exporters in the same period and current process innovators have a higher probability of becoming new exporters in the next period. On the reverse direction, current exporters will more likely become new process innovators in the same period but not in a future period. Furthermore, for small and medium-sized firms such as Australian SMEs – most of whose product innovation involves products that are not new to the world and that are more likely to be financially constrained, relative to large firms – the type of innovative activities that appears to matter most regarding export market participation is process innovation. Such higher relative importance of process innovation as a key to enter the export market seems to be consistent with the findings of Iacovone and Javorcik (2010).

In summary, the findings highlight that, to enter the export market, SMEs may need to first discover or create their own comparative advantage (Rodrik, 2004).[13] As also found in other countries,[14] the SMEs in this study did this by introducing product and/or process innovation before entering the export market. Intuitively, the former seems to be more important for firms in the goods-producing sector (primary and manufacturing) and the latter for firms in the services sector. Thus, if any market failure results in inefficient resource allocation while comparative advantage is being created, the government may complement the private sector by considering inter-sectoral differences.

Also, the evidence that exporters will more likely become process innovators in the same period suggests the existence of externalities from the comparative advantage discovery process. Such externalities and the strong link between innovation and exports and their two-way causality call for industrial policy, which encompasses both innovation and international trade policies. If businesses cannot export because they are not innovative (in terms of either product or process), then traditional government policies aimed at facilitating export market entry (such as export promotion programmes or free trade agreements) would be less effective.

In other words, trade liberalisation policies, which focus only on taking advantage of existing comparative advantage and ignoring the necessity for comparative advantage discovery, may fail to produce the promised sustained economic growth (Rodrik, 2004). Such failure is possible, even if trade liberalisation results in 'better resource' allocation to traditionally comparative advantaged sectors, when the increase in export revenues fails to induce investment in new technology (Bustos, 2011).[15] On the other hand, the design of innovation policy would also need to address factors that hinder the ability of innovating firms to create comparative advantages and enter the export market in the first place. In either case, a closely coordinated effort is needed between the government and the private sector to identify the bottlenecks and that considers the fact that the government does not know and cannot do everything and that the private sector has its own incentive to capture all gains from favourable government policy (Rodrik, 2010).

In closing, while the findings of this study contribute to our understanding of the link between innovation and export, there are limitations that can potentially be fruitfully addressed in the future. For example, I did not model the joint determination of the different types of innovation. Redoing the analysis following a similar methodology such as that used by Egger and Becker (2013) may yield further insights on the link between product innovation, process innovation, and export. In addition, the empirical analysis of this study may be subject to data-related limitations, including a short period, small sample size at the sector level, and, most importantly, a restrictive data access method. An extension of this study that incorporates the newly released BLD panel data covering 2004–2005 to 2009–2010 (ABS, 2011) with a better method for accessing the data could address time dynamics better, to say the least. For example, a longer data period would enable the investigation of what happens to new exporters and new innovators after the switch. I leave all of these for future research.

2.6 Acknowledgements

The author acknowledges and thanks the Economic Research Institute of ASEAN and East Asia (ERIA), under the ERIA Research Project on Globalization and Innovation in East Asia, for financing the study. The author also thanks the Australian Bureau of Statistics for providing online data access via RADL to the business level panel data 2004/2005–2006/2007 of the Business Longitudinal Database. Finally, the author is grateful to have received valuable comments and suggestions from Ari Kuncoro, Dionisius Narjoko, John Haisken-DeNew, and participants of the 41st Australian Conference of Economists in Melbourne in 2012 and participants of ERIA Working Group Workshop on Globalization and Innovation in East Asia in Jakarta, Denpasar and Bangkok in 2010 and 2011, where earlier versions of the paper were presented.

The author claims responsibility for all the views expressed in this paper. Email: apalangkaraya@swin.edu.au

Notes

1 See also Tuhin (2016).

2 Marin and Vögtlander (2013) argued that learning effects might be masked by price reduction if sales revenue data are used to measure performance.

3 The ABS uses the term 'businesses' while in this paper, I use the term 'enterprises' to be consistent with the term (that is, SMEs) used in the existing literature.

4 Here, 'new' may refer to 'new to the business' (74% of product innovation), 'new to the industry' (10%), 'new to Australia' (10%), or 'new to the world' (6%).

5 The Australian Export Awards has run for 48 years and has provided recognitions and honours to exceptional Australian exporters, based on the criterion of sustainable export growth achieved through innovation and commitment. See http://www.exportawards.gov.au/default.aspx (11 accessed March 2011) for more details.

6 See the case studies for the award winners provided by the Australian Export Awards website mentioned in the previous endnote.

7 Marginal effect estimates were obtained using STATA's dprobit command.

8 The coefficient estimates of the propensity to innovate equation estimated at the sector level are omitted for space consideration but they are available upon request. The three sectors are defined according to ANZSIC Version 1993: Primary is A (agriculture, forestry, and fishing); B (mining); Manufacturing is C (manufacturing); Services is E (construction); F (wholesale trade); G (retail trade); H (accommodation, cafes, and restaurants); I (transport and storage); J (communication services); L (property and business services); P (cultural and recreational services); and Q (personal and other services).

9 In addition, I also conduct a matching process using the radius matching method. The results (available upon request) are roughly similar to the results presented in the paper based on the nearest neighbour approach; except, the radius approach tends to produce estimates with weaker statistical significance due to fewer matched samples obtained. I refer to Imbens (2004) and the cited references therein for an excellent survey of the implications of the different matching approaches. Unfortunately, due to data access restrictions put in place by the Australian Bureau of Statistics, which required us to access the data indirectly via an online STATA do file submission and limited the types of STATA commands that I could issue to only built-in statistical analysis command – programming commands such as the FOR loop command and non-standard ADO files were not allowed – I was not able to conduct other more sophisticated propensity matching estimation techniques, such as the kernel density–based matching or bootstrapping for standard errors.

10 The balancing property tests (omitted due to space constraints but available upon request) support the validity of the results of the matching process when all sectors are pooled. Despite the relatively weak estimates of the propensity models, the results of the matching process appear quite reasonable in identifying valid matched control observations. In other words, balancing property tests appear to be satisfied for almost all nearest neighbour matching exercises (similar covariate balance results, available upon request, were also obtained for the sector-level estimation). Furthermore, it appears that the balancing property of the results based on the radius matching method is weaker compared to that of the nearest neighbour results. Similar covariate balance results are also obtained for the sector-level estimation.

11 Ideally, we would want to condition all other preceding periods ($t - 2$, $t - 3$, and so on) to identify new exporters more accurately. However, this is not possible with the limited data period. Hence, the analysis rests on an assumption that there is enough persistence in the export market.

12 However, these findings are not robust in terms of matching method, with none of the results based on the radius matching method being statistically significant. Also, other studies employing a similar methodology, such as Damijan et al. (2010), are also sensitive to the matching methods used.
13 The author would like to thank an anonymous referee for raising this point.
14 For recent examples, see Iacovone and Javorcik (2010) and Bustos (2011).
15 This, however, does not mean that the traditional comparative advantage sectors should be ignored because export market discovery can also occur in these sectors (Klinger and Lederman, 2004).

References

ABS (Australian Bureau of Statistics) (2001), *Small Business in Australia*, ABS Catalogue No. 1321.0.

ABS (Australian Bureau of Statistics) (2006), *Number and Characteristics of Australian Exporters*, ABS Catalogue No. 5368.0.55.006.

ABS (Australian Bureau of Statistics) (2007), *Patterns in Innovation in Australian Businesses 2005*, ABS Catalogue No. 8163.0.

ABS (Australian Bureau of Statistics) (2008), *Australian Industry 2006–07*, ABS Catalogue No. 8155.0.

ABS (Australian Bureau of Statistics) (2009), *Business Longitudinal Database, Expanded CURF, Australia 2004–05, 2005–06 and 2006–07.* Technical Manual, Catalogue No. 8168.055.002.

ABS (Australian Bureau of Statistics) (2010), *Characteristics of Australian Exporters 2008–09*, ABS Catalogue No. 5368.0.55.006.

ABS (Australian Bureau of Statistics) (2011), *Business Longitudinal Database, CURF, Australia, 2004–05 to 2009–10.* Technical Manual, ABS Catalogue No. 8168.0.55.002.

Acs, Z.J., and B. Audretsch (1988), 'Innovation in Large and Small Firms: An Empirical Analysis', *American Economic Review* 78: 678–90.

Arundel, A., and I. Kabla (1998), 'What Percentage of Innovations Are Patented? Empirical Estimates for European Firms', *Research Policy* 27(2): 127–41.

Aw, B.Y., X. Chen, and M.J. Roberts (1997), 'Firm-level Evidence on Productivity Differentials, Turnover, and Exports in Taiwanese Manufacturing', Mimeo. Pennsylvania State University, June.

Aw, B.Y., M.J. Roberts, and D.Y. Xu (2008), 'R&D Investments, Exporting and the Evolution of Firm Productivity', *American Economic Review: Papers & Proceedings* 98(2): 451–56.

Aylward, D.K. (2004), 'Innovation-Export Linkages within Different Cluster Models: A Case Study from the Australian Wine Industry', *Prometheus* 22(4): 423–37.

Aylward, D.K. (2006), 'Global Pipelines: Profiling Successful SME Exporters within the Australian Wine Industry', *International Journal of Technology, Policy and Management* 6(1): 49–65.

Becker, S.O., and P. Egger (2013), 'Endogenous Product versus Process Innovation and a Firm's Propensity to Export', *Empirical Economics* 44(1): 329–54.

Bernard, A.B., and J.B. Jensen (1999), 'Exceptional Exporter Performance: Cause, Effect, or Both?', *Journal of International Economics* 47: 1–25.

Bernard, A.B., and J.B. Jensen (2004), 'Exporting and Productivity in the USA', *Oxford Review of Economic Policy* 20: 343–57.

Bustos, P. (2011), 'Trade Liberalization, Exports and Technology Upgrading: Evidence on the Impact of MERCOSUR on Argentinean Firms', *American Economic Review* 101: 304–40.

Cassiman, B., and E. Golovko (2007), 'Innovation and the Export-Productivity Link', *CEPR Discussion Papers* no. 6411. London: CEPR.

Cassiman, B., and E. Martinez-Ros (2007), *Product Innovation and Exports. Evidence from Spanish Manufacturing. Mimeo.* Madrid: IESE Business School.

Chadha, A. (2009), 'Product Cycles, Innovation, and Exports: A Study of Indian Pharmaceuticals', *World Development* 37(9): 1478–83.

Constantini, J.A., and M.J. Melitz (2008), 'The Dynamics of Firm-Level Adjustment to Trade Liberalization', in E. Helpman, D. Marin, and T. Verdier (eds.), *The Organization of Firms in a Global Economy*, Cambridge, MA: Harvard University Press. pp. 107–141.

Crespi, G., C. Criscuolo, and J. Haskel (2008), 'Productivity, Exporting, and the Learning-by-Exporting Hypothesis: Direct Evidence from UK Firms', *Canadian Journal of Economics* 41(2): 619–37.

Damijan, J.P., C. Kostevc, and S. Polanec (2010), 'From Innovation, to Exporting or Vice Versa', *The World Economy* 33(3): 374–98.

Dehejia, R.J., and S. Wahba (2002), 'Propensity Score-Matching Methods for Nonexperimental Causal Studies', *The Review of Economics and Statistics* 84(1): 151–61.

De Loecker, J. (2007), 'Do Exports Generate Higher Productivity? Evidence from Slovenia', *Journal of International Economics* 73(1): 69–98.

Fernandes, A.M., and C. Paunov (2010), 'Does Trade Stimulate Innovation? Evidence from Firm-Product Data', *OECD Working Paper* No. 286. Paris: OECD.

Girma, S., D. Greenaway, and R. Kneller (2003), 'Export Market Exit and Performance Dynamics: A Causality Analysis of Matched Firms', *Economic Letters* 80(2): 181–87.

Girma, S., H. Görg, and A. Hanley (2008), 'R&D and Exporting: A Comparison of British and Irish Firms', *Review of World Economics* 144(4): 751–73.

Iacovone, L., and B.S. Javorcik (2010), 'Multi-Product Exporters: Product Churning, Uncertainty and Export Discoveries', *The Economic Journal* 120(544): 481–99.

Imbens, G. (2004), 'Nonparametric Estimation of Average Treatment Effects under Exogeneity: A Review', *The Review of Economics and Statistics* 86(1): 4–29.

Ito, K. (2012), 'Sources of Learning-by-Exporting Effects: Does Exporting Promote Innovation', *Working Papers* DP-2012–06, Jakarta: Economic Research Institute for ASEAN and East Asia (ERIA).

Ito, K., and S. Lechevalier (2010), 'Why Some Firms Persistently Out-Perform Others: Investigating the Interactions between Innovation and Exporting Strategies', *Industrial and Corporate Change* 19(6): 1997–2039.

Jensen, P.H., and E. Webster (2006), 'Firm Size and the Use of Intellectual Property Rights', *The Economic Record* 82256: 44–55.

Klinger, B., and D. Lederman (2004), 'Discovery and Development: An Empirical Exploration of 'New' Products', *World Bank Policy Research Working Paper* 3450, November.

Kirbach, M., and C. Schmiedeberg (2008), 'Innovation and Export Performance: Adjustment and Remaining Differences in East and West German Manufacturing', *Economics of Innovation and New Technology* 17(5): 435–57.

Long, N.V., H. Raff, and F. Stähler (2011), 'Innovation and Trade with Heterogeneous Firms', *Journal of International Economics* 84: 149–59.

MacGarvie, M.J. (2006), 'Do Firms Learn From International Trade', *The Review of Economics and Statistics* 88(1): 46–60.

Mansfield, E., M. Schwartz, and S. Wagner (1981), 'Imitation Costs and Patents: An Empirical Study', *The Economic Journal* 91(364): 907–918. Aldershot: Edward Elgar.

Marin, A.G., and Voigtländer (2013), 'Exporting and Plant-Level Efficiency Gains: It's In the Measure', *NBER Working Paper* 19033, http://www.nber.org/papers/w19033.

Melitz, M.J. (2003), 'The Impact of Trade on Intra-Industry Reallocations and Aggregate Industry Productivity', *Econometrica* 71: 1695–725.

Palangkaraya, A., and J. Yong (2007), 'Exporter and Non-Exporter Productivity Differentials: Evidence from Australian Manufacturing Establishments', *Melbourne Institute Working Paper* 4/07. Melbourne, Australia: The University of Melbourne.

Palangkaraya, A., and J. Yong (2011), 'Trade Liberalisation, Exit, and Output and Employment Adjustments of Australian Manufacturing Establishments', *The World Economy* 34(1): 1–22.

Rodrik, D. (2004), 'Industrial Policies for the Twenty-First Century', John F. Kennedy School of Government, Harvard University, September.

Rodrik, D. (2010), 'The Return to Industrial Policy', *Project Syndicate*, https://www.project-syndicate.org/commentary/the-return-of-industrial-policy.

Schumpeter, J.A. (1934), *The Theory of Economic Development: An Inquiry into Profits, Capital Credit, Interests, and the Business Cycles.* Cambridge, MA: Harvard University Press.

Tuhin, R. (2016), 'Modelling the Relationship between Innovation and Exporting: Evidence from Australian SMEs', *Research Paper* 3/2016, Australian Government Department of Industry, Innovation and Science.

Wagner, J. (2007), 'Exports and Productivity: A Survey of the Evidence from Firm-level Data', *The World Economy* 30(1): 60–82.

3 Trade reforms, competition, and innovation in the Philippines

Rafaelita M. Aldaba

3.1 Introduction

Innovation is defined as the implementation of a new or significantly improved product or process, marketing method, or organisational method in business practices, workplace organisation, or external relations (OECD, 2007). In general, there is broad consensus among economists that research and development (R&D)/innovation is a major source of economic growth (Gilbert, 2006). As Aghion and Howitt (1999) argue, innovation is a crucial ingredient in long-run economic growth. Moreover, research shows that the social return on investment in R&D is higher than private return (Griliches, 1992).

Since the 1980s, the Philippines has implemented market-opening reforms such as trade and investment liberalisation, deregulation, and privatisation to encourage competition in the economy, increase productivity, and stimulate economic growth. Using the country's newly created manufacturing firm-level panel data, the paper will examine the impact of trade reforms through increased competition on the innovative activities of domestic firms. The study is relevant given not only the substantial trade reforms implemented in the last two decades but also in the light of the country's low R&D expenditures and the urgent need for technology upgrading. It will address the following questions: What is the impact of the removal of trade barriers on firms' innovation activities? Did the increase in competition arising from trade reforms lead to increases in innovation?

The paper is divided into six parts. After the introduction, Section 3.2 focuses on the trade and industrial policies and economic performance of the Philippine manufacturing industry. Section 3.3 reviews selected literature on competition and innovation. Section 3.4 presents the methodology of the paper while Section 3.5 analyses the results. Section 3.6 concludes and discusses the implications of the paper.

3.2 Philippine manufacturing industry: trade policy reforms, performance, and structure

3.2.1 Government trade liberalisation policy

Like most developing countries, the Philippines adopted an import substitution strategy from the 1950s up to the late 1970s. The manufacturing sector is the country's most favoured industry, given the high level of protection and substantial investment incentives that it enjoyed during the last two decades. In the 1980s, the government started liberalising the trade regime by removing tariff and non-tariff barriers. In the 1990s, tariff reforms were continued, to further narrow down the tariff range and remove quantitative restrictions. In 2001, additional legislation was passed to adjust the tariff structure towards a uniform tariff rate of 5% by the year 2004, except for a few sensitive agricultural and manufactured items. In October and December 2003, the Arroyo government issued Executive Orders 241 and 264, respectively, to modify the tariff structure such that the rates on products that were not locally produced were made as low as possible while the rates on products that were locally produced were adjusted upward. This resulted in tariff increases on a group of agricultural and manufactured products.

Table 3.1 presents the statutory tariff rates from 1998 to 2004 for the country's major economic sectors. Note that since 2004, no major most favoured nation tariff changes have been implemented. The tariff changes pursued were mainly those arising from regional trading agreements such as the ASEAN Free Trade Agreement. It is evident from the data that the overall level of tariff rates is already low, with the average tariff rate for all industries at 6.82%. Agriculture has the highest average tariff rate of 11.3%.

While the average tariff rate for all industries dropped from 11.32% in 1998 to 6.82% in 2004, tariff dispersion widened as the coefficient of variation went up from 0.96 to 1.07. The ad valorem tariffs for mining and quarrying as well as those for fishing and forestry show the most uniformity, while those for agriculture and manufacturing exhibit the most dispersion. Note that a lower level of tariff protection does not always imply that the tariff schedule is less distorting. In general, the more dispersion in a country's tariff schedule, the greater the distortions caused by tariffs on production and consumption patterns.

Table 3.1 also indicates that the percentage of tariff peaks (those greater than three times the mean) went up from 2.24% in 1998 to 2.71% in 2004. The

Table 3.1 Average Tariff Rates by Major Economic Sector, 1998–2004

	Implementation of Major Tariff Policy Changes						
Major sectors	*1998*	*1999*	*2000*	*2001*	*2002*	*2003*	*2004*
All industries	11.32	10.25	8.47	8.28	6.45	6.6	6.82
Coefficient of variation	0.96	0.91	0.99	1.04	1.17	1.06	1.07
% of tariff peaks	2.24	2.24	2.48	2.5	2.69	2.53	2.71
Agriculture	15.9	13.2	11.5	12.3	10.4	10.4	11.3
Coefficient of variation	1.07	1.14	1.3	1.23	1.31	1.22	1.17
Fishing and forestry	9.4	8.9	6.7	6.7	5.8	5.7	6
Coefficient of variation	0.63	0.7	0.66	0.62	0.45	0.48	0.57
Mining and quarrying	3.3	3.3	3.1	3.2	2.8	2.7	2.5
Coefficient of variation	0.42	0.41	0.24	0.23	0.38	0.4	0.48
Manufacturing	11.38	10.35	8.5	8.28	6.39	6.57	6.76
Coefficient of variation	0.93	0.88	0.95	1	1.13	1.03	1.03

Source: Aldaba (2005).

greater the percentage of tariff peaks in a country's tariff schedule, the greater the potential economic distortions, particularly when highly substitutable products are present in both domestic and world markets. The sectors with tariff peaks consisted mostly of agricultural products with in-quota rates and out-quota rates.

3.2.2 Economic performance of the manufacturing industry: 1980s–2000s

The overall performance of the manufacturing industry, in terms of output and employment generation, has been generally weak. Table 3.2 shows that from the 1980s up to the 1990s, manufacturing growth was very slow – averaging 1% and 2% in each respective decade. Growth picked up in the 2000s, with manufacturing expanding by 3.4% on average. However, there seems to have been very little movement of resources in the manufacturing industry, as its share of total industrial output declined from 26% in the 1980s to 25% in the 1990s and to about 24% in the 2000s. As in manufacturing, growth in the agriculture sector remained sluggish up to the 1990s and averaging a rate of 4% during the most recent period. The services sector has been the best performer in all three decades. On average, its growth rate went up from 2.3% in the 1980s to 5% in the 2000s. Broad growth took place, as its sub-sectors consistently experienced rising growth rates. Services also accounted for the bulk of the economy's output with the sector's average share rising substantially from 49% in the 1980s to 55% in the current period.

In terms of employment generation, the manufacturing industry failed in creating enough jobs to absorb new entrants to the labour force. Table 3.3 indicates that its share of total employment remained stagnant at 10% in the 1980s until the 1990s and dropped to 9.2% in 2000–2008. The services sector is the most important provider of jobs in the recent period with its average share increasing from 40% in the 1980s to 47% in the 1990s. Currently, it accounts for almost 54%. Agriculture's share in total employment dropped

Table 3.2 Average Value-Added Growth Rates and Structure

	Average Growth Rate			*Average Value-Added Share*		
Year	*1981–1989*	*1990–1999*	*2000–2009*	*1981–1989*	*1990–1999*	*2000–2009*
Agriculture, fishery, and forestry	1.3	1.5	3.5	23.5	21.6	19.2
Industry sector	0.9	2.1	3.9	27.6	26.4	25.4
Mining and quarrying	3	–1.4	12.7	1.7	1.3	1.5
Manufacturing	0.9	2.3	3.4	25.9	25.1	23.8
Services sector	2.3	3.7	5.2	48.9	52	55.4
Total GDP	1.7	2.8	4.6	100	100	100

Source: National Income Accounts, NSCB.

continuously from 50% in the 1980s to 43% in the 1990s and to 37% in the current period.

Table 3.4 shows the distribution of value added in the manufacturing industry. Consumer goods comprised the bulk of manufacturing value added, although their share declined from 57% to 50% between the 1980s and the 1990s. Currently, the sector's share is still at 50%. Food manufacturing represents the most important sub-sector, accounting for an average share of 39% of the total in the current period. Intermediate goods follows with a share of 27% in the 2000s, a decline from 35% in the 1990s and 31% in the 1980s. With the growing importance of electrical machinery, the share of capital goods increased steadily from 10% in the 1980s to 13% in the 1990s and 19% in the 2000s. Electrical machinery posted an average share of 3% in the 1980s, 6% in the 1990s, and 12% in the 2000s.

Table 3.3 Employment Growth Rate and Structure

Economic Sector	*Average Growth Rate*			*Average Share*		
	1981–1989	*1990–1999*	*2000–2009*	*1981–1989*	*1990–1999*	*2000–2009*
Agriculture, fishery, and forestry	1.2	0.7	1.4	49.6	42.8	36.6
Industry	2.5	1.7	0.8	10.6	10.6	9.6
Mining and quarrying	5.3	-4.6	7.9	0.7	0.5	0.4
Manufacturing	2.5	2.1	0.6	9.9	10.2	9.2
Services	4.8	4.2	3.6	39.8	46.6	53.8
Total employed	2.7	2.5	2.5	100	100	100

Source: National Income Accounts, NSCB.

Table 3.4 Average Value-Added Structure and Growth

Industry Group	*Average Growth Rate*			*Average Value-Added Share*		
	1980–1989	*1990–1999*	*2000–2008*	*1981–1989*	*1990–1999*	*2000–2008*
Consumer goods	0	2	5	57	50	50
Food manufactures	-1	2	6	44	36	39
Beverage industries	7	2	4	4	4	4
Tobacco manufactures	1	1	-6	3	3	1
Footwear wearing apparel	6	2	2	5	6	5
Furniture and fixtures	2	2	7	1	1	1
Intermediate goods	2	2	2	31	35	27
Textile manufactures	0	-5	0	4	3	2
Wood and cork products	-5	-4	-4	2	2	1
Paper and paper products	4	-1	2	1	1	1
Publishing and printing	3	1	0	1	2	1
Leather and leather products	-3	5	0	0	0	0
Rubber products	1	-2	0	2	1	1

(*Continued*)

Industry Group	*Average Growth Rate*			*Average Value-Added Share*		
	1980–1989	*1990–1999*	*2000–2008*	*1981–1989*	*1990–1999*	*2000–2008*
Chemicals and chemical products	–1	2	3	7	6	6
Petroleum and coal	6	4	3	12	17	14
Non-metallic minerals	2	2	3	2	3	2
Capital goods	2	6	6	10	13	19
Basic metal industries	10	–2	13	3	2	2
Metal industries	4	0	7	2	2	2
Machinery ex. electrical	0	6	2	1	1	2
Electrical machinery	7	13	6	3	6	12
Transport equipment	–5	2	5	1	1	1
Miscellaneous manufactures	8	5	7	2	2	3
Total manufacturing	1	2	4	100	100	100

Source: Authors' computation.

3.2.3 Price cost margins

Table 3.5 presents four-firm concentration ratio (CR4) calculations for the manufacturing industry adjusted for the presence of imports. In general, given the relatively low tariff rates affecting the industry, the calculated ratios seem to indicate that the industry is already contestable. In most sectors, the concentration ratios are below 35%. However, high ratios ranging from 60% to 82% are still prevalent in sectors such as refined petroleum, tobacco, beverages, and flat glass (non-metallic products).

Table 3.6 presents price cost margin (PCM) estimates with an average of 29% for the manufacturing industry. In many sectors, PCMs were already low in 2003, ranging from 8% to 19% covering leather, fabricated metal, transport equipment, garments, machinery (excluding electrical), and printing and publishing. Moderate PCMs that range from 22% to 38% are found in food, plastic, wood, rubber, and furniture products. Finally, PCMs are high in beverages, tobacco, non-metallic products, and glass and glass products. In these sectors, PCMs range from 45% to 62%. These sectors are also the most highly concentrated within the manufacturing industry.

3.2.4 Total factor productivity growth

Table 3.7 presents estimates of total factor productivity (TFP) growth. The growth figures are normalised and interpreted as growth relative to 1996. From 1996 to 2006, aggregate productivity gains are evident in the leather, textiles, furniture, other manufacturing, and basic and fabricated metal sectors. Meanwhile, six sectors – (i) food, beverages, and tobacco; (ii) garments; (iii) wood, paper, and publishing; (iv) coke, petroleum, chemicals, and rubber; (v) non-metallic products; and (vi) basic and fabricated metal products, as well as machinery and equipment, motor vehicles, and other transport – registered

Table 3.5 Four Firm Concentration Ratios, 2003

PSIC	*Description*	*CR4*
23	Coke, refined petroleum and other fuel products	79.8
16	Tobacco products	72
15	Beverages	62.4
26	Other non-metallic: flat glass	82.4
34	Motor vehicles, trailers, and semi-trailers	57.2
15	Food	55.7
26	Other non-metallic mineral products	54.3
26	Other non-metallic: cement	52.7
19	Tanning and dressing of leather; luggage, handbags, and footwear	45.1
35	Manufacture of other transport equipment	44.8
24	Chemicals and chemical products	40.6
22	Publishing, printing and reproduction of recorded media	36.3
28	Fabricated metal products, except machinery and equipment	35.8
29	Machinery and equipment, n.e.c.	34.5
27	Basic metals	30.5
33	Medical, precision and optical instruments, watches and clocks	29.4
21	Paper and paper products	29
25	Rubber and plastic products	28.3
36	Manufacture and repair of furniture	22.7
20	Wood, wood products and cork, except furniture; articles of bamboo, cane, rattan and the like; plaiting materials	20.4
17	Textile	4.4

Source: Authors' computation.

CR4 = 4-firm concentration ratio calculated as the value of output by the four largest firms to the total for each 5-digit industry level. The CR4 calculations are adjusted for import penetration (MPR), i.e., (1-MPR)*CR4. Import penetration shares are estimated as the ratio of imports to output plus imports less exports.

Table 3.6 Price Cost Margins

Code	*Description*	*PCM Based on Roeger Method*	*Standard Errors*	*PCM Based on Simple Method*
313	Beverages	0.62***	0.06	0.53
314	Tobacco	0.59***	0.04	0.47
361,363, and 369	Pottery, cement, and other non-metallic products	0.60***	0.1	0.57
362	Glass and glass products	0.50***	0.04	0.52
352	Other chemicals	0.45***	0.04	0.37
341	Paper and paper products	0.38***	0.03	0.36
351	Industrial chemicals	0.38***	0.03	0.35
355	Rubber products	0.34***	0.05	0.28
332 and 386	Furniture including metal furniture	0.32***	0.03	0.22
385	Professional and scientific equipment	0.31***	0.29	-0.06
331	Wood and cork	0.31***	0.02	0.26
372	Nonferrous metal	0.31***	0.05	0.21
390	Miscellaneous manufactures	0.30***	0.04	0.2

(*Continued*)

Code	*Description*	*PCM Based on Roeger Method*	*Standard Errors*	*PCM Based on Simple Method*
356	Plastic products	0.30***	0.02	0.25
353	Petroleum refineries	0.29***	0.11	0.21
383	Electrical machinery	0.28***	0.01	0.25
354	Petroleum and coal	0.27***	0.12	0.21
321	Textiles	0.26***	0.02	0.27
311 and 312	Food processing and manufacturing	0.24***	0.03	0.28
371	Iron and steel	0.22***	0.01	0.26
342	Printing and publishing	0.19**	0.11	0.16
382	Machinery except electrical	0.18***	0.04	0.11
322	Wearing apparel except footwear	0.16**	0.12	-0.01
384	Transport equipment	0.12***	0.04	0.14
381	Fabricated metal	0.10**	0.04	0.17
323 and 324	Leather and leather footwear	0.08***	0.04	0.16
	All manufacturing	*0.29****	*0.02*	*0.3*

Source: Aldaba (2008).

Note: PCMs in column 3 are estimated using Roeger regression while those in column 4 are based on accounting data using average variable costs as proxy for marginal costs. *** indicates significance at the 1% level.

Table 3.7 Total Factor Productivity Growth

Sector	*Year*	*TFP Growth Relative to Base Year 1996*	*Sector*	*Year*	*TFP Growth Relative to Base Year 1996*
Food, beverages, and tobacco	1996	0	Non-metallic products	1996	0
	1997	0.45		1997	0.11
	1998	3.01		1998	1.47
	2000	-0.82		2000	-1.12
	2002	-1.83		2002	-7.38
	2003	-2.25		2003	-2.2
	2005	-1.36		2005	0.39
	2006	-1.44		2006	-0.65
Textile	1996	0	Basic metal and fabricated metal products	1996	0
	1997	1.8		1997	-0.2
	1998	1.01		1998	-4.39
	2000	0.95		2000	-1.77
	2002	-0.46		2002	-3.18
	2003	1.2		2003	-2.7
	2005	6		2005	-4.47
	2006	2.35		2006	1.32
Garments	1996	0	Machinery and equipment, motor vehicles and other transport	1996	0
	1997	1.12		1997	0.37
	1998	2.46		1998	-4.92
	2000	0.51		2000	0.9
	2002	0.49		2002	-2
	2003	0.62		2003	-2.75
	2005	-0.75		2005	-1.7
	2006	-0.99		2006	-0.86

Sector	*Year*	*TFP Growth Relative to Base Year 1996*	*Sector*	*Year*	*TFP Growth Relative to Base Year 1996*
Leather	1996	0	Furniture	1996	0
	1997	-1.35		1997	1.16
	1998	0.81		1998	1.64
	2000	0.63		2000	3.12
	2002	7.2		2002	3.46
	2003	12.1		2003	2.03
	2005	8.09		2005	2.59
	2006	9.54		2006	1.86
Wood, paper, and publishing	1996	0	Other manufacturing	1996	0
	1997	0.61		1997	-0.18
	1998	0.29		1998	3.01
	2000	-2.46		2000	0.27
	2002	-1.06		2002	1.49
	2003	-3.85		2003	0.63
	2005	-3.64		2005	1.18
	2006	-5.39		2006	2.87
Coke, petroleum, chemicals, and rubber	1996	0	All manufacturing	1996	0
	1997	-0.61		1997	-0.23
	1998	-2.68		1998	-1.59
	2000	2.94		2000	-0.44
	2002	-6.65		2002	-4.86
	2003	4.19		2003	-1
	2005	-1.11		2005	-2.53
	2006	-4.76		2006	-3.37

Source: Aldaba (2010).
Note: These growth figures are normalised and interpreted as growth relative to base year 1996.

negative productivity growth rates from 1996 to 2006. On the whole, the manufacturing sector's aggregate productivity declined by 3.4% from 1996 to 2006.

3.2.5 R&D/innovation

Using gross domestic expenditure on R&D as a percentage of GDP as a measure, it is shown that research intensity is low in the Philippines. Figures from the Institute for Statistics[1] of the United Nations Educational, Scientific and Cultural Organization (UNESCO) showed that the country's investment in R&D was only 0.14% in 2013. Singapore registered 1.99%, Thailand had 0.44%, and Indonesia posted 0.08%. In terms of gross domestic R&D expenditures per capita measured in terms of purchasing power parity dollar (constant PPP$), the Philippines registered PPP$7.75 in 2013 in contrast to Singapore's PPP$1,405.1, Thailand's PPP$58.09, and Indonesia's PPP$7.27.

In terms of number of R&D personnel measured in full-time equivalent, the UNESCO data showed that the Philippines had a total of 26,576.9 in 2013 while Singapore had 41,582.2. Expressed in terms of R&D personnel per million inhabitants, the Philippines posted 269.9 while Singapore had 7,756.7.

These figures seem to indicate that the Philippines has been under-investing in R&D. In a study on R&D gaps in the Philippines, Cororaton (1999) estimated a gap of 0.6% of GDP based on the average ratio in the 1980s. In terms of R&D manpower, the results showed the need for an additional 197 scientists and engineers per million population based on the average level in the 1980s. Cororaton (1999) also pointed out the large gap in the country's institutional structure, characterised by a weak national science and technology system, including incentives and protection of intellectual property rights.

3.3 Brief review of selected literature

Three strands of literature on international trade and growth are important in assessing the effects of trade liberalisation on innovation: (i) trade and competition, (ii) competition and innovation, and (iii) trade and innovation.

3.3.1 Competition and innovation

The existing theoretical models on competition and innovation point to two opposing views. Early endogenous growth and industrial organisation models suggest that competition appears to be detrimental to innovation and technical progress. Rents are seen as the major source of innovation for companies wishing to engage in R&D. Increased competition leads to a decline in innovative activity as more competition reduces the monopoly rents that reward successful innovators. Hence, large firms provide a more stable platform for investment in R&D. In contrast, the opposite view contends that competition may foster innovation as firms need to escape increased competition from rival firms. Competition will force firms to innovate in order to survive.

In an effort to reconcile the two views, Aghion et al. (2005) extended the basic Schumpeterian model by allowing incumbent firms to innovate. Traditional models were based on the assumption that innovation was done by outsiders or new entrants competing against incumbents with conventional technology and that the payoff of innovation was equal to post-innovation rent (pre-innovation rent was zero). The Aghion et al. model assumes that innovation incentives depend on the difference between post- and pre-innovation rents. Firms innovate to reduce production costs and this is done in a step-by-step manner where a laggard firm must first catch up with the technological leader before becoming a leader itself. Greater competition may foster innovation and growth as it may reduce a firm's pre-innovation rents by more than it reduces post-innovation rents. Competition may increase incremental profits from innovation and encourage R&D investments aimed at escaping competition. Competition is particularly intense in 'neck-and-neck' industries, where it is so close that it is hardly possible to determine which firm is leader; the 'escape competition' effect is strongest in these industries. On the other hand, in less neck-and-neck or unlevelled industries, more competition may reduce innovation as the reward for laggard firms catching up with the technological leader may fall; this is the Schumpeterian effect.

The model predicts an inverted-U-shaped relationship between competition and innovation. At low levels of competition, the escape competition effect dominates, while at higher levels of competition, the Schumpeterian effect dominates. To test the model, Aghion et al. (2002) used a panel data set of United Kingdom firms. The results confirmed the presence of a strong inverted-U relationship and that the gradient of the curve tends to be steeper for firms in more neck-and-neck industries.

Looking at entry and innovation, Aghion and Burgess (2003) showed that competition can affect innovation depending on the firm's level of efficiency. In particular, firms close to the efficiency frontier are expected to survive and deter entry by innovating. An increased entry threat leads to greater innovation aimed at escaping that threat. In contrast, firms that are far below the frontier are in a weaker position to fight external entry. An increased entry threat reduces the payoff from innovating, since the innovation's expected life horizon has become shorter. Competition thus provides incentives for more efficient firms to innovate and a disincentive for less efficient ones. In a related model, Aghion et al. (2005) predict that firms located in more pro-business environments are more likely to respond to competition by innovating.

Empirical studies that investigated the relationship between competition and innovation showed mixed results. The Schumpeterian argument predicts a negative relationship. Earlier studies that used market concentration as proxy for competition showed a positive relationship between industry concentration and R&D intensity (implying a negative relationship). However, more recent studies showed that this disappears when inter-industry differences such as industry characteristics and technological opportunities are taken into account (Gilbert, 2006). Geroski (1990) did not find support for the Schumpeterian assertion that monopoly power stimulates innovation. More recent empirical studies on the relationship between competition and innovation pointed to a positive relationship. Empirical work by Geroski (1995), Nickell (1996), and Blundell et al. (1999) found a positive correlation between competition and innovation. Creusen et al. (2006) also found a positive relationship between competition and innovation but no evidence for the existence of an inverted U.

Hopman and Rojas-Romagosa (2010) analysed the relationship between changes in competition levels and innovation efforts. Using the panel data of the Organisation for Economic Co-operation and Development, the authors found a monotonic relationship between the variables but did not find an inverted-U relationship as in the influential Aghion et al. (2002) paper. Using data on firms in 27 transition economies, Gorodnichenko et al. (2009) tested predictions about the impact of competition and linkages with foreign firms on domestic firms' innovative efforts. Their findings showed that competition has a negative effect on innovation, especially for firms that are far from the efficiency frontier. Firms that have market power tend to innovate more, but greater pressure from foreign competition also stimulates innovation. The paper did not find support for an inverted-U effect of competition on innovation. In testing the same hypothesis, Carlin et al. (2004) showed that innovation is higher in monopolistic industries.

3.3.2 Trade and competition

Since the early 1980s, the new trade theory has shown that aside from the gains from trade due to specialisation based on comparative advantage, trade liberalisation can lead to additional gains by reducing the 'deadweight losses' created by the ability of domestic firms to exercise market power. An open trade regime is a powerful instrument for disciplining the firms that have market power. Competition from imports constrains the ability of domestic producers to engage in anti-competitive activities, which would otherwise reduce welfare (Cadot et al. 2000). This is known in industrial organisation literature as the 'imports-as-competitive discipline' hypothesis. When confronted with intensified competition, domestic industries that may have accumulated oligopoly profits in heavily protected markets are forced to behave more competitively.

In general, the empirical evidence provides strong support for the imports-as-competitive discipline hypothesis. Based on industry-level cross-section data, Schmalensee (1989) indicated that the ratio of imports to domestic consumption tends to be negatively correlated with the profitability of domestic sellers, especially when domestic concentration is high. Pugel (1980) also found that import penetration has a stronger negative relationship with domestic profitability when conventional measures of entry barriers are high.

Reviewing the literature on the impact of trade liberalisation on PCMs, Erdem and Tybout (2003) and Tybout (2001) concluded that, based on numerous empirical studies of firm- and plant-level liberalisation episodes, mark-ups decline with import competition. This empirical evidence provides robust confirmation for the import discipline hypothesis. Among import-competing firms, trade liberalisation squeezes PCMs, inducing some intra-plant efficiency gains as well as additional efficiency gains due to the closure of weak plants. The authors added that the effect was particularly marked among large plants. As Roberts and Tybout (1996) wrote, relatively high industry-wide exposure to foreign competition is associated with lower margins and the effect is concentrated in larger plants.

Using panel data sets on firms, Harrison (1994) found that mark-ups were negatively related to import competition in Cote d'Ivoire. In India, Krishna and Mitra (1998) also showed that mark-ups fell during the trade reform period. Earlier studies by De Melo and Urata (1986) and Tybout (1996) for Chile, and Grether (1996) for Mexico showed the same finding. Erdem and Tybout (2003) cautioned that care must be exercised in interpreting the results. The authors noted that the studies only describe the short-run effects of trade liberalisation. Reforms in trade regimes trigger a dynamic adjustment process that may take a long time to play out (plausibly lasting more than a decade).

Other studies showing further evidence that trade liberalisation has a pro-competitive effect include those by Levinsohn (1993) for Turkey; Warzynski (2002) and Konings et al. (2002) for Romania and Bulgaria; and Goldar and Agarwal (2004), Kambhampati and Parikh (2003), and Srivastava et al. (2001) for India. These country studies support the import discipline hypothesis indicating that trade liberalisation can lead to substantial reductions in price cost margins at least in those industries that are imperfectly competitive.

With the availability of micro data, the recent literature on trade liberalisation and productivity has increased substantially. This body of literature shows that industries facing the greatest tariff reduction and import competition have faster productivity growth than relatively protected industries. This is due to resource allocation arising from the exit of inefficient plants and productivity improvements within existing plants. Empirical studies showing these results were pioneered by Pavcnik (2000) for Chile; Topalova (2004) for India; Muendler (2002) and Amite and Konings (2007) for Indonesia; Schor (2004) for Brazil; and Fernandes (2003) for Columbia. For the Philippines, Aldaba (2010) also provided some evidence that trade liberalisation leads to productivity increases.

3.3.3 Trade and innovation

Recent literature on trade and growth shows that international trade affects firms' innovative activities through increased competition. As Licandro (2010) noted, increasing evidence supports the claim that international trade enhances innovation and productivity growth through an increase in competition.

In an earlier work based on Schumpeterian growth theory and using firm panel data sets for India and the United Kingdom, Aghion and Burgess (2003) found that reducing barriers to entry of foreign products and firms has a more positive effect on economic performance for firms and industries that are initially closer to the technological frontier. Incumbent firms that are sufficiently close to the technological frontier can survive and deter entry by innovating. On the other hand, firms that are far below the frontier are in a weaker position to fight external entry since this will reduce their expected payoff from innovating. Thus, liberalisation encourages innovation in industries that are close to the frontier and discourages innovation in industries that are far from it. Productivity, outputs, and profits should be higher in the industries and firms that are initially more advanced. The authors suggested that, for countries to benefit from liberalisation, policies that allow firms to upgrade their technological capabilities or workers to move from low to high productivity sectors are important.

Griffith et al. (2006) assessed the impact of product market reforms under the European Union's Single Market Programme (SMP) on innovation activity using an unbalanced panel of nine countries and 12 two-digit manufacturing industries covering the period 1987–2000. Their results suggest that the SMP's product market reforms led to an increase in product market competition, measured by a reduction in average profitability. Moreover, increased competition led to an increase in R&D intensity in manufacturing industries. Increased R&D intensity translated into faster TFP growth. The authors indicated that reforms that put pressure on profitability are likely to lead to increased innovation.

Fernandes and Paunov (2009) examined the effects of increased import competition on the upgrading of product quality using Chilean manufacturing plant data. The results showed a positive and significant effect from import competition on product-level product quality upgrading. The author suggested that increased exposure to import competition, including China and India, may be beneficial because it encourages producers to focus on offering upgraded and differentiated products rather than 'mundane' labour-intensive ones.

Bloom, Draca, and Van Reenen (2010) examined the impact of Chinese import competition on patenting, information technology, R&D, and TFP in 12 countries of the European Union using a panel data set for the period 1996–2007. The key results are, first, Chinese import competition increases innovation and TFP within surviving firms. Firms facing higher levels of import competition from China create more patents, spend more on R&D, and raise the intensity of their information technology and TFP. Second, Chinese import competition reduces job and survival probabilities in low-tech firms, whose TFP declines. These firms exit much more rapidly than high-tech firms in response to Chinese competition. The authors noted that the results suggest that increased import competition from China has caused a significant technological upgrading in European firms through faster diffusion and innovation. This implies that reducing import barriers against low wage countries like China can bring about welfare gains through technical change.

3.4 Description of methodology and data

3.4.1 Overall framework

The foregoing review highlights three important effects of trade liberalisation: (i) trade reforms increase competition, (ii) trade reforms have positive effects on innovation, and (iii) trade reforms lead to the selection of the most productive firms. Trade liberalisation thus has *pro-competitive effects* and, as Bhagwati (1968) wrote, is seen as a powerful and administratively simple way to enhance competition. Helpman and Krugman (1989) further noted that international trade increases competition. With trade liberalisation, imports can discipline the market by forcing domestic firms to lower their prices and behave competitively. Based on a comprehensive review of empirical studies of firm- and plant-level liberalisation episodes in various countries, Erdem and Tybout (2003) concluded that mark-ups decline with import competition.

Through the competition channel, trade liberalisation also has *innovation effects*. Newer studies by Fernandes and Paunov (2009) and Bloom, Draca and Van Reenen (2010) have shown some evidence of the positive impact of trade liberalisation on innovation. Economic profits or rents can serve as rewards for entrepreneurship and encourage innovation. An increase in competition may increase incentives for incumbent firms to adopt more or to innovate in order to prevent an erosion of their market position. Note, however, that increased competition may also reduce the incentive or reward for innovation or entry and may discourage these activities.

Through the competition channel, trade liberalisation also leads to *selection effects*. As trade liberalisation squeezes price cost margins, some intra-plant efficiency gains are made, and additional efficiency gains are induced due to the closure of weak plants. In the presence of within-industry firm heterogeneity, trade liberalisation may lead to improved productivity through the exit of inefficient firms and the reshuffling of resources and outputs from less to more efficient firms. Melitz (2003) points out that trade opening may induce a market share reallocation towards more efficient firms and generate an aggregate productivity gain, without any change at the firm level.[2] As Pavcnik (2000) showed, trade liberalisation induces the least productive firms to exit the market and the most productive non-exporters to become exporters.

Impulliti and Licandro (2009, 2010) introduced a framework that attempted to link together these three effects of trade liberalisation. Basically, trade affects both firm selection and innovation through the competition channel. Trade liberalisation leads to an increased number of firms in the domestic market, raising product market competition and lowering the mark-up rate. The selection effect of trade operates through endogenous mark-ups resulting from oligopolistic competition[3] among firms. The reduction in the mark-up rate (or increase in competition) due to trade liberalisation reduces profits, raises the productivity threshold above which firms can profitably produce, and forces less productive firms out of the market. Resources are reallocated from exiting firms to the more productive surviving firms, which innovate at a faster pace.

Given the relationship between trade liberalisation and innovation operating through the competition channel, the impact of trade liberalisation on innovation is examined through a two-stage approach where competition is endogenous. The same framework was used by Griffith et al. (2006) to address the endogeneity of competition in analysing the relationship between product market reform and innovation in the European Union. The following basic econometric model is tested:

Competition function

$$\text{Competition}_{ijt} = f\left(\text{Trade}_{jt},\ Z_{ijt}\right) \tag{1}$$

Innovation function

$$\text{Innovation}_{ijt} = g\left(\text{Competition}_{ijt},\ Z_{ijt}\right) \tag{2}$$

Where i indexes firms, j industries, and t years. Equation (1) describes the relationship between trade reforms and competition while equation (2) characterises the relationship between innovation and competition and links trade reforms with innovation through competition. Z is a vector of control variables that may affect the firm's innovation efforts.

Following Aghion et al. (2002), the PCM is used as an indicator of product market competition, while R&D expenditures are used as a proxy for innovation. The authors noted that the PCM has several advantages over other indicators such as market shares, the Herfindahl index, or the concentration index. These measures require a definition of both the geographic and product boundaries of the market in which the firm operates. This becomes important particularly for firms that operate in international markets where such traditional market concentration measures could be extremely misleading.

The specific competition and innovation functions are described by Equations (3) and (4) below:

$$\text{PCM}_{\text{ijt}} = \beta_0\text{Tariff}_{\text{jt}} + \beta_1\text{TGap}_{\text{ijt}} + \beta_2\text{Age}_{\text{ijt}} + \beta_3\text{Size}_{\text{ijt}} + \beta_4\text{Time} + \beta_5\text{Ind} + \beta_{\text{ijt}} \quad (3)$$

$$\text{RD}_{\text{ijt}} = \alpha_0\text{PCM}_{\text{ijt}} + \alpha_1\text{TGap}_{\text{ijt}} + \alpha_2\text{Age}_{\text{ijt}} + \alpha_3\text{Size}_{\text{ijt}} + \alpha_4\text{Time} + \alpha_5\text{Ind} + \alpha_{\text{ijt}} \quad (4)$$

where *PCM* is price cost margin, *Tariff* is a trade reform indicator, *TGap* or technology gap is the distance to the technological frontier and is a measure of efficiency, *RD* is R&D expenditures, *Age* and *Size* are firm characteristics measured by firm age and total number of workers, respectively; *Time* and *Ind* are time and industry dummies, and ε and ω are error terms. Apart from output tariff, the effective protection rate (EPR) will also be used as a trade reform indicator. EPRs represent rates of protection of value added and measure the net protection received by domestic producers from the protection of their outputs and the penalty from the protection of their inputs.

To control for the effects of the selection process on competition and innovation, net entry is also incorporated in the model:

$$\begin{aligned}\text{PCM}_{\text{ijt}} = {} & \lambda_0\text{Tariff}_{\text{jt}} + \lambda_1\text{TGap}_{\text{ijt}} + \lambda_2\text{Age}_{\text{ijt}} + \lambda_3\text{Size}_{\text{ijt}} + \lambda_4\text{NetEntry}_{\text{jt}} \\ & + \lambda_5\text{Time} + \lambda_6\text{Ind} + \rho_{\text{ijt}} \end{aligned} \quad (3a)$$

$$\begin{aligned}\text{RD}_{\text{ijt}} = {} & \delta_0\text{PCM}_{\text{ijt}} + \delta_1\text{TGap}_{\text{ijt}} + \delta_2\text{Age}_{\text{ijt}} + \delta_3\text{Size}_{\text{ijt}} + \delta_4\text{NetEnty} \\ & + \delta_5\text{Time} + \delta_6\text{Ind} + \gamma_{\text{ijt}} \end{aligned} \quad (4a)$$

A positive relationship is expected between competition (as measured by *PCM*) and trade liberalisation (with *Tariff* and *EPR* as indicators). As tariffs or EPRs are lowered, PCM or profitability is reduced, which indicates increased competition. This is the main channel through which trade liberalisation affects innovation. Hence, the trade indicators (*Tariff* and *EPR*) do not directly enter Equation (4).

A negative relationship is expected between *PCM* (measure of competition) and *RD* (measure of innovation). As PCM or profitability is reduced due to trade reforms, competition increases, raising the productivity threshold above which firms can profitably produce. This forces less productive firms out of the market. Resources are reallocated from exiting firms to the higher-productivity surviving firms, which innovate at a faster pace.

The PCM or Lerner index is an indicator of the level of competition or degree of monopoly power of firms in industries. It is often used as an indicator of the strength of competition in the market. In theory, it is defined as price minus marginal cost over price and reflects the degree of monopoly power measured by the mark-up pricing above marginal costs. It should be noted that high PCMs are not necessarily an indication of bad market performance or that a firm is less competitive. While a high PCM implies market power, it could also indicate high firm efficiency. If these high mark-ups or margins are the result of internal efficiency-improving measures or represent gains from product innovation or techniques that a firm employs, then the firm is still considered competitive.

The empirical measurement of the PCM is difficult since marginal costs are not directly observable and are quite hard to estimate. Indirect measures have been developed based on accounting data, with average variable costs acting as proxy for marginal costs. Critiques have noted that, measured in this manner, the PCM omits capital costs and becomes a poor indicator of excess profits.

Aghion et al. (2002) used operating profits net of depreciation and provisions less the financial cost of capital. This is represented by the following equation:

$$B = \frac{\text{Operating profits} - \text{Financial cost of capital}}{\text{Sales}} \quad (5)$$

where *Financial cost of capital* is defined as [*capital cost* * *capital stock*]. They assumed the cost of capital to be 0.085 for all firms and time periods, while capital stock is measured using the perpetual inventory method. This way, it is more like the ratio of price less average cost to price.

In this paper, the PCM is defined as:

$$B = \frac{\text{Total revenue} - \text{Compensation} - \text{Total cost} - \text{Financial cost of capital}}{\text{Total revenue}} \quad (6)$$

where Total costs = Raw materials + Fuel + Electricity + Depreciation + Other costs

*Financial cost of capital = [Index of investment goods*Real interest rate]*Book value of assets* The implicit price index for gross domestic capital formation is used as a price index of investment goods, while the 180-day Treasury Bill interest rate less inflation is used as measure of real interest rate.

Aghion et al. (2002) measured the technology gap between firms within an industry as the proportional distance a firm is from the technological frontier. In this paper, this is calculated as the difference between the TFP of the most productive firm in a given industry and log TFP of each firm in the industry.

3.4.2 Data

The paper uses firm-level panel data set consisting of firm-level information on revenues, employment, compensation, physical capital, R&D expenditures, and production costs from the Annual Survey and Census of Establishments of the National Statistics Office. The firm-level panel data set built covered the period 1996 to 2006, with three missing years (1999, 2001, and 2004). Both 2000 and 2006 are census years while the remaining six are survey years.

The panel data set is unbalanced and covers all firms with two or more overlapping years during the period 1996–2006. Firms with missing zero or negative values for the variables listed above as well as firms with duplicates were dropped. Firms with missing R&D expenditures and those with less than 10 workers were also excluded. Firm exit is indicated by firms that

Table 3.8 Summary Statistics

Variable	*Observations*	*Mean*	*Standard Deviation*	*Minimum*	*Maximum*
Total revenue (in million pesos)	8296	736	5200	0.065	233000
Compensation (in million pesos)	8296	43	141	0	2640
Total costs (in million pesos)	8296	594	4510	0.026	203000
Book value of fixed assets (in million pesos)	8296	180	1000	0	47600
Capital cost	8296	0.07	0.059	0.03	0.219
Financial cost of capital (in million pesos)	8296	15	102	0	5750
Price cost margin	8296	0.053	0.259	-6.086	0.96
R&D expenditure share (as % of value added)	8296	0.005	0.068	0	5.373
Age of firm (in years)	8263	17	14	0	100
Total number of workers	8296	264	703	10	14647
TFP gap	8296	0.371	0.146	0	1.054
Tariff (in %)	8296	9.087	6.309	1.073	60
Net entry	8296	-3	6.9	-52	6

Source: Authors' computation.

are no longer included in the 2006 census as well as those whose two-digit PSIC codes have changed. Firm entry is defined based on the firm's year of establishment or year when it started operating. Net entry by PSIC code is calculated as firm entry less exit. Firm age is calculated based on the firm's year of establishment or year when it started operating. Table 3.8 presents a summary of the data along with the calculated PCMs and financial cost of capital.

The TFP Gap indicator was calculated based on the TFP estimates obtained from an earlier study by Aldaba (2010). The TFP is defined as the residual of a Cobb-Douglas production function and is estimated using the methodology of Levinsohn and Petrin (2003). The estimates of firm i's TFP is obtained by subtracting firm i's predicted y (or log of output) from its actual y at time t. To make the estimated TFP comparable across industry sectors, a productivity index is created. The TFP Gap is given by the difference between the TFP index of the most productive firm in a given industry j at year t and the TFP index of each firm i in the industry j at year t.

Table 3.9 presents the yearly exit and entry rates. Exit rates increased from 6% in 1998 to about 22% in 2000 and 32% in 2001 but dropped to 26% in 2003 and

Table 3.9 Entry and Exit Rates, 1996–2006

Year	*Exit Rate*	*Entry Rate*	*Total Number of Firms*
1996			
1997			
1998	6.14	5.05	277
2000	21.96	1.63	551
2001	31.71		1,009
2003	26.14	1	903
2005	13.05	0.24	1,226
2006		0.09	4,330

Source: Authors' computation.

further to 13% in 2005. Entry rates were low and declined continuously from 5% in 1998 to 1% in 2003 and to less than 1% in 2005 and 2009.

3.5 Analysis of results

To examine the impact on innovation of the increased competitive pressure arising from trade reforms, a two-stage approach is applied, as specified in Equations (3) and (4). The profitability level measured by the PCM is the main channel through which trade liberalisation affects innovation. The *PCM* and *RD* are simultaneously determined.

The model is estimated using two methods. First, a two-stage instrumental variables (IV) technique is applied. Equation (3) is the first stage in the IV estimation of the second stage given by equation (4). The *PCM* and *RD* are estimated by instrumental variables where *Tariff* is the excluded instrument. Two estimators, fixed effects (FE) and random effects (RE), are used. The Hausman test is implemented to decide between FE and RE.

Second, a Tobit estimation method is also applied where observations on *RD* are censored at 0. Note that *RD* observations contain either zeroes for firms that do not engage in innovation or a positive value for those that decided to innovate.

Table 3.10.1 presents the results of the first stage of the IV estimation, which evaluates the degree of correlation between trade reforms, as measured by *Tariff*, and the endogenous regressor, *PCM*, which is our measure of profitability. The results show that the coefficient on *Tariff* is positive and highly significant, indicating that trade reforms have a strong positive impact on the level of profitability. The results also indicate that the coefficient on *TFP Gap* is negative and highly significant in both FE and RE methods. This implies that firms that are farther from a technological frontier (less productive firms) have lower profitability than efficient firms, which tend to have higher profitability.

Using EPR as a trade indicator, the random effects method shows that the coefficient on *EPR* is positive but not significant. The coefficient on *Total Workers* is negative and highly significant. The coefficient on *TFP Gap* is also negative

Table 3.10.1 First Stage IV Results: FE and RE

PCM	*Tariff*		*EPR*	
	(1) FE	*(2) RE*	*(1) FE*	*(2) RE*
Age	0.00031	-0.000458*	-0.0039674	-0.0008581*
	0.0026855	0.0002743	0.0022206	0.000539
Total workers	-0.00001	-0.000028***	-8.15E-06*	-0.0000241***
	0.0000128	0.0000054	0.0000128	6.94E-06
TFP gap	-2.54176***	-1.483633***	-2.557112	-2.08648***
	0.1052527	0.04587	0.1052544	0.0568845
Trade	0.0069049***	0.002489***	0.0006741	0.0004895
	0.0022272	0.0007028	0.0004289	0.0002319
Constant	1.096718***	0.5535773***	1.254195	
	0.1022577	0.0254748	0.0889347	
Year dummies	Y	Y	Y	Y
Industry dummies	Y	Y	Y	Y
F-Statistic	1.65		1.65	
Prob>F	0		0	
Observations	8263	8263	8263	8263
R-squared	0.0672			
Hausman Test				
Chi2	45.22			8.27
Prob>chi2	0.0001			0.9605

Source: Authors' computation.
EPR = effective protection rate, FE = fixed effects, PCM = price cost margin, RE = random effects, TFP = total factor productivity.
Note: *10% level of significance, **5% level of significance, ***1% level of significance.

and highly significant while the coefficient on *Age* is negative and significantly different from zero.

Table 3.10.2 presents the results of the second stage IV estimation, which looks at the relationship between profitability and innovation where *RD* is the dependent variable. The FE results based on *Tariff* as trade indicator show a significant negative relationship between *PCM* and *RD*, which indicates that reduced profitability (suggesting high competition) due to trade reform is associated with increased *RD*. The RE results show the same negative relationship between *PCM* and *RD*, but not at a significant level. The coefficient on *TFP Gap* is negative in both FE and RE methods but is insignificant.

Using *EPR* as trade indicator, the RE method shows that none of the explanatory variables is significant. The coefficient on *PCM* is negative but is insignificant.

To test the appropriateness of RE, a Hausman test was implemented. Using *Tariff* as the trade indicator, the result shows a rejection of the null hypothesis that the RE estimator is consistent. Using *EPR* as trade indicator, the result indicates an acceptance of the null hypothesis.

The model is refitted as a Tobit with *lnRD* being left censored at zero. The first stage results presented in Table 3.11.1 show that *Tariff* has a highly significant positive effect on profitability. *TFP Gap* has a highly significant negative impact

Table 3.10.2 Second Stage IV Results: FE and RE

RD	*Tariff*		*EPR*	
	(1) FE	*(2) RE*	*(1) FE*	*(2) RE*
PCM	-0.114983*	-0.095598	-0.074743	-0.111575
	-0.0704618	-0.0776039	-0.129896	-0.111468
Age	-0.00044	0.0001051	-0.000256	0.0000963
	-0.0005744	-0.000084	-0.000737	-0.000158
Total workers	-0.00000538*	-2.25E-06	-5.06E-06*	-4.56E-06
	-0.00000285	-0.00000265	-2.81E-06	-3.16E-06
TFP gap	-0.11871	-0.0520831	-0.015795	-0.096095
	-0.1816651	-0.1146816	-0.332906	-0.232484
Constant	0.09242	0.027075	0.0419677	0.0494711
	-0.0904484	-0.0444074	-0.163868	-0.095103
Year dummies	Y	Y	Y	Y
Industry dummies	Y	Y	Y	Y
F-Statistic	3.13		3.57	
Prob>F	0		0	
Observations	8263	8263	8263	8263
R-squared	0.0044			
Hausman test				
Chi2	45.22			8.27
Prob > chi2	0.0001			0.9605

Source: Authors' computation.
EPR = effective protection rate, FE = fixed effects, PCM = price cost margin, RD = R&D expenditures, RE = random effects, TFP = total factor productivity.
Note: *10% level of significance, **5% level of significance, ***1% level of significance.

Table 3.11.1 First Stage IV Results: Tobit

PCM	*Tariff*	*EPR*
Trade	0.0012992***	0.0000996
	-0.000547	-0.0001304
Total workers	-0.0000211***	-0.000021***
	-0.00000405	-4.05E-06
Age	-0.0003406*	-0.0003545*
	-0.0002017	-0.0002018
TFP gap	-1.242917***	-1.234866***
	-0.0393622	-0.039239
Constant	0.4478913***	0.4647943
	-0.0196814	-0.0182534
Year dummies	Y	Y
Industry dummies	Y	Y
Observations	8263	8263
R-squared	0.1207	0.12

Source: Authors' computation.
EPR = effective protection rate, PCM = price cost margin, TFP = total factor productivity.
Note: *10% level of significance, **5% level of significance, ***1% level of significance.

Table 3.11.2 Second Stage IV Results: Tobit

LnRD	*Tariff*	*EPR*
PCM	-10.44935*	-10.05107
	-5.906214	-17.95807
Total workers	-0.0005009***	-0.0004926
	-0.0001365	-0.0003815
Age	-0.0064991*	-0.0063593
	-0.0035068	-0.0068841
TFP gap	-5.04204	-4.551069
	-7.30149	-22.14417
Constant	-0.5995352	-0.7849602
	-2.761603	-8.364468
Year dummies	Y	Y
Industry dummies	Y	Y
Observations	8263	8263
R-squared	0.1207	0.12

Source: Authors' computation.
EPR = effective protection rate, PCM = price cost margin, TFP = total factor productivity.
Note: *10% level of significance, **5% level of significance, ***1% level of significance.

on profitability. Similarly, *Total Workers* also has a highly significant negative impact while *Age* has a significant negative effect on profitability. We expect trade reforms to increase the probability that a firm will face more competition and lower profitability. The lower *TFP Gap* will increase the probability that profitability will be higher. The smaller the firm in terms of number of workers and the younger the firm, the higher the probability that profitability will be higher.

With *EPR* as trade indicator, the first stage results show that the coefficient on *EPR* is positive but not significant. The coefficient on *TFP* is negative and highly significant. The coefficient on *Total Workers* is also negative and highly significant. For *Age*, the coefficient is negative and significant.

The second stage Tobit results are presented in Table 3.11.2. The results show that with *Tariff* as trade indicator, *PCM* has a significant negative effect on *lnRD*. The lower profitability (suggesting higher competition) will increase the probability that a firm will engage in R&D activities and will increase its R&D intensity. The Tobit results also show a highly significant negative effect for *Total Workers* and negative effect for *Age*. With *EPR* as trade indicator, none of the explanatory variables is significant. The coefficient on *PCM* is negative but insignificant.

On the whole, using tariffs as trade indicator, the results tend to confirm that trade liberalisation may stimulate firms to innovate through competition. For *EPR*, however, this is not the case. While the correct signs on the coefficient of *EPR* and *PCM* are obtained, these are not significant. For *TFP Gap*, the expected negative relationship is found; however, the result is also not statistically significant.

Tables 3.12.1 and 3.12.2 show the results with an additional control variable for exit and entry, measured by *Net Entry*. Using IV, the first stage results

Table 3.12.1 First Stage IV Results with Net Entry

PCM	*EPR*		*Tariff*	
	(1) FE	*(2) RE*	*(1) FE*	*(2) RE*
Age	-0.0039215*	-0.0007018*	0.0003441	-0.0004529*
Standard error	0.0022208	0.0004111	0.0026855	0.0002718
Total workers	-0.00000818	-0.0000282***	-5.38E-06	-0.0000279***
Standard error	0.0000128	0.00000648	0.0000128	5.37E-06
TFP gap	-2.557469***	-1.864594***	-2.54216***	-1.475161***
Standard error	0.1052466	0.0532788	0.1052451	0.0456886
Net entry	-0.0007582	-0.000508	-0.0007556	-0.0001445
Standard error	0.0006247	0.0004102	0.0006239	0.0004494
Trade indicator	0.0006674	0.000427**	0.006884***	0.0024462***
Standard error	0.0004289	0.0002165	0.0022271	0.0006985
Constant	1.255121		1.098123***	
Standard error	0.088931		0.1022564	
Year dummies	Y	Y	Y	Y
Industry dummies	Y	Y	Y	Y
Observations	8263	8263	8263	8263
R-squared (overall)	0.0694		0.0669	
Hausman test				
Chi2		13.32	52.66	
Prob>chi2		0.7145	0.0000	

Source: Authors' computation.
EPR = effective protection rate, FE = fixed effects, PCM = price cost margin, RE = random effects, TFP = total factor productivity.
Note: *10% level of significance, **5% level of significance, ***1% level of significance.

Table 3.12.2 Second Stage IV Results with Net Entry

RD	*EPR*		*Tariff*	
	(1) FE	*(2) RE*	*(1) FE*	*(2) RE*
PCM	-0.0739931	-0.1189551	-0.1148789*	-0.0916575
Standard error	0.1310972	0.1272509	0.0706754	0.0784155
Age	-0.0002561	0.0000955	-0.0004381	0.0001054
standard error	0.0007356	0.000136	0.000573	0.0000833
Total workers	-0.00000505*	-0.00000422	-0.00000538*	-2.09E-06
Standard error	0.00000282	0.00000396	0.00000285	2.65E-06
TFP gap	-0.0138511	-0.1017999	-0.1184321	-0.0459054
Standard error	0.3360179	0.2370014	0.1822321	0.1152147
Net entry	0.0000574	0.0000826	0.0000259	0.0001785
Standard error	0.0171815	0.0001225	0.0001468	0.0001243
Constant	0.0409574	0.0471517	0.0922571	0.0306018
Standard error	0.1654865	0.092097	0.0907753	0.0469146
Year dummies	Y	Y	Y	Y
Industry dummies	Y	Y	Y	Y
Observations	82633	8263	8263	8263
R-squared (overall)	0.0047	0.0102	0.0044	0.0118

Source: Authors' computation.
EPR = effective protection rate, FE = fixed effects, PCM = price cost margin, RD = R&D expenditures, RE = random effects, TFP = total factor productivity.
Note: *10% level of significance, **5% level of significance, ***1% level of significance.

indicate a strong positive impact of trade liberalisation on competition based on both *Tariff* and *EPR* as trade indicators. As tariffs (and EPRs) decline, price cost margin or profitability is reduced, indicating increased competition. The coefficient on *TFP Gap* is negative and highly significant. The coefficient on *Net Entry* is also negative but insignificant.

In the second stage, the results based on the FE method with *Tariff* as trade indicator show some evidence of a positive effect of competition on innovation brought about by trade liberalisation. The coefficient on *PCM* is negative and significant at the 10% level. The coefficient on *Total Workers* is negative and significant. The coefficient on *TFP Gap* is negative but not statistically significant. In the case of *EPR* as trade indicator, the RE results show that although the coefficient on *PCM* is negative, it is not significant. It is important to note that the EPRs used are based only on output and input tariff rates and do not take into account the presence of non-tariff barriers, such as import controls and restrictions, which are more binding than tariffs. Although tariff rates are reduced, importation is still limited due to the presence of these restrictions. This may be one possible explanation why in most cases, though *EPR* has the correct sign, it is not significant.[4]

Tables 3.13.1 and 3.13.2 present the results of the Tobit regression. Based on *Tariff* as trade indicator, trade liberalisation has a positive effect on innovation through competition. The results show a positive relationship between *Tariff* and *PCM* and a negative relationship between *PCM* (measure of competition) and *RD* (measure of innovation).

In the first stage, the coefficients on *TFP Gap* and *Total Workers* are negative and highly significant while the coefficient on *Net Entry* is negative but is insignificant. In the second stage, the coefficient on *Net Entry* is negative and

Table 3.13.1 First Stage Tobit with Net Entry

PCM	*EPR*	*Tariff*
Trade Indicator	0.0000993	0.0012991***
Standard error	0.0001304	0.0005476
Total workers	-0.000021***	-0.0000211***
Standard error	0.00000405	0.00000405
Age	-0.0003541*	-0.0003405*
Standard error	0.0002018	0.0002018
TFP gap	-1.234975***	-1.242921***
Standard error	0.0392628	0.0393829
Net entry	-0.0000404	-0.00000138
Standard error	0.0004832	0.0004833
Constant	0.4647379***	0.4478903***
Standard error	0.0182669	0.0196862
Year dummies	Y	Y
Industry dummies	Y	Y
Observations	8263	8263
Adj R-squared	0.118	0.1186

Source: Authors' computation.

EPR = effective protection rate, PCM = price cost margin, TFP = total factor productivity.

Table 3.13.2 Second Stage Tobit with Net Entry

LnRD	*EPR*	*Tariff*
PCM	-11.70061	-11.17755*
Standard error	19.68247	6.144492
Total workers	-0.0005295	-0.0005185***
Standard error	0.0004182	0.000142
Age	-0.0067569	-0.0065736*
Standard error	0.0075315	0.0036446
TFP gap	-6.638679	-5.993806
Standard error	24.27343	7.596961
Net entry	-0.0188524***	-0.0188251***
Standard error	0.0073079	0.0070451
Constant	-0.0445921	-0.2880717
Standard error	9.166121	2.872541
Year dummies	Y	Y
Industry dummies	Y	Y
Observations	8263	8263
R-squared		

Source: Authors' computation.
EPR = effective protection rate, PCM = price cost margin, TFP = total factor productivity.
Note: *10% level of significance, **5% level of significance, ***1% level of significance.

highly significant, indicating that higher net exit will increase the probability that surviving firms will engage in R&D activities. As tariffs decline, PCM or profitability is reduced, competition increases, and less efficient firms are forced out of the market. The coefficient on *Age* is negative and significant; similarly, the coefficient on *Total Workers* is negative and highly significant. Based on *EPR* as trade indicator, the evidence that trade liberalisation leads to innovation is relatively weaker. The coefficient on *PCM* is negative but not significant.

3.6 Conclusions and policy implications

Both the IV and Tobit results show that trade liberalisation affects innovation through competition. In the first stage, *Tariff* is highly correlated with *PCM* while in the second stage, a significant relationship between *PCM* and *RD* is obtained. This suggests that reduced profit (which implies high competition) is associated with increased R&D.

Given the crucial role of competition in the relationship between trade liberalisation and innovation, it is important for the government to maintain the contestability of markets. Contestability is the essence of effective competition; for as long as markets remain contestable (when entry is easy), large firms in an oligopolistic environment are expected to act independently and monopolies to act competitively. If entry is easy and costless, the potential threat from imports or from domestic competitors will make incumbent firms behave competitively.

It is important to note that the presence of market imperfections – such as abuse of the dominant position and other anti-competitive business practices along with trade barriers or government regulations – limits market entry and creates inefficiencies, leading to reduced long-term growth. These weaken competition and prevent structural changes from taking place, resulting in resources being tied to low-productivity industries. Weak competition reduces the pressure on firms to adopt new technology or innovate, resulting in low growth of productivity and a loss of competitiveness.

The Philippine experience has shown that after two decades of implementing liberalisation and other market-opening policies, competition and productivity growth has remained weak not only due to the presence of structural and behavioural barriers to entry, but also due to the country's inadequate physical and institutional infrastructure. Due to the fundamental weakness of competition in many major economic sectors, the gains from liberalisation remained limited, slowing down the country's economic growth.

The results have a bearing on the possible impact of the government's selective protection policy on competition and innovation. This policy, which was adopted in 2003, increased the tariff rates on selected agriculture and manufacturing products, leading to a sizeable proportion of products with tariff peaks. The paper's findings suggest that an increase in tariffs will reduce competition, which would likely result in reduced innovation, holding all else equal. The selective protection policy must thus be reviewed, given its likely negative impact on competition and innovation and considering the current low level of R&D spending and overall innovation activity in the country.

It is necessary to address the remaining barriers to market entry (and exit), such as selective tariff protection and non-tariff measures in rice, sugar, automotive parts and components, and other manufacturing products. The government needs to carefully review its protectionist policies and mechanisms that intervene in the market and try to decide and select which firms should survive and which ones should die. In the light of the findings of this paper and increasing globalisation and economic integration, which have made industries more mobile through production networks and supply chains, the government should focus on designing an overall policy and strategy that would ensure competition, innovation, and the productivity growth of firms. Note, also, that other important determinants of innovation, including human capital, infrastructure, and institutional factors, must be closely examined, along with their interaction with trade policy reform indicators.

3.7 Acknowledgements

The author is grateful to Ms. Estela de Guzman, Director of the Industry and Trade Statistics Department, and Ms. Dulce Regala, Chief of the Industry Statistics Division of the National Statistics Office, and also acknowledges the research assistance of Mr. Donald Yasay and Ms. Jocelyn Almeda of PIDS.

Notes

1 http://data.uis.unesco.org/Index.aspx?DataSetCode=SCN_DS&lang=en (accessed 13 October 2019).

2 The channel through which selection happens is the labour market; trade liberalisation increases labour demand. These bids increase wages and the cost of production, forcing least productive firms to exit the market.
3 In Melitz (2003), the model assumes monopolistic competition.
4 Import ratios were also calculated as an alternative trade indicator. However, the inconsistencies in using matched aggregated import data at the industry level with the survey and census data prevented their use.

Bibliography

Aghion, P., R. Burgess, S. Redding, and F. Zilibotti (2005), 'Entry Liberalisation and Inequality in Industrial Performance', *Journal of the European Economic Association*, Papers and Proceedings 3(2–3): 291–302.

Aghion, P., and R. Burgess (2003), 'Liberalization and Industrial Performance: Evidence from India and the UK', in Ernesto Zedillo (ed.), *The Future of Globalization: Explorations in Light of Recent Turbulence*, London: Routledge, pp. 557–592.

Aghion, P., N. Bloom, R. Blundell, R. Griffith, and P. Howitt (2002), 'Competition and Innovation: An Inverted U Relationship', *Working Paper* 9269. Cambridge, MA: National Bureau of Economic Research.

Aghion, P., and P. Howitt (1999), *Endogenous Growth Theory*. Cambridge: Massachusetts Institute of Technology.

Aldaba, R. (2010), 'Does Trade Protection Improve Firm Productivity? Evidence from Philippine Micro Data', Paper submitted to ERIA in March 2010.

Aldaba, R. (2005), "Policy Reversals, Lobby Groups and Economic Distortions." PIDS Discussion Paper No. 2005-04. Makati City: Philippine Institute for Development Studies.

Amiti, M. and J. Konings (2007), "Trade Liberalization, Intermediate Inputs and Productivity: Evidence from Indonesia." IMF Working Paper No. WP/05/146. International Monetary Fund.

Bhagwati (1968), *The Theory and Practice of Commercial Policy*. Princeton, NJ: Princeton University Press.

Bloom, N., M. Draca, and J. Van Reenen (2010), 'Trade Induced Technical Change? The Impact of Chinese Imports on Innovation, IT and Productivity'. NBER Working Paper Series, No. 16717, Cambridge, MA: NBER.

Blundell, R., R. Griffith, and J. Van Reenen (1995), 'Dynamic Count Data Models of Technological Innovation', *Economic Journal* 105(429): 333–44.

Cadot, O., J-M. Grether, and J. de Melo (2000), 'Trade and Competition Policy: Where Do We Stand?' *Journal of World Trade* 34(3): 1–20.

Carlin, W., M.E. Schaffer, and P. Seabright (2004), 'A Minimum of Rivalry: Evidence from Transition Economies on the Importance of Competition for Innovation and Growth', *Contributions to Economic Analysis & Policy* 3(1). Berkeley, CA: Berkeley Electronic Press.

Cororaton, C. (1999), 'R&D Gaps in the Philippines', *PIDS Discussion Paper Series* No. 99-16, Makati City, Philippines: PIDS.

Creusen, H., B. Vroomen, H. van der Wiel, and F. Kuypers (2006), 'Dutch Retail Trade On The Rise?: Relation Between Competition, Innovation And Productivity', *CPB Document 137*. City: CPB Netherlands Bureau for Economic Policy Analysis.

De Melo and Urata (1986), "The Influence of Increased Foreign Competition on Industrial Concentration and Profitability," *International Journal of Industrial Organization* 4(1986): 287–304.

Domowitz, I., R. Hubbard, and B. Petersen (1986), 'The Intertemporal Stability of the Concentration-Margins Relationship', *Journal of Industrial Economics* 35(1): 13–34.

Erdem and Tybout (2003), "Trade Policy and Industrial Sector Responses: Using Evolutionary Models to Interpret the Evidence." Working Paper 9947, National Bureau of Economic Research.

Fernandes, A. (2003), "Trade Policy, Trade Volumes and Plant Level Productivity in Columbian Manufacturing Industries." World Bank Working Paper 3064.

Fernandes, A. and C. Paunov (2009), 'Does Tougher Import Competition Foster Product Quality Upgrading?' Policy Research Working Paper, No. 4894, Washington, DC: World Bank.

Geroski, P. (1995), *Market Structure, Corporate Performance and Innovative Activity.* Oxford: Oxford University Press.

Geroski, P. (1990), 'Innovation, Technological Opportunity and Market Structure', *Oxford Economic Papers* 42: 586–602.

Gilbert, R. (2006), 'Looking for Mr. Schumpeter: Where Are We in the Competition–Innovation Debate?', *Innovation Policy and the Economy* 6: 159–215. Chicago, IL: The University of Chicago Press.

Goldar and Agarwal (2004), 'Trade Liberalization and Price-Cost Margin in Indian Industries.' ICRIER Working Paper No. 130, Indian Council for Research on International Economic Relations.

Gorodnichenko, Y., J. Svejnar, and K. Terell (2009), 'Globalization and Innovation in Emerging Markets', *Policy Research Working Paper* 4808, Washington: The World Bank.

Grether, J-M. (1996), 'Mexico: 1985–90: Trade Liberalization, Market Structure and Manufacturing Performance', in Mark Roberts and James Tybout (eds.), *Industrial Evolution in Developing Countries*, Oxford: Oxford University Press.

Griffith, R., R. Harrison, and H. Simpson (2006), 'The Link between Product Market Reform, Innovation and EU Macroeconomic Performance', *European Economy Economic Papers* 243, Brussels.

Griliches, Z. (1992), 'The Search for R&D Spillovers', *Scandinavian Journal of Economics* 94: 29–47.

Hall, R. (1988), 'The Relation between Price and Marginal Cost in US Industry', *Journal of Political Economy* 96: 921–47.

Harrison, A. (1994), "Productivity, Imperfect Competition and Trade Reform." *Journal of International Economics* 36: 53–73.

Helpman, E. and P. Krugman (1989), *Trade Policy and Market Structure*, Cambridge, MA: MIT Press.

Hopman, C., and H. Rojas-Romagosa (2010), 'The Relation between Competition and Innovation: Empirical Results and Implementation into WorldScan', CPB Memorandum, City: Netherlands Bureau for Economic Policy Analysis.

Impulliti, G., and O. Licandro (2009), 'Trade, Firm Selection, and Innovation: The Competition Channel', The University of Nottingham. Discussion Papers in Economics No. 13/04.

Kambhampati and Parikh (2003), 'Disciplining Firms? The Impact of Trade Reforms on Profit Margins in Indian Industry', *Applied Economics* 35(4): 461–70.

Konings, J., P. Van Cayseele, and F. Warzynski (2005), 'The Effects of Privatization and Competitive Pressure on Firms' Price-Cost Margins: Micro Evidence from Emerging Economies', *Review of Economics and Statistics* 87(1): 124–34.

Krishna, P. and D. Mitra (1998), 'Trade Liberalization, Market Discipline and Productivity Growth: New Evidence from India.' *Journal of Development Economics* 56(2): 447–62.

Levinsohn, J. (1999), 'Employment Responses to International Liberalization in Chile,' *Journal of International Economics* 47(April 1999): 321–44.

Levinsohn, J., and A. Petrin (2003), 'Estimating Production Functions Using Inputs to Control for Unobservables', *Review of Economic Studies* 70(2): 317–41.

Licandro, O., and A. N. Ruiz (2010), 'Trade Liberalization, Competition and Growth', UFAE and IAE Working Papers 806.10, Unitat de Fonaments de l'Anàlisi Econòmica (UAB) and Institut d'Anàlisi Econòmica (CSIC).

Melitz, M. (2003), 'The Impact of Trade on Intra-Industry Reallocations and Aggregate Industry Productivity', *Econometrica* 71(6): 1695–725, City: Economics Society.

Muendler, M-A. (2004), 'Trade, Technology, and Productivity: A Study of Brazilian Manufactures, 1986–1998.'*Mimeo*. UC San Diego.

Nickell, S.J. (1996), 'Competition and Corporate Performance', *Journal of Political Economy* 104(4): 724–46.

Olley, S., and A. Pakes (1996), 'The Dynamics of Productivity in the Telecommunications Equipment Industry', *Econometrica* 64: 1263–98.

Organisation for Economic Co-operation and Development (OECD) Secretariat (2007), *Discussion Paper on Trade, Innovation and Growth*. Paris: OECD.

Pavcnik, N. (2000), 'Trade Liberalization, Exit, and Productivity Improvements: Evidence from Chilean Plants.' NBER Working Paper No. W7852.

Pugel, T. (1980), Profitability, Concentration and the Interindustry Variations in Wages. *Review of Economics and Statistics* 62, 248–53.

Roberts, M. and J. R. Tybout (eds.). (1996), *Industrial Evolution in Developing Countries*, New York: Oxford University Press.

Srivastava, V., P. Gupta and A. Datta (2001), *The Impact of India's Economic Reforms on Industrial Productivity, Efficiency and Competitiveness: A Panel Study of Indian Companies, 1980–97*, Report, National Council of Applied Economic Research, New Delhi.

Schmalensee, R. (1989), 'Inter-Industry Studies of Structure and Performance,' in R. Schmalensee and R. D. Willig (eds.), *Handbook of Industrial Organization*, Volume II, Elsevier Science Publishers BV.

Schor, A. (2004). 'Heterogeneous Productivity Response to Tariff Reduction: Evidence from Brazilian Manufacturing Firms.' NBER Working Paper 10544.

Schumpeter, J. (1942), *Capitalism, Socialism, and Democracy*. New York: Harper.

Topalova, P. (2004). 'Trade Liberalization and Firm Productivity: The Case of India.' IMF Working Paper WP/04/28.

Tybout, J. R. (2001), 'Plant -and Firm-Level Evidence on "New" Trade Theories.' NBER Working Paper No. 8418.

Tybout, J. R. (1996), 'Chile: 1979–86: Trade Liberalization and its Aftermath,' in M. Roberts and J. R. Tybout (eds.), *Industrial Evolutions in Developing Countries: Micro Patterns of Turnover, Productivity and Market Structure*, Oxford University Press.

Warzynski, F. (2002), 'The Dynamic Effect of Competition on PCMs and Innovation', PhD dissertation, Katholieke Universiteit Leuven.

4 FDI forward linkage effect and local input procurement

Evidence from Indonesian manufacturing

Sadayuki Takii and Dionisius Narjoko

4.1 Introduction

Developing countries always consider the establishment of foreign firms a high priority in their policy agenda. Providing evidence of this, history has demonstrated investment liberalisations and increasing foreign direct investment (FDI) in many developing Asian countries since the early 1990s. Policymakers in these countries are interested not only in the efficient technology brought by FDI but also in the positive productivity impact for local firms through technological spillovers to them (Saggi, 2006).

FDI channels therefore play an important role in materialising positive productivity impact. One of these channels is connection; that is, the linkage between multinational enterprises (MNEs) with other firms within an industry (horizontal linkage) or with firms in other industries (vertical linkage). FDI spillovers through backward linkage occur when MNEs establish an inter-firm relationship with firms in downstream industries with a purpose to supply intermediate inputs for the MNEs. The backward spillover effect then takes place through direct knowledge transfer, requirement for higher quality input, and increased demand that allows firms in downstream industries to benefit from economies of scale (Javorcik, 2004). Meanwhile, spillovers through FDI in upstream industries (forward linkages) occur when domestic firms in downstream industries benefit from high-quality and less costly intermediate inputs produced by MNEs operating in the upstream industries. The analytic of FDI spillovers puts forward a hypothesis that vertical linkages, either through backward or forward linkages, are relatively more important than the horizontal FDI linking MNEs with other firms within the same industry. MNEs will likely protect their knowledge from possible use by their competitors, whereas this is unlikely in the case of vertical linkage because there is no competition threat from sharing knowledge with firms in other industries.[1] Several recent empirical works, such as Javorcik (2004), Blalock and Gertler (2008), Havranek and Irsova (2011), and Xu and Sheng (2011) support this hypothesis.

Evidence of vertical linkages, however, has been skewed towards backward linkages. As Saggi (2006) wrote, 'A voluminous informal and empirical literature exists on backward linkages'. Reflecting this, Javorcik (2004) found strong evidence for spillovers from backward linkages but weak evidence for spillovers from forward linkages. The skewed evidence may have been, to some extent, affected by the nature of FDI in developing countries, who usually promote export-oriented industries or experience a rapidly growing demand as a result of population growth. In other words, much of this FDI is located in downstream industries; hence, it is not surprising if evidence for a backward linkage effect appears more frequently.

This paper focuses on forward linkages. It examines whether the productivity of a plant is correlated with the presence of MNEs in upstream industries, using the case study of Indonesian manufacturing. In other words, this study tests the existence of FDI spillovers coming through forward linkages.

This study essentially extends the work previously done by Blalock and Gertler (2005), which only considered the backward linkage effect. Examining FDI spillovers through forward linkages, particularly in the context of industrialisation in Indonesia, is important at least for three reasons. First, over more than two decades of industrialisation with a relatively open trade and investment regime, the FDI in the country has gone to both downstream and upstream industries, even though in terms of magnitude FDI in the latter may have been lower than in the former, as argued by Blalock and Gertler (2008). As described in Section 4.3 (Table 4.1), FDI in the group of capital-intensive sectors of Indonesian manufacturing, such as resource-based capital intensive (RCI), electronics (ELE), and footloose capital intensive (FCI) has increased over time since the 1990s.[2] Moreover, the spillovers through forward linkages – if any – should arguably have been much stronger more recently, after a rather long-term engagement of FDI in upstream industries in the country.

Second, the large size and resource abundance of Indonesia support the establishment of a relatively complete supply chain. As indicated by Blalock and Gertler (2008), these characteristics could incentivise foreign firms to establish themselves in both downstream and upstream industries.

Third, for policymaking purposes, inviting FDI for upstream industries not only brings new knowledge or technology but also introduces competitive pressure for incumbents, which, in some developing countries, are dominated by state-owned enterprises (SOEs). SOEs in upstream industries are likely inefficient and tend to be 'protected'; hence, directing FDI to upstream industries may pose a credible threat of competitive pressure, which could eventually improve efficiency in upstream industries.

In examining the forward linkages, this study further tests whether the benefits stemming from them depend on the extent to which inputs are locally procured. The conjecture is that the productivity-enhancing effect of forward linkages should be higher for a firm that sources many of its intermediate inputs locally. The availability of high-quality inputs produced locally by MNEs, but at relatively cheaper price/cost than imported inputs, allows any firm to switch from sourcing low-quality locally produced inputs to procuring high-quality ones.

The rest of this paper is organised as follows. Section 4.2 presents the methodology of our study, outlining the empirical model and the testable hypotheses, as well as describing the dataset and variables used. Section 4.3 presents and discusses our empirical results and Section 4.4 offers policy implications from the analysis.

4.2 Data and methodology

4.2.1 Specifications and hypotheses

Previous studies of technology spillovers through vertical linkages typically estimate the following function (Javorcik, 2004; Blalock and Gertler, 2008):

$$\Delta\omega_{ijt} = \beta_{ijt} + \beta_F Forw_{jt} + \beta_H Horz_{jt} + \beta_B Bacw_{jt} + \varepsilon_{it},$$

where ω_{ijt}, $Forw_{jt}$, $Horz_{jt}$, and $Bacw_{jt}$ are the natural logarithm of total factor productivity of plant i in year t, and the proxies for forward, horizontal, and backward spillover effects in industry j of year t, respectively. The Δ stands for difference operator. The linkage variables are measured as output shares of foreign-owned plants in upstream (forward effect), own (horizontal effect), and downstream (backward effect) industries, respectively. The *Horz* variable is calculated as the output share produced by foreign-owned plants in industry j and the *Forw* and *Bacw* variables are calculated as weighted average of *Horz* variables for upstream and downstream industries of industry j with weights taken from Input-Output (IO) tables.[3]

In our current analysis, we extend the basic model focusing on spillovers through forward linkages, which was not examined in the study by Blalock and Gertler (2008) on Indonesian manufacturing. In our empirical analysis, the following equation is estimated:

$$\omega_{ijt} = \beta_{ijt} + \beta_\omega \omega_{ijt-1} + \beta_F Forw_{jt} + \beta_{F*Rdm} Forw_{jt} * Rdm_{it} + \beta_H Horz_{jt} + \beta_B Bacw_{jt} + \varepsilon_{it}. \quad (1)$$

This specification is consistent with an assumption that productivity is dependent on its lagged variables in an estimation technique used in our analysis (see Section 4.2.2) and is different from that of previous studies. First, Javorcik (2004) regressed the growth of productivity ($\Delta\omega_{ijt}$) on the linkage variables, assuming that the coefficient β_ω in our estimated model is one. Second, Blalock and Gertler (2008) regressed the level of productivity on the backward linkage variable, assuming that the coefficient β_ω is zero. In our analysis, the coefficient – and thus the lag structure – is to be estimated in more general specification with a lagged dependent variable on the right-hand side. Second, we hypothesise that the magnitude of forward linkage effect varies among benefiting plants depending on the extent to which they procure inputs locally or import them. The variable *Rdm* is the share of material inputs procured locally in total material inputs. If the coefficient β_{F*Rdm} is positive, it suggests that plants procuring more material inputs locally can benefit more from forward linkage effects. The hypotheses of our interest can be written as:

$$\mathrm{H}_0 : \beta_F = 0,\ \mathrm{H}_1 : \beta_F > 0$$

and

$$\mathrm{H}_0 : \beta_{F*Rdm} = 0,\ \mathrm{H}_1 : \beta_{F*Rdm} > 0.$$

4.2.2 Variables and estimation issues

Previous studies estimated the productivity variable ω_{ijt} with a technique suggested by Olley and Pakes (1996) (the OP method) to account for endogeneity of input choice, using investment as a proxy for unobservable productivity shocks in the production function.[4] However, the technique requires that investment respond to productivity shocks smoothly and that positive (non-zero) investment was reported by plants in sample observations. In our analysis, productivity is estimated with a technique suggested by Levinsohn and Petrin (2003) (the LP method), using material inputs as a proxy for unobservable productivity shocks. This methodology is more appropriate for Indonesian manufacturing, where the number of plants reporting positive material inputs is greater than plants reporting positive investment. Furthermore, the OP method avoids selection bias by considering the exit decision of plants, while the LP method does not. However, the latter is more appropriate for our analysis because a relatively large number of plants did not report capital stock, resulting in missing values of the variable. In the OP method, capital stock is a key determinant of the plant's exit decision. In the case where the dataset contains many missing values of capital stock for existing plants, we cannot properly estimate the probability of exit.

In the estimation process, we set up a following production function:

$$y_{it} = \alpha_0 + \alpha_l l_{jt} + \alpha_l k_{it} + \alpha_m m_{it} + \omega_{it} + \eta_{it},$$

where y_{it} is the logarithm of output calculated as the sum of value added and expenses for material inputs or revenue minus the expenses for energy and fuel, assuming additive separability of energy and fuel inputs in the production function. The logarithm of the number of workers, capital stock, and material input are l_{it}, k_{it}, and m_{it}, respectively. The output, capital stock, and material inputs are deflated values.[5] Similarly with the OP and LP methods, productivity ω_{it} is presumed to follow a first-order Markov process (in the estimation process of the productivity). It is also assumed that material inputs are a strictly monotone function of the productivity and respond to productivity shocks smoothly. Under these assumptions, the total factor productivity ω_{it} is estimated by applying the LP method for each industry at a two-digit ISIC level.

The horizontal effect variable, *Horz*, is calculated as:

$$Horz_{jt} = \frac{\text{sum of output produced by foreign owned plants in industry } j, \text{ year } t}{\text{sum of output produced in inudstry } j, \text{ year } t}.$$

Conceptually, this effect mainly captures the demonstration and competition effects of productivity spillovers within the 'own' industry. However, it should be noted that this variable also captures forward and backward linkage effects within the 'own' industry. The backward linkage effect variable, *Bacw*, measures the presence of foreign-owned plants in the downstream industries procuring from industry *j*. It is calculated as:

$$Bacw_{jt} = \sum_{k=1}^{K} \alpha_{jk} Horz_{kt},$$

where the coefficient α_{jk} is the proportion of output in industry *j* supplied to industry *k* and is taken/calculated from Indonesia's IO tables for 2000 and 2005.[6] Similarly, the forward linkage effect variable, *Forw*, is defined as:

$$Forw_{jt} = \sum_{k=1}^{K} \alpha_{kj} Horz_{kt}.$$

These two variables capture vertical linkage effects, including both inter-industry and intra-industry effects because in the definition of these variables, there is a term of foreign presence in the 'own' industry $\left(\alpha_{jj} Horz_{jt}\right)$. Therefore, the estimated model based on these definitions has a limitation in estimating the magnitude of spillovers through backward and forward linkages and through horizontal separately for the reason that backward and forward linkage effects *within* the 'own' industry have been captured by both the *Bacw/Forw* and *Horz* variables. Javorcik (2004) used different definitions of backward and forward variables wherein α_{jj} is set to zero. This means there is no backward/forward linkage effect *within* the 'own' industry.[7] However, this is not a well-grounded solution because it is unrealistic to assume no intra-industry linkage effect, even if we use a highly aggregated industrial classification. Therefore, we do not impose $\alpha_{jj} = 0$ in the definitions of the *Bacw/Forw* variable.

Using these definitions, equation (1) is estimated with the other control variables including capital intensity, ratio of non-production workers in total employment, and plant size measured by output in previous year. When we estimate the model, another estimation issue arises because the model is a dynamic panel data model that requires strict exogeneity of independent variables in order to be estimated by OLS/DVLS consistently. A generalised method of moment (GMM) estimator for a dynamic panel data model with endogenous/predetermined variables was developed by Arellano and Bond (1991) and Blundell and Bond (1998). We apply the estimator suggested by Blundell and Bond (1998), assuming that the spillover variables are exogenous while plant size is predetermined and the ratio of material input procured domestically, capital intensity, and the ratio of non-production workers are endogenous, as well as the lagged dependent variable. In this estimation method, two-year and further lags of the independent and dependent variables can be used as instruments for (orthogonal) difference equation, and one-year and further lag of difference dependent variables can be used as an instrument for level equation. When we seek a set of valid instrumental variables, the possibility of the presence of measurement errors in variables is considered by excluding/including two-year lags of instruments for difference equation and 1-year lag for level equation, as Bond (2002) suggested.[8]

4.2.3 Data and sample

This study uses a plant-level panel dataset of Indonesian manufacturing. The dataset was constructed by collecting data for relatively large manufacturing plants with 50 or more workers from annual surveys conducted by Indonesia's statistical agency since 1975. This study considers 2000–2008 as the period for the analysis and, therefore, a panel dataset for this period was constructed. It contains useful information related to both locally and foreign-owned plants, including value added, employment, capital stock, intermediate inputs, and other variables necessary for the calculation of TFP. However, there were several outliers and apparently incorrect data entries in the original dataset. To avoid misleading results, data that appeared to be outliers or contain measurement errors were modified/eliminated from the panel dataset.

The data modification process took following steps. First, incorrect data entries were modified. For example, a plant reported 100% foreign ownership share in a year but it reported a share of 0% in previous and subsequent years. In this case, the data entry of 100% foreign ownership share was replaced with 0%. Second, the dataset contained estimates by the statistical agency for non-responses to the surveys. In general, the agency does not provide information on whether data entries were original replies from plants or were estimated by the agency because the plants did not respond. However, in some cases, we can speculate. For example, original datasets for 2001–2005 contained data entries indicating that labour productivity (value added divided by the number of workers) was exactly the same for several plants within a 5-digit ISIC level.[9] Observations for these plants were totally excluded from our sample because the entries appear to be estimates by the agency. Third, before estimating a production function by the LP method, it was estimated by OLS and the residual was calculated. If observations with the residual whose absolute value was 2.5 times greater than estimated standard error, then the observations were excluded from the sample for the LP estimation. This step eliminated outliers and incorrect entries in value added and other production factor variables.

Another data used in this analysis were the IO tables for 2000 and 2005. Indonesia's statistical agency publishes four types of IO tables every five years. In our analysis, a table for domestic transaction at producers' prices is used to calculate the *Forw/Bacw* variables.[10] For 2000 and 2005, α_{jk}s are calculated from the tables. The α_{jk}s for 2001–2004 and 2006–2008 are interpolated or extrapolated using α_{jk}s for 2000 and 2005.

4.3 Results and analysis

4.3.1 Descriptive analysis

Indonesia has adopted a policy to attract FDI to develop its manufacturing sector. In the late 1980s and during the first half of the 1990s before the 1997/1998 economic crisis, the government consistently introduced measures to liberalise the country's investment regime.[11] The policy direction to attract FDI continued after the crisis; in fact, the emphasis was greater in this period because of the perceived decline in the extent of FDI entering Indonesia after the 1997/1998 crisis. Reflecting the greater emphasis, the government introduced a new investment law in 2007 in an effort to increase FDI flow into the country.

The picture of foreign ownership in Indonesian manufacturing points to a rising pattern over 1990–2008 (Table 4.1). The share of manufacturing output produced by firms with foreign equity rose from 22% in 1990 to 47% in 2008. It rose continuously throughout the period, but particularly immediately before and after the crisis, 1993–1999. It is important to note a jump in 2008, which may have been the result of an immediate impact of the new investment law introduced in early 2007. Overall, the crisis had no major impact on this secular trend of rising foreign ownership. The increase in foreign ownership is evident in most industries, except for paper and chemical products where local firms have become more active. As expected, foreign presence is greatest in the two most MNE–intensive industries, automotive products and electronics, as well as in the resource-based capital-intensive (RCI) and footloose capital-intensive industry. Recalling the definition of *Forw*, the increase in the presence of MNEs in an industry indicates an increased share of intermediates produced by MNEs. If the MNEs in upstream industries produce similar products with imported inputs, there should be a higher chance for plants in the downstream industry to procure inputs locally.

Table 4.2 presents the average value of *Forw* and *Bacw* for 2000–2008 for the whole and by industry groups of Indonesian manufacturing. The table shows that for the whole manufacturing sector, the value of *Bacw* is higher than that of *Forw*. This reflects that large extent of FDI in Indonesian manufacturing went to downstream industries, which is consistent with the export orientation and large domestic demand of the Indonesian economy.

Another important observation is the variation in the *Forw* value across industries, ranging from the lowest 19.7% in food products and beverages (ISIC 15) to the highest 68.3% in radio, TV, and communications (ISIC 32). More importantly, there is a rather skewed pattern in the distribution of *Forw*, with many capital-intensive industries, such as electrical machinery, office and computing, radio, TV and communications, precision machinery, and motor vehicles (ISIC

Table 4.1 Foreign Ownership Share, Indonesian Manufacturing, 2000–2008

Foreign Ownership (Share, in %)

		1990	*1993*	*1996*	*1999*	*2002*	*2005*	*2008*
31	Food, beverages, and tobacco	8.5	9.7	14.0	15.8	9.4	24.9	24.4
32	Textile, clothes, and leather industry	17.8	21.8	29.3	37.4	32.1	32.8	44.5
33	Wood and wood products	10.1	11.7	22.9	15.8	11.6	11.2	19.1
34	Paper and paper products	30.2	14.9	33.8	23.5	46.4	29.0	27.3
35	Chemicals and chemical products	33.1	36.6	43.0	44.8	29.7	26.3	53.5
36	Non-metallic mineral products	18.0	23.3	33.4	34.6	28.3	35.9	39.2
37	Basic metal industries	24.8	35.3	24.3	43.1	29.4	30.5	28.2
38	Fabricated metal, machinery, and eq.	46.1	36.4	42.4	58.0	67.6	68.3	77.9
39	Other manufacturing industries	19.5	44.4	51.9	56.1	33.7	46.9	71.2
1-ULI	Unskilled labour intensive	16.2	21.1	27.3	35.4	28.8	30.0	42.2
2-RLI	Resource based, labour intensive	9.0	10.2	16.8	15.9	9.8	22.8	24.4
3-RCI	Resource based, capital intensive	29.5	32.5	35.9	40.0	34.9	29.9	45.6
4-ELE	Electronics	41.7	43.0	48.7	82.4	71.5	68.9	76.0
5-FCI	Footloose capital intensive	47.2	34.7	39.5	44.0	66.0	68.1	78.5
	Non-oil and gas manufacturing	**21.9**	**23.4**	**30.9**	**35.5**	**33.5**	**37.2**	**47.6**

Source: *Statistik Industri* (SI), various years.

30, 31, 32, 33, and 34, respectively), recording a value well above the average for the whole manufacturing sector. These are the industries where MNEs are likely to locate. It is interesting to note that the value of *Forw* in apparel (ISIC 18) is slightly above the whole manufacturing average. This is interesting because this industry is labour intensive in nature, deviating from the skewness pattern the table has just revealed. The cross-section pattern of *Bacw* seems to resemble closely the one of *Forw*, including the concentration of the value above whole-industry average in capital-intensive industries. Moreover, it is observed that the values of *Bacw* are significantly high for motor vehicle (the highest); precision machinery; radio, TV, and communications; and electrical machinery (ISIC 34, 33, 32, and 30, respectively).

The cross-section variation in the value of *Forw* and *Bacw* also varies over the time, as shown by the changes over 2000–2008 (Figures 4.1 and 4.2). Consider the pattern of *Forw* (see Figure 4.1), about half of two-digit ISIC industries registered positive change over this period, while the other half recorded a negative change. Assuming the technical coefficient does not change substantially over the period, the positive change therefore suggests an increase in the foreign share of output produced by upstream industries. Observing Figure 4.1, industries

Table 4.2 Forward and Backward, Indonesian Manufacturing, 2000–2008

ISIC 2 Digit	*Sectors*	*Forward*	*Backward*
15	Food products and beverages	19.72	33.63
16	Tobacco	22.79	21.81
17	Textiles	26.35	33.41
18	Wearing apparel	37.46	36.40
19	Leather products and footwear	31.34	22.39
20	Wood products	32.08	28.70
21	Paper	27.03	11.74
22	Publishing	31.32	38.36
23	Petroleum products	41.21	30.47
24	Chemicals	32.01	37.00
25	Rubber and plastics products	45.25	42.87
26	Non-metallic mineral products	35.04	32.49
27	Basic metals	33.10	45.90
28	Fabricated metals	34.98	40.53
29	General machinery	31.44	62.44
30	Electrical machinery	58.71	70.94
31	Office and computing machinery	52.91	57.26
32	Radio, TV, and communication	68.27	78.30
33	Precision machinery	49.93	75.11
34	Motor vehicles	45.38	82.28
35	Other transport equipment	43.20	65.92
36	Furniture and miscellaneous	33.03	40.08
37	Recycling	23.36	26.54
	Manufacturing	36.67	43.43

Source: Authors' computation.

that significantly increased their foreign-shared output are capital-intensive, such as motor vehicles, fabricated metal products, and general machinery. The pattern is similar for *Bacw* (see Figure 4.2) where there is wide cross-section variation over time. Most industries that gained here are those coming from capital-intensive industries.

There is an indication of a decline in the use of imported inputs over time, suggesting a higher use of locally produced inputs. This is derived from observing the cross-section and overtime patterns of imported input ratio over 2000–2008 (Table 4.3). The use of imported inputs declined from 7.1% in 2000–2004 to 6.5% in 2005–2008. This is observed in almost all broader industry groups, with a large decline occurring in electrical machinery (ISIC 31), precision machinery (ISIC 33), and to some extent in basic metal (ISIC 27) and motor vehicles (ISIC 34). Notwithstanding this decline, eight industries experienced an increase in their average ratio of imported inputs. However, the increase was marginal, except that recorded for the other transportation equipment industry (ISIC 35), which increased from 8% to 14%.

The change in the average ratio of imported input can be broken down into two factors: one is the change in average imported input in importing plants (an average after excluding plants not importing) (columns 3 and 4) and the other is the change in the number of importers (columns 4 and 5). The importers'

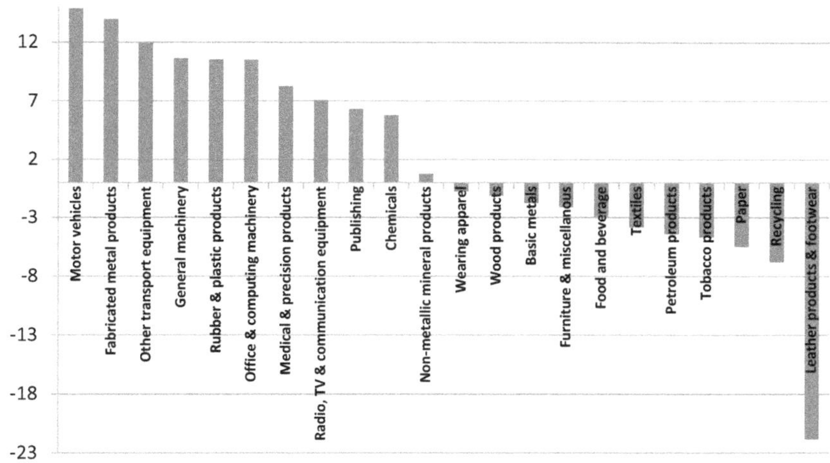

Figure 4.1 Change in Forward in Indonesian Manufacturing, 2000–2008.
Source: Authors' computation.

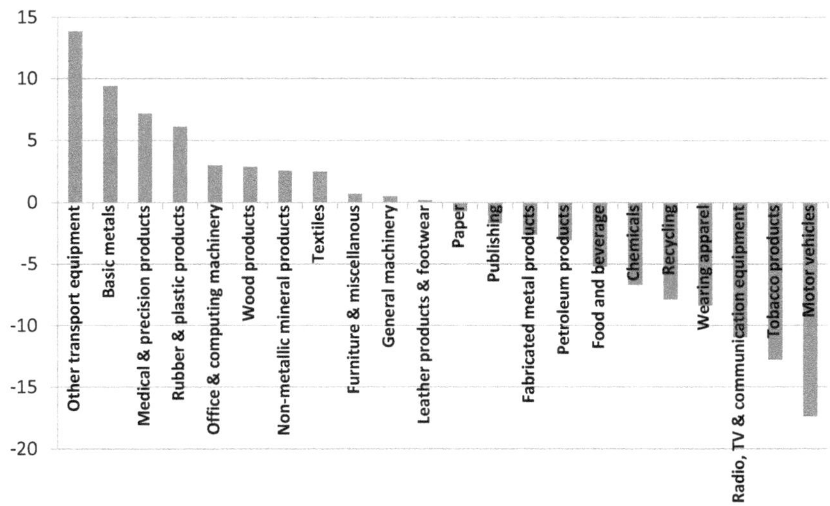

Figure 4.2 Change in Backward in Indonesian Manufacturing, 2000–2008.
Source: Authors' computation.

average imported input increased only in three industries: wood products (ISIC 20); paper (ISIC 21); and radio, TV, and communication (ISIC 32). The average for the whole manufacturing sector decreased from 47% to 44% over the periods 2000–2004 and 2005–2008, respectively. Meanwhile, for the change in the

Table 4.3 Imported Input Ratio of Indonesian Manufacturing, 2000–2008

		Average of Imported Input Ratio (%)	*Average of Imported Input Ratio Only for Importers (%)*	*Percentage of # of Importers (%)*			
	Period	*2000–2004*	*2005–2008*	*2000–2004*	*2005–2008*	*2000–2004*	*2005–2008*
	Column	*[1]*	*[2]*	*[3]*	*[4]*	*[5]*	*[6]*
15	Food products and beverages	2	2	28	25	8	8
16	Tobacco	1	1	18	16	4	5
17	Textiles	12	9	50	46	23	18
18	Wearing apparel	11	11	63	61	15	16
19	Leather products and footwear	9	6	38	37	23	17
20	Wood products	1	1	16	17	7	8
21	Paper	8	8	35	38	22	21
22	Publishing	5	3	28	17	16	17
23	Petroleum products	10	11	65	43	15	25
24	Chemicals	24	23	57	56	42	40
25	Rubber and plastics products	11	10	48	45	22	20
26	Non-metallic mineral products	3	3	41	37	8	8
27	Basic metals	28	26	57	52	48	47
28	Fabricated metals	12	12	58	56	20	21
29	General machinery	15	16	56	56	26	28
30	Office and computing machinery	–	–	–	–	–	–
31	Electrical machinery	32	29	61	58	50	47
32	Radio, TV, and communication	59	58	85	87	62	54
33	Precision machinery	34	27	66	55	48	43
34	Motor vehicles	15	13	59	54	25	24
35	Other transport equipment	8	14	52	50	15	26
36	Furniture and miscellaneous	4	4	38	35	10	10
37	Recycling	–	–	–	–	–	–
	Manufacturing	7.1	6.5	47	44	15	14

Source: Authors' computation.

number of importers, importing plants decreased, albeit slightly, by one percentage point over these two sub-periods.

To sum up and to reiterate, all figures described by Table 4.3 show that plants in Indonesia's manufacturing sector tend to have lowered their purchase of imported inputs, suggesting, at the same time, that they may have procured inputs locally. This is somewhat inconsistent with the fact that Indonesia has liberalised international trade since the mid-1980s. It is however consistent with, and provides some support to, the idea of development in upstream industries.

4.3.2 Estimation results and analysis

This subsection reports the estimation results to address the hypothesis of this study. Table 4.4 presents these for all continuing plants in our dataset, which covers the period 2000–2008. Consider, first, the results of specifications in columns [1] and [2], which follow the modelling strategy of Blalock and

Table 4.4 Productivity Estimation Results

Column	*[1]*	*[2]*	*[3]*	*[4]*	*[5]*	*[6]*
Dependent variable	w_t	Δw_t	w_t	w_t	w_t	w_t
Estimation	*DVLS*	*DVLS*	*Sys-GMM*	*Sys-GMM*	*Sys-GMM*	*Sys-GMM*
w_{t-1}			0.144	0.145	0.147	0.146
			[0.040]***	[0.039]***	[0.039]***	[0.039]***
Forw	0.291	-0.101	0.146	-5.281	-5.843	-4.413
	[0.226]	[0.283]	[0.278]	[3.172]*	[3.678]	[2.334]*
*Rdm*Forw*				6.643	7.294	5.291
				[3.799]*	[4.424]*	[2.859]*
Horz	0.168	0.254	0.009	0.044	0.086	0.005
	[0.084]**	[0.107]**	[0.096]	[0.097]	[0.121]	[0.096]
Bacw	1.049	0.914	0.934	1.027	1.127	0.872
	[0.216]***	[0.257]***	[0.261]***	[0.253]***	[0.297]***	[0.235]***
HI	0.095	0.019	0.116	0.106	0.091	0.118
	[0.113]	[0.145]	[0.109]	[0.112]	[0.116]	[0.110]
Rmd	0.002	-0.054	-0.668	-0.673	-0.572	-0.722
	[0.040]	[0.054]	[0.353]*	[0.368]*	[0.369]	[0.373]*
Rln	0.014	0.023	-0.018	-0.014	-0.002	-0.043
	[0.007]**	[0.010]**	[0.074]	[0.076]	[0.075]	[0.075]
Rlk	0.029	0.026	0.137	0.123	0.122	0.121
	[0.004]***	[0.006]***	[0.054]**	[0.053]**	[0.053]**	[0.053]**
Plants	7,673	5,311	5,311	5,311	5,311	5,311
Observations	32,749	24,462	24,462	24,462	24,462	24,462
F-value	0.000	0.000	0.000	0.000	0.000	0.000
AR1 (*p*-value)			0.000	0.000	0.000	0.000
AR2 (*p*-value)			0.969	0.905	0.899	0.958
Hansen (*p*-val.)			0.012	0.113	0.105	0.118
Instruments			64	75	75	75

Notes: In Sys-GMM estimation, w_{t-2}, w_{t-3}, Rmd_{t-3}, Rmd_{t-4}, Rln_{t-3}, Rln_{t-4}, Rlk_{t-3}, Rlk_{t-4}, $Rdm*Forw_{t-3}$ and $Rdm*Forw_{t-4}$ (for difference equation) and Δw_{t-2} (for level equation) were used as instruments. The results of two-step estimation with Windmeijer's (2005) finite-sample correction of standard errors are reported. "***", "**", "*" indicate statistical significance at 1%, 5%, or 10%, respectively. Year dummies are included in all models.

Gertler (2008) and Javorcik (2004), respectively, in treating the lag of natural logarithm of total factor productivity (see discussion in subsection 4.2.1). It turns out that there is no support for the impact of the forward linkage effect on productivity if we consider these modelling strategies. The estimated coefficient of *Forw* is very statistically insignificant and, in the case of the results of specification in column [2], shows a negative sign, which is not expected based on the theory.

Turning to the next column, which shows the result from the specification that includes the lag of dependent variable (i.e., specification in column [3]), there is a hint of a positive impact of forward linkage on productivity. The estimated coefficient of *Forw* is positive although not statistically significant. Examining further, it turns out that the result is not reliable; the p-value of the Hansen test rejects the null of valid overidentifying restrictions. In the dynamic panel GMM estimation, rejecting the null means a higher chance for the estimates, although efficiency of the estimator at the same time also increases (Baltagi, 2008).

Specification in column [4] specifies the hypothesis that the impact of forward linkage depends on the extent of locally procured inputs. The estimation result of this specification supports this hypothesis; the estimated coefficient of the interactive variable *Forw* and *Rdm* is positive and statistically significant, albeit only at 10%. The overall or net impact of forward linkage on productivity is also positive, although the estimated coefficient of *Forw* is negative when it enters the specification individually. The result is likely to be robust, given that specification in column [4] passes the Hansen test where the p-value of the Hansen statistics fail to reject the null of overidentifying restrictions.

The finding on the positive effect of the interactive *Forw* and *Rdm* variables supports the argument that the availability of cheaper – but high-quality – intermediate inputs produced by MNEs in the local economy can make a firm switch from importing inputs to sourcing them locally. It is important to note, however, that the coefficient of the interactive term does not reflect the extent of the switching; it merely suggests that such switching behaviour may occur.

Specifications in columns [5] and [6] are estimated to test the robustness of the key finding on the impact of forward linkage. First, in specification in column [5], and following Javorcik (2004), the output produced by a foreign plant in the formula to compute horizontal linkage is adjusted by the foreign share in the plant; that is, by multiplying it with the foreign ownership share, or

$$Horz_{j,t} = \frac{\sum_{i \in j} (\text{foreign share})_{i,t} \times (\text{output})_{i,t}}{\sum_{i \in j} (\text{output})_{i,t}}$$

Thus, now, unlike the *Horz* variable used by specification in column [4], the *Horz* variable adopted by specification in column [5] reflects the extent of output from foreign plants more precisely because it reflects the share of foreign ownership in an industry. The value of *Bacw* and *Forw* is adjusted accordingly. Looking at the estimation result of this specification, it turns out that the key finding is robust even with the alternative measurement of horizontal, forward, and backward linkages; that is, the impact of forward linkage is positive but dependent on the extent of locally procured input.

Another robustness test considers the value of *Forw* and *Bacw* that excludes the 'within industry' effect. Recalling the explanation in Section 4.2.2, this means the definition of *Forw* and *Bacw* imposes a restriction of $\alpha_{jj} = 0$. This is done by specification in column [6]. The key message from the results accords the one derived by a previous estimation where the forward and backward effects within an industry are included. However, the dependency of the forward linkage effect on the extent of locally procured inputs appears to be lower than the dependency when the 'within industry' effect is assumed. The estimated coefficient of interactive term *Rdm*Forw* in specification in column [6] is higher than the one produced by the estimation of specifications in columns [4] and [5].

Table 4.5 reports our experiment that focuses on testing the hypothesis on the group of local plants. This extends the exercise reported in Table 4.4 and is motivated both by a more policy-oriented argument and cleaner, more convincing test to detect the presence of spillovers from the presence of multinationals. While it does not necessarily apply only to domestic or local firms, FDI spillovers analytically and commonly refer to an increase in productivity of domestic firms as a consequence of the presence of foreign firms in the domestic economy. From the perspective of policy, policymakers are usually interested to know the extent of knowledge transferred from multinationals to local firms.

In an attempt to carefully examine the impact on this group of plants, the experiment is conducted among three more specific groups of local plants: (i) whole local plants, (ii) groups of local plants differentiated by whether they procured inputs from importing, and (iii) groups defined by (ii) but with addition of plants that have some share of foreign ownership. Two specifications, i.e., with and without the interacted *Forw* and *Rdm* variables, are applied/estimated on each of these more specific groups.

Consider, first, the estimation results for the group of whole local plants (see the results of specifications in columns [7] and [8] in Table 4.5). There is no evidence for the impact of forward linkage on productivity, shown by the statistical insignificance of the *Forw* and *Forw*Rdm* variables. The positive impact of forward linkages on productivity only appears in the results of estimations for the remaining more specific groups (see the results of specifications in columns [9] to [12]). Specifically, forward linkages positively affect productivity for the group of non-importing local plants (the results of specification in column [9]), indicated by the positive and statistically significant estimated coefficient of *Forw*. The productivity impact of forward linkages that depend on the extent of locally procured input is positive for the group of local plants that, at the same time, also import some of their inputs (the results of specification in column [10]).

Table 4.5 Productivity Estimation Results: Focusing on Local Plants

Column	*[7]*	*[8]*	*[9]*	*[10]*	*[11]*	*[12]*
Subsample	*Local plants*	*Local plants*	*Non-importing local plants*	*Importing local plants*	*Non-importing plants including foreign plants*	*Importing plants including foreign plants*
Estimation	*Sys-GMM*	*Sys-GMM*	*Sys-GMM*	*Sys-GMM*	*Sys-GMM*	*Sys-GMM*
w_{t-1}	0.127	0.133	0.182	0.141	0.197	0.113
	[0.041]***	[0.040]***	[0.047]***	[0.070]**	[0.045]***	[0.060]*
Forw	0.363	-2.378	0.659	-2.45	0.659	-3.71
	[0.277]	[2.527]	[0.308]**	[1.306]*	[0.299]**	[1.575]**
*Rdm*Forw*		3.208		4.241		6.165
		[2.945]		[2.230]*		[2.693]**
Horz	-0.063	-0.06	-0.021	-0.114	0.009	0.039
	[0.094]	[0.094]	[0.116]	[0.136]	[0.112]	[0.143]
Bacw	1.049	1.138	1.345	0.197	1.286	0.644
	[0.276]***	[0.268]***	[0.311]***	[0.463]	[0.298]***	[0.428]
HI	-0.001	-0.014	0.04	-0.091	0.037	0.094
	[0.095]	[0.095]	[0.118]	[0.138]	[0.115]	[0.169]
Rmd	-0.491	-0.509		-0.564		-0.658
	[0.419]	[0.392]		[0.344]		[0.366]*
Rln	-0.053	-0.06	0.005	0.197	0.017	0.244
	[0.080]	[0.078]	[0.087]	[0.120]	[0.079]	[0.124]**
Rlk	0.088	0.075	0.121	0.059	0.13	0.089
	[0.057]	[0.056]	[0.061]**	[0.113]	[0.057]**	[0.081]
Plants	4,645	4,645	4,099	1,132	4,414	1,617
Observations	21,065	21,065	16,727	4,338	17,954	6,508
F-value	0.000	0.000	0.000	0.012	0.000	0.011
AR1 (*p*-value)	0.000	0.000	0.000	0.000	0.000	0.000
AR2 (*p*-value)	0.761	0.720	0.243	0.649	0.175	0.780
Hansen (*p*-value)	0.003	0.021	0.015	0.653	0.009	0.816
Instruments	64	75	53	75	53	75

Notes: In Sys-GMM estimation, w_{t-2}, w_{t-3}, Rmd_{t-3}, Rmd_{t-4}, Rln_{t-3}, Rln_{t-4}, Rlk_{t-3}, Rlk_{t-4}, $Rdm{*}Forw_{t-3}$ and $Rdm{*}Forw_{t-4}$ (for difference equation) and Δw_{t-2} (for level equation) were used as instruments. The results of two-step estimation with Windmeijer's (2005) finite-sample correction of standard errors are reported. "***", "**", "*" indicate statistical significance at 1%, 5%, or 10%, respectively. Year dummies are included in all models.

These findings persist even when plants with some foreign ownership are added to the sample groups, shown by the results of specifications in columns [11] and [12].

These findings support the inference produced by the results presented in Table 4.4 on the positive impact of forward linkage on productivity. This seems to further suggest that the impact of a forward linkage is greater for local plants or firms that do have strong international linkages. In this context, international linkage is broadly defined by how much a plant imports its inputs. Following a strand of literature in importing (and exporting), this could be explained by the theory that importing is costly, particularly the high sunk costs associated with it.

So far this section has focused on the presentation and comments on the results for the question asked by this study. In addition to these, it is also worth noting the results of the other spillover-linkage variables (i.e., *Horz* and *Bacw*). Referring back to the results of specification in column [4] in Table 4.4, evidence suggests strong FDI spillovers through backward linkages. The estimated coefficient is positive and statistically significant at the very high level of confidence (at 1%). Moreover, the impact through this channel is suggested to be economically very important, owing to the very large estimated coefficient. This finding is consistent with numerous other studies, which have demonstrated the existence of backward-linkage spillovers. In particular, it supports the work of Blalock and Gertler (2008) that also found positive impact from backward linkages in Indonesian manufacturing. This finding also confirms the particular characteristic of inward FDI into developing countries that mostly targets downstream industries.

Turning to horizontal linkages, the results do not find evidence that FDI spillovers take place through horizontal linkages. The *Horz* estimated coefficient is very statistically insignificant. Moreover, the sign of the coefficient is negative, which indicates a possible adverse competition effect in the local market as an impact of MNE operation. This finding, however, is consistent with other studies (e.g., Aitken and Harrison 1999; Javorcik 2004; Blalock and Gertler 2008) in which the evidence for the presence of horizontal linkage spillovers cannot be found.

Also, worth commenting on is the rather strong persistency in the outcome of productivity. The coefficient of ω_i is very statistically significant not only with the one-year lag of the variable ω_{ijt-1} but it is also for the two-year lag variable ω_{ijt-2}. The impact of the two-year lag of the variable, however, is not so strong in terms of magnitude; the estimated coefficient of ω_{ijt-2} is about half of the estimated coefficient of ω_{ijt-1}.

4.4 Summary and policy implications

This paper addresses the topic of FDI spillovers through forward linkages using the case study of Indonesian manufacturing over 2000–2008. It examines whether the productivity of a plant in an industry is correlated with the presence of MNEs in upstream industries. Examining the forward linkage effect tests whether the benefits stemming from the forward linkages depend on the extent of inputs locally procured by a plant. An exercise of dynamic panel data model econometric was undertaken to examine the forward linkage effect. The study also includes a descriptive analysis that provides some basic facts about forward linkage and its pattern over time and across industries. The descriptive analysis also provides a picture of some pattern or characteristics of input procurement of plants in the manufacturing sector.

The descriptive analysis indicates an increase in the presence of MNEs in upstream industries. The value of the forward variable is recorded to have increased over 2000–2008 in about half of the industries defined at the two-digit ISIC level. More importantly, and more interestingly, almost all these industries where FDI is usually located are capital intensive. Consistent with this, many two-digit ISIC industries that record well above the whole manufacturing sector average – in the value of forward variable – are capital intensive. The descriptive analysis also indicates that plants in the manufacturing sector tended to lower their purchase of imported inputs, which suggests that they should have procured more locally.

The econometric results provide evidence on the positive spillovers impact through forward linkages. The impact, however, seems to depend on the extent, or share, of locally procured inputs. This supports the hypothesis about the existence of a spillover effect through forward linkages. The dependence of the forward linkage effect suggests that the availability of cheaper but high quality inputs produced by MNEs in the local economy may encourage firms to switch from importing inputs to procuring them locally. The econometric analysis also found evidence of the existence of backward linkage effects, which appear to be quite strong.

At least two policy implications can be drawn from this study. First, this study underlines the importance of a strategic investment policy for FDI. Usually, in many cases, the government tends to direct FDI only to downstream industries. While this has proved to be beneficial, as shown in this study in the convincing results of the backward linkage effect, the government could actually apply a more strategic policy by directing, or promoting, FDI in upstream industries. As indicated by this study, the forward linkage effect is proved to be positive and may actually trigger firms to switch from importing to procuring their inputs locally. Procuring inputs locally definitely reduces costs, meaning a potential increase in the growth rate of many firms. Second, considering the positive impact of the vertical linkages in facilitating technology transfers from MNEs, it is important for policy to promote FDI in the sectors that are still experiencing a low level of vertical linkage with MNEs. Recalling the insight from the descriptive analysis of this study, many of these industries at the moment are labour, and some are resource, intensive.

Notes

1 See Blalock and Gertler (2008) for the conceptual framework that explains the behaviour of MNEs in sharing their knowledge and technology with firms in other industries vis-à-vis firms within the same industry.

2 The five categories are based on the following ISIC groups (and corresponding SITC groups for export statistics). Unskilled labour-intensive: ISIC 32 (textiles and garments), 332 (furniture), 342 (printing and publishing), and 39 (other manufacturing). Resource-based, labour-intensive: ISIC 31 (food and beverages) and 331 (wood products). Resource-based, capital-intensive: ISIC 341 (paper and paper products); 35 (chemicals, rubber, and plastics); 36 (non-metallic minerals); and 37 (basic metals).

Electronics: ISIC 383 (electrical machinery). Footloose capital-intensive: ISIC 381 (metal products), 382 (non-electrical machinery), 384 (transport equipment), and 385 (professional and scientific equipment).

3 The coefficients used as weights are not weight because the sum of the weight is not equal to 1. The *Horz* variable was calculated as a three-year moving average.

4 Another related previous study on Indonesian manufacturing by Negara and Firdausy (2011) does not take account for the endogeneity.

5 Output is deflated by the wholesale price index, which appears to be appropriate for each 3-digit ISIC classification. Deflated capital stock is calculated by the following steps: (i) buildings, machinery and equipment, vehicles and other fixed capital are respectively deflated using wholesale indices for construction materials of buildings, imported machinery, transport machinery, and the general wholesale price index, respectively; (ii) then the sum of the four categories is calculated as the measure of deflated capital stock for each plant. Because of lack of sufficient information on prices, intermediate input is deflated by corresponding wholesale price index of output.

6 This variable corresponds to Downstream_FDI in Blalock and Gertler (2008).

7 Another purpose of setting to zero is to avoid colinearity with the horizontal variable.

8 For the estimation, xtabond2 command was used in the Stata programme. 'Forward orthogonal deviations' was used instead of first difference because the dataset is an unbalanced panel with 'gap', as suggested by Roodman (2009).

9 For example, calculated labour productivity is exactly the same for 497 plants in industry 18101 in 2001. For these plants, the value of calculated labour productivity is integer, which is usually a non-integer. The number of such data entries decreased year by year and disappeared in the dataset for 2006.

10 Other options are (i) total transaction including imports and (ii) at consumers' prices. Thus, there are four combinations of these options.

11 See, for example, Pangestu (1996) and Aswicahyono et al. (2010) for details of the FDI policy in Indonesia before and after the 1997/1998 economic crisis, respectively.

References

Aitken, B., G. Hanson, and A. Harrison (1997), 'Spillover, Foreign Investment and Export Behaviour', *Journal of International Economics* 43(1–2), pp. 103–32.

Aitken, B., and A. Harrison (1999), 'Do Domestic Firms Benefit from Direct Foreign Investment? Evidence from Venezuela', *American Economic Review* 89(3), pp. 605–618.

Arellano, M., and S.R. Bond (1991), 'Some Tests of Specification for Panel Data: Monte Carlo Evidence and an Application to Employment Equations', *Review of Economic Studies* 58, pp. 277–97.

Aswicahyono, H., H. Hill, and D. Narjoko (2010), 'Industrialisation after a Deep Economic Crisis: Indonesia', *Journal of Development Studies* 46, pp. 1084–1108.

Baltagi, B.H. (2008), *Econometric Analysis of Panel Data*. Chichester: John Wiley & Sons Ltd.

Blalock, G. and P.J. Gertler (2008), 'Welfare Gains from Foreign Direct Investment through Technology Transfer to Local Suppliers', *Journal of International Economics* 74(2), pp. 402–21.

Blundell, R.W., and S.R. Bond (1998), 'Initial Conditions and Moment Restrictions in Dynamic Panel Data Models', *Journal of Econometrics* 87, pp. 115–43.

Bond, S.R. (2002), 'Dynamic Panel Data Models: A Guide to Micro Data Methods and Practice', *Portuguese Economic Journal* 1, pp. 141–62.

Havranek, T., and Z. Irsova (2011), 'Estimating Vertical Spillovers from FDI: Why Results Vary and What the True Effect Is', *Journal of International Economics* 85, pp. 231–44.

Javorcik, B.S. (2004), 'Does Foreign Direct Investment Increase the Productivity of Domestic Firms? In Search of Spillovers Through Backward Linkages', *The American Economic Review* 94, pp. 605–27.

Levinsohn, J., and A. Petrin (2003), 'Estimating Production Functions Using Inputs to Control for Unobservables', *Review of Economic Studies* 70(2), pp. 317–41.

Negara, S.D., and C.M. Firdausy (2011), 'The Development of Foreign Direct Investment and Its Impact on Firm's Productivity, Employment and Exports in Indonesia', in C.Y. Sussankarn, C. Park, and S.J. Kang (eds.), *Foreign Direct Investments in Asia*. London: Routledge, pp. 18–50.

Olley, G.S., and A. Pakes (1996), 'The Dynamics of Productivity in the Telecommunications Equipment Industry', *Econometrica* 64(6), pp. 1263–97.

Pangestu, M. (1996), *Economic Reform, Deregulation, and Privatization: The Indonesian Experience*. Jakarta: CSIS.

Roodman, D. (2009), 'How to do xtabond2: An Introduction to Difference and System GMM in Stata', *Stata Journal* 9(1), pp. 86–136.

Saggi, K. (2006), 'Foreign Direct Investment, Linkages, and Technology Spillovers', in B. Hoekman and B.S. Javorcik (eds.), *Global Integration and Technology Transfer*. Washington, DC: World Bank, pp. 51–65.

Xu, X. and Y. Sheng (2011), 'Productivity Spillovers from Foreign Direct Investment: Firm-Level Evidence from China', *World Development* 40, pp. 62–74.

5 Exporting, productivity, innovation and organization

Evidence from Malaysian manufacturing

Cassey Lee Hong Kim

5.1 Introduction

Economic globalization in the form of export-oriented industrialization driven by foreign direct investment (FDI) has been the main industrialization strategy in the Southeast Asian region since the early 1970s. The sustainability of this strategy has been intensely debated, especially in the aftermath of the 1997/1998 Asian Financial Crisis. Today, there is widespread concern amongst policy makers in the region about whether their economies can graduate from a middle-income to a high-income country, i.e., the so-called "middle-income trap". In Malaysia, this policy concern is manifested in the country's recent industrial policies such as the *Third Industrial Master Plan* (2008–2020), which put emphasis on upgrading the country's manufacturing base towards activities characterized by higher value-adding, productivity and innovation.

The key challenge in overcoming the "middle income trap" problem is finding ways to upgrade the industrial and technological capabilities of firms such that they are globally competitive – measured in terms of their ability to operate at the frontiers of global productivity and technology. The process of industrial and technological upgrading can take place either internally within a firm such as through undertaking research activities or externally via its interactions with suppliers, customers and universities (Griliches, 1979). In this regard, foreign sources of knowledge and technology are particularly important, especially for developing countries. Knowledge and technology can diffuse from developed to developing countries through trade and FDI (Keller, 2004). It is therefore important to understand how trade is related to both productivity and innovation. In addition, a deeper understanding of the relationship between trade, productivity and innovation requires an analysis of the nature and role of organization (Helpman, 2006; Antras & Rossi-Hansberg, 2009). This is reflected by the recent convergence of four areas of research in the study of trade, innovation, productivity and organization, i.e., international trade, industrial organization, innovation studies and the economics of organization.

The main purpose of this paper is to empirically examine the relationship between exporting on one hand, and productivity, innovation and firm organization on the other. The relationship between exporting and organization is studied using proxies of several aspects of firm organization, such as outsourcing/insourcing and the decentralization of decision-making. It will also investigate evidence for productivity premium of exporters as well as whether exporting causes innovation.

The outline of the rest of this chapter is as follows. Section 5.2 will briefly review the literature. This is followed by a discussion of the research methodology, which covers the framework utilized, econometric specifications and data source in Section 5.3. Section 5.4 provides a discussion of the results. Policy implications are discussed in Section 5.5. Finally, Section 5.6 is the conclusion.

5.2 Brief literature review

This study draws from a number of related literature. The first strand focuses on the relationship between trade (exporting), productivity and innovation. The second strand deals with trade and organizations.

5.2.1 Exporting, productivity and innovation

The seminal work by Melitz (2003) provides a theoretical framework that relates trade to industry and firm-level changes in productivity. In his model, trade brings about intra-industry and inter-firm reallocation of resources, which raises the average productivity level of the industry. This is brought about by the engagement (or self-selection) of firms with higher productivity in exporting as well as the exit of less productive (non-exporting) domestic firms. The empirical evidence on the role of self-selection at the firm-level in exporting is documented in Greenaway and Kneller (2007) and Wagner (2007). The role of innovation activities such as R&D (via their impact on productivity) on exporting has been highlighted by recent works such as Aw et al. (2007) and Damijan et al. (2010). Using three-year panel data from the Taiwanese electronics industry, Aw et al. (2007) found evidence of self-selection. In addition, they concluded that exporting firms benefit from R&D investment and worker training in terms of higher future productivity. These activities are related to firms' in-house capabilities to assimilate new information. Using innovation survey data from Slovenia, Damijan et al. (2010) provided evidence that product and process innovation does not increase the probability of a firm becoming a first time exporter. Furthermore, past exporting does not have impact on product innovation but there is some indirect evidence of past exporting on process innovation – thus providing some evidence of learning-by-exporting.

5.2.2 Trade and organization

Yeaple (2003) extends the theory of FDI using a three-country model to show that, aside from just undertaking horizontal or vertical integration strategies, firms may undertake complex integration strategies in which they may simultaneous adopt both types of integration strategies. Such situations can arise due to complementarities between vertical FDI (benefit from factor price differentials) and horizontal FDI (minimize transport cost). Helpman et al. (2004) provides an analysis of firm's choice between exporting or horizontal FDI (defined by the authors as "investment in a foreign production facility that is designed to serve customers in the foreign market"). They demonstrate that heterogenous firms (in terms of productivity) sort-out across the different forms of ownerships such that globalized firms (exporting and/or FDI) are more productive than non-globalized ones (serving domestic markets) and that globalized firms that engage in FDI are more productive than those engaged in exporting only. Tomuira (2007) investigated the relationship between productivity and the different modes of globalization such as FDI, exporting and foreign outsourcing. In the case of outsourcing, Tomuira (2007) used unique cross section survey data from the Japanese manufacturing sector that contains data on outsourcing to find some evidence of FDI firms being more productive than both foreign outsourcers and exporters.

5.3 Methodology

5.3.1 Exporting and productivity

The relationship between exporting and productivity can be analyzed by examining the average differences in productivity between firms that always export, those entering into exporting and those exiting exporting. This is undertaken by regressing productivity (proxied by labor productivity) of firm i in industry j against dummies representing different types of establishments with regards to changes in exporting status. The specification is as follows:

$$LProd_{ij} = \alpha_1 AE_{ij} + \alpha_2 NE_{ij} + \alpha_3 EE_{ij} + I_j + \varepsilon_{ij} \tag{1}$$

where AE is a dummy for firms that export in t and t+1, NE represents firms that do not export in t but export in $t+1$, EE is firms that export in t but do not export in t+1, $LProd$ is labor productivity and Ij are industry dummies. The reference category for these exporting/non-exporting status variables is non-exporters (in both t and t + 1). Two versions of the performance variable, namely productivity ($LProd$) are used – level and changes. By and large, the exporting premium in terms of productivity is expected to be larger for firms that export (AE and NE) compared to those that exit from exporting (EE). If the productivity premium from exporting is larger for continuing exporters (AE) than new exporters (NE), then there might be a learning-by-exporting effect.

5.3.2 Exporting and innovation

Following Damijian et al. (2010) and Hahn and Park (2011), the bi-directional causality between exporting and innovation can be investigated by using propensity score matching. The propensity score specification for the probability of undertaking innovation is given by:

$$\text{Prob}(Innov_{t-1}) = f(X_{t-1}) \tag{2}$$

where Xt_{-1} is the vector of lagged explanatory variables. Three measures of innovation are used – namely, product innovation, process innovation and organizational innovation.

The lagged explanatory variables include the natural log of the number computers (COMP), firm size measured by natural log of number of employees (SIZE), labor productivity (LPROD), foreign ownership dummy when the firm's headquarters are located abroad (FOREIGN), research and development dummy variable (RND), average wage of employee (WAGE), managerial experience by dummy for more than 10 years' experience (MGREXP), percent of employees with degrees (EMPDEGREE), trade liberalization by average MFN tariff (TARIFF), dummy for government assistance in research (GOVRES), dummy for government financial assistance (GOVFIN) and industry dummies.

The propensity scores from the probit estimations of the probability to innovate (equation 2) are used to match innovators and non-innovators and test the effects of lagged innovation on current exporting status. Matching was undertaken using the STATA command "psmatch2", which relies on nearest neighbor matching.

A similar exercise was undertaken for exporting:

$$\text{Prob}(Exp_{t-1}) = f(X_{t-1}) \tag{3}$$

5.3.3 Productivity and innovation

Productivity has been traditionally theorized in terms of a growth accounting production function framework. Within this framework, technological factors augment growth and are measured as a residual. In addition, human capital can also be included as an augmenting factor. Process innovation is generally understood to reduce fixed or variable costs (Swann, 2009). Thus, process innovation could reduce the use of factor inputs, resulting in higher productivity. Product innovation can be conceived as involving the introduction of new product. Its effect on productivity is more ambiguous depending on whether new products increase or reduce the total output of the firm.

Following Griffith et al. (2006), the relationship between productivity and innovation for firm *i* in industry *j* can estimated using an augmented production function in the form of:

$$\Upsilon_{ij} = f\left(K_{ij},\ H_{ij}, \mathbf{T}_{ij}\right) \tag{4}$$

where Υ is labor productivity (LPROD), K is capital intensity proxied by the number of computers per employee (COMPEMP), H human capital proxied by the percentage of employees with degrees (EMPDEGREE), $\mathbf{T}$ is the vector of innovation comprising product innovation (INNOVPROD), process innovation (INNOVPROC) and organizational innovation (INNOVORG).

5.3.4 Exporting and organization

There have been a number of theoretical and industry/macro-level empirical studies that link trade and organization. Organizations have several characteristics such as horizontal boundaries (scale of production), vertical boundaries (make or buy/outsourcing decisions) and span of control.

Similar to the approach used by Bustos (2011), differences in organization characteristics of firm *i* in industry *j* are estimated using the following specification:

$$\Upsilon_{ij} = \alpha AE_{ij} + \alpha_2 NE_{ij} + \alpha_3 EE_{ij} + I_j + ij \quad (5)$$

where *AE* are firms that exported in 2002 and 2006, *NE* is firms that did not export in 2002 but did in 2006, *EE* is firms that exported in 2002 but did not export in 2006, Υ is firm characteristic(s) and *I* are industry dummies. The reference category for these exporting/non-exporting status variables is non-exporters (in both 2002 and 2006).

In the empirical exercise, the scale of production is provided by natural log of revenue (REV) and natural log of employment size measured in full-time equivalent (EMP). The vertical boundary variables are proxied by four dummies for outsourcing (OUTSOURCE), local outsourcing (LOUTSOURCE), insourcing (INSOURCE) and local insourcing (LINSOURCE). The span of control is proxied by two dummies created for responses, indicating "agree" or "strongly agree" to the questions on whether "senior managers and middle managers frequently supervise our workers on tasks" (SUPERVISEMGR) and "our workers are directly involved in work-task decisions, and are not frequently supervised by middle or senior management" (SUPERVISEWKR).

5.3.5 Data

The firm-level data used in this study come from two sets of surveys for the *Study on Knowledge Content in Economic Sectors in Malaysia* (MyKE Study). The two waves of surveys were conducted by the Department of Statistics for the Economic Planning Unit in the Prime Minister's Department (EPU) in 2002 and 2006. The dataset is not available publicly and was obtained from the EPU by the author. The original dataset contains firms from the manufacturing as well as services sectors. Only firms from the manufacturing sector were used for this study.

There are 1,228 firms and 1,148 firms in the 2002 and 2006 datasets, respectively. A balanced panel is constructed for 753 firms. Table 5.1 provides summary statistics for some key variables. There is significant diversity in the sample, judging from the mean and standard deviation for firm size and total revenues. The majority of the firms in the sample are headquartered in Malaysia. A high

Table 5.1 Basic Descriptive Statistics

Year 2002				
Variable	*Mean*	*Standard Deviation*	*Min*	*Max*
Size (no. Employees)	232	442	3	6086
Revenues (RM, million)	124	1040	0,14	24500

Year 2006				
Variable	*Mean*	*Standard Deviation*	*Min*	*Max*
Size (no. Employees)	265	562	11	8471
Revenues (RM, million)	183	1180	0,15	21300

	Year 2002		*Year 2006*	
	Number	*%*	*Number*	*%*
HQ in Malaysia	630	83,7	607	80,6
HQ outside Malaysia	123	16,3	146	19,4

	Year 2002		*Year 2006*	
	Number	*%*	*Number*	*%*
Exporting	630	83,7	607	80,6
Non-exporting	123	16,3	146	19,4

	Year 2002		*Year 2006*	
	Number	*%*	*Number*	*%*
Product innovation	23	3	50	6,6
Process innovation	176	23,4	154	20,5
Prod & proc innovation	134	17,8	147	19,5
Non-innovators	420	55,8	402	53,4

Source: Economic Planning Unit, Malaysia.

proportion of firms in the sample are exporters, about 77.8% in 2002 and 61.5% in 2006. Innovation is defined as per the OSLO

Manual's definition. Non-innovators make up about half the firms in the sample.

Industry dummies at the two-digit level are included in all regressions.

5.4 Result

5.4.1 Exporting and productivity

The results from this study provide some evidence of a higher productivity premium of continuing exporters (Table 5.2). Only this result is statistically significant (at the 1% level). Surprisingly, the value of the coefficients indicate that the exporting premium of exiting exporters is higher than of new exporters – even though only the exiting exporter variables are significant for the regression involving the productivity level in 2006. This might be due to the relatively smaller productivity gains achieved by new exporters. This is confirmed by separate regressions for the two different class sizes, namely small and medium-sized enterprises (SMEs) (< 51 employees) and large sized firms (> 50 employees) [Note: Both definitions are based on official definitions adopted by the Malaysian government]. In fact, SME entry exporters may have lower productivity compared to their counterpart non-exporters (Table 5.3).

Table 5.2 Exporting and Productivity

Variables	*LPROD*	*LPROD*	*LPROD*
	Year 2002	*Year 2006*	*Change*
Always export	0.442***	0.628***	1.427
	(0.125)	(0.117)	(1.338)
Entry export	0,121	0.0955	0.687
	(0.252)	(0.247)	(2.730)
Exit export	0.214	0.249*	-0.114
	(0.150)	(0.138)	(1.602)
Industry dummies	Yes	Yes	Yes
Observations	633	749	630
R-squared	0.148	0.173	0.009

Source: Author.
Note: Standard errors in parenthesis, *, ** and ** indicate statistical significance at 10%, 5%, and 1%, respectively.

Table 5.3 Exporting and Productivity – SMEs and Large Firms

Variables	*SME Firms*	*Large Firms*
	LPROD	*LPROD*
	Year 2002	*Year 2002*
Always export	0.482**	0.316*
	(0.224)	(0.164)
Entry export	-0.269	0.0671
	(0.555)	(0.296)
Exit export	0.155	0.132
	(0.238)	(0.194)
Industry dummies	Yes	Yes
Observations	134	499
R-squared	0.150	0.168

Source: Author.
Note: Standard errors in parenthesis, *, ** and ** indicate statistical significance at 10%, 5%, and 1%, respectively.

5.4.2 Exporting and innovation

The results from this study indicate that the causal direction between exporting and innovation is from exporting to innovation, and not vice versa (Table 5.4). This applies for both product and process innovations. Thus, with regards to these two types of innovations, learning-by-exporting effects seem to apply. These results are similar to those from Damijan et al. (2010). Since both the results from this study and Damijan's (based on Slovenian data) differ from the selection hypothesis, it may indicate that the experience of developing countries may differ from that of more developed countries (such as Taiwan or South Korea). This would be consistent with the general observation that technology diffuses from developed to developing countries (Keller, 2004). For the latter, this occurs partly through exporting. Finally, there is no causal relationship between exporting and organizational innovation.

5.4.3 Productivity and innovation

Productivity is driven by capital intensity and human capital (proxied by percentage of employees with degrees; Table 5.5). This is consistent with both the theoretical framework underlying growth theory as well as empirical results from firm-level studies. Productivity is also driven by process innovation – which indirectly confirms Damijan et al.'s (2010) suggestion that exporting leads to productivity improvements via process innovation rather than product innovation. However, it should be noted that product innovation is not well measured when productivity is measured using a production function approach. This is

Table 5.4 Average Treatment Effects of Lagged Innovation (Exporting) on Current Exporting Status (Innovation)

Causality	*Average Treatment Effects*	*Standard Error*	*Treatment Observations*	*Control Observations*
Lagged product innovation on current exporting status	-0,056	0,066	125	460
Lagged exporting status on product Innovation	0.150**	0.080	452	133
Lagged process innovation on current exporting status	-0.012	0.058	253	332
Lagged exporting status on process Innovation	0.272***	0.090	452	133
Lagged organization innovation on current exporting status	-0.116	0.064	277	308
Lagged exporting status on organization Innovation	0.051	0.100	452	133

Source: Author.

Note: Standard errors in parenthesis, *, ** and ** indicate statistical significance at 10%, 5%, and 1%, respectively.

Table 5.5 Productivity and Innovation

Variables	*LPROD*	*LPROD*	*LPROD*
COMPEMP	0.406***	0.357***	0.351***
	(0.0329)	(0.0352)	(0.0356)
EMPDEGREE		0.0142***	0.0141***
		(0.0036)	(0.0036)
INNOVPROD			-0.0415
			(0.0740)
INNOCPROC			0.140**
			(0.0699)
INNOVORG			0.0173
			(0.0648)
Industry dummies	Yes	Yes	Yes
Observations	633	749	630
R-squared	0.148	0.173	0.009

Source: Author.
Note: Standard errors in parenthesis, *, ** and ** indicate statistical significance at 10%, 5%, and 1%, respectively.

Table 5.6 Exporting and Horizontal Boundaries

Variables	*Revenue*	*Employment*	*Revenue*	*Employment*
	Year 2006	*Year 2006*	*Change*	*Change*
Always export	2.154 e + 08*	241.0***	5.671 e + 07	46.30*
	(1.191 e + 08)	(55.15)	(1.276 e + 08)	(26.22)
Entry export	-1.575 e + 07	57.9	-1.060 e + 07	12.18
	(2.481 e + 08)	(114.9)	(2.660 e + 08)	(54.63)
Exit export	4.660 e + 07	71.83	3.033 e + 07	11.15
	(1.405 e + 08)	(65.08)	(1.506 e + 08)	(30.94)
Industry dummies	Yes	Yes	Yes	Yes
Observations	753	753	753	753
R-squared	0.027	0.077	0.017	0.026

Source: Author.
Note: Standard errors in parenthesis, *, ** and ** indicate statistical significance at 10%, 5%, and 1%, respectively.

because the total output does not sufficiently capture product variety that arises from product innovation. Thus, the role of product innovation may be underestimated in such exercises.

5.4.4 Exporting and organization

The evidence on organizational differences between exporters and non-exporters is complex. In terms of horizontal boundaries or scale or production, continuing exporters do have larger revenues or employment size compared to non-exporters (Table 5.6). The scale exporting premium of continuing exporters is larger than that enjoyed by new and exiting exporters (the latter two are not

Table 5.7 Exporting and Vertical Boundaries

Variables	*Outsourcing*	*Outsourcing*	*Insourcing*	*Insourcing*
		Local		*Local*
Always export	0.210	0.191	0.197	0.117
	(0.139)	(0.142)	(0.160)	(0.163)
Entry export	0.0923	0.136	0.431	0.362
	(0.289)	(0.291)	(0.302)	(0.310)
Exit export	-0.134	-0.106	0.173	0.187
	(0.170)	(0.172)	(0.186)	(0.189)
Industry dummies	Yes	Yes	Yes	Yes
Observations	753	753	753	753

Source: Author.
Note: Standard errors in parenthesis, *, ** and ** indicate statistical significance at 10%, 5%, and 1%, respectively.

Table 5.8 Exporting and Decentralization

Variables	*SUPERVISEMGR*	*SUPERVISEWORKER*
Always export	-0.513***	0.182
	(0.156)	(0.152)
Entry export	-0.511*	-0.0201
	(0.295)	(0.327)
Exit export	-0.301*	0.346**
	(0.182)	(0.173)
Industry dummies	Yes	Yes
Observations	753	753

Source: Author.
Note: Standard errors in parenthesis, *, ** and ** indicate statistical significance at 10%, 5%, and 1%, respectively.

statistically significant). New exporters performed worse than exiting exporters in terms of both revenue and employment size – similar to earlier findings on productivity.

In terms of vertical boundaries (measured by outsourcing and insourcing), there are no statistically significant differences between continuing exporters, entry exporters and exit exporters (Table 5.7). There is strong evidence on exporting on decentralization (Table 5.8). This confirms the theoretical predictions that the accumulation of knowledge may lead to hierarchies in which many routine-type decisions are delegated to production workers (see Caliendo & Ross-Hansberg, 2011).

5.5 Policy implications

A number of policy implications can be drawn from the findings of this study. The continued emphasis on exporting as a development strategy for the manufacturing sector is the right approach, given the productivity premium associated with exporting. However, given the productivity differentials between continuing, new and exiting exporters (compared to non-exporters), the government should consider focusing on new exporters, especially SMEs.

With regards to innovation and exporting, the results on the direction of causality between the two (exporting → innovation) suggest that there is perhaps a need for policies to encourage more product innovation rather than to promote exporting per se. The findings on productivity and innovation imply that human capital development should be a key area of focus.

Whilst organizational innovation is likely to be mostly an endogenous and adaptive phenomenon, it is possible that human capital development plays an important role, as suggested by the current theoretical literature on knowledge accumulation and hierarchies. The empirical evidence linking decentralization to exporting may constitute an early indirect evidence of this – thus reinforcing the importance of policies on human capital development.

5.6 Conclusions

Many developing countries continue to focus on export-driven industrialization as an engine for growth and development. There is a greater need to understand how exporting is related to productivity and innovation at the micro-level. Using firm-level data from Malaysian manufacturing, this study has found some evidence of strong productivity premium for continuing exporters (compared to non-exporters). Such premiums are much weaker (even negative) for new exporters, especially for smaller firms. There is evidence on the causality of exporting to innovation, which supports the learning-by-exporting hypothesis. The impact of exporting on productivity may take place through process innovation. There are also important organizational changes associated with exporting, namely scale effects (horizontal boundaries) and the decentralization of decision-making, especially for continuing exporters. In terms of policy implications, findings from this study suggest that export entry is a difficult process, especially for smaller firms. As the productivity gains from exporting are likely to come from learning-by-exporting, there is perhaps a need for the government to provide incentives and support for human capital investment to increase firm-level productivity (rather than providing incentives for exporting per se).

References

Antras, P. and Rossi-Hansberg, E. (2009), 'Organizations and Trade', *Annual Review of Economics* 1(1), pp. 43–64.

Aw, B., Roberts, M., and Winston, T. (2007), 'Export Market Participation, Investments in R&D and Worker Training, and the Evolution of Firm Productivity', *World Economy* 30(1), pp. 83–104.

Bustos, P. (2011), 'Trade Liberalization, Exports, and Technology Upgrading: Evidence on the Impact of MERCOSUR on Argentinian Firms', *American Economic Review* 101(1), pp. 304–40.

Caliendo, L. and Ross-Hansberg, E. (2011), 'The Impact of Trade on Organization and Productivity', *NBER Working Paper* No.17308.

Damijan, J., Kostevc, C., and Polanec, S. (2010), 'From Innovation to Exporting or Vice Versa', *World Economy* 33(3), pp. 374–98.

Greenaway, D. and Kneller, R. (2007), 'Firm Heterogeneity, Exporting and Foreign Direct Investment', *Economic Journal* 117(517), pp. F134–61.

Griffith, R., Huergo, E., Mairesse, J., and Peters, B. (2006), 'Innovation and Productivity across Four European Countries', *Oxford Review of Economic Policy* 2(4), pp. 483–98.

Griliches, Z. (1979), 'Issues in Assessing the Contribution of R&D to Productivity Growth', *Bell Journal of Economics* 10(1), pp. 92–116.

Hahn, C.-H. and Park, C.-G. (2011), 'Direction of Causality in Innovation-Exporting Linkage: Evidence from Microdata on Korean Manufacturing', *Korea and the World Economy* 12(2), pp. 367–98.

Helpman, E. (2006), 'Trade, FDI, and the Organizations of Firms', *Journal of Economic Literature* 44(3), pp. 589–630.

Helpman, E., Melitz, M., and Yeaple, S. (2004), 'Exports Versus FDI with Heterogeneous Firms', *American Economic Review* 94(1), pp. 300–16.

Keller, W. (2004), 'International Technology Diffusion', *Journal of Economic Literature* 42(3), pp. 752–82.

Melitz, M. (2003), 'The Impact of Trade on Intra-industry Reallocation and Aggregate Industry Productivity', *Econometrica* 71(6), pp. 1695–725.

Swann, G. (2009), *The Economics of Innovation: An Introduction.* Edward Elgar: Cheltenham.

Tomuira, E. (2007), 'Foreign Outsourcing, Exporting, and FDI: A Productivity Comparison at the Firm Level', *Journal of International Economics* 72(1), pp. 113–27.

Wagner, J. (2007), 'Exports and Productivity: A Survey of the Evidence from Firm-level Data', *World Economy* 30(1), pp. 60–82.

Yeaple, S. (2003), 'The Complex Integration Strategies of Multinationals and Cross Country Dependencies in the Structure of Foreign Direct Investment', *Journal of International Economics* 60(2), pp. 293–314.

6 Trade liberalization and the wage skill premium in Korean manufacturing plants

Do plants' R&D and investment matter?

Chin Hee Hahn and Yong-Seok Choi

6.1 Background and objective

For the past several decades, the impact of globalization on wage inequality between skilled and unskilled workers (wage skill premium) has drawn much attention in academic and policy circles. Earlier studies based on the traditional Heckscher-Ohlin theory were generally skeptical of the view that trade is an important cause of rising wage inequality. Recent theories, however, highlight several new mechanisms—interaction between skill-biased technological progress (SBTC) and trade (Wood 1995; Thoenig and Verdier 2003; Bustos 2011a, 2011b), complementarity between imported capital goods and skilled workers (Acemoglu 2003) or a trade-induced compositional change in a firm's product portfolio (Verhoogen 2008), for example—by which trade liberalization increases wage skill premium. Although there are a growing number of empirical studies that find that globalization increases the wage skill premium,[1] whether and how it does so is an issue that deserves further scrutiny.

In this paper, we examine empirically the effect of trade liberalization on within-plant wage inequality between skilled and unskilled workers[2] utilizing plant-level dataset in the Korean manufacturing sector. As in Amiti and Davis (2012) and Amiti and Cameron (2012),[3] we examine separate roles of output and input tariffs and consider possibly differential effects among plants. The latter approach is broadly in line with the spirit of recent heterogeneous firm trade theories, which predict differential responses of firms to trade liberalization depending on the firm's characteristics.

In this paper, we focus on plants' R&D and investment behavior as the key characteristics determining the effect of import tariff reductions on within-plant wage skill premiums. So, our paper can be broadly related to the literature examining the possible interaction between trade and SBTC as a mechanism through which trade affects the wage skill premium. While there is a growing interest in this subject, empirical studies that examine this mechanism explicitly are surprisingly scant.[4]

Following is a brief sketch of the story that explains our focus on plants' R&D and investment behavior. According to well-known heterogeneous firm trade theories, such as those developed and reviewed by Amiti and Davis (2012), trade liberalization or reductions of trade costs increase the revenue and profit of firms with higher productivity while decreasing them for firms with lower productivity. The increase (decrease) of the revenue and profit, or the prospect of it, will enhance (reduce) the incentive to engage in R&D[5] and/or to make investments in production facilities, since these are basically investment activities motivated by profit opportunities. However, the effect of import tariff reductions on within-plant wage skill premiums might differ depending on firms' behaviors in R&D and facility investment in response to import tariff reductions. Above all, R&D itself is likely to be a skilled labor-intensive activity. Thus, if a firm increases R&D activity in response to trade liberalization, it will increase the relative demand for skilled workers, leading to an increase in the wage skill premium when wages are determined at the firm level. Furthermore, R&D might be aimed at more skill-intensive products or processes under the increased import competition.[6] Alternatively, if a firm decides to increase its production capacity by investing in equipment and production lines given existing technologies, it is likely to boost relative demand for the production or unskilled workers, or at least their increase of relative demand for the non-production workers will be weaker than R&D-doing firms. So, firms that increase production capacities in response to trade liberalization may experience a reduction in the wage skill premium or a weaker increase in it than R&D-doing firms.[7] So, our analysis allows for differential effects of tariff reductions among plants engaged in R&D, those making facility investments and those that do neither. We find evidence consistent with the above conjecture. We think that this is a novel feature of our paper.

As mentioned above, we are interested in estimating the separate effects of output and input tariff reductions on the wage skill premium as in Amiti and Cameron (2012). We think that conducting similar analyses for Korea's case is a meaningful exercise per se. Amiti and Cameron (2012) found that the reduction in intermediate input tariffs *lowers* the wage skill premium in Indonesian manufacturing and no significant effect from the output tariff reductions. Their interpretation of the wage inequality reducing effect of input tariff reductions is as follows. As Indonesian manufacturing plants import more skill-intensive intermediate inputs mostly from developed countries, the reduction in input tariffs induces firms to switch from in-house production of skill-intensive intermediate inputs to importing, which decreases the relative demand for skilled labor within firm. They give no detailed explanations on the insignificant effect from output tariff reductions.

In our view, however, there is no guarantee that similar results will be found for Korea or in other countries or contexts. First and foremost, we expect that the reduction of output tariffs widens the wage skill premium mostly in R&D-doing plants and narrows it mostly in plants expanding their production capacity. Next, regarding the effect of input tariff reductions, we think that the expected effect of the reduction in input tariffs is ambiguous on empirical and theoretical grounds. Amiti and Cameron's interpretation of their own results was based on the observation that Indonesia is a skill-scarce country that imports intermediate inputs from skill-abundant developed countries. However, the source-country composition of Korea's intermediate input imports is different from that of Indonesia's. Although high-income countries accounted for a major share of Korea's intermediate input imports during the period 1992–2003, the share of low-income countries has steadily risen, from 22% to 32%.

More importantly, in our view, the effect of the reduction in intermediate input tariffs is likely to be theoretically ambiguous even if imported intermediate inputs are typically more skill-intensive than domestically produced ones. The relative-cost-based choice between in-house production of and importing intermediate inputs, as explained by Amiti and Cameron, is one mechanism. However, there could be another mechanism through which the reduction in input tariffs affect the within-firm wage skill premium. As theoretically shown by Amiti and Davis (2012), for example, when there are increasing returns from a greater number of input varieties, the increase in the number of available intermediate inputs caused by input tariff reductions lowers the marginal cost of production for firms that import intermediate inputs, which increases their revenues and profits. If, again, the increase in profit opportunity strengthens the incentive to do R&D, input tariff reductions are expected to increase, rather than decrease, the wage skill premium within plants.[8] So, the combined effect is ambiguous. Under this story, which we think is very plausible, the effect of input tariff reductions on the within-plant wage skill premium is an empirical matter.

This paper is organized as follows. In the next section, we explain our data and present trends in wages and employments of skilled and unskilled workers in the aggregate manufacturing. We also review trends in the average tariff rate. In Section 6.3, we explain estimation strategy and provide summary statistics in the key variables in our regressions. In Section 6.4, we provide our main empirical results. The final section is the conclusion.

6.2 Data and descriptive statistics

In our empirical analyses, we will utilize two data sources. The first one is the "Mining and Manufacturing Census" conducted by the KNSO (Korea National Statistical Office) during 1992–2003. This data covers all plants with five or more employees in the mining and manufacturing sectors.[9] For each year, the numbers of and the wage bills paid to production and non-production workers are available at the plant-level in this survey. We construct the within-plant wage inequality between production and non-production workers by dividing average wage of non-production workers by that of production workers. This data also provides information about various plant characteristics: status of R&D, investment and export, size (measured by the level of total employment) and skill intensity (measured by the ratio of the number of non-production workers to that of production workers).

Finally, the yearly import tariff data comes from the KCS (Korea Customs Service) at the ten-digit level with the HS code system. They provide data on the value of applied tariffs and imports for each HS category; the output tariff can be directly calculated by dividing the value of the applied tariff by the value of import. This tariff data with the HS code system has been converted to 141 Korea's Input-Output industry codes to calculate the weighted average of industry-level output tariffs using the matching table provided by the Bank of Korea. Here, the weights are based on import value in 1992 (initial year of our sample period) in the HS code system. In turn, we combine these industry-level output tariffs with the Korea's Input-Output table in 2000 to calculate the weighted average of input tariffs for the corresponding industry, where the weights are based on the input-output coefficients from the Bank of Korea.[10]

Tables 6.1 and 6.2 report some basic statistics of the major variables in our analyses. In Table 6.1, the output and input tariffs are listed for each year. As we can see, both tariff rates display decreasing trends although it is not monotonic.[11] Table 6.2 show the summary statistics of the other variables. The average skilled wage premium in our sample is 1.151 with substantial heterogeneity across plants. On average, R&D, investment and export activities are implemented by 8.4%, 48.6% and 12.9% of plants, respectively.

One emphasis of our empirical work in Section 6.3 lies in the different responses to tariff reduction depending on plant characteristics. Thus, according to the status of plants' behavior in terms of R&D, investment and exporting, Table 6.3 presents the mean values of our major variables. Consistent with our expectations, plants engaged in R&D, investment and export activities (i.e., plants with R&D, investment and export dummies are equal to 1) pay a relatively higher wage to skilled workers, are bigger in size, have higher productivity and employ relatively more skilled workers.

Table 6.1 Korea's Output Tariffs and Input Tariffs: 1992–2003

Year	*Output Tariff*		*Input Tariff*	
	Mean (1)	*Std. Dev. (2)*	*Mean (3)*	*Std. Dev. (4)*
1992	0.109	0.083	0.053	0.023
1993	0.092	0.077	0.046	0.020
1994	0.089	0.084	0.043	0.020
1995	0.111	0.160	0.050	0.035
1996	0.094	0.085	0.044	0.023
1997	0.092	0.077	0.043	0.025
1998	0.094	0.079	0.042	0.022
1999	0.088	0.069	0.044	0.019
2000	0.087	0.071	0.044	0.020
2001	0.084	0.069	0.043	0.021
2002	0.086	0.072	0.043	0.021
2003	0.086	0.081	0.041	0.022
1992–2003	0.091	0.084	0.044	0.022

Note: Table reports the means and standard deviations of output and input tariffs across 141 industries. Input tariffs are constructed using 2000 input-output table provided by the Bank of Korea.

Table 6.2 Summary Statistics of Other Variables

	Observation	*Mean*	*Std. Dev.*	*Min*	*Max*
Skilled wage premium	509,211	1.151	0.676	0.020	107.143
R&D dummy	742,585	0.084	0.278	0.000	1.000
Investment dummy	706,503	0.486	0.500	0.000	1.000
Export dummy	633,506	0.129	0.335	0.000	1.000
Size	737,558	2.544	0.920	0.693	10.219
Ln(TFP)	742,574	0.194	0.400	-11.905	15.787
Skill intensity	722,642	0.393	0.878	0.000	85.000

Note: Skilled wage premium is defined by the ratio of the average wage of non-production workers relative to that of production workers. Export, R&D and Investment dummies take the value of 1 if the value of export, R&D and investment are positive, respectively and the value of 0 otherwise. Size is the natural logarithm of employment. TFP is measured using the chained-multilateral index number approach as developed in Good (1985) and Good, Nadiri and Sickles (1997). Skill intensity is defined by the ratio of non-production workers to production workers.

Table 6.3 Mean Values of Variables According to R&D, Investment and Export Dummies

	R&D dummy		*Investment dummy*		*Export dummy*	
	0	*1*	*0*	*1*	*0*	*1*
Skilled wage premium	1.139	1.251	1.094	1.194	1.125	1.315
R&D dummy	0.000	1.000	0.040	0.127	0.059	0.264
Investment dummy	0.462	0.752	0.000	1.000	0.447	0.710
Export dummy	0.104	0.400	0.070	0.186	0.000	1.000
Size	2.459	3.467	2.254	2.823	2.413	3.520
Ln(TFP)	0.186	0.282	0.181	0.206	0.181	0.273
Skill intensity	0.352	0.842	0.298	0.480	0.360	0.608
Number of observation	1,051,654	86,347	555,519	529,728	893,502	131,867

Note: The definitions of the variables are given in the note of Table 6.2.

Figure 6.1 shows the trends of wage and employment of non-production and production workers during our sample period.[12] In Panel (a), we can see that the levels of average wages of non-production and production workers show increasing trends (except in 1998 when a severe economic crisis took place in Korea), while their difference has been generally enlarged, especially since 1995. This latter point can be seen more conveniently by looking at Figure 6.2 where the relative wage and employment of non-production workers are drawn throughout the sample period. In Panel (b) of Figure 6.1, we observe again a sharp decrease in employment (both for non-production and production workers) in the year of economic crisis, after which employment of non-production workers increased relatively more rapidly than production workers. This also can be seen in Figure 6.2 where the relative employment of non-production workers shows an increasing trend. In this paper, we use non-production and production workers

Figure 6.1 Trends of Wage and Employment of Non-production and Production Workers.

Figure 6.2 Trends of Relative Wage and Employment of Non-production Workers (Log Level in Each Year – Log Level in 1992).

as proxies for skilled and unskilled workers, respectively. Then, trends shown in Figures 6.1 and 6.2 suggest that the relative demand for skilled workers has been rising in Korean manufacturing in our sample period.

6.3 Empirical specification

In order to investigate how (both output and input) tariff reduction and its interaction with R&D, investment and export activity affect within-plant wage inequality, we run the following regression:

$$\begin{aligned}\ln\left(w_s / w_u\right)_{p,\, i,\, t} = {} & \alpha_p + \alpha_t + \beta_1 \text{ * output tariff}_{i,\, t} + \beta_2 \text{ * input tariff}_{i,\, t} \\ & + \beta_3 \text{ * output tariff}_{i,\, t} {}^{*} CH_{p,\, t} + \beta_4 \text{ * input tariff}_{i,\, t} {}^{*} CH_{p,\, t} \\ & + \Gamma' X_{p,\, i,\, t} + \varepsilon_{p,\, i,\, t} \qquad (1)\end{aligned}$$

where the dependent variable is the skilled wage premium, measured by the log of the ratio of the average wage of non-production workers to that of production workers (w_s / w_u). The output and input tariffs are measured at 141 input-output industry-level. *CH* denotes three different channels that can interact with trade liberalization: R&D, physical investment and the export activity of each plant. *X* represents a vector of plant-specific characteristics such as size, total factor productivity and skill intensity. α_p and α_t are plant-fixed and year-fixed effect, respectively.

The coefficient β_1 has the meaning of the effect of output tariff on the within-plant skilled wage premium for the plants with $CH = 0$: for example, the effect of output tariff on the wage premium without doing any R&D activity. The coefficient on the interaction term, β_3, represents the heterogeneous response of R&D-doing plants in response to an output tariff reduction: if an output tariff reduction leads to increased demand for skilled labor in the R&D-doing plants (and therefore to a widening of the skilled wage premium), we expect that β_3 would be significantly negative. This interpretation can be applied to the other different channels, investment and export activity.

Likewise, β_2 measures the effect of input tariffs on the skilled wage premium for plants with $CH = 0$. If an input tariff reduction affects the skilled wage premium of, for example, R&D-doing firms differently, β_4 would be significantly different from zero.

6.4 Empirical results

6.4.1 Main results

We first estimate Equation (1) with plant fixed effects and Table 6.4 shows the results. In all specifications, we include plant-specific characteristics of size, TFP and skill intensity, all of which are statistically different from zero at 1% level. It shows that the skilled wage premium is higher when the size is larger, the

Table 6.4 Fixed Effects Estimation Results: Skill Premium

	(1)	(2)	(3)	(4)	(5)
Output tariff	-0.040*		-0.024	-0.062**	-0.059**
	(0.022)		(0.023)	(0.028)	(0.029)
Input tariff		-0.249**	-0.226**	-0.221*	-0.057
		(0.098)	(0.104)	(0.127)	(0.140)
Output tariff * R&D			-0.076*	-0.103**	-0.105**
			(0.043)	(0.044)	(0.049)
Input tariff * R&D			0.135	0.216	0.160
			(0.193)	(0.201)	(0.222)
Output tariff * INV				0.073***	0.076***
				(0.026)	(0.028)
Input tariff * INV				0.006	-0.045
				(0.118)	(0.129)
Output tariff * EXP					-0.022
					(0.056)
Input tariff * EXP					-0.138
					(0.221)
R&D			0.008	0.007	0.011
			(0.008)	(0.008)	(0.010)
INV				-0.004	-0.002
				(0.005)	(0.006)
EXP					0.018*
					(0.010)
Size	0.126***	0.126***	0.125***	0.128***	0.133***
	(0.002)	(0.002)	(0.002)	(0.003)	(0.003)
Ln(TFP)	-0.066***	-0.066***	-0.066***	-0.066***	-0.067***
	(0.003)	(0.003)	(0.003)	(0.003)	(0.003)
Skill intensity	-0.345***	-0.345***	-0.346***	-0.342***	-0.383***
	(0.008)	(0.008)	(0.008)	(0.008)	(0.009)
Constant	-0.269***	-0.259***	-0.257***	-0.266***	-0.279***
	(0.009)	(0.010)	(0.010)	(0.011)	(0.012)
Year effect	Yes	Yes	Yes	Yes	Yes
Plant effect	Yes	Yes	Yes	Yes	Yes
Number of plants	157,409	157,409	157,409	155,275	143,589
Number of observations	506,376	506,376	506,376	478,424	413,072
R-squared	0.026	0.026	0.026	0.027	0.028

Note: Robust standard errors clustered at the plant level are in parentheses. *, **, and *** denote that the estimated coefficients are significant at 10%, 5% and 1% level, respectively. The dependent variable is the skill premium defined by the natural logarithm of average wage of non-production workers to production workers.

productivity is lower and the skill intensity is lower. These results are almost identical to the case of Indonesia as shown in Amiti and Cameron (2012).[13]

In Columns (1)–(3) of the table, we include either output/input tariffs or both. When we include output or input tariffs separately, both coefficients on these variables are estimated to be significantly negative. This means that the reductions of both output and input tariffs are associated with the increase of the skilled wage premium, which is in sharp contrast with the main findings from the Indonesian data by Amiti and Cameron (2012). In the case of Korea, it seems that trade liberalization (in terms of both output and input) leads plants to increase the demand for skilled labor. Then, what are the important channels through which trade liberalization affects demand for skilled labor?

As explained in Section 6.4.2, the interaction of trade liberalization and R&D might be an important channel that explains this skilled wage premium in the Korean context. To explore this, in Column (3) of Table 6.4 we include the interaction term of output tariff and R&D dummy and we find that its coefficient is estimated to be significantly negative. This suggests that trade liberalization, as measured by output tariff reductions, had an effect of increasing the skilled wage premium within R&D-performing plants compared to R&D non-performing plants. This result is supportive of the view that trade liberalization, in interaction with SBTC, contributed to the increase in the skilled wage premium. We do not find, however, any significant effect of the reduction in intermediate input tariffs on within-plant skilled wage premium, which is in contrast to the results by Amiti and Cameron (2012).

As explained in Section 6.4.2, if trade liberalization affects the skilled wage premium of R&D-doing plants differently, it would be a natural empirical question to ask whether investment-doing plants also respond differently to trade liberalization. Thus, in Column (4) of Table 6.3, we additionally include the interaction term of investment with trade liberalization. After adding investment-related variables, the coefficient on output tariff becomes significantly negative again, which means that even the plants without any R&D and physical investment increase the demand for skilled labor. In addition, the coefficient on the interaction of R&D with output tariff becomes larger in its absolute value and more significant. R&D-performing plants further increase the demand for skilled labor. However, the coefficient of the interaction of the investment dummy with output tariff is estimated to be positively significant. This means that plants with physical investment respond in the opposite direction compared those with R&D investment.[14] To the extent that R&D activity is associated with higher demand for human capital (or skilled labor) and physical investment with lower demand for skilled labor, the positive sign of the estimated coefficient on the interaction of investment with output tariffs is not surprising.

In Column (5) of the table, we include export-related variables in the regression additionally. None of the coefficients on the interaction terms of export with output and input tariffs are significant but the coefficients on the interactions terms of R&D and investment remain significant and have the same sign as in Column (4).[15]

As an alternative specification, we estimate Equation (1) in five-year differences. Using five-year differencing would reduce the problems of measurement errors and any concern of unit roots that may exist in a levels equation. The dependent variable is the log difference of skilled wage premium and output tariffs, input tariffs and other plant characteristics (size, productivity and skill intensity) are also differenced at five-year interval. For the R&D, investment and export dummies, we take the initial year's value.[16] Table 6.5 reports the estimation results of this specification, which are very similar to those in Table 6.4 with

Table 6.5 Alternative Specification (Five-year Differences): Skill Premium

	(1)	*(2)*	*(3)*
ΔOutput tariff	-0.037	-0.132**	-0.134**
	(0.038)	(0.059)	(0.059)
ΔInput tariff	-0.011	0.404	0.460*
	(0.167)	(0.273)	(0.278)
ΔOutput tariff * $R\&D_{t0}$	-0.184*	-0.256**	-0.258**
	(0.109)	(0.115)	(0.117)
ΔInput tariff * $R\&D_{t0}$	0.323	0.344	0.386
	(0.453)	(0.468)	(0.471)
ΔOutput tariff * INV_{t0}		0.163**	0.161**
		(0.074)	(0.074)
ΔInput tariff * INV_{t0}		-0.605*	-0.557
		(0.338)	(0.342)
ΔOutput tariff * EXP_{t0}			0.028
			(0.117)
ΔInput tariff * EXP_{t0}			-0.352
			(0.378)
$R\&D_{t0}$	-0.017**	-0.018**	-0.018***
	(0.007)	(0.007)	(0.007)
INV_{t0}		-0.010**	-0.011**
		(0.005)	(0.005)
EXP_{t0}			0.003
			(0.006)
ΔSize	0.099***	0.099***	0.100***
	(0.004)	(0.004)	(0.004)
ΔLn(TFP)	-0.059***	-0.058***	-0.058***
	(0.005)	(0.005)	(0.005)
ΔSkill intensity	-0.409***	-0.405***	-0.405***
	(0.014)	(0.014)	(0.014)
Year effect	Yes	Yes	Yes
Number of observations	74,110	70,403	70,403
R-squared	0.028	0.028	0.028

Note: Robust standard errors are in parentheses. *, **, and *** denote that the estimated coefficients are significant at 10%, 5% and 1% level, respectively. The dependent variable is the five-year difference in the natural logarithm of the skill premium. The skill premium is defined as in the note in Table 6.3.

fixed effects. R&D-doing plants and physical investment-doing plants respond differently to output tariff reduction in the opposite direction in terms of the skilled wage premium.[17]

6.4.2 *Further discussion*

The empirical results in the previous subsection implies that an output tariff reduction is more likely to affect within-plant skilled wage premium than an input tariff reduction. In addition, there is strong evidence supporting the idea that the skilled wage premium of R&D-performing plants has increased, but such an effect could not be found for investment-performing plants. Our conjectured mechanism in interpreting these results was that an output tariff reduction is more likely to increase the incentive to implement R&D, which requires relatively more skilled workers (than physical investment activity), explaining why the increase of the skilled wage premium took place most prominently in R&D-performing plants.

In this subsection, we would like to investigate and clarify this mechanism a little bit further by doing some supplementary analyses. First, Table 6.6 shows the conditional logit regression results of R&D and investment dummies on output and input tariffs.[18] It shows that while both output and input tariff reductions increase the probability of plants being engaged in investment activity, it is the output tariff reduction that increases the probability of R&D activity of plants. This is consistent with our conjecture that an output tariff reduction increases the plants' incentive to implement R&D activity. Also, as we mentioned in Section 6.1, this may reflect a defensive innovation phenomenon in the face of import competition of final goods.[19]

Second, in Table 6.7, the fixed effect regression results of total employment and employment of non-production and production workers are reported. When the output tariff falls, plants' total employment does not change in any statistically significant way. This is because an output tariff reduction increases the employment of non-production workers (skilled workers) and decreases the employment of production workers. By contrast, plants facing input tariff reductions increase total employment by boosting both non-production and production workers. Therefore, an output tariff reduction (which is more closely related with R&D activity as seen in Table 6.6) will increase the relative demand for skilled workers.

Finally, in Table 6.8 the same dependent variables as in Table 6.7 were regressed on the R&D and investment dummy. Here, both activities increase non-production and production workers but in relative terms R&D-performing plants demand more non-production workers than production workers

Table 6.6 Conditional Logit Regression of R&D, Investment and Export Dummies on Tariffs

	Dependent Variables	
	R&D Dummy	*Investment Dummy*
Output tariff	-0.592**	-0.486***
	(0.249)	(0.104)
Input tariff	-0.456	-2.479***
	(0.870)	(0.468)
Year effect	Yes	Yes
Plant effect	Yes	Yes
Number of plants	26,702	97,545
Number of observations	152,509	454,606
R-squared	0.011	0.009

Note: Robust standard errors are in parentheses. *, **, and *** denote that the estimated coefficients are significant at 10%, 5% and 1% level, respectively.

Table 6.7 Fixed Effect Estimation of Employment on Tariffs

	Dependent Variables		
	Employment	*Employment of non-Production Workers*	*Employment of Production Workers*
Output tariff	0.001	−0.069***	0.065***
	(0.017)	(0.026)	(0.019)
Input tariff	−0.961***	−0.767***	−0.650***
	(0.073)	(0.120)	(0.996)
Year effect	Yes	Yes	Yes
Plant effect	Yes	Yes	Yes
Number of plants	219,020	163,470	214,465
Number of observations	742,332	529,113	722,627
R-squared	0.015	0.004	0.012

Note: Robust standard errors are in parentheses. *, **, and *** denote that the estimated coefficients are significant at 10%, 5% and 1% level, respectively.

Table 6.8 Fixed Effect Estimation of Employment on R&D and Investment

	Dependent Variables		
	Employment	*Employment of Non-production Workers*	*Employment of Production Workers*
R&D dummy	0.143***	0.170***	0.107***
	(0.003)	(0.004)	(0.003)
Investment dummy	0.084***	0.085***	0.075***
	(0.001)	(0.002)	(0.001)
Ln(TFP)	0.033***	0.001	0.040***
	(0.002)	(0.004)	(0.002)
Year effect	Yes	Yes	Yes
Plant effect	Yes	Yes	Yes
Number of plants	285,142	211,597	280,152
Number of observations	1,077,848	752,603	1,056,182
R-squared	0.037	0.016	0.031

Note: Robust standard errors are in parentheses. *, **, and *** denote that the estimated coefficients are significant at 10%, 5% and 1% level, respectively.

compared to investment-performing plants. In other words, R&D-performing plants employ non-production workers more by approximately 17% and that of production workers more by 10.7%, thus their relative demand for non-production workers is higher. However, investment-performing plants employ non-production and production workers more by almost the same magnitude: 8.5% and 7.5%, respectively. Therefore, R&D-performing plants' relative demand for skilled workers is much higher than that of investment-performing plants, which seems to be consistent with our findings in the previous subsection, where an increasing skilled wage premium is visible most prominently for R&D-performing plants.

6.4.3 Endogeneity issue

As in other empirical studies focusing on the effects of tariff reduction, we may address the concern of the potential endogeneity of trade liberalization if politically powerful industries are able to successfully lobby governments for trade protection. However, in previous literature, the degree of endogeneity of tariff reduction seems to vary depending on the specific country and the sample period being analyzed. For example, in the case of Indonesia, Amiti and Cameron (2012) used an instrumental variable approach in order to treat the endogeneity issue but it turns out that the endogeneity problem was not that severe. On the other hand, Topalova and Khandelwal (2011), who analyzed the effect of industry-level output and input tariffs on plants' total factor productivity using Indian data, provided several evidences for the exogeneity of tariff reductions in India and did not treat the endogeneity issue explicitly.

In this subsection, we follow the methodologies in Topalova and Khandelwal (2011) in order to check whether Korea's tariff reduction should be treated as endogenous in our sample. Before we proceed, it would be worthwhile to note that in Korea two major tariff reforms took place in 1984 and 1988, before our sample period of 1992–2003, as mentioned in Section 6.4.2. Moreover, during our sample period, there were several international events under which any political consideration in favor of some industries is unlikely to have played an important role in determining tariffs endogenously: the end of the Uruguay Round in 1994, the establishment of the WTO in 1995, Korea's accession to OECD in 1996 and the IMF-supported program for Korea starting from 1997, after the financial crisis.

Nevertheless, we first follow Topalova and Khandelwal (2011) to test whether tariff reductions are correlated with politically important characteristics by regressing the changes in output and input tariffs over 1992–2003 on various industrial characteristics in 1992. These industrial characteristics include average wage, production worker share, capital/labor ratio, shipment and employment. The results are shown in Table 6.9. In Panel A, the correlation between changes in output tariffs and these characteristics are reported and there exists no statistical correlation between output tariff and any of them. In Panel B, with the only exception being a significantly positive correlation between changes in input tariffs and shipment, none of the other industry characteristics are correlated with input tariff reductions.

The second way to check the endogeneity of a tariff reduction is to investigate whether tariffs were adjusted in response to the industry's skilled wage premium. If this were the case, the current level of the skilled wage premium would be able to predict future measures of tariffs. In Panel A and B of Table 6.10, we regress the changes in output and input tariffs from t to $t + 1$ on the skilled wage premium at time t. For the whole sample period (1992–2003) and before and after the Korean financial crisis (1992–1996 and 1998–2003), the correlations between the current skilled wage premium and future changes in tariffs were not different from zero.

Table 6.9 Initial Industrial Characteristics and Subsequent Tariff Change

Ln(wage)	*Production Worker Share*	*Capital/Labor Ratio*	*Ln(shipment)*	*Ln(employment)*
(1)	*(2)*	*(3)*	*(4)*	*(5)*
Panel A: Regression of Changes in output tariff on				
0.002	−0.035	−0.000	0.004	0.004
(0.004)	(0.025)	(0.001)	(0.003)	(0.005)
Panel B: Regression of Changes in input tariff on...				
0.002	0.002	0.000	0.003***	0.002
(0.002)	(0.016)	(0.001)	(0.001)	(0.002)

Note: Each cell represents a separate regression of either changes in output tariffs (Panel A) or changes in input tariffs (Panel B) during 1992–2003 on the variable in the column heading in 1992. The number of observation in each regression is 141 industries. Robust standard errors are in parentheses. *, **, and *** denote that the estimated coefficients are significant at 10%, 5% and 1% level, respectively.

Table 6.10 Current Wage Premium and Subsequent Tariff Change

Period	*1992–2003*	*1992–1996*	*1998–2003*
	(1)	*(2)*	*(3)*
Panel A: Regression of Changes in output tariff from t to t + 1 on ...			
Skilled wage premium at *t*	−0.009	−0.051	−0.003
Observations	(0.007)	(0.034)	(0.007)
	1,183	332	755
Panel B: Regression of Changes in input tariff from t to t + 1 on ...			
Skilled wage premium at *t*	0.001	−0.003	0.002
Observations	(0.002)	(0.005)	(0.003)
	1,183	332	755

Note: The table regresses either changes in output tariffs (Panel A) or changes in input tariffs (Panel B) from t to $t + 1$ on industry-level skilled wage premium in period t. Industry-level skilled wage premium is calculated as a real shipment-weighted average of plant-level skilled wage premium. All regressions include industry and year fixed effects. Robust standard errors are in parentheses. *, **, and *** denote that the estimated coefficients are significant at 10%, 5% and 1% level, respectively.

Overall, we conclude that Korea's tariff reduction, at least during our sample period, does not suffer from endogeneity problem, as in the case of Indian data investigated by Topalova and Khandelwal (2011).

6.5 Summary and policy implications

In this paper we examined the effects of output and input tariff reductions on within-plant wage skill premiums in Korean manufacturing plants during the period of 1992–2003. Our empirical results can be summarized as follows. First, both output and input tariff reductions are associated with an increase in the skilled wage premium, unlike in the case of Indonesia. Second, trade liberalization, as measured by output tariff reduction, had the effect of increasing the skilled wage premium within R&D-performing plants. This result is supportive of the view that trade liberalization, in interactions with SBTC, contributed to an increase in the skilled wage premium. But there is no significant and robust effect of the reduction in intermediate input tariffs on within-plant skilled wage premiums. Third, for investment-performing plants an output tariff reduction had the effect of decreasing the skilled wage premium (or increasing it to a lesser extent in comparison to R&D-performing plants). These results may reflect the point that, while R&D activity is associated with relatively higher demand for human capital (or skilled labor), physical investment is associated with relatively higher demand for unskilled labor.

The results found in this study suggest that trade liberalization brings about not only benefits but also costs: increased disparity between skilled and unskilled workers in labor market outcomes. So, a country liberalizing its trade should also consider strengthening its general social protection scheme in order to make the benefits from liberalized trade more equally shared among economic agents. Another policy implication from this study is that we can maximize the benefits from trade liberalization and make it more politically supported when it is pursued as part of a broader growth strategy. Given the interdependence of trade, innovation and income distribution, as shown in this study, key elements of such growth strategy should at least include trade policy, innovation policy and redistribution policies. Establishing an effective policy governance scheme for such a strategy is likely to be an important issue.

6.6 Acknowledgements

This research was financially supported by ERIA (Economic Research Institute for ASEAN and East Asia) under the project entitled 'Impact of Globalization on Labor Market.' We are grateful to Professor Chris Milner and an anonymous referee for many detailed comments on this paper. The revision of this paper was made when Choi was at the Division of Politics and Economics at Claremont Graduate University as a visiting scholar. Choi would like to thank Professor Thomas Willett for his generous hospitality. All remaining errors are our own.

Notes

1 See Goldberg and Pavcnik (2007) for an extensive review of the related literature.
2 Our focus on within-plant wage skill premium is motivated by Hahn and Park (2012), who showed that around half of the increase in the aggregate share of the skilled employment and wages is accounted for by the within-plant effect in Korean manufacturing during the period of our analysis.
3 While Amiti and Cameron (2012) focus on the effects on within firm wage inequality between skilled and unskilled workers as in this paper, Amiti and Davis (2012) analyze the effects on between-firm wage inequality.
4 Bustos (2011a, 2011b) are a few exceptions.
5 Costantini and Melitz (2008) and Aw, Roberts and Xu (2011) theoretically analyze this mechanism in the context of heterogeneous firms and trade.

6 Thoenig and Verdier (2003) theoretically show that firms respond to globalization by engaging in "defensive innovation", i.e., by biasing the direction of their innovations towards skilled-labor-intensive technologies.

7 It is well known that only a small fraction of plants are engaged in R&D and a much higher fraction, although not all, are making positive investments at a point in time. This pattern is also observed for Korean manufacturing, as we will show below. Thus, focusing on R&D alone in response to trade liberalization might not be sufficient to understand the effect of import tariff reductions on within-plant wage skill premiums and might lead to an omitted variable bias problem.

8 We must acknowledge that, unlike Indonesia, which was analyzed by Amiti and Cameron (2012), plant-level intermediate input imports data is not available for Korea. So, the results of this paper are not directly comparable to their paper.

9 In our empirical analyses below, we exclude the mining sector from our sample, focusing on only manufacturing industries.

10 The correlation between output tariffs and input tariffs calculated in this way is 0.302.

11 Korea's major tariff reform took place in 1984 and 1989 (See Cheung and Ryu 2004). In each year, the average output tariffs for manufacturing goods were reduced to around 20% and 15%. It would be ideal to include these early periods in our sample. But unfortunately, detailed tariff data is not available for these reform periods.

12 In Drawing (a) in Figure 6.1, we used simple average wage of non-production and production workers.

13 Amiti and Cameron (2012) did not include the TFP level in their regressions. But our empirical results do not change in any material way when we drop the TFP variable in our analyses.

14 Note that in estimating Table 6.4 [Column (3)-(5)] all the dummy variables are time-varying. To check the robustness of these results, we can use time-invariant dummy variables by taking each plant's initial year's dummy values for R&D, investment and export variables. In this case, the coefficients on time-invariant dummies themselves are inestimable in our fixed effect specification. However, we can still estimate the coefficients on the interaction terms between (time-variant) tariff variables and (time-invariant) initial values of each dummy, which is of our major interest. The estimated coefficients in this alternative specification does not change the major implications of our results in any material way. We would like to thank an anonymous referee who raised this point.

15 To be more precise, for example in Column (5) of Table 6.4, the estimated marginal effect of output tariff on skilled wage premium would be $(-0.059 - 0.105 * \text{R\&D} + 0.076 * \text{INV} - 0.022 * \text{EXP})$. Then these marginal effects of non-R&D plants and R&D plants at the means of investment and export dummies can be estimated by $(-0.059 + 0.076 * \overline{\text{INV}} - 0.022 * \overline{\text{EXP}})$ and $(-0.059 - 0.105 + 0.076 * \overline{\text{INV}} - 0.022 * \overline{\text{EXP}})$ where upper bar above the variable means its sample mean. Then we can test whether each of these estimates are significant and whether these two estimates are significantly different from each other. The results are reported in Table 6.A1 in the Appendix. It shows that wage skill premiums in R&D (and investment)-performing plants respond differently to output tariffs but not input tariffs, confirming our argument above. That is, compared to non-R&D-performing plants, R&D-performing plants tend to increase the skill premium with output tariff reductions. And compared to non-investment-performing plants, investment-performing plants tend to decrease the skill premium with output tariff reductions. But in the case of input tariffs, there exists no such heterogeneous effect on the skill premium. We thank the anonymous referee who raised this issue.

16 The reason why we take the initial year's values for these dummy variables instead of taking five-year differences is due to the convenience of the interpretation. If we

mechanically take five year differences of these dummies then they will have the values of –1, 0 or 1 whose coefficients are difficult to interpret.

17 In Column (3) of Table 6.5, the coefficient on input tariff becomes positive, meaning that as input tariffs decrease the skilled-wage premium decreases as well. This is the same finding as in Amiti and Cameron (2012) in their study on Indonesia (see our introduction for a brief summary on this paper). However, in our empirical work this positive effect does not seem to be robust if we take into account the signs and the significance levels in all other specifications of Tables 6.4 and 6.5.

18 Adding other control variables such as size and TFP in the regression does not change the implications of the results in any material way. Thus, we report the simplest specification here.

19 See Endnote 6 in Section 6.1.

References

Acemoglu, Daron (2003) "Patterns of Skill Premia," *Review of Economic Studies*, vol. 70, pp. 199–230.

Amiti, Mary and Donald R. Davis (2012) "Trade, Firms, and Wages: Theory and Evidence," *Review of Economic Studies*, vol. 79, no. 1, pp. 1–36.

Amiti, Mary and Lisa Cameron (2012) "Trade Liberalization and the Skilled Wage Premium: Evidence from Indonesia," *Journal of International Economics*, vol. 87, pp. 277–87.

Aw, Bee Yan, Mark J. Roberts and Daniel Yi Xu (2011) "R&D Investment, Exporting, and Productivity Dynamics," *American Economic Review*, vol. 101, no. 4, pp. 1312–44.

Bustos, Paula (2011a), 'The Impact of Trade Liberalization on Skill Upgrading: Evidence from Argentina', Working Paper 559, Barcelona GSE, Barcelona.

Bustos, Paula (2011b), 'Trade Liberalization, Exports, and Technology Upgrading: Evidence on the Impact of MERCOSUR on Argentinian Firms," *American Economic Review*, vol. 101, no. 1, pp. 304–40.

Cheung, Jaeho and Deockhyun Ryu (2004) A Study on the Tariff and Industrial Structure in Korea, Korea Institute of Public Finance, Seoul.

Costantini, James and Marc Melitz (2008) "The Dynamics of Firm-Level Adjustment to Trade Liberalization," in E. Helpman, D. Marin, and T. Verdier (eds.), *The Organization of Firms in a Global Economy*, Harvard University Press, Boston, pp. 107–141.

Goldberg, Pinelopi K. and Nina Pavcnik (2007) "Distributional Effects of Globalization in Developing Countries," *Journal of Economic Literature*, vol. 45, no. 1, pp. 39–82.

Good, David H. (1985) "The Effect of Deregulation on the Productive Efficiency and Cost Structure of the Airline Industry," Ph.D. dissertation, University of Pennsylvania.

Good, David H., M. Ishaq Nadiri and Robin C. Sickles (1997), "Index Number and Factor Demand Approaches to the Estimation of Productivity," in M. H. Pesaran and P. Schmidt (eds.), *Handbook of Applied Econometrics*, Volume 2: Microeconomics. Oxford: Blackwell, pp. 14–80.

Thoenig, Mathias and Thierry Verdier (2003) "A Theory of Defensive Skill-Based Innovation and Globalization," *American Economic Review*, vol. 93, no. 3, pp. 709–28.

Topalova, Petia and Amit Khandelwal (2011), "Trade Liberalization and Firm Productivity: the Case of India," *Review of Economics and Statistics*, vol. 93, no. 3, pp. 995–1009.

Verhoogen, Eric (2008) "Trade, Quality Upgrading and Wage Inequality in the Mexican Manufacturing Sector," *Quarterly Journal of Economics*, vol. 123, no. 2, pp. 489–530.

Appendix

Table 6.A1 Marginal Effects of Output and Input Tariffs

	(1)	*(2)*	*(3)*	*(4)*	*(5)*	*(6)*
A. Marginal effect of output tariff on skill premium						
(a) when R&D = 0	−0.023					
	(0.024)					
when R&D = 1	−0.115**					
	(0.053)					
(b) when INV = 0		−0.067**				
		(0.029)				
when INV = 1		−0.005				
		(0.028)				
(c) when EXP = 0			−0.029			
			(0.024)			
when EXP = 1			−0.055			
			(0.057)			
B. Marginal effect of input tariff on skill premium						
(a) when R&D = 0				−0.099		
				(0.117)		
when R&D = 1				0.012		
				(0.223)		
(b) when INV = 0					−0.061	
					(0.136)	
when INV = 1					−0.108	
					(0.125)	
(c) when EXP = 0						−0.067
						(0.120)
when EXP = 1						−0.183
						(0.212)
p-value	0.066*	0.029**	0.647	0.620	0.714	0.597
Rejection of the null (equality of marginal effects)	Yes	Yes	No	No	No	No

Note: Robust standard errors are in parentheses. *, **, and *** denote that the estimated coefficients and the statistics are significant at 10%, 5% and 1% level, respectively. The *p*-values are for testing the null hypothesis, the equality of marginal effects when corresponding dummies are equal to zero and one.

Table 6.A2 Fixed Effects Estimation Results with Industry Fixed Effects

	(1)	*(2)*	*(3)*	*(4)*	*(5)*
Output tariff	-0.051**		-0.043*	-0.081***	-0.068**
	(0.025)		(0.025)	(0.030)	(0.031)
Input tariff		-0.192	-0.150	-0.157	0.086
		(0.131)	(0.135)	(0.154)	(0.165)
Output tariff * R&D			-0.078*	-0.103**	-0.103**
			(0.043)	(0.045)	(0.049)
Input tariff * R&D			0.195	0.263	0.173
			(0.194)	(0.202)	(0.223)
Output tariff * Investment				0.074***	0.075***
				(0.026)	(0.028)
Input tariff * Investment				0.022	-0.038
				(0.118)	(0.129)
Output tariff * Export					-0.036
					(0.056)
Input tariff * Export					0.015
					(0.226)
R&D dummy			0.006	0.005	0.010
			(0.008)	(0.009)	(0.010)
Investment dummy				-0.005	-0.003
				(0.005)	(0.006)
Export dummy					0.012
					(0.010)
Size	0.125***	0.125***	0.124***	0.128***	0.132***
	(0.002)	(0.002)	(0.002)	(0.002)	(0.003)
Ln(TFP)	-0.066***	-0.067***	-0.067***	-0.067***	-0.067***
	(0.003)	(0.003)	(0.003)	(0.003)	(0.003)
Skill intensity	-0.345***	-0.345***	-0.346***	-0.342***	-0.383***
	(0.008)	(0.008)	(0.008)	(0.008)	(0.009)
Constant	-0.279***	-0.272***	-0.270***	-0.279***	-0.301***
	(0.009)	(0.012)	(0.012)	(0.012)	(0.014)
Year effect	Yes	Yes	Yes	Yes	Yes
Plant effect	Yes	Yes	Yes	Yes	Yes
Industry effect	Yes	Yes	Yes	Yes	Yes
Number of plants	157,409	157,409	157,409	155,275	143,589
Number of observations	506,376	506,376	506,376	478,424	413,072
R-squared	0.026	0.026	0.026	0.027	0.028

Note: Robust standard errors clustered at the plant level are in parentheses. *, **, and *** denote that the estimated coefficients are significant at 10%, 5% and 1% level, respectively. The dependent variable is the skill premium defined by the natural logarithm of average wage of non-production workers to production workers.

Wood, Adria (1995) "How Trade Hurt Unskilled Workers," *Journal of Economic Perspectives*, vol. 9, no. 3, Summer, pp. 15–32.

Table 6.A3 Alternative Specification: Five-year Differences with Industry Fixed Effects

	(1)	*(2)*	*(3)*
ΔOutput tariff	-0.046	-0.135**	-0.136**
	(0.040)	(0.062)	(0.062)
ΔInput tariff	-0.166	0.210	0.251
	(0.204)	(0.300)	(0.302)
ΔOutput tariff * $R\&D_{t0}$	-0.204*	-0.271**	-0.272**
	(0.110)	(0.116)	(0.118)
ΔInput tariff * $R\&D_{t0}$	0.384	0.397	0.452
	(0.459)	(0.474)	(0.477)
ΔOutput tariff * INV_{t0}		0.157**	0.155**
		(0.074)	(0.074)
ΔInput tariff * INV_{t0}		-0.536	-0.490
		(0.340)	(0.344)
ΔOutput tariff * EXP_{t0}			0.026
			(0.120)
ΔInput tariff * EXP_{t0}			-0.367
			(0.390)
$R\&D_{t0}$	-0.016**	-0.017**	-0.018**
	(0.007)	(0.007)	(0.007)
INV_{t0}		-0.010**	-0.010**
		(0.005)	(0.005)
EXP_{t0}			0.003
			(0.006)
ΔSize	0.100***	0.100***	0.101***
	(0.004)	(0.004)	(0.004)
ΔLn(TFP)	-0.063***	-0.062***	-0.062***
	(0.006)	(0.006)	(0.006)
ΔSkill intensity	-0.410***	-0.405***	-0.405***
	(0.014)	(0.014)	(0.014)
Year effect	Yes	Yes	Yes
Industry effect	Yes	Yes	Yes
Number of observations	74,110	70,403	70,403
R-squared	0.031	0.031	0.031

Note: Robust standard errors are in parentheses. *, **, and *** denote that the estimated coefficients are significant at 10%, 5% and 1% level, respectively. The dependent variable is the five-year difference in the natural logarithm of the skill premium. The skill premium is defined as in the note in Table 6.2.

7 Trade, technology, foreign firms, and the wage gap

Case of Vietnam manufacturing firms

Shandre Mugan Thangavelu

7.1 Introduction

The growing amount of recent research in the area of international economics has associated the phenomenon of widening wage differentials between skilled and unskilled workers in developed countries with technological changes and globalisation. Recent studies highlight that the rising wage differentials in most developed countries are mainly due to technological advances and skill-biased technological change that have increased the demand for skilled workers relative to unskilled labour (Autor, et al., 1998; Card and DiNardo, 2002; Acemoglu, 2002; Acemoglu and Autor, 2011). However, Card and DiNardo (2002) highlight that the key issue in skill-biased technology change is that it fails to explain wage inequality due to gender and racial wage gaps and the age gradient in the return to education.

In contrast, with the prevalence of globalisation and trade activities, Feenstra and Hanson (1996, 1997, 1999) highlight that we can observe widening wage differentials when production shifts to higher value-added activities due to competition in the global markets. Several empirical studies have examined the relationship between trade (outsourcing) and wage inequality at the industrial level such as Anderton and Brenton (1999) for the United Kingdom (UK), Geishecker (2002) for Germany, Chongvilaivan and Thangavelu (2012) and Thangavelu and Chongvilaivan (2011) for Thailand, and Hsieh and Woo (2005) for Hong Kong. These studies produce rather consistent evidence that points to trade and international outsourcing such as the uses of parts and components imports that allow firms to specialise in their core-competent activities, to enhance cost efficiency, and to maintain competitiveness in the globalised market as the key catalyst for wage inequality by increasing the demand for skills (Arndt and Kierzkowski, 2001; Autor, et Al., 1998, 2003). This development is also attributed to the advancement of information and communication technology and to closer trade ties with the international market, which have led to substantial surges in outsourcing less skill-intensive activities to developing countries where unskilled workers are relatively abundant.

The objective of this study is to examine the impact of trade and technology on the wage gap of skilled and unskilled workers in the Vietnamese manufacturing firms. In particular, we will examine the impact of skill-biased technological changes induced by globalisation that increases the demand for skilled relative to unskilled workers. Particularly, we will examine the impact of trade on the wage gap of skilled and unskilled workers. It is expected that import is likely to have a different impact on the demand of skilled and unskilled workers as compared to exports. In particular, if technology is embodied in imported intermediate inputs such as machines and equipment, then the impact on skilled workers is expected to be greater than on unskilled workers. In this study, we examine the effect of capital investment, imported intermediate inputs, and exports on the wage gap of skilled and unskilled workers.

The organisation of paper is as follows. Section 7.2 depicts the recent trends and developments in Vietnam. Section 7.3 develops the empirical methodology based on the translog cost function approach. Section 7.4 presents and discusses the empirical results. Section 7.5 is the conclusion.

7.2 Overview of globalisation and the Vietnamese manufacturing industry

The one of the key factors for the strong growth of the Vietnamese economy is the economic and trade liberalisation policy of the government, in an effort to increase the competitiveness of the domestic economy by opening it to foreign competition and investment. Since the economic liberalisation, the government has put in market-friendly policy to attract foreign activities in the domestic economy. In 2007, Vietnam joined the WTO and hence increased its participation in the global economy.

The role of the government is also emerging as an important factor for the stability of the Vietnamese economy. Its pro-business approach tends to attract significant foreign direct investment into the country. Current economic policies were triggered by a series of reforms in the 1980s known as *doi moi* (new thought). The government is now more receptive to the involvement of foreign activities in its domestic economy, especially in high value-added industries.

Recent evidence also indicates that the Vietnamese government is liberalising the key high value-added sectors, for foreign investment and export competitiveness. Deregulation is taking the form of restructuring state-owned enterprises into private ones and increasing foreign ownership in domestic industries. In terms of infrastructure, the government has devoted resources to building Vietnam's most modern industrial parks.

The effects of liberalisation of the Vietnamese economy are reflected in terms of robust growth of real GDP as seen in Figure 7.1. Vietnam tend to experience an average real growth of around 7.1% from 2000 to 2011, which is much higher than the average of ASEAN countries and it is only surpassed by recently by emerging ASEAN countries of Cambodia and Myanmar. The real growth rate peaked at 8.4% before the global financial crisis in 2006 and then we observe a lower trend in real GDP of 5.9% from 2008 to 2011.

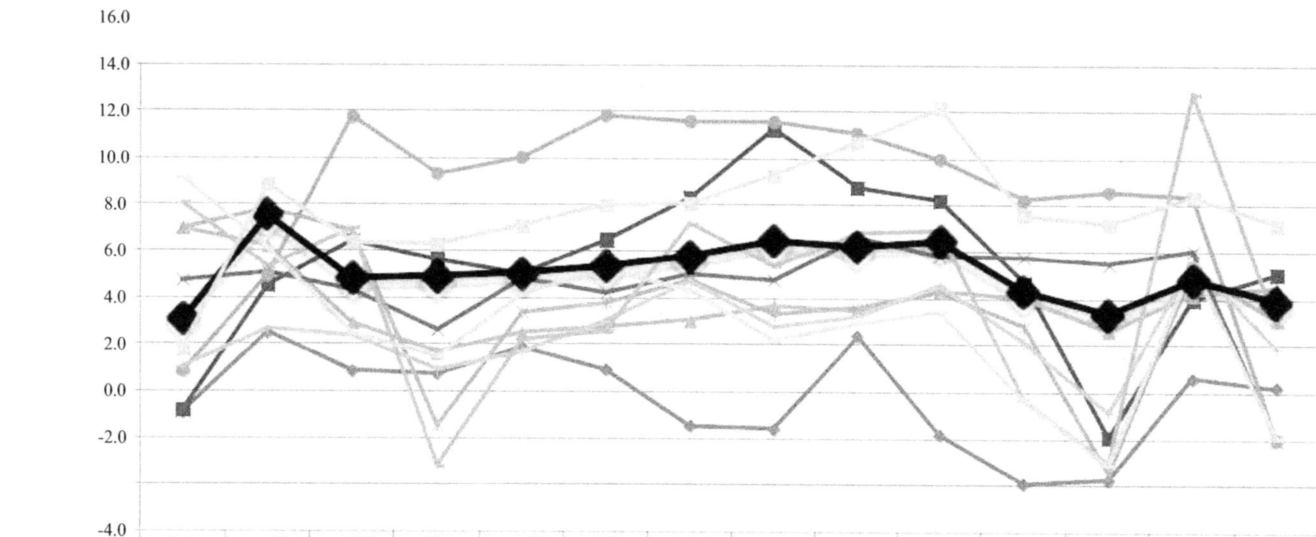

	1990	1995	2000	2001	2002	2003	2004	2005	2006	2007	2008	2009	2010	2011
Brunei	1.1	4.5	2.8	2.7	3.9	2.9	0.5	0.4	4.4	0.2	-1.9	-1.8	2.6	2.2
Cambodia	1.2	6.5	8.4	7.7	7.0	8.5	10.3	13.3	10.8	10.2	6.7	0.1	6.0	7.1
Indonesia	9.0	8.2	4.9	3.6	4.5	4.8	5.0	5.7	5.5	6.3	6.0	4.6	6.2	6.5
Lao PDR	6.7	7.1	6.3	4.6	6.9	6.2	7.0	6.8	8.6	7.8	7.8	7.5	8.1	0.0
Malaysia	9.0	9.8	8.9	0.5	5.4	5.8	6.8	5.3	5.6	6.3	4.8	-1.5	7.2	5.1
Myanmar	2.8	6.9	13.7	11.3	12.0	13.8	13.6	13.6	13.1	12.0	10.3	10.6	10.4	0.0
Philippines	3.0	4.7	4.4	2.9	3.6	5.0	6.7	4.8	5.2	6.6	4.2	1.1	7.6	3.9
Singapore	10.1	7.3	9.0	-1.2	4.2	4.6	9.2	7.4	8.8	8.9	1.7	-1.0	14.8	4.9
Thailand	11.2	8.1	4.5	3.4	6.2	7.2	6.3	4.2	4.9	5.4	1.6	-1.1	7.5	0.1
Viet Nam	5.1	9.5	6.8	6.9	7.1	7.3	7.8	8.4	8.2	8.5	6.3	5.3	6.8	5.9
China	3.8	10.9	8.4	8.3	9.1	10.0	10.1	11.3	12.7	14.2	9.6	9.2	10.4	9.2

Figure 7.1 Real Growth Rate of GDP of Vietnam and Selected Asian Countries.
Source: ADB, Macroeconomic Indicators.

The growth of the Vietnamese economy also reflects the rising importance of high value-added manufacturing in the domestic economy. Table 7.1 clearly shows the rising share of manufacturing with the declining share of the agricultural sector. The share of manufacturing to GDP ratio increased from 22% in 1990 to over 40% in 2011, and with the agricultural sector declining to 22% in 2011 from over 39% in 1990. We also observer the share of services sector in GDP remained at 38% from 1990 to 2001. We also observe similar trends for Cambodia, Indonesia, Lao PDR, and Myanmar. In particular, Cambodia, Lao PDR, and Myanmar also experienced strong and double-digit increases in the share of the manufacturing to GDP ratio from 1990 to 2011, with the concurrent declines in the agricultural sector (Figure 7.2).

Table 7.1 Share of Key Sectors to GDP Ratio for Vietnam and Selected Asian Countries

	Agriculture			*Manufacturing*			*Services*		
	1990	*2000*	*2011*	*1990*	*2000*	*2011*	*1990*	*2000*	*2011*
Brunei	1.0	1.0	0.6	61.6	71.6	71.7	37.5	35.3	27.7
Cambodia	56.5	37.9	36.7	11.3	26.4	23.5	32.2	39.1	39.8
Indonesia	19.4	15.6	14.7	39.1	46.5	47.2	41.5	38.5	38.1
Lao PDR	61.2	48.5	30.3	14.5	23.5	27.7	24.3	32.4	42.0
Malaysia	15.0	8.3	12.0	41.5	46.9	40.7	43.5	44.9	47.3
Myanmar	57.3	57.2	36.4	10.5	17.5	26.0	32.2	33.1	37.6
Philippines	21.9	14.0	12.8	34.5	33.8	31.5	43.6	51.6	55.7
Singapore	0.3	0.1	0.0	31.9	31.6	26.6	67.8	65.4	73.4
Thailand	10.0	8.5	10.9	37.2	38.8	40.1	52.8	54.6	49.0
Vietnam	38.7	24.5	22.0	22.7	41.0	40.3	38.6	38.7	37.7
China	27.1	15.1	10.1	41.3	47.4	46.8	31.5	39.0	43.1

Source: ADB.

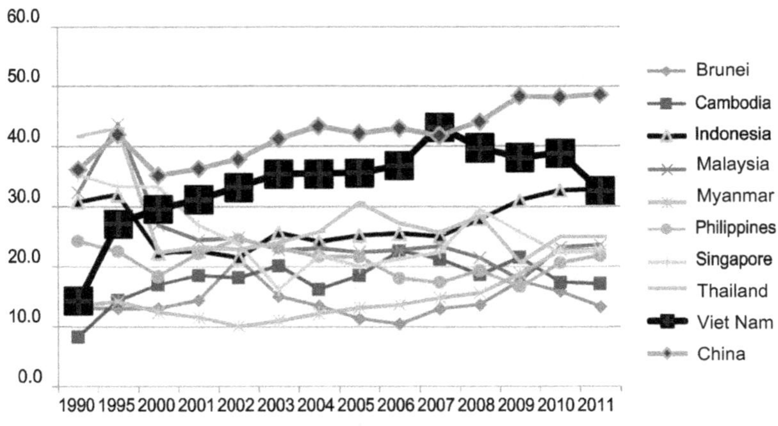

Figure 7.2 Share of Gross Domestic Capital Formation of Vietnam and Selected Asian Countries.

Source: ADB.

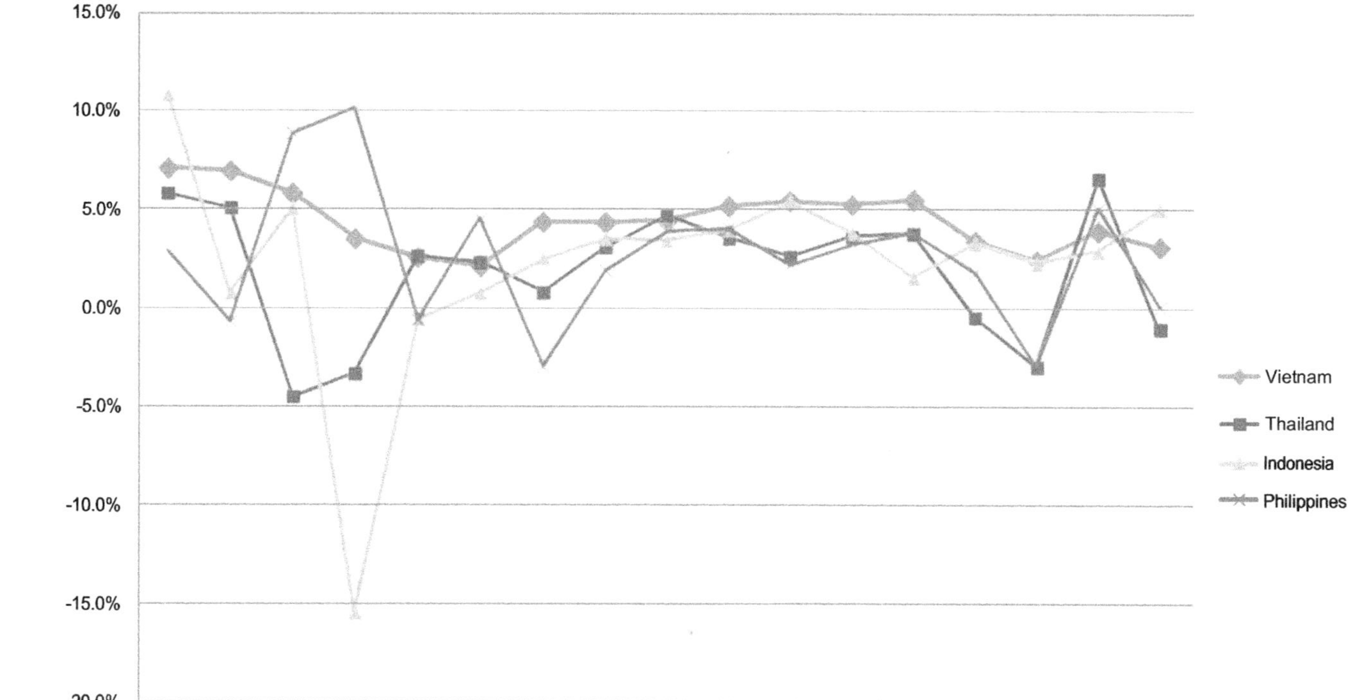

	1995	1996	1997	1998	1999	2000	2001	2002	2003	2004	2005	2006	2007	2008	2009	2010	2011
Vietnam	7.1%	7.0%	5.9%	3.5%	2.6%	2.2%	4.4%	4.4%	4.4%	5.2%	5.5%	5.3%	5.5%	3.4%	2.5%	3.9%	3.1%
Thailand	5.9%	5.1%	-4.4%	-3.3%	2.7%	2.4%	0.8%	3.1%	4.7%	3.6%	2.6%	3.7%	3.8%	-0.5%	-2.9%	6.6%	-1.0%
Indonesia	10.8%	0.8%	5.1%	-15.4%	-0.5%	0.8%	2.5%	3.5%	3.5%	4.0%	5.4%	3.8%	1.6%	3.3%	2.3%	2.9%	5.0%
Philippines	2.9%	-0.6%	8.9%	10.2%	-0.5%	4.6%	-2.9%	1.9%	3.9%	4.1%	2.2%	3.3%	3.9%	1.9%	-2.9%	5.1%	0.1%

Figure 7.3 Labour Productivity of Vietnam and Selected Asian Countries.
Source: Statistics from ADB.

A recent study by the World Bank (Vietnam Development Report, 2012) reports the importance of declining labour productivity growth for Vietnam and its impact on sustaining the economic growth momentum in the region. The trends of labour productivity for Vietnam and selected ASEAN countries are given in Figure 7.3. Labour productivity is fairly stable for Vietnam but shows a downward trend after the global financial crisis. The average labour productivity was around 4.9% from 2000 to 2007 and it declined to nearly 3.2% in 2008–2011. Although the decline in the post-crisis period is of concern, as compared to other selected ASEAN countries, the productivity for Vietnam is quite stable and shows similar trend as other ASEAN countries.

In addition to the productivity growth, the other key concern is the distribution of productivity gains and growth in the economy. Together with declining labour productivity, the widening income (wage) gap between the top 20 percentile income earners and the lower 20th percentile is a major concern in the Vietnamese economy (see Table 7.2). The gap between high income earners as compared to low income earners has widened over the years. We also noted the widening income gap across most selected Asian countries except for Indonesia, Malaysia, and Philippines. The widening income (wage) gap may be driven by technological innovation and trade, as the economy transits to higher value-added activities, thus increasing the demand for more skilled workers.

It is important to highlight that the economic liberalisation of Vietnam is mainly driven by the growth in global trade. The share of exports in GDP increased to 87% in 2011 from 26% in 1990. The impact of openness is also observed with the rising share of imports to GDP, which increased from 36% in 1990 to nearly 91% in 2011. The rising trend of imports suggests that Vietnamese and foreign firms might be increasing their outsourcing activities in the domestic economy (Figure 7.4).

Table 7.2a The Income Gap in Vietnam and Selected ASEAN Countries

Income Ratio of Highest 20% to Lowest 20%		
	1995	*Latest year*
China	5.0	9.6 (2005)
Cambodia	5.8 (1994)	6.1 (2008)
Indonesia	5.0 (1996)	5.1 (2005)
Lao PDR	5.4 (1997)	5.9 (2008)
Malaysia	12.0	11.3 (2009)
Philippines	8.3 (1994)	8.3 (2009)
Thailand	8.1 (1996)	7.1 (2009)
Vietnam	5.6 (1993)	5.9 (2008)

Source: ADB.

Table 7.2b Share of Exports and Imports to GDP Ratio for Vietnam and Selected Asian Countries

	Exports			*Imports*		
	1990	*2000*	*2011*	*1990*	*2000*	*2011*
Brunei	61.8	67.4	81.3	37.3	35.8	29.1
Cambodia	2.4	49.9	54.1	8.4	61.7	59.5
Indonesia	25.3	41.0	26.3	23.7	30.5	24.9
Malaysia	74.5	119.8	91.6	72.4	100.6	75.7
Myanmar	1.9	0.5	0.1	3.6	0.6	0.1
Philippines	27.5	51.4	31.0	33.3	53.4	36.0
Singapore	177.4	192.3	209.0	167.4	179.5	182.3
Thailand	33.1	65.0	66.7	40.6	56.6	60.4
Vietnam	26.4	55.0	87.0	35.7	57.5	91.2
China	19.0	23.3	28.6	15.6	20.9	26.0

Source: ADB.

The rising ratio of imports to GDP clearly indicates that the economic liberalisation in Vietnam has reduced the barriers to trade in terms of import tariffs and tax on capital goods. The effects of this liberalisation is the rising share of imports to GDP, where domestic firms are likely to outsource some of their key services and other activities to the global production value-chain. The rising share of imports and, hence, outsourcing is shown in Figure 7.2; the share of imports increased from 36% in 1990 to nearly 91% in 2011.

7.2.1 Impact of trade on the wage gap

Vietnam is endowed with young and competitive labour force. The average wages in Vietnam are much lower than that of India and the Vietnamese government is also increasing its investment in education of the workers. Increasingly the Vietnamese workforce is improving its skills in technical and science education, thereby boosting the incentive for firms to adopt new technologies. Further, recent evidence indicates that Vietnamese workers are educated in English, thus enabling the country to absorb and diffuse new technologies faster.

Vietnam has an educated and young labour force. The young population less than aged 25 years old accounts for nearly 60% of the population. It also has very high literacy rate of nearly 97%. Primary education focuses on mathematics and the sciences, and cultivates the interest of the students in technology fields. Annually, about 20,000 Vietnamese people graduate as technical engineers. Another key characteristic of the Vietnamese labour force is the low turnover, which helps create strong client and customer relationships. The nominal wages of workers by educational attainment from 1998 to 2006 is given in Figure 7.5. It is clear that wages of educated workers have increased significantly in Vietnam, where tertiary and higher-educated workers experienced an average annual wage

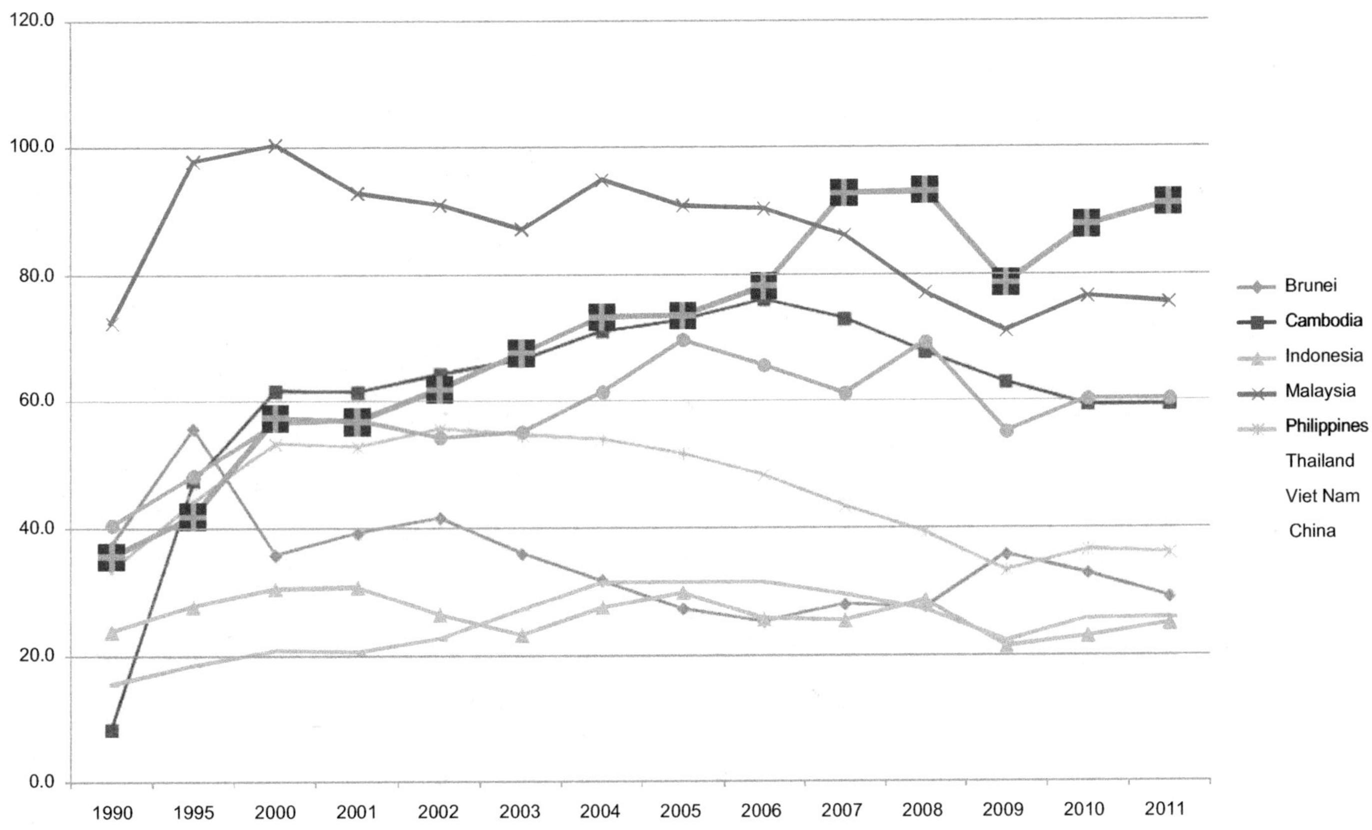

Figure 7.4 Share of Imports to GDP Ratio for Vietnam and Selected Asian Countries.
Source: ADB.

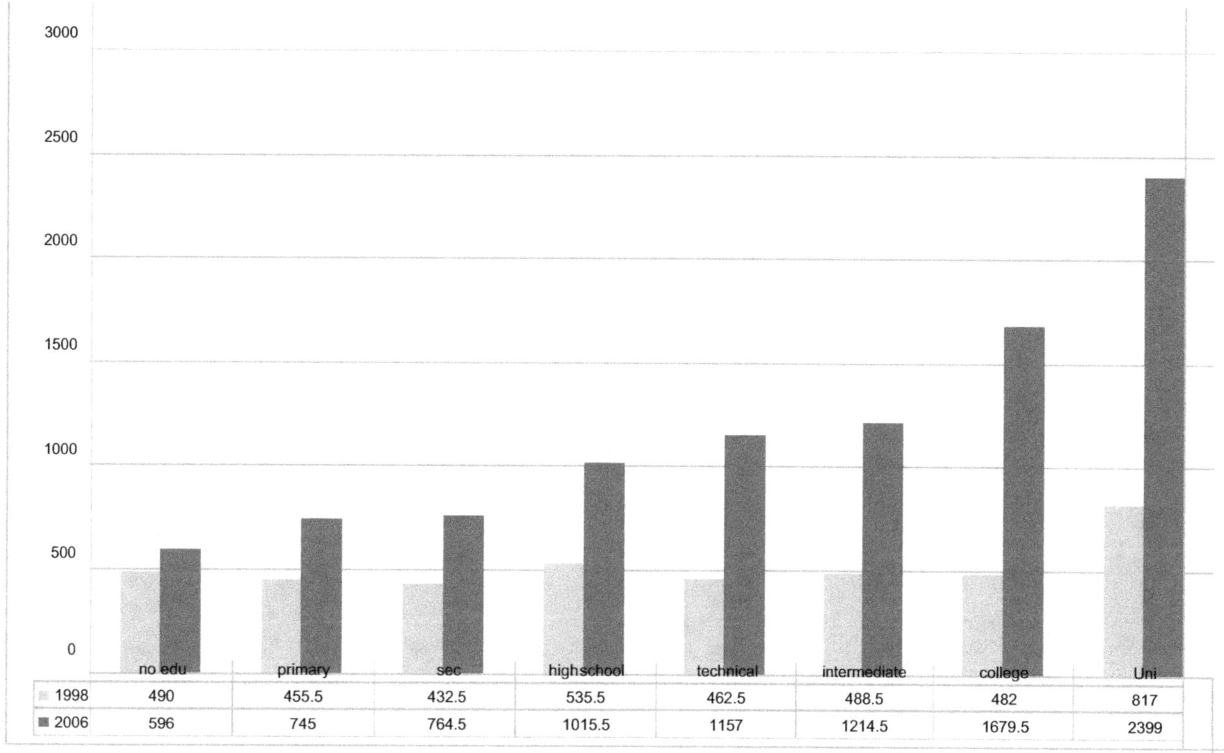

Figure 7.5 Nominal Wages of Workers by Educational Attainment at Vietnam: 1998–2006.

Source: Nguyen Thi Lan Huong (2008).

increase of nearly 16% from 1998 to 2006. In contrast, the annual average wages of primary and secondary and high school increased at 5% and 6.5%, respectively, from 1998 to 2006. This clearly indicates that the demand for skilled and educated workers has risen over the years and that the wage gap between skilled and unskilled workers is widening.

The plots of share of skilled and unskilled workers' compensation against fixed capital, export and import of materials are given below. The negative impact of fixed capital on the share of unskilled workers' compensation as compared to skilled workers' compensation is clear in Figures 7.6 and 7.7. This suggests a technological change that is biased towards skilled workers from capital investment.

Figures 7.8 and 7.9 show the relationship between exports and the compensation share of skilled and unskilled workers. It is clear that trade activities are more in favour of skilled workers as compared to unskilled ones. This indicates that Vietnam is becoming more competitive in the trade of capital-intensive goods and is moving away from labour-intensive goods that reduce the wage share of unskilled workers.

Both the share of skilled and unskilled compensation tend to rise with imports of intermediate inputs. However, the correlation between the share of skilled workers and the import of intermediate inputs is 1.34 as compared to only 0.6 for unskilled labour. This indicates that the importing activities of firms increase the compensation share of skilled workers relative to unskilled workers. This impact is likely to be driven by skilled-biased technological change, especially if technology is embodied in the imports of machines and equipment (Figures 7.10 and 7.11).

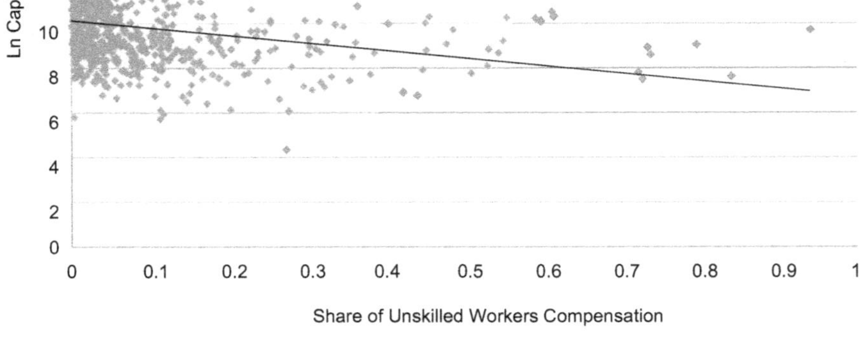

Figure 7.6 Share of Unskilled Compensation to Fixed Capital.

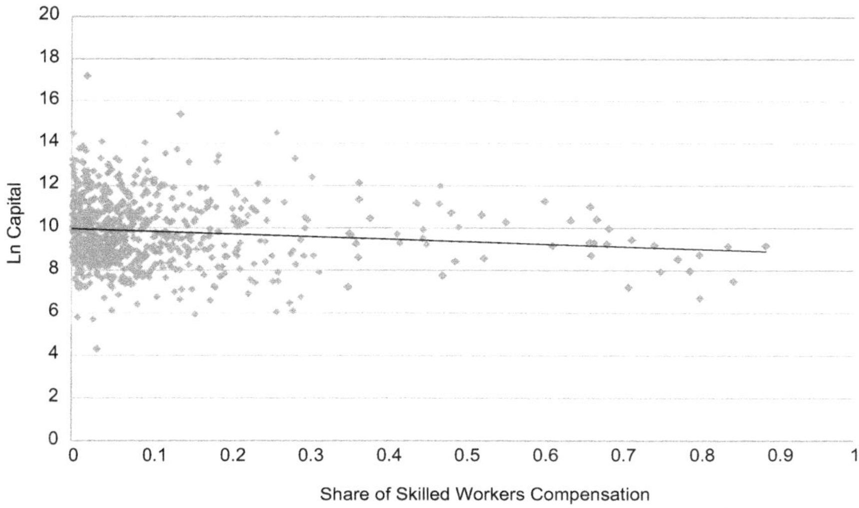

Figure 7.7 Share of Skilled Workers Compensation to Fixed Capital.

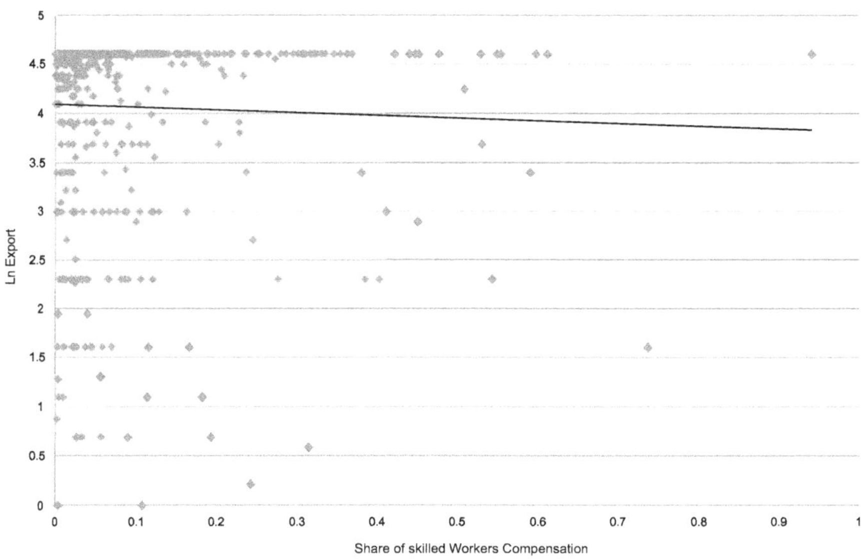

Figure 7.8 Share of Skilled Workers Compensation to Export.

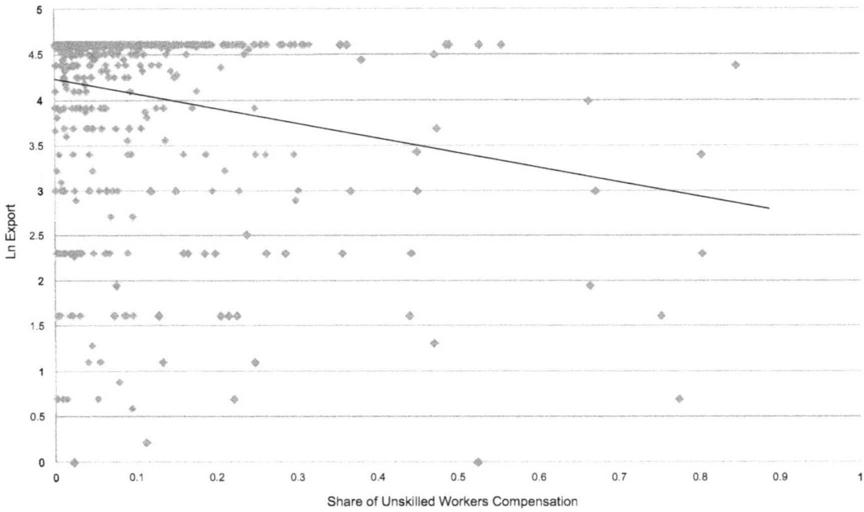

Figure 7.9 Shared of Unskilled Workers Compensation to Export.

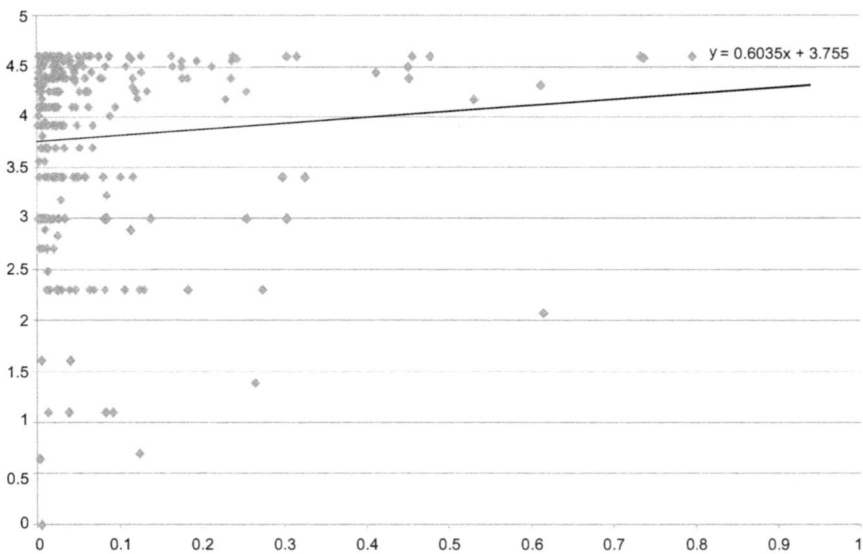

Figure 7.10 Share of Unskilled Workers Compensation and Imports of Material Inputs (Log) in Vietnamese Firms.

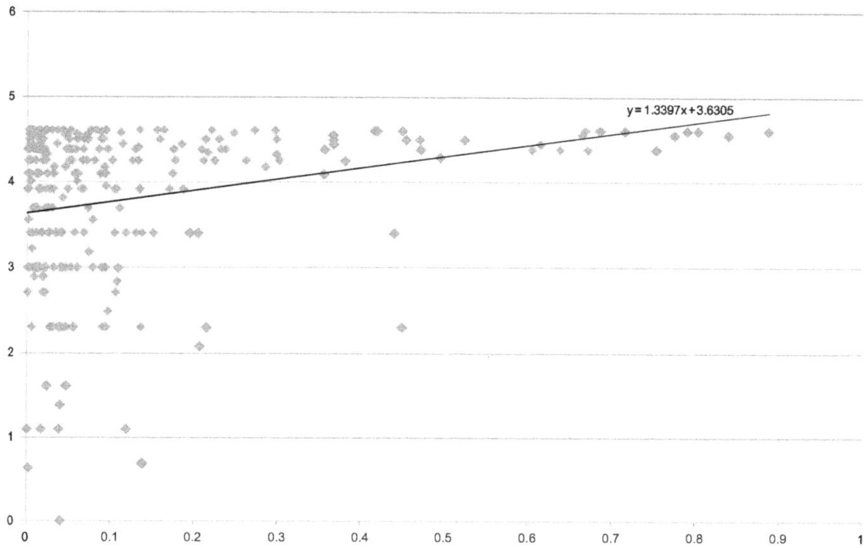

Figure 7.11 Share of Skilled Workers Compensation to Import of Materials (Log) in Vietnamese Firms.

7.3 Empirical model

The empirical model of the skilled-biased effects of outsourcing is implemented using the cost function (short-run cost function with capital as fixed input). We derived the relative demands for skilled and unskilled labour by differentiating the cost function (*Translog*) with respect to factor prices of skilled (lnW_{Hi}) and unskilled wages (lnW_{Li}). To empirically investigate the economic impacts of outsourcing on the relative demands for skilled and unskilled workers, it is important to estimate a cost function that is sufficiently flexible and also to show the effects of outsourcing on firms' labour demands. Following Morrison and Siegel (2001), our model is based on a non-homothetic variable cost function specification, incorporating quasi-fixed capital and *external shift* factors.[1]

For a given industry i, where $i = 1,\ldots, N$, the short-run (dual) cost function can be expressed in an implicit form as:

$$G_i = G(w_i, K_i, \Upsilon_i, T_i) \tag{1}$$

Where w_i is a vector of variable input prices, including unskilled workers, skilled workers, and raw materials; K_i is quasi-fixed capital stock; Υ_i is output; and T_i is a vector of external trade and technological factors, including the variables of material and service outsourcing. Therefore, the short-run total cost function is equal to $C_i = G(w_i, K_i, \Upsilon_i, T_i) + W_K K_i$, where wK is the price of capital stock.

Following Berman et al. (1994), by assuming that capital is a quasi-fixed factor, we will employ the non-homothetic translog functional form of a variable cost function.

By assuming symmetry such that $\gamma_{ij} = \gamma_{ji}$, $\varnothing_{ij} = \varnothing_{ji}$ and $\delta_{ij} = \delta_{ji}$, and temporarily dropping the time and industry subscripts, the cost function is given as:

$$
\begin{aligned}
Ln\ G &= \alpha_0 + \alpha_H \ln(w_H) + \alpha_M \ln(w_M) + \gamma_{HL} lnw_H lnw_L + \gamma_{HM} lnw_H lnw_M \\
&+ \gamma_{LM} lnw_L lnw_M + \frac{1}{2}\gamma_{HH}(lnw_H)^2 + \frac{1}{2}\gamma_{LL}(lnw_L)^2 + \frac{1}{2}\gamma_{MM}(lnw_M)^2 + \beta_K lnK \\
&+ \varnothing_{LK} lnw_L lnK + \varnothing_{HK} lnw_H lnK + \varnothing_{MK} lnw_M lnK + \frac{1}{2}\delta_{KK}(lnK)^2 + \beta_y ln\Upsilon \\
&+ \phi_{L\Upsilon} lnw_L ln\Upsilon + \phi_{H\Upsilon} lnw_H ln\Upsilon + \phi_{M\Upsilon} lnw_M ln\Upsilon + \delta_{K\Upsilon} lnK ln\Upsilon + \frac{1}{2}\delta_{\Upsilon\Upsilon}(ln\Upsilon)^2 \\
&+ \beta_O lnO + \varnothing_{LO} lnw_L lnO + \varnothing_{HO} lnw_H lnO + \varnothing_{MO} lnw_M lnO + \delta_{KO} lnK lnO \\
&+ \delta_{\Upsilon O} ln\Upsilon lnO + \frac{1}{2}\delta_{OO}(lnO)^2 + \beta_T lnT + \phi_{LT} lnw_L lnT + \phi_{HT} lnw_H lnT \\
&+ \phi_{MT} ln W_M lnT + \delta_{KT} lnK lnT + \delta_{\Upsilon T} ln\Upsilon lnT + \delta_{OT} lnO lnT + \frac{1}{2}\delta_{TT}\ (lnT)^2
\end{aligned} \tag{2}
$$

where O is the variable of outsourcing and T is the index of technological progress. A well-defined cost function must satisfy the condition of linear homogeneity in variable factor prices. This implies that we have to impose the following parameter restrictions on Equation (3).

$$\alpha_L + \alpha_H + \alpha_M = 1, \tag{3}$$

$$\gamma_{HL} + \gamma_{HH} + \gamma_{HM} = \gamma_{LL} + \gamma_{LH} + \gamma_{LM} = \gamma_{ML} + \gamma_{MH} + \gamma_{MM} = \phi_{Lj} + \phi_{Hj} + \phi_{Mj}, \tag{4}$$

where $j \mp K$, Υ, O, and T.

By employing Sheppard's Lemma and logarithmically differentiating Equation (3) with respect to variable input prices, we can show that $S_k = {}^{w_k K}\!/_{C} = {}^{\partial lnC}\!/_{\partial lnw_k}$, where $k = L$, H, and M. Furthermore, the adding-up condition requires that the summation of three factor shares must be equal to unity ($S_L + S_H + S_M = 1$), and therefore only two equations are linearly independent. Hence, we choose to drop the material share equation and estimate the following:

$$
\begin{aligned}
S_L = \alpha_L &+ \gamma_{LL} lnw_L + \gamma_{HL} lnw_H + \gamma_{ML} lnw_M + \phi_{KL} lnK \\
&+ \phi_{Ly} ln\Upsilon + \phi_{LO} lnO + \phi_{LT} lnT
\end{aligned} \tag{5}
$$

$$S_H = \alpha_H + \gamma_{HH} lnw_H + \gamma_{HL} lnw_L + \gamma_{HM} lnw_M + \phi_{HK} lnK + \phi_{Hy} ln\Upsilon + \phi_{HO} lnO + \phi_{HT} l \quad (6)$$

The share Equations of (5) and (6) can be deemed a composite representation of the demands for unskilled and skilled labour, respectively. To estimate these share equations empirically, we must specify a stochastic framework. Typically, a random disturbance term u_K is added to each share equation and assumed to be multivariate, normally distributed with a mean vector zero, $E(\mathrm{u}) = 0$, and a constant variance matrix, $Var(\mathrm{u}) = \Omega$. Furthermore, our econometric model specifications also include the time-specific (μ_t) and industry-specific (λ_i) dummies. These time- and industry-specific effects are meant to capture persistent industrial differences and overall technological progress affecting the industries. Accordingly, our fully specified econometric model is given as follows:

$$S_{Lit} = \alpha_L + \gamma_{LL} lnw_{Lit} + \gamma_{HL} lnw_{Hit} + \gamma_{ML} lnw_{Mit} + \phi_{KL} lnK_{it} + \phi_{Ly} ln\Upsilon_{it} + \phi_{LO} lnO_{it} + \phi_{LT} lnT + \mu_t + \lambda_i + \mu_{Lit} \quad (5A)$$

$$S_{Hit} = \alpha_H + \gamma_{HH} lnw_{Hit} + \gamma_{HL} lnw_{Lit} + \gamma_{HM} lnw_{Mit} + \phi_{HK} lnK_{it} + \phi_{Hy} ln\Upsilon_{it} + \phi_{HO} lnO_{it} + \phi_{HT} l + \mu_t + \lambda_i + \mu_{Hit} \quad (6A)$$

One attractive feature of the non-homothetic translog functional form of the dual-cost Equation (2) is that it does not impose any restrictions on the elasticities of substitution between two variable inputs in priori. It may also be interesting to investigate the impacts of outsourcing on substitution among unskilled labour, skilled labour, and raw materials.

In the above analysis we have three variable inputs: skilled, unskilled, and material inputs. For the adding-up condition to hold, the summation of shares of factor inputs should add up to unity. To account for the adding-up condition, we dropped the share of material inputs and estimated only the labour share equations given above. We introduced dummies for technology adoption, number of branches, and foreign ownership, respectively. They take the value of unity if a firm adopts new technology, has at least one branch, and is foreign-owned; and nil otherwise.

The data for the estimation is from *Annual Statistical Censuses & Surveys: Enterprises*, gathered by General Statistics Office of Vietnam. It provides firm-level information on foreign ownership and production characteristics, like the number of workers, gross revenue, working capital, materials, profits, levels of export and imports, etc. However, the survey does not provide any information on the wages of workers by occupation. We also obtained wage data from the *World Bank Business Survey* at the occupational level to derive the wages for skilled and unskilled workers. Since wage data is only available for 2006, we are only able to implement the model for 2006. As with other studies (Amiti and Wei, 2009; Ahn, et al., 2008; Chongvilaivan and Thangavelu, 2012), we define the imports of intermediate inputs as:

$$OM_i = \sum_j \frac{imported\ intermediate\ input\ j\ by\ industry\ i}{total\ intermediate\ inputs\ used\ by\ industry\ i}.$$

The skilled labour share (S_H) is measured by the ratio of the non-production wage bill to total cost as in Feenstra and Hanson (1996, 1997, 1999). Likewise, production workers represent unskilled labour. By definition, non-production workers are those engaged in factory supervision, executive roles, financing, legal, and professional and technical services, whereas production workers are those engaged in assembling, packaging, inspecting, repair, and maintenance. Therefore, non- production and production workers are conventionally acknowledged as promising candidates of proxies for skilled and unskilled workers, respectively. Since wage data by occupation is not available in the survey, we derived the occupation wage data by industry from the *World Bank Business Survey*. This information is matched to workers at the industry to derive the weighted wages for the skilled (w_H) and unskilled (w_L). Furthermore, capital stock (K) is measured by the values of land, building and construction, and machinery and equipment at the end of each consecutive year, whereas total output (Y) is proxied by the total sales of goods produced (Figure 7.12).

The share of skilled and unskilled compensation to total cost is given in Figure 7.9. As expected, the share of skilled compensation to total cost is much higher for both domestic and foreign firms relative to the share of unskilled compensation. We also observed that the share of skilled compensation is much higher for foreign firms as compared to local ones, suggesting that allowing more foreign firms into the market tends to push the wages of skilled workers higher. It is likely that foreign workers use more advanced technology that complements skilled workers, hence increasing the demand and wages for skilled workers.

Two issues should be highlighted. First, since we have three variable factors of production, it follows that the summation of the three factor shares must be unity; that is, the adding-up condition must be satisfied: $\sum S_K = S_H = S_L = S_M = 1$.

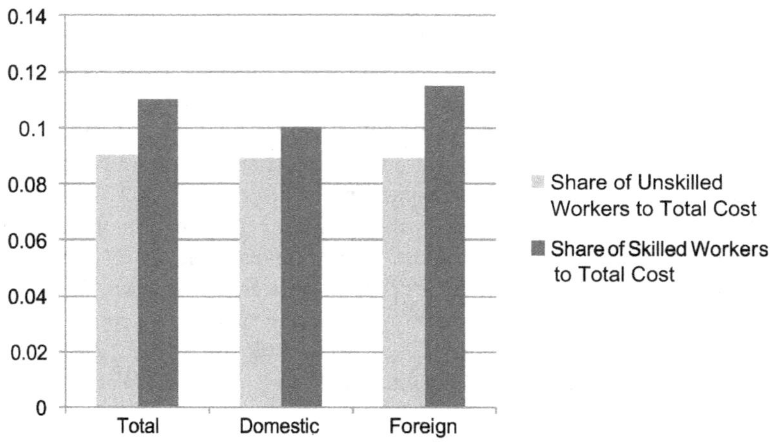

Figure 7.12 Share of Unskilled and Skilled Labour in Vietnamese Manufacturing Sector.

This condition requires us to drop one of the three equations from the system estimation to make it linearly independent. In doing so, we choose to drop the material share equation and estimate only the labour share equations. In light of this, we employ the two-step Iterative Seemingly Unrelated Regression (ISUR) to estimate the labour share equations (5A and 6A). The major advantage of ISUR is that the estimates are invariant to the choices of factor share equations dropped.

7.4 Empirical results

Table 7.3 portrays the ISUR estimates of (5A and 6A) with the perturbed specifications. We also undertook 3SLS-SURE estimation to address any endogeneity issues in the estimation. The results for the 3SLS-SURE are given in Table 7.4. We find that our estimates are robust with respect to the inclusion of the trade and technology variables for ISUR and 3SLS-SURE.

Table 7.3 Impact of Technology and Trade on Skilled and Unskilled Labour in Vietnamese Firms (ISUR)

	Share of Skilled Wages			*Share of Unskilled Wages*		
	1	*2*	*3*	*1*	*2*	*3*
Log (skilled wages/price of materials)	0.006 (0.008)	0.011 (0.007)	-0.011 (0.013)	0.004 (0.007)	−0.0004 (0.007)	0.012 (0.011)
Log (unskilled wages/price of materials)	0.004 (0.007)	−0.0004 (0.007)	0.012 (0.011)	0.011 (0.007)	0.0149** (0.007)	0.001 (0.012)
Log of material imports	–	–	0.037** (0.010)	–	–	0.009 (0.008)
Log (capital)	0.199*** (0.046)	0.2004*** (0.043)	0.189** (0.073)	0.201*** (0.040)	0.151*** (0.041)	0.192** (0.053)
Log of export	–	0.112** (0.039)	–	–	−0.139*** (0.037)	–
Adopted technology dummy	0.007 (0.107)	0.010 (0.009)	0.024 (0.020)	−0.0008 (0.009)	−0.0009 (0.009)	−0.009 (0.014)
Branches dummy	−0.033* (0.017)	0.002 (0.015)	−0.051* (0.027)	0.0029 (0.015)	−0.010 (0.015)	−0.0007 (0.020)
Foreign owned	−0.0001 (0.002)	−0.0004 (0.002)	−0.0003 (0.002)	−0.001 (0.001)	−0.0012 (0.0023)	−0.0008 (0.002)
Constant	−0.696 (0.051)	−0.070 (0.044)	−0.181** (0.087)	−0.117** (0.044)	−0.1222** (0.042)	−0.156** (0.063)
Industry dummies	Yes	Yes	Yes	Yes	Yes	Yes
Observations	623	535	535	623	535	535
R-Square	0.074	0.089	0.118	0.116	0.166	0.121

Source: Authors' compilation.

Notes: *10% level of statistical significance, **5% level of statistical significance, ***1% level of statistical significance. The parentheses indicate standard errors.

Table 7.4 Impact of Technology and Trade on Skilled and Unskilled Labour in Vietnamese Firms (3SLS-SURE)

	Share of Skilled Wages			*Share of Unskilled Wages*		
	1	*2*	*3*	*1*	*2*	*3*
Log (skilled wages/price of materials)	0.005 (0.007)	0.014 (0.008)	-0.012 (0.013)	0.004 (0.008)	-0.0002 (0.007)	0.012 (0.012)
Log (unskilled wages/price of materials)	0.004 (0.007)	-0.0002 (0.007)	0.012 (0.011)	0.011 (0.008)	0.0143** (0.007)	0.004 (0.013)
Log of material imports	–	–	0.012** (0.012)	–	–	0.008 (0.007)
Log (capital)	0.176*** (0.048)	0.198*** (0.044)	0.167** (0.074)	0.200*** (0.042)	0.150*** (0.042)	0.190** (0.054)
Log of export	–	0.115** (0.040)	–	–	-0.138*** (0.038)	–
Adopted technology dummy	0.007 (0.018)	0.010 (0.009)	0.024 (0.020)	-0.0008 (0.009)	-0.0009 (0.010)	-0.008 (0.015)
Branches dummy	-0.034* (0.018)	0.002 (0.016)	-0.055* (0.028)	0.0029 (0.015)	-0.010 (0.015)	-0.0005 (0.020)
Foreign owned	-0.0001 (0.003)	-0.0004 (0.002)	-0.0003 (0.002)	-0.001 (0.001)	-0.0011 (0.002)	-0.0008 (0.002)
Constant	-0.047 (0.053)	-0.067 (0.044)	-0.151** (0.088)	-0.116** (0.045)	-0.119** (0.049)	-0.153** (0.065)
Industry dummies	Yes	Yes	Yes	Yes	Yes	Yes
Observations	623	535	535	623	535	535
R-Square	0.070	0.094	0.112	0.120	0.167	0.117

Source: Authors' compilation.

Notes: *10% level of statistical significance, **5% level of statistical significance, ***1% level of statistical significance. The parentheses indicate standard errors.

We observed very interesting results from Tables 7.3 and 7.4. The results are robust and consistent for both ISUR and 3SLS-SURE. We observe technological changes in Vietnamese firms (statistically significant) and it tends to be neutral in terms of increasing both skilled and unskilled wage shares. This suggests that technological changes are neutral and are not the key factor for the widening wage gap observed in the Vietnamese economy. Nevertheless, this result is not surprising as capital accumulation like automated machineries, computers, and equipment typically require more skilled workers. As Vietnamese firms are moving towards higher value-added manufacturing activities through high-tech capital investment, one would expect the complimentary effect, wherein building up capital escalates the demand for skilled workers and thus wage inequality between skilled and unskilled workers.

The results based on the trade variables of export and import are very interesting. Imports of intermediate inputs increase the skilled wage share and is statistically significant. In contrast, the impact of import of intermediate inputs on unskilled workers is not statistically significance. This is intuitive, as technology is embodied in imports of machines and equipment that complement and increase returns for skilled workers. These complementary effects increase the demand for skilled workers relative to unskilled workers.

The impact of export on the wage share of skilled and unskilled workers indicates that it increases the demand for skilled workers relative to unskilled ones. The coefficient of export is positive and statistically significant for the wage share of skilled workers. The results clearly indicate that trade tends to increase the returns for skilled workers as both imports and exports tend to have positive impacts on the wage share of skilled workers.

Vietnamese firms with branches tend to employ less skilled workers than those without branches. The coefficient of the branches dummy is negative and statistically significant at the 5% level. This evidence may be explained by the fact that skill-intensive activities like research and development (R&D) and product design are typically subject to knowledge spill-overs, and therefore Vietnamese firms strategically retain them within a single location.

Lastly, we find only weak evidence that foreign-owned firms tend to employ more skilled workers than domestic firms. Even though the coefficients of the foreign ownership dummy are positive and negative in the skilled and unskilled share equations respectively, both are statistically insignificant.

7.5 Policy conclusion

In this study, we explored the impacts of trade and, in particular, the effects of international activities among Vietnamese firms. The results indicate that firms that adopt new technologies and restructure their organisation are likely to move part of their activities to more value-added and skill-based activities. These restructuring activities increase the wage gap between skilled and unskilled workers due to the increase in demand for the former.

We also observe that firms that are part of global production networks and value-chains are likely to undertake more restructuring and international activities. As Vietnam liberalises and integrates with the regionally and globally, we should expect more international activities in trade and investment among Vietnamese firms.

The implications of economic liberalisation with regards to foreign investment and global competition are that it is likely to increase restructuring activities in domestic firms. It is clear from our results that trade-related activities are skill-biased towards skilled workers, thereby increasing the demand for them and their wages. Thus, we are likely to see a more widening wage gap between skilled and unskilled workers in the Vietnamese economy. This has implications for the country in terms of increasing the skills and human capital of workers and reducing any job mismatches that might emanate from the economic restructuring.

Several key challenges still exist in Vietnam. Firstly, there is still rent-seeking in the economy and this is likely to create inefficiencies. The importance of transparency and the protection of property rights are important for conducting business in Vietnam. Thus, the flow of foreign investment is slow-moving and there are concerns that the government's economic reforms have been sluggish.

The other challenge for Vietnam is inadequate investment in public infrastructure such as digital and telecommunications. The digital and telecommunication industry is heavily regulated by the government and there are restrictions on foreign ownership. Greater economic liberalisation of this sector is expected to increase the competitiveness and efficiency of the domestic sector.

There are several important policy implications from the study. If manufacturing activities in Vietnam are moving towards more capital and technology intensive, the impact of globalisation will have important impact on rising wage inequality and also on skill development in the economy.

Our results indicate that there are negative effects on unskilled workers and, thus, the government has an important role in managing negative effects without sacrificing the positive effects from trade and globalisation. This clearly reflects domestic human capital development as a key component of growth in an economy open to globalisation. The training and upgrading of skill programmes will be crucial to moving unskilled workers to more productive sectors in the economy. The improvement and upgrading of the education and innovation systems in Vietnam will be important factors to augment the potential benefits of globalisation. The government should focus on retraining unskilled workers as they are displaced from technological changes and globalisation. As new jobs are created from structural changes, it is important to train and move workers to competitive industries. Thus, the government could consider policies targeted at continuing education such as industrial education for the working population to upgrade their skills and remain relevant in the labour market.

The importance of domestic capacity building and linkages will be crucial to increasing technological development and the innovation capabilities of the domestic economy. In particular, the next phase of development for Vietnam will be based on how well they are able to harness the development of local human capital and domestic enterprises.

Note

1 Despite these three variable factors, our framework, unlike Morrison and Siegel's (2001), is based on the non-homothetic translog cost function rather than the Generalized Leontief cost function.

References

Acemoglu, D. (2002), 'Technical Change, Inequality and the Labor Market', *Journal of Economic Literature*, issue 40, pp. 7–72.

Acemoglu, D. and D. H. Autor (2011), 'Skills, Tasks and Technologies: Implications for Employment and Earnings', in Ashenfelter, O. and D. Card, (eds.), *Handbook of Labor Economics*, chapter 12, Vol. 4B, Amsterdam: North Holland, pp. 1044–1155.

Ahn, S., K. Fukao, and K. Ito (2008), 'Outsourcing in East Asia and Its Impact on the Japanese and Korean Labor Markets', OECD Trade Policy Working Papers, No. 65, Paris: OECD.

Amiti, M. and S. Wei. (2009), 'Services Offshoring and Productivity: Evidence from the United States', *The World Economy, Blackwell Publishing* 32(2), pp. 203–20.

Anderton, B. and P. Brenton, (1999), 'Outsourcing and Low-skilled Workers in the UK', *Bulletin of Economic Research* 51(4), pp. 267–85.

Arndt, S. W. and H. Kierzkowski (2001), *Fragmentation: New Production Patterns in the World Economy.* Oxford: Oxford University Press.

Autor, D., L. Katz and A. Krueger (1998), 'Computing Inequality: Have Computers Changed the Labor Market?', *Quarterly Journal of Economics* 113, pp. 1169–213.

Autor, D. H., F. Levy, and R. J. Murnane (2003), 'The Skill Content of Recent Technological Change: An Empirical Exploration', *Quarterly Journal of Economics* 116, pp. 1279–334.

Card, D. and J. E. DiNardo (2002), 'Skill Biased Technological Change and Rising Wage Inequality: Some Problems and Puzzles', *Journal of Labour Economics* 20(4), pp. 733–83.

Chongvilaivan, A. and S. M. Thangavelu (2012), 'Does Outsourcing Provision Leads to Wage Inequality? New Evidence from Thailand's Establishment-Level Data', *Review of International Economics* 20, pp. 364–76.

Feenstra, R. C. and G. H. Hanson (1996), 'Foreign Direct Investment, Outsourcing, and Relative Wages', in Feenstra, R. C., G. M. Grossman, and D. A. Irwin (eds.), *The Political Economy of Trade Policy: Papers in Honor of Jagdish Bhagwati*, Cambridge: MIT Press, pp. 89–127.

Feenstra, R. C. and G. H. Hanson (1997), 'Productivity Measurement and the Impact of Trade and Technology on Wages: Estimates for the U.S., 1972–1990', NBER Working Paper, No. 6052.

Feenstra, R. C. and G. H. Hanson (1999), 'The Impact of Outsourcing and High-Technology Capital on Wages: Estimates for the United States, 1979–1990', *Quarterly Journal of Economics* 114(3), pp. 907–40.

Hsieh, C. and K. T. Woo (2005), 'The Impact of Outsourcing to China on Hong Kong's Labor Market', *American Economic Review* 95(5), pp. 1673–87.

Morrison, C. J. Paul and D. S. Siegel (2001), 'The Impacts of Technology, Trade, and Outsourcing on Employment and Labor Composition', *Scandinavian Journal of Economics*, 103(20, pp. 241–64.

Thangavelu, S. M. and A. Chongvilaivan, (2011), 'Impacts of Outsourcing on Employment and Labour Substitution: New Firm level Evidence from Manufacturing Industries in Thailand', *Applied Economics* 43(27), pp. 3931–44.

World Bank (2012), 'Vietnam Development Report 2012: Market Economy for Middle Income Vietnam', Joint Donor Report to the *Vietnam Consultative Group Meeting*, December 2011.

8 Does real exchange rate depreciation increase productivity?

Analysis using Korean firm-level data

Bo-Young Choi and Ju Hyun Pyun

8.1 Introduction

The literature has long debated whether changes in real exchange rate (RER)—a measure for international price competitiveness—affect a country's total factor productivity (TFP) and further economic growth. While one strand shows the positive effect of RER depreciation on productivity, another focuses on its negative consequences. The positive effect implies that currency depreciation is like a positive demand shock to the economy that results in higher productivity growth via increased factor utilization, learning-by-doing effects, or increasing returns to scale (IRS) (Verdoorn, 1949).[1] Previous studies such as Eichengreen (2007) and Rodrik (2008) point out that currency undervaluation stimulates economic growth, particularly in developing countries.[2]

However, some studies emphasize the negative effect of RER depreciation on TFP. For instance, Porter (1990) argues that it is, in fact, counterproductive for governments to intervene in factor and currency markets, hoping that the devaluation will help domestic firms compete more effectively in international markets. This is because such intervention would discourage firms from searching for a more sustainable competitive advantage. In short, costs as well as benefits exist in keeping the RER low, especially if RER depreciation persists.

This study attempts to find RER depreciation effects on firm-level productivity and examine the mechanism leading to such effects using rich South Korean firm-level data for 2006–2013. The effect of external RER shocks on productivity is particularly important for Korea, because as a small open economy, a change in RER can greatly affect the profitability of many firms.[3] Furthermore, we exploit the sharp and persistent depreciation of the Korean Won during 2007–2009 as a natural experiment to study exogenous RER depreciation effects on firm productivity (see Figure 8.1).

In the literature, RER changes are generally believed to affect the price of products or firm assets and this price effect has been thoroughly investigated (Berman, Martin, and Mayer, 2012; Li, Ma, and Xu, 2015). In this study, however, we elucidate that the impact of RER changes is more than that of price

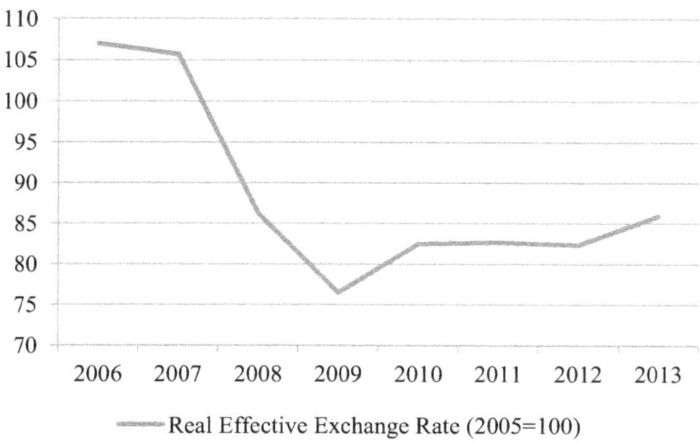

Figure 8.1 Real Effective Exchange Rate in Korea.
Note: A decrease in RER index indicates currency depreciation.

changes and assess the channels through which RERs affect firm productivity. We also identify the heterogeneous effects of a common RER shock on productivity base on firms' exposure to international trade.

Our year-by-year analysis finds a positive effect of RER depreciation on productivity. This effect is more pronounced for firms with higher export exposure. However, we find that the significant productivity gain in response to immediate RER depreciation disappears when RER depreciation "persists" over time. More importantly, we dissect the channels through which RERs influence productivity differently. The immediate RER effect on productivity is greater for firms (industries) exhibiting IRS, which suggests that RER depreciation increases TFP through economies of scale. Yet, the nullifying effect of "persistent" depreciation is particularly observed for firms with a negative R&D growth. This implies that the persistent depreciation slackens the innovation effort and discourages firms from allocating resources more efficiently, thereby reducing productivity. Several robustness checks strongly support our results.

Previous studies show that the RER affects firm performance. Baggs, Beaulieu, and Fung (2009) find that appreciations of Canadian currency decrease the probability of Canadian firms' survival and this effect is less pronounced for more productive firms. Tomlin (2014), using dynamic structural parameter estimates, confirms the negative effect of RER appreciation on the probability of firm survival in the market. While previous findings of the RER effect on firm survival are quite consistent, the literature on how it affects firm productivity has yielded mixed results. Fung, Baggs, and Beaulieu (2011) found that RER appreciation led Canadian plants in the manufacturing industry to decrease shipments, resulting in lower productivity, but Ekholm, Moxnes, and Ulltveit-Moe (2012) found that a sharp and persistent RER appreciation increased Norwegian firms' productivity through labor shedding.

Our work contributes to the existing literature on RERs and within-firm productivity in several ways. First, we find heterogeneous effects of RER depreciation on productivity not only across firms but also "over time." We compare and contrast the consequences of year-by-year RER depreciation with those of persistent RER depreciation and finally reconcile somewhat contrasting findings in previous studies. Positive productivity gains from RER depreciation for exporting firms are observed in our yearly analysis, consistent with the scale effect in RER depreciation as shown in Fung, Baggs, and Beaulieu (2011). However, the negative consequences of persistent RER depreciation on productivity are consistent with Ekholm, Moxnes, and Ulltveit-Moe (2012) in that the persistent RER changes influence the competitive environment that firms face and lead to changes in firm productivity.

Methodologically, we address the problem of revenue based TFP by controlling for the RER effect on firm markup. Because a change in RERs is closely associated with firm pricing, it is important to net out the price effect from changes in the measured TFP. We show that RER depreciation shocks affect firm productivity through not only prices but also through efficiency by controlling for firm-level markups derived by using the De Loecker and Warzynski (2012) method. Finally, yet importantly, this micro-study adds an interesting insight to the enduring debate on RER undervaluation and economic growth.

The remainder of the paper is organized as follows. Section 8.2 introduces the channels through which RERs affect firm-level productivity. Section 8.3 describes our data and empirical research design, Section 8.4 gives our empirical results, Section 8.5 presents our robustness checks, and Section 8.6 is the conclusion.

8.2 Theoretical discussions

Several studies examine the effect of RERs on firm-level productivity through the efficiency channel.[4] Fung, Baggs, and Beaulieu (2011) and Tomlin and Fung (2015) show that firms increase their productivity through economies of scale during RER depreciation.[5] However, Ekholm, Moxnes, and Ulltveit-Moe (2012) show that productivity gains occur during persistent RER appreciation as firms are restructuring (e.g., shedding labor) in response to intense competition. In line with this, if we assume the symmetric effect of RERs on firm productivity, depreciation may loosen competition and discourage a firm's innovation effort to search for a more sustainable competitive advantage (e.g., Porter, 1990).

Furthermore, as RER change is a common shock across firms, previous studies have specified the following three firm or industry characteristics that identify the effect of RER shocks on productivity: (i) export shares of exporting firms, (ii) intermediate input import shares of importing firms, and (iii) import competition of import-competing domestic firms (Campa and Goldberg, 1995, 2001; Ekholm, Moxnes and Ulltveit-Moe, 2012). We discuss each below.

When the RER depreciates, firms with higher export shares become more competitive on final goods prices and impose higher markups.[6] In addition, they expand their output through increased factor utilization. If firms' technology exhibits IRS and their export shares are large enough, productivity would increase (à la scale effect; Krugman, 1979). Thus, the positive effect of RER depreciation on productivity would be more pronounced for firms with higher export exposure.

However, if RER depreciation persists, the sustainability of the positive productivity gain from the RER depreciation needs to be assessed. Persistent depreciation may affect a firm's resource allocation, so it would rather have a negative effect on an exporting firm's efficiency. That is, lower competition in foreign markets owing to depreciation discourages the effective internal reallocation of resources within exporting firms (by reducing investment in innovation), leading to a decrease in firm productivity (e.g., Porter, 1990). Eckel and Neary (2010); Bernard, Redding, and Schott (2011); and Mayer, Melitz, and Ottaviano (2014) suggest that tougher competition encourages firms' resource reallocation through changes in the scope of products—tougher competition induces firms to drop their worst performing products and focus on core competencies. The effect of export market competition on firms' product mix translates into differences in measured firm productivity as they allocate relatively more workers to the production of core competencies and raise overall sales per worker. Thus, depreciation is likely to moderate competition and encourage firms to expand their product scope further away from core competence, resulting in lower firm productivity. Although the change in the scope of products is not observable in our data, the theoretical predictions of the literature justify our conjecture. Again, this negative effect may be amplified when a firm's export share increases.

Secondly, the RER depreciation leads to higher prices for foreign inputs, so importing firms would not be able to afford the cheaper foreign inputs they had used earlier. Thus, higher input costs due to depreciation would lower productivity. This negative RER depreciation effect on productivity may be stronger for firms with higher intermediate input import shares. However, if RER depreciation persists, this cost disadvantage may encourage surviving firms to reallocate their resources more efficiently. Again, the response of firm-level productivity to RER depreciation could vary with the firms' input import shares.

Finally, the effects of RER depreciation on firm productivity vary with the import penetration (industry-wide import share) in the domestic market. RER depreciation hurts importing firms' price competitiveness on imported goods, whereas domestic import-competing firms would enjoy relative price gains against the importing firms and expand output (scale expansion). However, if the RER depreciation persists, domestic firms in the industry with higher import penetration would face mild competition against the importing firms. The persistent depreciation may discourage investment in innovation or efficient resource allocation within domestic import-competing firms, affecting their efficiency negatively. Thus, the positive price gains of domestic import-competing firms from immediate depreciation may be canceled out by the efficiency loss from persistent RER depreciation.

The numerous channels through which RERs affect productivity indicate that the productivity responses of firms to immediate RER depreciation shocks as well as persistent depreciation are indeed heterogeneous, in terms of exposure to trade and industrial competition.[7]

8.3 Data and empirical methodology

8.3.1 Data

We use firm-level data of South Korean manufacturing industries for the period 2006–2013. Statistics Korea collected this data via the Survey of Business Activities from 2006. These data are collected annually from all enterprises operating in South Korea that have at least 50 regular workers and a capital of 300 million Korean Won. This firm-level dataset is a good representation of the whole population of firms in the Korean manufacturing industry in that the total output of all firms accounts for about 80% of the total manufacturing industry's output. Manufacturing industries are classified into 24 types based on the Korea Standard Industrial Classification (KSIC) system. The dataset provides rich information on sales, export activity, employees, wages, material costs, foreign capital share, assets, and so forth.

We estimate the firm-level productivity by industry following Levinsohn and Petrin (2003) (hereafter LP), who proposed a method to control for the endogeneity of input choices influenced by productivity shocks. Productivity is often estimated as the residual of ordinary least squares (OLS) estimation based on the Cobb–Douglas production function. Such estimates could be biased from the simultaneity problem that may arise because a simple OLS estimation does not take into account unobserved productivity shocks, although firms choose their input levels based on the productivity shock. For instance, firms expand their output and consequently increase their inputs in response to a positive productivity shock. Here, without addressing the simultaneity issue, the input estimates of the production function would be biased upward.

Olley and Pakes (1996) (hereafter OP) and LP propose a novel approach to addressing the simultaneity problem. While OP uses investment as a proxy for an unobserved time-varying productivity shock, LP states that the OP methodology is valid only when investments respond smoothly to productivity shocks and sample observations report positive investment. In our data, since 56% of our sample reports zero investment, we choose the LP methodology for our firm-level TFP estimation (see Appendix I for details). Applying this method, we estimate the production function by industry.

Table 8.1 presents the firm- and industry-level descriptive statistics and correlations among variables. Export/sales represent the annual total export divided by total sales. Intermediate imports/cost indicates a firm's imported intermediate

Table 8.1 Descriptive Statistics

Panel A. Summary

Variable	*Obs.*	*Mean*	*Std.*	*Min.*	*Max.*
ln TFP (LP)	36146	3.745	1.279	-4.703	9.025
Labor productivity (VA/L)	36146	3.853	0.982	-4.259	9.307
ln TFP (System GMM)	28134	4.234	7.901	-74.288	40.267
ln Industry RER	36146	4.477	0.150	4.074	4.737
Export/sales (*t*–1)	28139	0.205	0.317	0	2
Intermediate import/cost (*t*–1)	28139	0.018	0.087	0	1.774
Net exposure (*t*–1)	28139	0.187	0.314	-1.670	2
Import penetration (*t*–1)	28139	0.291	0.283	0.034	1.479
Export dummy (*t*–1)	28827	0.604	0.489	0	1
Import dummy (*t*–1)	28827	0.449	0.497	0	1
Size (employment) (*t*–1)	28139	4.931	0.862	2.485	10.999
R&D intensity (*t*–1)	28139	0.017	0.043	0	3.721
HHI (*t*–1)	28827	0.075	0.084	0	0.526
GFC dummy (*t*–1)	36146	0.241	0.428	0	1
Markup (*t*–1)	28134	1.816	8.159	0.0009	1352.799

(*Continued*)

Panel B. Correlation matrix

	ln TFP (LP)	*Labor prod.*	*ln TFP (System GMM)*	*ln (Ind. RER)*	*Export/ sales (t–1)*	*Inter. input import/ cost (t–1)*	*Net exp. (t–1)*	*Import penetration (t–1)*	*Export dummy (t–1)*	*Import dummy (t–1)*	*Employment (t–1)*	*R&D intensity (t–1)*	*HHI (t-1)*	*GFC dummy (t–1)*	*Markup (t–1)*
ln TFP (LP)	1.000														
Labor productivity	0.645	1.000													
ln TFP (S-GMM)	0.186	–0.137	1.000												
ln industry RER	0.200	–0.025	–0.044	1.000											
Export/sales (*t*–1)	0.012	0.090	0.003	–0.107	1.000										
Import/cost (*t*–1)	0.056	0.115	–0.033	–0.055	0.179	1.000									
Net exposure (*t*–1)	–0.003	0.059	0.012	–0.093	0.962	–0.096	1.000								
Import penetration(*t*–1)	–0.140	–0.067	0.038	–0.114	0.159	0.054	0.146	1.000							
Export dummy (*t*–1)	0.032	0.151	-0.061	–0.061	0.507	0.133	0.476	0.075	1.000						
Import dummy (*t*–1)	0.104	0.201	–0.075	–0.066	0.282	0.223	0.224	0.073	0.485	1.000					
Employment (*t*–1)	0.227	0.227	–0.013	0.017	0.198	0.092	0.175	0.034	0.241	0.240	1.000				
R&D intensity (*t*–1)	–0.107	0.009	–0.022	–0.080	0.080	–0.011	0.084	0.147	0.098	0.072	0.005	1.000			
HHI (*t*–1)	–0.125	–0.112	0.059	–0.198	0.108	0.039	0.099	0.689	0.029	0.015	0.022	0.059	1.000		
GFC dummy (*t*–1)	–0.010	–0.021	0.001	–0.254	–0.005	0.016	–0.010	–0.022	0.000	0.021	–0.010	–0.001	–0.017	1.000	
Markup (*t*–1)	0.040	0.062	–0.019	–0.029	0.004	0.004	0.003	–0.015	0.008	0.023	0.027	–0.009	–0.020	–0.003	1.000

input divided by its total cost, and industry import penetration is defined as the total imports relative to total absorption in industry j in year t, where the total absorption is calculated as (production value$_j$) – (export value$_j$) + (import value$_j$). This measure captures industry j's dependence on foreign imports. We include employment after taking a log as a proxy for firm size. R&D intensity is R&D expenditure divided by total sales. The Herfindahl index is calculated as $\sum_{k \in j} s_{kt}^2$, where s_{kt} is the market share of firm k in industry j at time t. This is a proxy for the degree of industry concentration capturing the level of competition. The global financial crisis (GFC) dummy is included to capture the external negative shock during 2008–2009. The variable is coded as 1 if the year is 2008 or 2009 and 0 otherwise.

As pointed out by Bernard et al. (2003) and many other studies, comparisons of measured productivity across firms/plants may only reflect differences in their markups; thus, value-based productivity measures provide information about market power and not about underlying efficiency. The standard solution in the literature has been to deflate firm-level sales by an industry-wide price index in the hope of eliminating price effects. However, the measured productivity is affected by the price component whenever individual firm price deviates from the average price level of the industry (i.e., in the case of imperfect competition).[8] Thus, an increase in measured productivity implies either an increase in price or an increase in efficiency.

De Loecker (2011) also points out that relying on deflated sales in the production function will generate productivity estimates that contain both the price and demand variation. Because RER changes may affect firm pricing, it suggests that a relationship between measured TFP and RER depreciation is simply through the depreciation effect on prices and demand. Hence, to identify the impact of the RER depreciation on firm efficiency, we include firm-level markups derived using the De Loecker and Warzynski (2012) method. Their empirical markup estimation method is tractable without any restrictive assumptions about the production function (i.e., returns to scale) and measuring the user cost of capital. Using standard cost minimization conditions for variable inputs free of adjustment costs, they estimate the output elasticity of an input and recover the firm markup with the share of that input's expenditure in total sales. We use two kinds of estimated markups: (i) value-added Cobb–Douglas production functions allowing an endogenous productivity process based on Ackerberg, Caves, and Frazer (2015) and (ii) value-added translog production functions. We use the first markup measure as our baseline measure. Note that markup estimation procedures are provided in Appendix II.

We use the annual industry-specific RER index published by the Research Institute of Economy, Trade and Industry (RIETI). The industry-specific RER index of Korea is classified into 13 manufacturing industries based on prices in Korea and its 26 major trade partners.[9] Because the country-level RER used by previous studies varies only through time, it is mixed with other macroeconomic shocks. Thus, the industry-level RER index is more appropriate to identify the pure RER effect on industries than the aggregate country-level RER. Although the correlation between industry RERs is high (see Table 8.2), we are able to exploit the industry variation in RERs.

Table 8.3 gives the firm dynamics in our dataset. Our sample includes the total number of firms and exporters over time. During 2006–2013, the total number of firms fluctuates, decreasing from 5,564 to 5,362 by 2010 and then increasing to 5,628 by 2013. The number of exporters increased from 3,093 to 3,412 during the sharp and persistent RER depreciation in 2006–2009. Thus, these firm entry and exit dynamics certainly show that the competitive environment has changed. Furthermore, the increase in the number of exporters suggests firm dynamics were influenced by persistent RER depreciation. However, the change in net number of firms entering the export market during the depreciation period is small: about 9% of total exporters. The low net entry rate during depreciation suggests that not only an RER depreciation shock but also that the negative GFC shock hit exporters simultaneously during the period, canceling out each other. Thus, disentangling the RER depreciation shock from the GFC shock is an important issue; we discuss this further in Section 8.5.2.

8.3.2 Empirical specifications

To study the heterogeneous effect of RER shocks on firm productivity over time, we employ year-by-year panel estimation and difference-in-difference (DID) analysis.

8.3.2.1 Year-by-year panel estimation.

First, we investigate the year-by-year effect of RERs on firm productivity as follows

$$\ln(TFP_{ijt}) = \beta_0 + \beta_1 RER_{jt} + \beta_2 RER_{jt} \times Export\ int._{ijt-1} + \beta_3 RER_{jt} \times Input\ dep._{ijt-1} + \beta_4 RER_{jt} \times Import\ penet._{jt-1} + X_{ijt-1} \cdot \gamma + \alpha_i + \varepsilon_{ijt} \quad (2)$$

where i indicates firm level, j indicates industry level, and t is a time descriptor; the dependent variable, $\ln(TFP_{ijt})$, is the log of firm-level productivity; RER_{jt} is the industry-level real effective exchange rate (a decrease in RER means depreciation); $Export\ int._{ijt-1}$ is firm i's export share of total sales; $Input\ dep._{ijt-1}$ is firm i's import share of total costs (for imported intermediate goods); $Import\ penet.jt{-}1$ is the import penetration measure of industry j at year t–1; and X_{ijt-1} is a vector of other control variables affecting productivity, such as firm size (employment), R&D intensity, Herfindahl index (HHI), and the global financial crisis dummy. To reduce the potential endogeneity problem, we use year-lagged variables of all controls including three variables that convey RER shocks to productivity. As mentioned previously, a change in price as well as efficiency can influence firm productivity. To exploit the effect of RERs on firm efficiency, we

Table 8.2 Correlation Table of Industry-Level RER

	Food	*Textile*	*Wood*	*Paper*	*Petrol.*	*Chemical*	*Rubber*	*Nonmetal*	*Metal*	*General Machinery*	*Electrical Machinery*	*Optical Instrument*	*Transport Equipment*
Food (10, 11, 12)	1												
Textile (13, 14, 15)	0.931	1											
Wood (16, 32)	0.9614	0.9491	1										
Paper (17)	0.9001	0.8188	0.9547	1									
Petroleum (19)	0.9367	0.9784	0.9417	0.8124	1								
Chemical (20, 21)	0.9624	0.9276	0.9935	0.9697	0.9166	1							
Rubber (22)	0.9703	0.9632	0.9966	0.9393	0.9542	0.99	1						
Nonmetal (23)	0.9299	0.9978	0.9437	0.811	0.9692	0.92	0.9585	1					
Metal (24, 25)	0.7696	0.6618	0.826	0.8794	0.7174	0.8303	0.8067	0.6409	1				
General machinery (26, 29, 33)	0.9641	0.9878	0.9787	0.8781	0.9785	0.9638	0.9875	0.9835	0.7578	1			
Electrical machinery (28)	0.803	0.9548	0.8263	0.6275	0.9274	0.7826	0.8493	0.9553	0.5049	0.9134	1		
Optical instruments (27)	0.8075	0.9518	0.8269	0.628	0.9334	0.7818	0.8509	0.9512	0.5292	0.9157	0.9981	1	
Transport equipment (30, 31)	0.9605	0.9652	0.9699	0.8728	0.9629	0.9516	0.9768	0.9633	0.7916	0.9908	0.8938	0.9017	1

Note: The table shows the correlation of the industry-level RER of RIETI classified by 13 subsectors of manufacturing.

Table 8.3 Firm Dynamics (Total Firms Observed: 8440)

Year	*N*	*No. of New Firms*	*No. of Shut Down Firms*	*Exporters*	*Entry*	*Exit*
2006	5564			3093		
2007	5605	394	353	3327	606	372
2008	5711	757	651	3345	564	546
2009	5490	120	341	3412	262	195
2010	5362	148	276	3231	358	539
2011	5677	740	425	3317	480	394
2012	5863	560	374	3513	458	262
2013	5628	652	887	3532	535	516

introduce the current firm-level markup estimates at t. By introducing a markup, we isolate the RER effects on firm prices from those on firm efficiency. Lastly, we also include α_i, firm fixed effects.

We consider the coefficients on the interaction terms of RER as the three channels introduced in Section 8.2. For instance, if exporting firms with IRS technology enjoy productivity gains by expanding their sales significantly in foreign markets following the RER depreciation, then firm productivity increases. Thus, we expect a negative sign for β_2, the coefficient on the interaction between RERs and export to sales.[10]

8.3.2.2 *Difference-in-difference (DID) analysis*

To examine the effect of sharp and persistent RER depreciation during 2007–2009 on firm productivity, we also introduce the DID approach, which is used widely to investigate the differences in outcomes between treatment and control groups. For instance, Trefler (2004) studied how Canadian firms responded to trade liberalization following the implementation of the North American Free Trade Agreement. In a similar context, Ekholm, Moxnes, and Ulltveit-Moe (2012) examined the effect of a persistent currency appreciation shock on Norwegian firm productivity. Following these previous studies, we define 2006–2010 as the RER shock period and 2010–2013 as the common period after the RER shock. The RER was relatively stable in 2010–2013, as Figure 8.1 shows. Note that for robustness of the results, we use a different set of shock periods.

Let $\Delta TFP_{ij,\,T}$ be the average annual change in the outcome variable of firm i in industry j at period T. The average annual changes in the two periods are as follows:

$$\begin{aligned} \Delta \mathrm{TFP}_{ij,S} &= (\ln TFP_{ij,2010} - \ln TFP_{ij,2006}) \,/\, (2010-2006) \\ \Delta \mathrm{TFP}_{ij,0} &= (\ln TFP_{ij,2013} - \ln TFP_{ij,2010}) \,/\, (2013-2010) \end{aligned} \tag{3}$$

where the period $T = 0$ denotes the period with stable RER movement—our reference point—and $T = S$ denotes the period with persistent RER depreciation shock. The RER decreased sharply for three years from 2007. Then, we propose the following DID model to explain the impact of a persistent RER shock on firm productivity:

$$\Delta TFP_{ij,S} - \Delta \mathrm{TFP}_{ij,0} = \theta + (\Delta RER_{j,S} - \Delta RER_{j,0})\tilde{\beta}_1 + \mathrm{E}_{ij,2006}(\Delta RER_{j,S} - \Delta RER_{j,0}) \cdot \tilde{\beta}_2 + W_{ij,2006}\delta + v_{ijt} \quad (4)$$

where θ is a constant term capturing the change in $\Delta TFP_{ij,\ T}$ due to any shock other than the RER shock. Firm fixed effects are differenced out. We define variable $(\Delta RER_{jS} - \Delta RER_{j0})$ as the difference in the "industry-wide" change in RER between the shock period and the common period. Note that when the countrywide RER is used, the change in RER growth between the shock and common period becomes a negative number, with no variation across industries or firms. $\mathrm{E}_{ij,2006}$ is a vector of variables measuring three channels—export sales, intermediate inputs, and import penetration in 2006. The firm or industry-level variation in $\mathrm{E}_{ij,2006}$ helps us interpret $\tilde{\beta}_2$. A negative $\tilde{\beta}_2$ means that depreciation has a greater positive impact on firm productivity with higher value of variable in $\mathrm{E}_{ij,2006}$.

We also add other control variables in 2006 ($W_{ij,2006}$). The choice of 2006 as the start of the RER shock period allows us to compare the year-end outcome through persistent RER change with its baseline level before the shock started. This ensures that the covariates are predetermined, minimizing concerns about reverse causality. In addition, for a robustness check we report our results with 2010 as base year for all covariates. However, the results remain unchanged.

Further, we include changes in markup growth $(\Delta Markup_{j,S} - \Delta Markup_{j,0})$ to address a problem in the revenue based productivity and also add $(\Delta DS_{j,\ S} - \Delta DS_{j,0})$, the difference in changes in total foreign demand (measured as a log of industry total export) between the shock period and the common period, to control for changes in business conditions between two periods that may bias the RER effect on TFP growth. This measurement also captures the effect of the global financial crisis during the shock period.

8.4 Empirical results

8.4.1 Main results: yearly analysis vs. DID analysis

Table 8.4 reports the effects of a year-by-year RER change on firm productivity. Since our controls include markup estimates, we report clustered bootstrap standard errors at the firm level. Column (1) shows the estimates for the sample including all types of firms while Column (2) represents the results when restricting our sample to only exporters. Column (3) shows the estimation results by combining the first two channels, export share and foreign input share, into net exposure. Column (4) introduces an alternative markup measure estimated from the value-added translog production function.

The estimated coefficients on RERs are negative but statistically insignificant over all columns. As mentioned earlier, we include the interaction terms of

RERs and the three channels to examine how firm characteristics and industry environments change the RER depreciation effect on firm productivity. The estimated coefficients on the interaction terms of RERs and export exposure are significantly negative in all columns of Table 8.4. This suggests that an RER depreciation affects productivity positively for firms with high export exposure. Note that in the next section, we examine whether the scale effect helps increase productivity in response to RER depreciation.

The estimated coefficients on the interaction terms of RERs and the share of intermediate input imports are positive, suggesting that firms that import more inputs face greater productivity loss in response to RER depreciation because the depreciation increases their import costs. Following RER depreciation, foreign intermediate inputs will become expensive and may no longer be affordable for some firms. This could result in lower productivity, similar to the findings of Amiti and Konings (2007), who show an increase in plant productivity from lower tariff rates on inputs via learning, variety, or quality effects.[11] However, the coefficient is statistically significant only for exporting firms in Column (2). This is possibly because exporting firms are often also importers; the correlation between the export dummy and import dummy is 0.476 (see Panel B of Table 8.1).

In Column (3), we consider net exposure, the difference between the export share and import input share, following Ekholm, Moxnes, and Ulltveit-Moe (2012). Export share is equal to elasticity of revenue with respect to RER changes, and import input share in total costs is equal to the elasticity of costs with respect to RER changes. Thus, a positive net exposure implies that RER depreciation has a positive effect on profits.[12]

The coefficients on the interaction terms of the RER and import penetration are significantly negative. This implies that RER depreciation leads to productivity gains for domestic firms with high industry import penetration via market expansion over foreign imported goods. Note that the coefficient of this interaction term in Column (1) shows a stronger effect compared to that in Column (2), which includes only exporters. This suggests that firms only operating in the domestic market are more sensitive to the depreciation effect through the import penetration channel than exporters.

Throughout Columns (1) to (4), firm size measured as employment has ambiguous effects on productivity. The coefficient of R&D intensity is negative and significant, but its squared term exhibits a positive sign. This finding is somewhat contradictory to common sense. However, our R&D variable of Korean manufacturing firms includes many zeros (about 29.1% of firms report zero R&D expenditure). Also, R&D investment occurs intermittently for some firms (e.g., positive R&D spending appears the current year and then zero R&Ds afterwards for some time), whereas TFP changes are continuously driven by R&D investment. Thus, this within variation between R&D and TFP may lead to a negative coefficient on R&D intensity. Kancs and Siliverstovs (2012) showed that R&D has a nonlinear effect on productivity: the R&D effect on productivity is negative for low-level R&D intensity and positive for high-level R&D intensity.

Table 8.4 Main Result I: The Effects of Year-By-Year RER Changes on TFPs

Dependent Variable	$ln(TFP_{ijt})$			
		Exporters	w/Net exposure	Markup from translog production
	(1)	(2)	(3)	(4)
$\ln(RER_{jt})$	-0.034	-0.154	-0.031	-0.043
	(0.095)	(0.133)	(0.089)	(0.105)
$\ln(RER_{jt})$ × Export Exposure (*t*–1)	-0.337***	-0.301**		-0.329***
	(0.130)	(0.144)		(0.111)
$\ln(RER_{jt})$ × Inter.input import/Cost (*t-1*)	0.578	0.807**		0.624
	(0.402)	(0.403)		(0.393)
$\ln(RER_{jt})$ × Net Exposure (*t*–1)			-0.347***	
			(0.111)	
$\ln(RER_{jt})$ × Import penetration (–1)	-0.584***	-0.437*	-0.586**	-0.587***
	(0.214)	(0.246)	(0.228)	(0.224)
Export Exposure (*t*–1)	1.501***	1.357**		1.471***
	(0.574)	(0.629)		(0.485)
Intermediate input import/ Cost (*t–1*)	-2.433	-3.417*		-2.636
	(1.764)	(1.747)		(1.708)
Net exposure (*t*–1)			1.538***	
			(0.482)	
Import penetration (*t*–1)	2.461***	1.794*	2.471**	2.470**
	(0.938)	(1.078)	(0.994)	(0.976)
Export dummy (*t*–1)	-0.003		0.000	-0.004
	(0.015)		(0.016)	(0.015)
Import dummy (*t*–1)	0.018*	0.012	0.021*	0.020*
	(0.010)	(0.016)	(0.011)	(0.012)
Employment (*t*–1)	0.030	-0.033	0.030	0.021
	(0.025)	(0.030)	(0.023)	(0.025)
R&D intensity (*t*–1)	-0.908***	-1.135***	-0.908***	-0.915***
	(0.333)	(0.410)	(0.305)	(0.334)
Squared R&D intensity (*t*–1)	0.586	1.496	0.586	0.416
	(0.511)	(1.067)	(0.554)	(0.516)
HHI (*t*–1)	0.098	0.222	0.095	0.103
	(0.163)	(0.204)	(0.153)	(0.156)
GFC dummy	-0.052***	-0.048***	-0.052***	-0.051***
	(0.010)	(0.015)	(0.011)	(0.010)
Markup	0.011	0.021	0.012	-0.017
	(0.023)	(0.032)	(0.025)	(0.023)
Firm fixed effects	Included	Included	Included	Included
Observations	28,134	17,775	28,134	27,037
R-squared	0.894	0.901	0.894	0.895

Note: Clustered bootstrap standard errors at firm level are reported in parentheses. *, **, and *** indicate significance at the 10%, 5%, and 1% levels, respectively. A constant term is included but not reported.

Industry competition measured as HHI has positive but statistically insignificant effects on firm productivity. During the GFC, many firms faced negative demand shocks. The coefficients on the GFC dummy are significant and negative, which means firm productivity decreased in response to the GFC shock.

As we control for markup, we are able to net out the price effect from changes in the revenue-based TFP. Markups are correlated positively with productivity [except for Column (4)] although the coefficient is statistically insignificant. In addition, the greater coefficient on markup in Column (2) than in Column (1) suggests that the markup gains of exporters increase more than those of firms serving only the domestic market. Note that our results do not alter even when we exclude the markup variable.

Table 8.5 Main Result II: Persistent RER Depreciation

Dependent Variable	$(\Delta TFP_{jS} - \Delta TFP_{j0})$			
		Exporters	*w/Net exposure*	*Markup from translog production*
	(1)	*(2)*	*(3)*	*(4)*
$(\Delta RER_{jS} - \Delta RER_{j0})$	-0.945**	-1.118*	-0.902**	-0.958**
	(0.394)	(0.584)	(0.414)	(0.391)
$(\Delta RER_{jS} - \Delta RER_{j0})$ × Export Exposure	0.330	-0.316		0.311
	(0.760)	(0.809)		(0.750)
$(\Delta RER_{jS} - \Delta RER_{j0})$ × Input import/Cost	0.957	0.671		-0.127
	(2.469)	(3.076)		(2.238)
$(\Delta RER_{jS} - \Delta RER_{j0})$ × Net Exposure			0.160	
			(0.793)	
$(\Delta RER_{jS} - \Delta RER_{j0})$ × Import penetration	2.848*	4.597**	2.745	2.993*
	(1.506)	(2.032)	(1.672)	(1.716)
Export exposure (Export/sales)	0.406	0.221		0.411*
	(0.252)	(0.261)		(0.242)
Intermediate input import/cost	0.548	0.553		0.061
	(0.919)	(1.154)		(0.796)
Net exposure			0.304	
			(0.262)	
Import penetration	1.061**	1.709**	1.031*	1.124*
	(0.522)	(0.712)	(0.582)	(0.599)
Export dummy	0.030	0.044*	0.033	0.039
	(0.020)	(0.025)	(0.022)	(0.024)
Import dummy	0.013		0.028	-0.007
	(0.048)		(0.047)	(0.046)
Employment	-0.021	-0.039	-0.002	-0.040
	(0.050)	(0.050)	(0.040)	(0.043)
R&D intensity	0.572	0.627	0.492	0.500
	(0.691)	(1.034)	(0.662)	(0.729)
HHI	0.082	-0.679	0.133	0.093
	(0.441)	(0.606)	(0.431)	(0.457)
$(\Delta Markup_{j,S} - \Delta Markup_{j,0})$	-0.083**	-0.084*	-0.081*	-0.129***
	(0.034)	(0.050)	(0.042)	(0.036)
$(\Delta DS_{j,S} - \Delta DS_{j,0})$	-0.023	0.001	-0.022	-0.011
	(0.016)	(0.025)	(0.016)	(0.017)
Observations (# of Firms)	2,573	1,585	2,573	2,464

Note: Bootstrap standard errors are reported in parentheses. *, **, and *** indicate significance at the 10%, 5%, and 1% levels, respectively. All controls used are values at base year, 2006.

Table 8.5 presents the results for the DID estimation that identifies the effect of a sharp and *persistent* RER depreciation during 2007–2009 on firm-level productivity. In parallel to Table 8.4, Column (1) shows the estimation results when we include all types of firms while Column (2) shows the result restricting the sample to only exporting firms. Column (3) includes the net exposure term instead of the export and import exposure separately and Column (4) shows the results when alternative markup estimates are used.

While the coefficients on RER change are significantly negative in all columns, we need to consider the interaction terms of RER changes together with this result to examine the total effect of RER changes on productivity. Interestingly, the coefficients on the interaction terms of export share and changes in RER growth between the shock period (2006–2010) and common period (2010–2013) are no longer significant. This suggests that the positive effect of RER depreciation on exporting firms' productivity shown in Table 8.4 is not sustained when the depreciation persists.

The coefficients on the interactions of RER changes and import penetration are significant and positive [except for Column (3)]. The result of this channel is in contrast to the yearly analysis of Table 8.4. This suggests that firms in industries with higher import penetration face greater productivity loss during *persistent* RER depreciation despite relatively better price conditions for domestic import competing firms than importing firms. The results of the export share and import penetration channels suggest efficiency losses in response to persistent RER depreciation. Moreover, the changes in markup growth between the shock and post-shock periods, rather, have negative effects on changes in TFP growth.

Our finding is consistent with Harris' (2001), who found a positive RER depreciation effect on productivity in the short run, which turns out to be negative in the long run, using industry-level data from 14 countries. In line with his research, our firm-level results also imply a downside to exchange rate manipulation for promoting exports.

8.4.2 Quantification of the marginal effect of RER depreciation

Using the results in both Tables 8.4 and 8.5, Figure 8.2 first evaluates the exact marginal effects of yearly and persistent RER depreciation shocks on productivity in terms of firm export exposure. In Panel A of Figure 8.2, we show the marginal effect of year-by-year RER change on productivity in a (thick) navy line. The dotted lines indicate the 90% confidence intervals. The results show the positive marginal effect of RER depreciation, which means that RER depreciation increases productivity over all values of export share. In addition, an upward sloping marginal effect curve indicates that firms with higher export share enjoy greater productivity gains in response to RER depreciation.

Panel B of Figure 8.2 shows that the marginal effects of persistent RER depreciation on productivity change in terms of export exposure in the initial year, 2006. While we observe a positive and upward sloping marginal effect curve in the year-by-year analysis, the DID approach identifying persistent RER

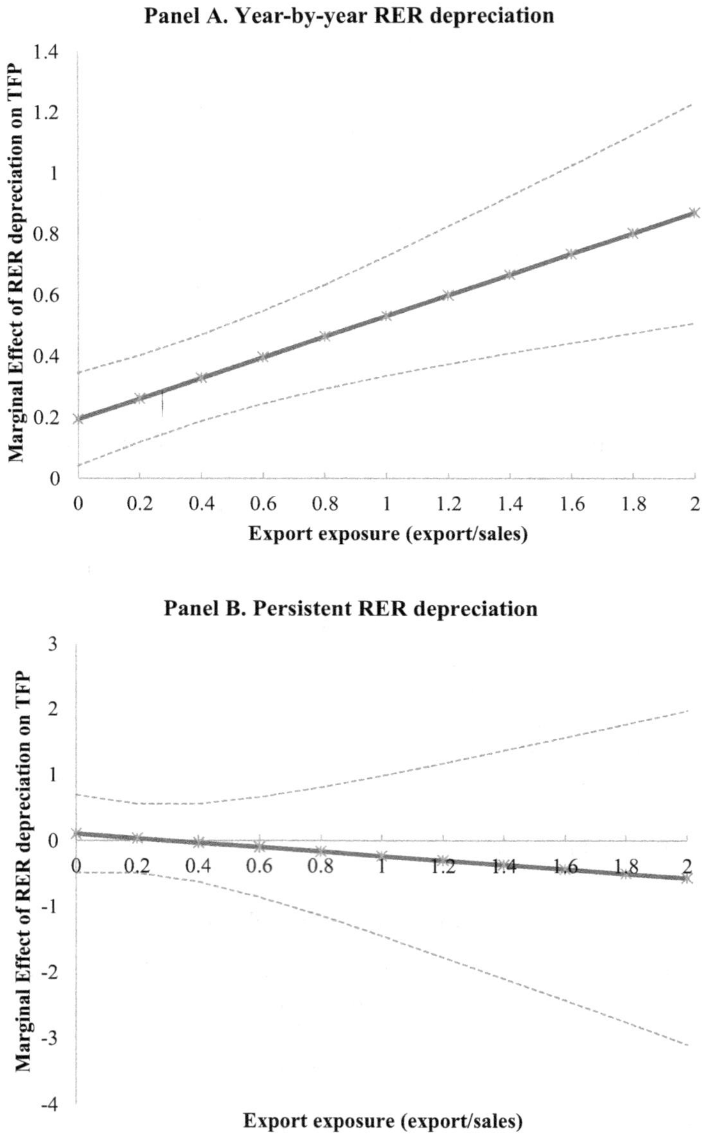

Figure 8.2 Marginal Effect of RER Depreciation on TFP in Export Exposure.

Note: The marginal effect of RER on TFP is given on the Y-axis in terms of firm's export exposure. Positive marginal effect indicates that RER depreciation increases TFP. The dashed lines indicate the 90% confidence intervals.

depreciation shows opposite results. The effect of persistent RER depreciation is close to zero for non-exporters while the effect turns negative for firms over a certain threshold of export share. Considering the 90% confidence intervals, we conclude that exporting firms do not enjoy any significant productivity gains in response to persistent RER depreciation.

8.4.3 Why did immediate and persistent RER depreciations affect productivity differently?

In this subsection, we attempt to examine the mechanism behind such different effects of RER depreciation illustrated in the previous two subsections. First, we simply plot our data. Figure 8.3 depicts the mean values of firm revenues (domestic sales + exports) and firm exports with the RER movement during 2006–2013. Despite the negative foreign demand shock during the 2008–2009 GFC, Korean manufacturing firms on average enjoyed an increase in both revenue and exports. Thus, the dramatic decline in RER of the Korean Won seems to have had stronger effects on sales of Korean firms than the negative demand shock. In addition, firm revenues and exports move very closely to firm TFPs. This positive relationship between revenues and TFPs drops a hint of the existence of the scale economy, which means that firms expanding their sales were able to increase productivity.

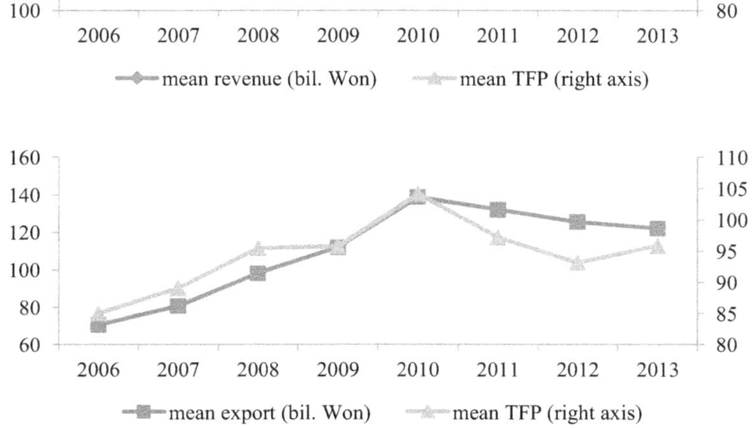

Figure 8.3 Changes in Revenue, Export and TFP.

For a detailed investigation of efficiency gain, we reiterate our main regression in Column (1) of Table 8.4 for the industries with IRS and non-IRS. Table 8.6 exhibits the estimates on industry production function. In addition, we test the null hypothesis that the firm production function exhibits constant returns to scale (CRS) and report this in the last column of Table 8.6. Using the two-sided test, we find that the production functions of 11 industries out of a total of 21 do not reject IRS, suggesting that firms in some industries indeed enjoy scale effects. In terms of estimated coefficients on output elasticities of labor and capital, the sum of coefficients are strictly greater than 1 in three industries such as coke, refined petroleum products, chemicals and chemical products, and pharmaceutical products.

For comparison purposes, we depict the marginal effects of yearly RER depreciation on productivity for firms in both industries together in Figure 8.4.[13] The navy line indicates the marginal effects of RER depreciation on productivity for firms in industries exhibiting IRS. The red line indicates those in industries exhibiting non-IRS. The dotted lines represent the 90% confidence intervals. We also describe the distribution of firms with respect to the mean value of their export shares during the sample period. The blue and red bars indicate a fraction of firms in IRS and non-IRS industries respectively at their value of export share (i.e., the blue bar at 0.2 means that about 60% of firms in the IRS industries have their export exposure between 0 and 0.2).

The results echo our main findings in that firms with a higher export share enjoy greater productivity gains in response to RER depreciation in both types of industries. More interestingly, our results reveal that firms in industries with IRS generally have greater productivity gains than those in industries with non-IRS. The positive marginal effect of yearly RER depreciation is greater for about 90% of the firms with IRS (export exposure less than 1) than those with non-IRS. This implies that RER depreciation increases productivity via scale expansion. This scale effect is more salient for firms in IRS industries.

While the year-by-year effect of depreciation had positive effects on firm productivity through economies of scale, the positive effect is not sustained in response to persistent RER depreciation. Persistent RER depreciation will lead domestic firms to less foreign competition, which in turn discourages them to innovate or to upgrade productivity. To examine this mechanism, we split our full sample into two sub-samples in terms of firms' R&D growth because investment in R&D is one of the most important attributes for productivity upgrade (e.g., Griliches 1986, 1992; Nadiri, 1993; Hall and Mairesse, 1995; Griffith et al. 2006). Since the median of R&D growth of total firms in our sample is zero during the RER shock period, we use a zero R&D growth as the threshold of splitting the sample.

In Figure 8.5, the navy line indicates the marginal effects of persistent RER depreciation on productivity (growth) for firms with positive R&D growth and the red line indicates those with negative R&D growth. The dotted lines indicate the 90% confidence intervals. We again depict the distribution of firms

Table 8.6 Estimates of Production Functions for 21 Manufacturing Industries

Industry	*KSIC Code*	*Estimated coeff.*		*TFP*	*(S.D.)*	*Test of Constant Returns to Scale:*
		Labor	*Capital*			
Food	10	0.55	0.09	5.26	(1.08)	30.65 ($p = 0.0000$)
Beverage	11	0.66	0.16	4.94	(0.91)	0.66 ($p = 0.4157$)*
Textiles	13	0.51	0.15	4.13	(0.95)	4.87 ($p = 0.0273$)
Wearing apparel	14	0.75	0.16	4.639	(1.049)	1.01 ($p = 0.3152$)*
Wood products (excl. furniture)	16	0.18	0.44	3.454	(1.255)	0.55 ($p = 0.4571$)*
Manufacture of pulp, paper, and paper products	17	0.64	0.13	4.457	(0.798)	4.66 ($p = 0.0309$)
Coke, refined petroleum products	19	0.97	0.46	0.308	(1.058)	1.11 ($p = 0.2912$)*
Chemicals and chemical products	20	0.77	0.24	3.258	(0.863)	0.01 ($p = 0.9367$)*
Pharmaceutical products	21	1.04	0.18	2.554	(0.669)	3.54 ($p = 0.0598$)*
Rubber and plastic products	22	0.4	0.41	2.66	(0.756)	5.08 ($p = 0.0242$)
Nonmetallic and mineral products	23	0.3	0.29	4.46	(0.938)	12.95 ($p = 0.0003$)
Basic metals	24	0.48	0.14	5.266	(0.982)	30.00 ($p = 0.0000$)
Manufacture of fabricated metal products (excl. machinery and furniture)	25	0.5	0.23	4.013	(0.802)	19.63 ($p = 0.0000$)
Manufacture of electronic components, boards, and computers	26	0.3	0.39	3.502	(1.062)	25.09 ($p = 0.0000$)
Manufacture of watches and clocks, optical instruments, and photographic equipment	27	0.6	0.4	2.223	(0.846)	0.00 ($p = 0.9931$)*
Electrical equipment	28	0.65	0.32	2.506	(0.833)	0.05 ($p = 0.8217$)*
Other machinery and equipment	29	0.4	0.28	4.123	(0.845)	29.80 ($p = 0.0000$)
Manufacture of bodies for motor vehicles, trailers, and semitrailers	30	0.4	0.35	3.14	(0.833)	11.96 ($p = 0.0005$)
Manufacture of other transport equipment n.e.c.	31	0.37	0.4	3.048	(0.919)	2.12 ($p = 0.1455$)*
Manufacture of furniture	32	0.43	0.3	3.987	(0.89)	1.07 ($p = 0.3014$)*
Other manufacturing	33	0.44	0.26	4.12	(1.018)	2.65 ($p = 0.1038$)*

Note: The table reports a two-sided test. For one side of the test for IRS, the p-value can be obtained by dividing the reported p-value in half. * denotes the industry with production function not rejecting IRS. Using this two-sided test, we find that the production functions of 11 industries of a total of 21 do not reject IRS, suggesting that firms in some industries indeed enjoy scale effects. In terms of estimated coefficients on output elasticities of labor and capital, the sum of coefficients are strictly greater than 1 in three industries in bold such as coke, refined petroleum products, chemicals and chemical products, and pharmaceutical products.

in terms of their export shares at the initial year, 2006. The blue and red bars indicate a fraction of firms with positive and negative R&D growth respectively at their value of export share in 2006 (i.e., the blue bar at 0.2 means that about 70% of firms with positive R&D growth have their export exposure between 0 and 0.2).

Persistent RER depreciation has almost a null effect on productivity for firms with positive R&D growth: the persistent RER depreciation effect turns out to be positive and becomes greater as the firm's export share increases (although it is statistically insignificant). However, the persistent depreciation has negative effects on productivity for those with negative R&D growth and its negative RER effect is amplified when export share increases. This sub-sample result supports the idea that persistent depreciation discourages innovation effort, thereby lowering firm efficiency.

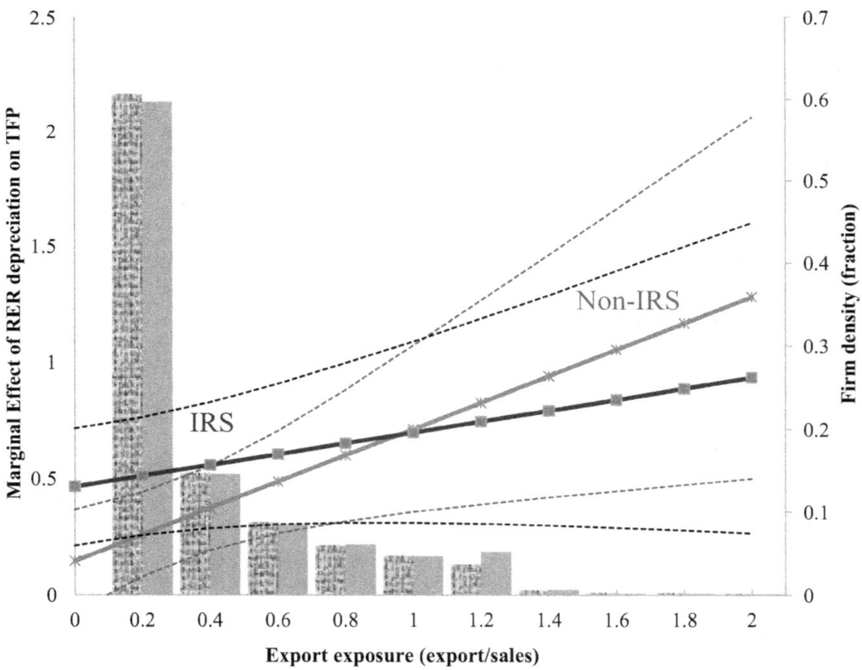

Figure 8.4 Yearly RER Deprecation: IRS vs Non-IRS.

Note: The marginal effect of RER depreciation on TFP is given on the Y-axis in terms of export exposure. Positive marginal effect indicates that RER depreciation increases TFP. The dashed lines indicate the 90% confidence intervals. IRS industries indicate the industries that cannot reject the null hypothesis the sum of coefficients on labor and capital is greater than 1, otherwise non-IRS industries. The blue and red bars indicate a fraction of firms in the IRS and non-IRS industry respectively at their value of export share.

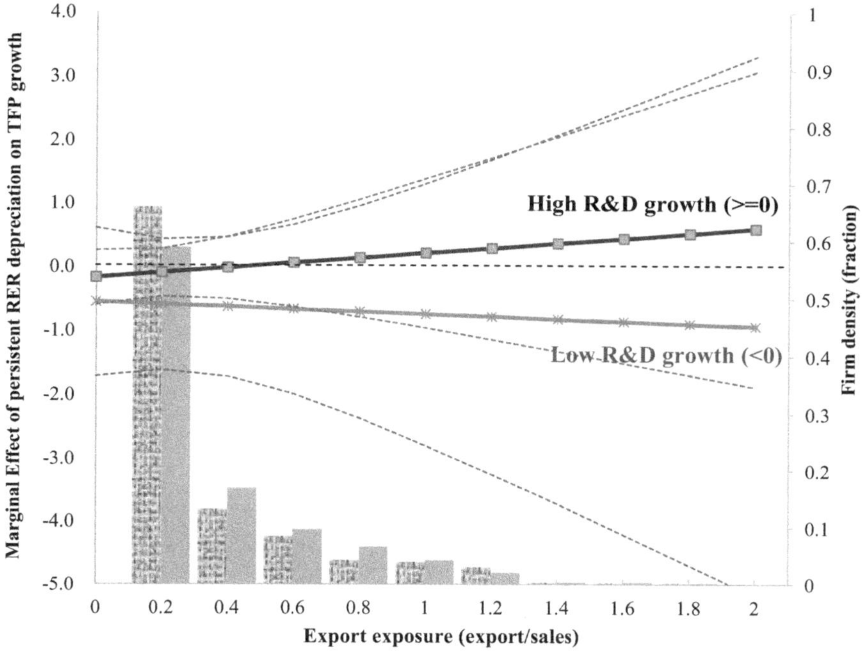

Figure 8.5 Persistent RER Depreciation: R&D Intensity Growth.

Note: The marginal effect of persistent RER depreciation on TFP growth is given on the Y-axis in terms of export exposure at the initial year, 2006. Positive marginal effect indicates that RER depreciation increases TFP. The dashed lines indicate the 90% confidence intervals. The median and mean values of R&D growth of firms during 2006–2010 are 0 and -0.002 respectively. High R&D growth indicates firms with R&D growth greater than and equal to zero during the RER shock period and low R&D growth indicates those with R&D growth less than zero. The blue and red bars indicate a fraction of firms with positive and negative R&D growth respectively at their value of export share in 2006.

8.5 Robustness checks

8.5.1 Alternative productivity measures and alternative base year

As various methods are proposed for measuring TFP, we run our yearly analysis in Table 8.4 on the alternative firm performance and productivity measures and present the results in Table 8.7. The first column shows the results with labor productivity as the dependent variable. Here, labor productivity is defined as a log of value added divided by number of workers. Column (2) presents the regression results using TFP based on system-generalized method of moments (GMM) as an alternative TFP measure to address endogeneity in TFP and factor use. Column (3) shows the estimation result when we restrict our sample to continuing firms during our sample period, 2006–2013.

Table 8.7 Robustness I: Y-b-Y Analysis with Alternative TFP Measures

Dependent Variable	*Labor Productivity*	*ln(TFP) (System GMM)*	*ln(TFP_{ijt})*
	Full sample		*Continuing firms since 2006*
	(1)	*(2)*	*(3)*
ln(RER_{jt})	-0.114	-0.177**	-0.025
	(0.100)	(0.075)	(0.105)
ln(RER_{jt}) × Export Exposure (*t*–1)	-0.380***	-0.223**	-0.350***
	(0.117)	(0.091)	(0.126)
ln(RER_{jt}) × Inter.input import/Cost (*t*–1)	0.805**	0.108	0.742*
	(0.325)	(0.283)	(0.387)
ln(RER_{jt}) × Import penetration (*t*–1)	-0.417**	-0.550***	-0.611***
	(0.209)	(0.129)	(0.230)
Export Exposure (*t*–1)	1.689***	1.007**	1.563***
	(0.514)	(0.404)	(0.556)
Intermediate input import/Cost (*t*–1)	-3.473**	-0.498	-3.147*
	(1.424)	(1.239)	(1.687)
Import penetration (*t*–1)	1.772*	2.287***	2.582**
	(0.910)	(0.566)	(1.006)
Export dummy (*t*–1)	0.002	0.001	-0.005
	(0.015)	(0.011)	(0.018)
Import dummy (*t*–1)	0.008	0.003	0.022
	(0.012)	(0.009)	(0.014)
Employment (*t*–1)	0.082***	0.168***	0.020
	(0.021)	(0.033)	(0.028)
R&D intensity (*t*–1)	-0.763**	-0.449	-0.959***
	(0.321)	(0.387)	(0.322)
Squared R&D intensity (*t*–1)	0.446	-0.184	0.466
	(0.638)	(0.679)	(0.609)
HHI (*t*–1)	0.011	0.098	0.054
	(0.156)	(0.106)	(0.176)
GFC dummy	-0.059***	-0.075***	-0.048***
	(0.010)	(0.007)	(0.010)
Markup	0.020	0.132***	0.011
	(0.025)	(0.024)	(0.027)
Firm fixed effects	Yes	Yes	Yes
Observations	32,582	28,134	22,781
R-squared	0.801	0.998	0.890

Note: Clustered bootstrap standard errors at firm level are reported in parentheses. *, **, and *** are significance at the 10%, 5%, and 1% levels, respectively. A constant term is included but not reported.

The first channel of export exposure appears robust through Columns (1)–(3). The results confirm our main message that the positive effect of RER depreciation on productivity is more salient among firms with higher export exposure in foreign markets. The effect of the second channel gains significance in Column (1) and Column (3). This supports our hypothesis that firms with high foreign input shares will suffer productivity losses because foreign inputs become more expensive, precluding some firms from importing high quality foreign inputs. Consistent with the main result presented in Table 8.4, the coefficients representing the third channel are all statistically significant and show negative signs.

Table 8.8 presents the robustness check of our DID analysis. First, Columns (1) and (2) introduce the alternative measures for TFP using labor productivity and TFP using system GMM. The coefficients on the interaction terms with export exposure are statistically insignificant. As the firm-level data pertain to only 2006–2013, we cannot compare the depreciation shock period with the pre-shock period as in the typical DID method. Instead, we compare the shock period with the post-shock period. To justify this methodology, we run a

Table 8.8 Robustness II: DID Analysis with Alternative TFP Measures and Base Year

Dependent variable	*($\Delta TFP_{jS} - \Delta TFP_{j0}$)*		
	Labor productivity	*TFP (System GMM)*	*TFP (Levinsohn and Petrin)*
			Alternative base year = 2010
	(1)	(2)	(3)
($\Delta RER_{jS} - \Delta RER_{j0}$)	-0.628	-0.379	-0.663
	(0.383)	(0.693)	(0.446)
($\Delta RER_{jS} - \Delta RER_{j0}$) × Export Exposure	0.136	-0.414	-0.475
	(0.671)	(0.665)	(0.663)
($\Delta RER_{jS} - \Delta RER_{j0}$) × Input import/ Cost	1.106	-2.369	2.131
	(2.647)	(2.473)	(2.756)
($\Delta RER_{jS} - \Delta RER_{j0}$) × Import penetration	1.841	0.092	1.525
	(1.635)	(4.228)	(1.714)
Export exposure (export/sales)	0.350	0.094	0.055
	(0.222)	(0.204)	(0.232)
Intermediate input import/cost	0.520	-0.709	0.863
	(0.973)	(0.717)	(0.921)
Import penetration	0.668	0.185	0.808
	(0.569)	(1.287)	(0.598)
Export dummy	0.021	-0.012	0.018
	(0.016)	(0.018)	(0.023)
Import dummy	0.023	0.054	0.034
	(0.050)	(0.038)	(0.057)
Employment	-0.034	-0.026	0.037
	(0.043)	(0.028)	(0.042)
R&D intensity	0.407	0.234	-3.716***
	(0.701)	(0.426)	(0.635)
HHI	0.531	0.407	-0.307
	(0.493)	(0.430)	(0.361)
($\Delta Markup_{j,S} - \Delta Markup_{j,0}$)	-0.078*	0.051	-0.103**
	(0.043)	(0.036)	(0.043)
($\Delta DS_{j,S} - \Delta DS_{j,0}$)	-0.028*	-0.021	-0.030*
	(0.015)	(0.015)	(0.018)
Observations (# of Firms)	2573	2573	2573

Note: Bootstrap standard errors are reported in parentheses. *, **, and *** are significance at the 10%, 5%, and 1% levels, respectively. A constant term is included but not reported.

robustness check using a different base year, 2010. The results are shown in Column (3). The results continue to support the loss of positive effect of persistent depreciation on productivity.

8.5.2 RER depreciation shock vs. negative demand shock during the global financial crisis

In the previous sections, we focused on the distinction between yearly RER depreciation and persistent RER depreciation. While an RER depreciation shock is possibly a positive attribute for better price conditions for firms to enjoy scale expansion, contributing to an increase in productivity, persistent RER depreciation can reduce productivity by hampering investment in innovation. However, the period we study includes the 2008–2009 GFC. While the overlap with the external shock period justifies that persistent RER depreciation in Korea was exogenous and was driven by external factors such as capital flight, one may argue that the RER shock can be mixed with other shocks such as a negative demand shock. The negative demand shock by the GFC is likely to decrease firm profitability, thereby reducing productivity. In contrast, this negative shock may also increase the competitive pressure. Surviving firms may have increased their productivity internally as low-productivity firms exited owing to deteriorating profitability. While our previous analyses control for this negative demand shock by including GFC dummies, Table 8.9 further compares the productivity responses of firms to two different shocks—the RER and GFC shocks—to better identify the RER shock.

Panels A and B of Table 8.9 give the results with yearly analysis and DID analysis respectively. In Column (1) of Panel A, we introduce the industry total export sales as an alternative measure for global demand shock to Korean firms. The first channel of export exposure by which yearly RERs affect productivity positively is still significant, even when we control for the negative demand shock during the GFC. Column (2) of Panel A shows the results with the net export exposure variable and its interaction terms, which are comparable to Column (3) of Table 8.5. Panel B shows the same analysis result of Table 8.6, including the negative demand shock, for our DID approach. Although we control for demand shocks with persistent RER depreciation shocks, our main results on persistent RER deprecation do not alter.

Table 8.9 RER Depreciation Shock vs. Negative Demand Shock

Panel A. Year-by-Year Analysis		
Dependent Variable	*ln* (TFP_{ijt})	
	(1)	(2)
$\ln(RER_{jt})$	0.110 (0.108)	0.120 (0.198)
Demand shock (DS)	−0.009 (0.016)	−0.007 (0.045)

Dependent Variable	*ln* (TFP_{ijt})	
$\ln(RER_{jt})$ × Export Exposure (*t*-1)	−0.416***	
	(0.152)	
DS × Export Exposure (*t*−1)	0.014	
	(0.016)	
$\ln(RER_{jt})$ × Int.inp.import/Cost (*t*−1)	0.897**	
	(0.394)	
DS × Int.inp. import/Cost (*t*−1)	0.058	
	(0.044)	
$\ln(RER_{jt})$ × Net Exposure (*t*-1)		−0.433**
		(0.153)
DS × Net Exposure (*t*−1)		0.012
		(0.016)
$\ln(RER_{jt})$ × Import penetration (*t*−1)	-0.743***	-0.743***
	(0.213)	(0.182)
DS × Import penetration (*t*−1)	0.133***	0.132
	(0.048)	(0.142)
Export exposure (export/sales) (*t*−1)	1.604**	
	(0.708)	
Intermediate input import/cost (*t*−1)	−4.852***	
	(1.818)	
Net exposure (*t*−1)		1.711**
		(0.645)
Import penetration (*t*−1)	0.737	0.754
	(1.244)	(3.156)
Export dummy (*t*−1)	0.001	0.004
	(0.015)	(0.024)
Import dummy (*t*−1)	0.025*	0.028
	(0.013)	(0.021)
Employment (*t*−1)	0.033	0.032
	(0.028)	(0.041)
R&D intensity (*t*−1)	−0.657*	−0.660**
	(0.347)	(0.257)
Squared R&D intensity (*t*−1)	−0.003	0.002
	(0.808)	(0.596)
HHI (*t*−1)	−0.047	−0.050
	(0.178)	(0.407)
Markup	0.019	0.019
	(0.027)	(0.056)
Firm fixed effects	Included	Included
Observations	23,686	23,686

Panel B. DID Analysis

Dependent Variable	$(\Delta TFP_{jS} - \Delta TFP_{j0})$	
	(1)	*(2)*
$(\Delta RER_{jS} - \Delta RER_{j0})$	−0.662	−0.652
	(0.465)	(0.463)
$(\Delta DS_{j,S} - \Delta DS_{j,0})$	−0.053*	−0.047
	(0.032)	(0.032)
$(\Delta RER_{jS} - \Delta RER_{j0})$ × Export Exposure	0.194	
	(0.835)	
$(\Delta DS_{j,S} - \Delta DS_{j,0})$ × Export Exposure	0.011	
	(0.059)	

(*Continued*)

Dependent Variable	*ln* (TFP_{ijt})	
$(\Delta RER_{jS} - \Delta RER_{j0})$ × Input import/Cost	-0.439 (2.228)	
$(\Delta DS_{j,S} - \Delta DS_{j,0})$ × Input import/Cost	0.405* (0.246)	
$(\Delta RER_{jS} - \Delta RER_{j0})$ × Net Exposure		0.291 (0.806)
$(\Delta DS_{j,S} - \Delta DS_{j,0})$ × Net Exposure		-0.020 (0.050)
$(\Delta RER_{jS} - \Delta RER_{j0})$ × Import penetration	1.574 (2.149)	1.322 (2.186)
$(\Delta DS_{j,S} - \Delta DS_{j,0})$ × Import penetration	0.134 (0.178)	0.159 (0.180)
Export exposure (export/sales)	0.376 (0.277)	
Intermediate input import/cost	-0.057 (0.754)	
Import penetration		0.349 (0.264)
Export dummy	0.784 (0.649)	0.722 (0.629)
Import dummy	0.030 (0.021)	0.033* (0.019)
Employment	0.006 (0.050)	0.026 (0.048)
R&D intensity	-0.019 (0.049)	-0.001 (0.039)
HHI	0.533 (0.613)	0.469 (0.686)
$(\Delta Markup_{j,S} - \Delta Markup_{j,0})$	0.108 (0.488)	0.144 (0.502)
Observations (# of Firms)	2,573	2,573

Note: DS indicates industry total foreign export that is a proxy for foreign demand. In Panel B, all controls are those in 2006. Bootstrap clustered standard errors are reported in parentheses. *, **, and *** indicate significance at the 10%, 5%, and 1% levels, respectively.

8.6 Conclusion and discussion

This study examined the effects of RER depreciation on productivity using Korean firm-level data for 2006–2013. In particular, we distinguished between yearly RER movements and the sharp and persistent RER depreciation of the Korean Won from 2007 to 2009 and analyzed the effect of each RER change on productivity.

Our year-by-year analysis shows that firm-level productivity increases for firms with higher export exposure in foreign markets in response to RER depreciation; however, this positive gain vanishes when we examine persistent RER depreciation through a DID analysis. RER depreciation leads to price competitiveness for domestic exporting firms relative to foreign firms, allowing exporting firms to enjoy scale expansion. In contrast, persistent RER depreciation hurts firm productivity especially for firms with negative R&D growth. We also find that persistent RER depreciation affects the productivity of domestic import-competing firms negatively in the industries with high import penetration, while RER depreciation temporarily increases their productivity through price competitiveness.

As Porter (1990) states, our result is so, possibly because the competitiveness gained by domestic firms from exchange rate depreciation is different from that gained by investment and innovation induced through competitive pressure. In addition, our result questions the policies of exchange rate undervaluation. Indeed, such policies help firms increase exports and achieve higher productivity temporarily. However, the positive effects on firm productivity may disappear when RER depreciation persists because sustained RER depreciation leads to less foreign competition and, in turn, discourages innovation.

8.7 Acknowledgements

We are grateful to Yong-Seok Choi, Chin Hee Hahn, Byungchae Jin, Dan Liu, Peter Morrow, Dionisius Narjoko, Shujiro Urata, Gregory Wright, Youzhi Yang, Miaojie Yu, an anonymous referee, and other participants in KAIST, Korea, SHUFE, China, Lipsey Memorial Panels, WEAI and ERIA workshop "Trade Policy Change and Firm Adjustment: A Search for the Underlying Mechanisms," Indonesia for their helpful comments and suggestions. This paper was prepared for 2014 Microdata Project, ERIA. We gratefully acknowledge financial support from ERIA. (ERIA-RD/RA-001-001-402/05/FY14). All remaining errors are our own.

Notes

1 Verdoorn's law implies a stable and positive causal relationship between output growth and productivity growth in manufacturing firms in the long run. Faster growth in output from higher demand increases productivity due to IRS, where the intuition is learning by doing (Verdoorn, 1949).

2 Eichengreen (2007) argues that first Japan, then Hong Kong, Singapore, South Korea, and Taiwan, and now China have gained economic growth through exchange rate undervaluation.

3 For example, Korea's trade dependence on international markets is high—the total trade volume of gross domestic product was 109.9% in 2012.

4 While previous models such as Bernard et al. (2003) and Melitz and Ottaviano (2008) suggest that increased efficiency yields higher markups, measured productivity is correlated positively with the efficiency component. Recent workhorse models in international trade such as Bernard, Eaton, Jensen, and Kortum (2003) and Melitz and Ottaviano (2008), show that RER mechanisms affect the productivity of exporters through changes in firm-level prices. In a Bertrand competition framework, Bernard, Eaton, Jensen, and Kortum (2003) imply that revenue-based productivity may increase in response to RER depreciation because limit pricing may force firms to charge higher prices in export markets. Melitz and Ottaviano (2008) suggest that revenue-based productivity increases owing to higher prices (markups) in export markets but less than proportional to the depreciation. Berman, Martin, and Mayer (2012) empirically find that exporters only partially counter depreciation by increasing prices. Thus, the measured productivity may increase from price changes even when the physical units sold by firms remain unchanged.

5 Note that Fung (2008) finds the scale effect of surviving firms under RER appreciation.

6 Previous studies on heterogeneous firms and endogenous markups suggest that firms with higher markups appear to be more productive. (e.g., Bernard, Eaton, Jenson, and Kortum 2003).

7 The last two channels could be analogous to the mechanism of how trade liberalization affects firm efficiency. Note that RER depreciation corresponds to an increase in import tariffs. Pavcnik (2002) finds that within plant productivity improves in the import-competing sector due to lower import tariffs. Schor (2004), Amiti and Konings (2007) and Topalova and Khandelwal (2011) find that both lower input tariffs and lower output tariffs lead to higher productivity gains. If we assume symmetry of the effect of RER on productivity, this implies that depreciation leads to lower productivity.

8 This omitted price variable bias in revenue based TFP was first discussed by Klette and Griliches (1996). The coefficient of the production function is potentially biased if the choice of inputs is correlated with the deviation of firm price from industry-level average prices.

9 The 26 major trade partners are Australia, Belgium, Canada, China, Germany, Spain, France, Greece, Indonesia, India, Ireland, Italy, Japan, Malaysia, the Netherlands, Norway, the Philippines, Russia, Singapore, South Africa, Sweden, Thailand, Turkey, Taiwan, the United Kingdom, and the United States.

10 This would hold even for firms selling goods only in the domestic market as foreign goods in this market lose price competitiveness. The scale effect would be pronounced for exporters as they easily expand their sales in both the domestic and foreign markets during depreciation.

11 Goldberg et al. (2010) also estimate that lower input tariffs lead to higher firm-level productivity. They argue that an increase of measured TFP comes from a wider range of intermediate inputs that have become available to Indian manufacturers.

12 The theoretic proof of this relation is shown in Campa and Goldberg (1995); Ekholm, Moxnes and Ulltveit-Moe (2012, p. 104).

13 The full regression results are available from the authors upon request.

References

Ackerberg, D. A., Caves, K., & Frazer, G. (2015). Identification properties of recent production function estimators. *Econometrica*, 83(6): 2411–2451.

Amiti, M., and Konings, J. 2007. Trade liberalization, intermediate inputs, and productivity: Evidence from Indonesia. *American Economic Review*, 97(5): 1611–38.

Baggs, J., Beaulieu, E., and Fung, L. 2009. Firm survival, performance, and the exchange rate. *Canadian Journal of Economics*, 42(2): 393–421.

Berman, N., Martin, P., and Mayer, T. 2012. How do different exporters react to exchange rate changes? *The Quarterly Journal of Economics*, 127(1): 437–92.

Bernard, A. B., Eaton, J., Jensen, J. B., and Kortum, S. S., 2003. Plants and productivity in international trade. *American Economic Review*, 93: 1268–90.

Bernard, A. B., Redding, S. J., and Schott, P. K. 2011. Multiproduct firms and trade liberalization. *The Quarterly Journal of Economics*, 126(3): 1271–318.

Campa, J. M., and Goldberg, L. S. 1995. Investment in manufacturing, exchange rates and external exposure. *Journal of International Economics*, 38(3–4): 297–320.

Campa, J. M., and Goldberg, L. S. 2001. Employment versus wage adjustment and the US dollar. *Review of Economics and Statistics*, 83(3): 477–89.

De Loecker, J. 2011. Product differentiation, multi-product firms and estimating the impact of trade liberalization on productivity. *Econometrica*, 79(5): 1407–51.

De Loecker, J., and Warzynski, F. 2012. Markups and firm-level export status. *American Economic Review*, 102(6): 2437–71.

Eckel, C., and Neary, J. P. (2010). Multi-product firms and flexible manufacturing in the global economy. *The Review of Economic Studies*, 77(1): 188–217.

Eichengreen, B. 2007. The real exchange rate and economic growth. *Social and Economic Studies*, 56(4): 7–20.

Ekholm, K., Moxnes, A., and Ulltveit-Moe, K. H. 2012. Manufacturing restructuring and the role of real exchange rate shocks. *Journal of International Economics*, 86: 101–17.

Fung, L. 2008. Large real exchange rate movements, firm dynamics, and productivity growth. *Canadian Journal of Economics*, 41(2): 391–424.

Fung, L., Baggs, J., and Beaulieu, E. 2011. Plant scale and exchange-rate-induced productivity growth. *Journal of Economics and Management Strategy*, 20(4): 1197–230.

Goldberg, P., Khandelwal, A., Pavcnik, N., and Topalova, P. 2010. Imported intermediate inputs and domestic product growth: Evidence from India. *Quarterly Journal of Economics*, 125(4): 1727–67.

Griffith, R., Huergo, E., Mairesse, J., and Peters, B. 2006. Innovation and productivity across four European countries. *Oxford Review of Economic Policy*, 22(4): 483–98.

Griliches, Z. 1986. Productivity, R and D, and basic research at the firm level in the 1970s. *The American Economic Review*, 76(1): 141–54.

Griliches, Z. 1992. The search for R&D spillovers. *The Scandinavian Journal of Economics*, 94: S29–47.

Harris, R.G. 2001. Is there a case for exchange rate-induced productivity changes? Department of Economics, Simon Fraser University, Canadian Institute for Advanced Research.

Kancs, D., and Siliverstovs, B. 2012. *R&D and non-linear productivity growth of heterogeneous firms*, KOF Working Papers No. 315, October, Zurich.

Klette, T.J. and Griliches, Z. 1996. The inconsistency of common scale estimators when output prices are unobserved and endogenous. *Journal of Applied Econometrics*, 11: 343–61.

Krugman, P.R. 1979. Increasing returns, monopolistic competition, and international trade. *Journal of International Economics*, 9(4): 469–79.

Levinsohn, J., and Petrin, A., 2003. Estimating production functions using inputs to control for unobservables. *Review of Economic Studies*, 70: 317–42.

Li, H., Ma, H., & Xu, Y. 2015. How do exchange rate movements affect Chinese exports?—A firm-level investigation. *Journal of International Economics*, 97(1): 148–61.

Mayer, T., Melitz, M.J., and Ottaviano, G. 2014. Market size, competition, and the product mix of exporters. *American Economic Review*, 104(2): 495–536.

Melitz, M. J., and Ottaviano, G. 2008. Market size, trade, and productivity. *Review of Economic Studies*, 75(1): 291–316.

Nadiri, M. I. (1993). *Innovations and technological spillovers* (No. w4423). National Bureau of Economic Research.

Olley, G. S., and Pakes, A. 1996. The dynamics of productivity in the telecommunications equipment industry. *Econometrica*, 64: 1263–97.

Pavcnik, N. 2002. Trade liberalization, exit, and productivity improvements: Evidence from Chilean plants. *The Review of Economic Studies*, 69(1): 245–76.

Porter, M. E. 1990. *The competitive advantage of nations*. Cambridge, MA: Harvard University Press.

Rodrik, D. 2008. The real exchange rate and economic growth. *Brookings Papers on Economic Activity*, 2008(2): 365–412.

Schor, A, 2004. Heterogeneous productivity response to tariff reduction. Evidence from Brazilian manufacturing firms. *Journal of Development Economics*, 75(2): 373–96.

Tomlin, B. 2014. Exchange rate fluctuations, plant turnover and productivity. *International Journal of Industrial Organization*, 35: 12–28.

Tomlin, B., and Fung, L. 2015. Exchange rate movements and the distribution of productivity. *Review of International Economics*, 23(4): 782–809.

Topalova, P., and Khandelwal, A. 2011. Trade liberalization and firm productivity: The case of India. *The Review of Economics and Statistics*, 93(3): 995–1009.

Trefler, D. 2004. The long and short of the Canada–U.S. Free Trade Agreement. *American Economic Review*, 94(4): 870–95.

Verdoorn, J. P. 1949. On the factors determining the growth of labor productivity. In L. Pasinetti (Ed.), *Italian Economic Papers: Vol. II.* Oxford: Oxford University Press, 1993.

Appendix I

Estimation of firm level productivity

To estimate our firm-level TFP, we specify the production function for each industry as follows:

$$v_{it} = \beta_0 + \beta_l l_{it} + \beta_k k_{it} + \omega_{it} + \eta_{it} \tag{A1}$$

where v_{it} is the logarithm of firm i's output measured as value added, l_{it} is the logarithm of freely variable labor input, and k_{it} is the logarithm of real capital, which is a state variable. Here, value added is calculated as revenue less cost and deflated with the producer price index by industry and year, labor input is measured with the number of workers, and real capital is defined as fixed assets deflated by the capital equipment price index. The deflators we use here are price indexes published by the Bank of Korea. The error term can be decomposed with the transmitted productivity component given as $\omega_{i,t}$ and an i.i.d. component $\eta_{i,t}$.

For the first stage of estimation, we have Equation (A2),

$$v_{it} = \beta_l l_{it} + \phi_t(k_{it}, m_{it}) + \eta_{it} \tag{A2}$$

where $\phi_t(k_{it}, m_{it}) = \beta_0 + \beta_k k_{it} + \omega_t(k_{it}, m_{it})$ and m_{it} the logarithm of material cost that proxies the unobserved productivity, ω_{it}. The material cost m_{it} is measured as the expenditure on the intermediate material inputs deflated by intermediate input deflators. In this study, we are able to deflate foreign inputs and domestic inputs separately by using a foreign intermediate deflator and a domestic intermediate deflator. We can consistently estimate the parameters of β_l and ϕ_t by substituting a third-order polynomial approximation in k_{it} and m_{it} in place of $\phi_t(k_{it}, m_{it})$ using OLS:

$$v_{it} = \delta_0 + \beta_l l_{it} + \sum_{i=0}^{3} \sum_{j=0}^{3-i} \delta_{ij} k_{it}^{i} m_{it}^{j} + \eta_{it} \tag{A3}$$

The second stage identifies the coefficient β_k by computing the estimated value of ϕ_{it} using $\hat{\phi}_{it} = \hat{v}_{it} - \hat{\beta}_l l_{it} = \hat{\delta}_0 + \sum_{i=0}^{3}\sum_{j=0}^{3-i}\hat{\delta}_{ij}k_{it}^{i}m_{it}^{j} - \hat{\beta}_l l_{it}$

For any candidate value β^*_k, we can compute a prediction for ω_{it}, using $\hat{\omega}_{it} = \hat{\phi}_{it} - \beta^*_k k_{it}$.

Appendix II

Estimation of firm-level markup (De Loecker and Warzynski, 2012)

Consider the cost minimization problem for a firm i at time t with value-added production technology, $Q_{it} = f(L_{it}, K_{it}\omega_{it})$, where L_{it} denotes labor, which is the only variable input, K_{it} is capital and ω_{it} denotes firm-level efficiency. Assume that $Q_{it}(\cdot)$ is continuous and twice differentiable for each of its arguments. Let w_{it} and r_{it} be firm-specific input prices for labor and capital, respectively. Then, the first-order condition for cost minimization indicates that

$$\frac{\partial Q_{it}(\cdot)}{\partial L_{it}} = \frac{1}{\lambda_{it}} w_{it} \tag{A4}$$

where λ_{it} measures the marginal cost of production. By multiplying both sides of Equation (A4) by labor share to output L_{it}/Q_{it} and rearranging it, we obtain

$$\frac{\partial Q_{it}(\cdot)}{\partial L_{it}} \frac{L_{it}}{Q_{it}(\cdot)} = \frac{1}{\lambda_{it}} \frac{w_{it} L_{it}}{Q_{it}} \tag{A5}$$

The markup, μ_{it} is simply defined as $\mu_{it} = \frac{P_{it}}{\lambda_{it}}$, where P_{it} denotes output price for a firm i at time t. Then, we can rearrange Equation (A5) as follows

$$\mu_{it} = \frac{\partial Q_{it}}{\partial L_{it}} \frac{L_{it}}{Q_{it}} \Big/ \frac{w_{it} L_{it}}{P_{it} Q_{it}} = \frac{\theta_{it}^{L}}{\alpha_{it}^{L}} \tag{A6}$$

where θ_{it}^{L} denotes the output elasticity of labor input and α_{it}^{L} is the share of expenditure on labor input in total sales $(P_{it}Q_{it})$. The latter can be obtained directly from the data and, thus, θ_{it}^{L} only needs to be estimated to obtain the markup measure, μ_{it} for a firm i at time t.

In order to estimate the output elasticity, De Loecker and Warzynski (2012) introduced a detailed procedure of production function estimation. In addition, they considered production functions with a scalar Hicks-neutral productivity term and common technology parameters across the set of producers. According to these two conditions, they express the production function as follows

$$Q_{it} = f(L_{it}, K_{it}, \beta_L)\exp(\omega_{it}) \tag{A7}$$

where a set of time-invariant coefficients β_L govern the transformation of labor to units of output, combined with the firm's productivity, ω_{it}. De Loecker and Warzynski (2012) argue that the main advantage of assuming production technologies of (A7) is its reliance on the proxy methods suggested by OP, LP, and Ackerberg, Caves and Frazer (2015) to obtain consistent estimates of β_L. Hence, by estimating the log version of Equation (A4), they recover the output elasticity of labor, $\theta_{it}^{L} = \frac{\partial \ln Q(\cdot)}{\partial \ln L_{it}}$. Refer to De Loecker and Warzynski (2012) for details of the estimation procedure of the production function parameters.

9 Worker training, firm productivity, and trade liberalization

Evidence from Chinese firms

Qing Liu, Larry Dongxiao Qiu and Miaojie Yu

9.1 Introduction

Firm productivity and trade liberalization is an important research topic in international trade and economic development. Growing empirical research using firm-level microdata has found evidence that trade liberalization from both input goods and final goods fosters firm productivity. Amiti and Konings (2007) used Indonesian firm-level data to find that firms' gains from reduction of input tariffs are at least twice as much as those from a reduction of output tariffs. Similarly, Topalova and Khandelwal (2011) found close evidence for Indian firms. Using a Chinese firm-level dataset, Yu (2015) found that the impact of input tariff reductions on productivity improvement, overall, is weaker than that of output tariff reductions, since processing imports is already duty-freein China. Both tariff reductions are found to contribute at least 14.5% to economy-wide productivity growth of China.

However, as noted by Bernard and Jensen (2004), a key unanswered question is how firms obtain the characteristics that allow them to easily enter the export market. Or equivalently, "What are the mechanisms through which trade policy changes affect welfare gains from trade?" Inspired by Melitz (2003), Lileeva and Trefler (2010) and Melitz and Trefler (2012) forcefully argue that foreign market access matters for firm innovation and, hence, for firm productivity. This paper argues that worker training is another important mechanism, in addition to firm innovation, through which productivity improvement and export growth are realized. With tariff reductions on final goods, Chinese domestic firms face tougher import competition. The competitive effect is stronger for low *ex-ante* productive firms, which in turn input more into labor training to boost their *ex-post* productive firms. With realized productivity growth, firms are able to maintain their international competitive advantage and export more. The idea can be illustrated by the following Figure 9.1.

Different from well-documented mechanisms such as firm innovation, in Figure 9.1 we introduce a new channel—labor training—through which trade liberalization affects firm productivity. Using Chinese firm-level production data from 2004 to 2006, we find strong evidence for such a mechanism. Our extensive empirical search supports the following novel findings.

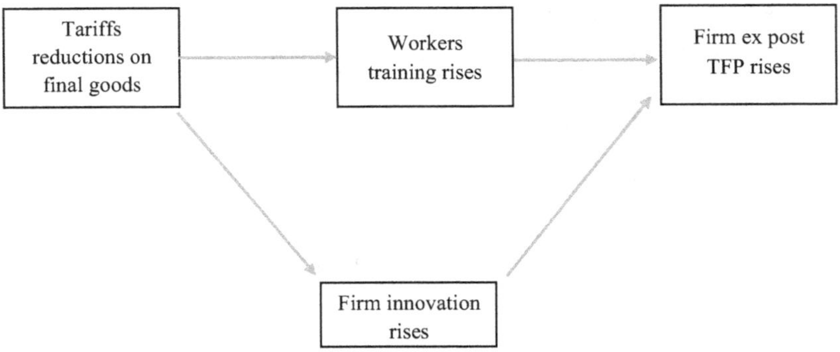

Figure 9.1 The Mechanism.

First, we find strong evidence that output trade liberalization fosters firm productivity as before. Second, with fiercer import competition, firms experience a decrease in profitability and hence are less likely to invest in firm training. Third, lower productive firms are more likely to train their workers, as otherwise they would collapse and exit from the market. The lower the firm's productivity, the higher the firm's worker training expenses. Finally, the effect of output trade liberalization on firm productivity is more pronounced for firms with more training investment.

Note that the first one is already well-documented in the literature. In this paper, we start from this exercise to echo to the well-accepted firm heterogeneity theory and to be in line with previous works. However, the other empirical predictions are novel. To emphasize the role of import competition, in this paper we focus on trade liberalization on final goods. Still, as robustness checks, we include foreign trade liberalization as control variables in our estimates and discuss the case with an input tariff cut.

We make the following three contributions to the literature. First, we identify a new mechanism through which trade liberalization affects firm productivity. Trade literature pervasively emphasizes the role of investment in research and development (R&D) for firms' exposure to global competition but neglects the role of investment in labor training, with only a few exceptions (e.g., Aw et al., 2011, Helpman et al., 2010, etc.). But the importance of worker training is recognized in development economics. For instance, Acemoglou and Pischke (1998) emphasized that firms invest in general skill of workers when labor market frictions compress the structure of wages. Such a theoretical thought is also warmly endorsed by reality.[1]

Second, we provide evidence on the nexus between trade liberalization, worker training, and productivity for China, the second largest economy and the largest trading country in the world. Due to increasing labor costs in recent years (Cai, 2010), Chinese firms have tried their very best to boost firm productivity to maintain their international competitiveness. In addition to inputting more into

R&D, Chinese manufacturing firms invest a lot in worker training, as illustrated in the next section using Chinese firm-level production data. However, previous firm-level research on China mainly focused on firm productivity and exports but kept silent on the role of firms' training behavior. Our paper also aims to fill in this gap.

Third, we make contributions to the related identification problem. The econometric challenges of this paper come from the following empirical identifications. In particular, we need to empirically distinguish between *ex-ante* and *ex-post* TFP. However, typical empirical research use a Solow residual to proxy firm TFP, which by definition is an *ex-post* measure. The recent developed semi-parametric techniques such as Olley and Pakes (1996), Levinsohn and Petrin (2003), and even system Generalized Method of Moments (GMM) cannot solve this challenge. In spired by Feenstra et al. (2014), we first estimate and calculate an *ex-ante* TFP measure in the estimates.

Our paper combines two strands of the growing literature. The first strand is on the nexus between trade liberalization and labor training. Baldwin (1992) was one of the pioneers who emphasized the dynamic effect of trade liberalization on human capital accumulation. However, not many empirical works directly investigate the importance of the specific channel—labor training. One outstanding exception is Li (2009) who investigated the effect of the import penetration ratio on firm training using American household-level data from the National Longitudinal Survey of Youth (NLSY). He found that import competition has a negative impact on training provision. Some recent theoretical papers such as Deardorff (2000) and Long et al. (2007) also looked at how trade liberalization affects workers' skill acquisition/accumulation decisions and, thus, how this affects wage inequality. Lai and Ng (2014) used a subjective measure of market competition and found that increased product market competition is strongly associated with more training provision. Gorlitz and Stiebale (2011) also found no impact of competition on firm training provision.

The second strand of literature is on the nexus between labor training and firm productivity, which has no conclusive results (see a review by Blundell et al. 1999). Early works like Blundell et al. (1996) generally used wage rates to proxy firm productivity to study the effect of training on productivity due to the unavailability of a direct productivity measure. Recent studies like Conti (2005) and Dearden et al. (2006) have made efforts to construct industry-level panel data to test the nexus between labor training and firm productivity. Finally, there is a small but growing subset of papers like Black and Lynch (2001) and Almeida and Carneiro (2009), who rely on firm-level panel data to investigate the effect of training on firm productivity. However, the results in these papers are constrained by the limited representativeness of the small sample size of the data.

The rest of this paper is organized as follows. Section 8.2 describes Chinese firm-level data. Section 8.3 sketches the bones of our empirical specifications. Section 8.4 presents our estimation results. Section 8.5 briefly discusses policy implications and our conclusions.

9.2 Data

Our sample is derived from a rich, firm-level panel dataset that covers between 162,885 firms (in 2000) and 336,768 firms (in 2007). The data are collected and maintained by China's National Bureau of Statistics (NBS) in an annual survey of manufacturing enterprises. Complete information on the three major accounting statements (i.e., the balance sheet, profit and loss account, and cash flow statement) is available. In brief, the dataset covers two types of manufacturing firms—all state-owned enterprises (SOEs) and non-SOEs whose annual sales exceed RMB 5 million (or equivalently, US$770,000, under current exchange rate).[2] The dataset includes more than 100 financial variables listed in the main accounting statements of these firms.

Although the dataset contains rich information, some samples are still noisy and are therefore misleading, largely because of misreporting by some firms.[3] Following Yu (2015), we clean the sample and omit outliers by using the following criteria: First, observations with missing key financial variables (such as total assets, net value of fixed assets, sales, and gross value of the firm's output productivity) are excluded. Second, we drop firms with fewer than eight workers since they fall under a different legal regime, as mentioned in Brandt et al. (2012). Thirdly, we delete observations according to the basic rules of Generally Accepted Accounting Principles.[4] After applying such a stringent filter to guarantee the quality of the production data, the filtered firm data are reduced by about 50% in each year. Since the CMS data provides information of worker training after 2004, our panel is shortened to cover the period during 2004–2007. As shown in Table 9.1, firms' worker training expenses increased during 2004–2007. Table 9.1 shows that firms' training investment increased over the sample period.[5]

Tariff data can be accessed directly from the WTO and the Trade Analysis and Information System (TRAINS).[6] China's tariff data are available at the Harmonized System (HS) six-digit disaggregated level for 2000–2006. Given that the product-level trade data are at the HS eight-digit level, the product-level trade data is aggregated to the HS six-digit level to correspond with the *ad valorem* tariff data. Table 9.2 provides the basic statistical information for key variables used in the estimations.

Table 9.1 TFP, Tariffs, and the Firm's Training Expenses

Year	*TFP*		*Training Dummy*		*Log Training*		*Ind. Output Tariffs*	
	Mean	Std. Dev.	Mean	Std. Dev.	Mean	Std. Dev.	Mean	Std. Dev.
	(1)	(2)	(3)	(4)	(5)	(6)	(7)	(8)
2004	1.055	0.317	0.437	0.496	4.244	4.920	8.321	1.863
2005	1.033	0.334	0.408	0.491	4.037	4.960	7.944	1.966
2006	1.046	0.342	0.409	0.492	4.054	4.981	7.582	1.583

Sources: Data compiled by the authors.

Table 9.2 Summary Statistics (2004–2006)

Key Variables	*Mean*	*Std. Dev.*
Log of export (RMB)	16.46	1.69
Training dummy	.412	.492
Log of training expenses (RMB)	4.11	4.95
Log of training expenses per capita (RMB)	1.99	2.53
Industry-level output tariffs	.090	3.66
Industry-level input tariffs	.004	.808
Firm-level external tariffs	.009	11.3
SOEs indicator	.035	.185
Foreign ownership indicator	.131	.338

Notes: $1 was equivalent to RMB 8.05 during the period.

9.3 Empirical specification

To investigate the effects of input and output tariff reductions on firm productivity, we consider the following empirical framework:

$$\ln TFP_{ijt}^{OP} = \beta_0 + \beta_1 OT_{jt} + \beta_2 TrainDummy_{it} + \theta \mathbf{X}_{it} + \varpi_i + \eta_t + \mu_{it}, \tag{1}$$

where ln $Export_{ijt}$ is the logarithm of firm i's export in industry j in year t and OT_{it} denotes industry-level output tariffs. $TrainDummy_{it}$ is a firm's training indicator, which equals one if a firm has any expenses on worker training and zero otherwise. $\mathbf{X}_{it}$ denotes other firm characteristics, such as type of ownership (i.e., state-owned-enterprises or multinational firms). State-owned enterprises (SOEs) usually have low productivity and, hence, export less (Hsieh and Klenow, 2009). By contrast, multinational firms have higher productivity due in part to fewer financial constraints (Feenstra et al., 2014) or more international technology spillover (Keller and Yeaple, 2009) and, hence, export more. Therefore, we construct two indicators to measure the roles of SOEs and multinational firms. In particular, a firm is classified as a foreign firm if it has any investments from other countries (regimes). A large proportion of the inflow of foreign investment comes from Hong Kong/Macao/Taiwan, so these investments are considered in the construction of such an indicator.[7] Similarly, we construct an indicator for SOEs, which is one if a firm has any investment from the government and zero otherwise.[8] Finally, the error term is divided into three components: (1) firm-specific fixed effects ϖ_i to control for time-invariant but unobservable factors such as managerial ability (Qiu and Yu, 2013); (2) year-specific fixed effects η_t to control for firm-invariant factors such as an appreciation of the Renminbi; and (3) an idiosyncratic effect μ_{it} with normal distribution $\mu_{it} \sim N\left(0, \sigma_i^2\right)$ to control for other unspecified factors.

However, the training indicator in the specification above is relatively crude. If a firm only spent a very small amount on worker training, it is still identified as a training firm though it is very unlikely that the small amount of worker training can boost its productivity. Hence, we use the firm's actual training expenses to capture its training activity with the following specification:

$$\ln TFP_{ijt}^{OP} = \beta_0 + \beta_1 OT_{jt} + \beta_2 \ln Train_{it} + \theta \mathbf{X}_{it} + \varpi_i + \eta_t + \mu_{it}, \tag{2}$$

9.3.1 Type-2 Tobit selection model

Thus far our estimates use firms' log of training expenses as a key variable, but such a variable is endogenous. First, it is possible that low-productivity firms self-select to provide more training since otherwise they would collapse and exit from the market. By the same token, tougher import competition raised by lower import tariffs would force firms to raise training to avoiding being swept out from the market. To control for this, we introduce a type-2 Tobit model, or equivalently, a bivariate sample selection model (Cameron and Trivedi, 2005). The type-2 Tobit specification includes: (i) a training participation equation,

$$TrainDummy_{ijt} = \left\{ \begin{pmatrix} 0 \\ 1 \end{pmatrix} \begin{matrix} if \ U_{ijt} < 0 \\ if \ U_{ijt} \geq 0 \end{matrix} \right\}, \tag{3}$$

where U_{it} denotes a latent variable faced by firm i in industry j; and (ii) an "outcome" equation whereby the firm's training expenses is modeled as a linear function of other variables.

In particular, we estimate the following selection equation using the Probit model:

$$\begin{aligned} \Pr(Training_{ijt} = 1) = \Pr(U_{ijt} \geq 0) = \Phi(\alpha_0 + \alpha_1 \ln TFP2_{it-1} + \alpha_2 OT_{jt-1} \\ + \alpha_3 FE_{it-1} + \alpha_3 SOE_{it-1} + \alpha_4 FIE_{it-1} + \alpha_5 \lg L_{it-1} + \alpha_6 Tenure_{it-1} + \lambda_j + \varsigma_t), \end{aligned} \tag{4}$$

where $\Phi(.)$ is the cumulative density function of the normal distribution. In addition to the logarithm of the firm's productivity, a firm's decision to training investment is also affected by other factors, such as its ownership (whether it is a SOE or a multinational firm) and output tariffs level. Note that the bivariate sample selection estimations require an excluded variable that affects the firm's training decision but does not appear in the level of training expenses (Cameron and Trivedi, 2005). Here the firm's age ($Tenure_{it-1}$) serves this purpose, since previous studies have found that older firms are more likely to invest in training (OECD, 1993). All regressors in the type-2 Tobit selection model are of a one-period lag since it usually takes times for such factors to affect the firm's training decision. Finally, we include the three-digit CIC industrial dummies λ_j and year dummies ς_t to control for other unspecified factors.

In addition, production productivity is also an important factor to determine the firm's training decision. We hence shall include it in the regressions in these binary estimates. However, an empirical identification challenge occurs. The conventional TFP measure is a "Solow" residual which is an *ex-post* measure whereas our model suggests that productivity shall be an *ex-ante* measure. Inspired by Feenstra et al. (2014), we construct an *ex-ante* productivity measure (TFP2) which differs from the standard *ex-post* productivity measure (TFP1) but is closer to the framework of Melitz (2003). We hence modify and tailor the standard Olley and Pakes (1996) TFP to construct the *ex-ante* TFP2. A detailed discussion of and method used to construct this measure will be included in the appendix. Finally, from the first-step Probit estimates (4), we obtain the estimation results for the type-2 Tobit selection model. Thus, after controlling for the endogenous selection of the firm's expenses on worker training, we obtain the fitted value of the expenses of worker training, which shall be used in related estimates.

9.4 Estimation results

9.4.1 Baseline results

We start off the estimations in Table 9.3 by using a firm's training dummy. The positive coefficient of training dummy in Column (1) as expected: training firms are more productive. Similarly, the coefficient of the industry output tariffs also has the anticipated negative sign. However, these two variables are insignificant statistically. We suspect this is due the coarse measure of the firm training variable as it cannot measure the extent of a firm's training expenses.

To overcome such a pitfall, from now on we use the firm's log training to capture its training activity. The two-way fixed-effects estimates in Column (2) abstract away the role of the firm's training expenses and still find that industry output tariffs have a significant negative impact on firm productivity, indicating that firms overall are more productive when they face tougher import competition due to output tariff reductions. Such results are consistent with previous findings (Amiti and Konings, 2007; Yu, 2015). We then include log firm training in estimates of Column (3). The coefficient of firm training is positive and significant, suggesting that the higher the firm's investment in worker training the more productive it is. In addition, exporters are more productive.

However, in reality, trade liberalization usually happens bilaterally. When China reduces its import tariffs, its trading partners are also likely to reduce their tariffs due to WTO commitments. We, hence, include a simple unweighted industry external tariff in Column (4). The negative, but insignificant, coefficient of external tariffs suggests that lower foreign trade barriers are helpful to boosting firms' productivity.

It is interesting to ask whether output trade liberalization boosts firm productivity through the channel of firm training. To check this out, we include an interaction term between output tariffs and firm training in Column (5). The coefficient of such a variable has the anticipated negative sign though it is insignificant. We suspect this is possibly due to two reasons. The first one is that we don't consider firm size since usually larger firms have more training expenses.

Table 9.3 Benchmark Estimates of Worker Training

Regressand: Firm TFP	*(1)*	*(2)*	*(3)*	*(4)*	*(5)*	*(6)*
Firm training dummy	0.002					
	(1.01)					
Log firm training			0.001**	0.001		
			(2.24)	(1.50)		
Log firm training per capita					0.004***	0.003**
					(4.08)	(1.99)
Industry output tariffs	-0.001	-0.002***	-0.001	-0.000	0.001	0.006*
	(-0.66)	(-4.67)	(-0.65)	(-0.24)	(0.14)	(1.80)
Industry output tariffs × Log firm training				-0.000	-0.000***	-0.000
				(-0.87)	(-3.04)	(-1.28)
Export Indicator	0.015***	0.015***	0.015***	0.016***	0.016***	0.011***
	(5.86)	(6.93)	(5.84)	(6.31)	(6.31)	(2.52)
Foreign indicator	0.008	0.007	0.008	0.009	0.009	0.003
	(0.85)	(1.15)	(0.84)	(0.98)	(0.97)	(0.28)
SOE indicator	0.020**	-0.009	0.020*	0.022**	0.022**	0.013
	(1.97)	(-1.62)	(1.96)	(2.15)	(2.17)	(0.90)
Log firm size				-0.023***	-0.022***	-0.032***
				(-12.27)	(-11.55)	(-10.82)
Industry external tariffs				-0.000	-0.000	0.001***
				(-1.29)	(-1.27)	(3.11)
Log R&D expenses						0.002***
						(3.14)
Firm-specific fixed effects	Yes	Yes	Yes	Yes	Yes	Yes
Year-specific fixed effects	Yes	Yes	Yes	Yes	Yes	Yes
Observations	226,513	335,681	226,513	226,513	226,513	147,548
R-squared	0.01	0.01	0.01	0.01	0.01	0.01

Notes: Robust *t*-values clustered at two-digit Chinese industry level are in parentheses, *, **, *** indicate significance at or below the 10%, 5%, and 1% level, respectively. Regressions in Columns (1)-(4) use log firm's total training expenses as a proxy of firm training whereas those in Columns (5)-(6) uses log firm's per-capita training expenses as a proxy of firm training.

To accurately capture the impact of firm training on productivity, we take firm's size into account. We hence replace total log training with log per-capita training and include log firm size as an additional regressor in Column (6). Once again, the coefficient of the firm's log per-capita training is positive and significant, confirming that the higher the firm's training expenses, the higher its TFP. Equally importantly, the negative and significant sign of the interaction term between output tariffs and firm training suggests that the effect of trade liberalization on firm productivity is more pronounced for firms with more training investment.

9.4.2 Self-selection of training

Table 9.3 uses a firm's training expenses to measure training activity and show that training firms are more productive. However, such a training variable is endogenous as less productive firms may self-select to provide worker training. To control for this, we introduce a bivariate sample selection model or, equivalently, a type-2 Tobit model (Cameron and Trivedi, 2005). As introduced above, the model includes two steps. The first step is to estimate a training participation equation, Equation (3), and the second step is a training extent function, Equation (4), which model the firm's training expenses as a linear function of other variables conditional on its participation in worker training.

Table 9.4 reports our type-2 Tobit estimation results. We first include one-period lag of log TFP in the first-step regression to see whether less productive firms self-select to provide worker training. To be consistent with the theoretical presumption that firm productivity is exogenously given, we therefore distinguish the difference between *ex-ante* measured TFP and standard *ex-post* measured TFP. The *ex-ante* measured TFP, *TFP*2, has an identical mean but different variance from the standard TFP, as introduced above and reported in Appendix 9.A1.

As reported in the first-stage estimations, less productive firms are more likely to engage in training behavior. The negative and significant coefficient of output trade liberalization seems striking at first glance. However, such a finding is reasonable. The tougher import competition caused by output trade liberalization results in lower firm profitability, which in turn causes them to invest less in training. Meanwhile, exporters and SOEs are more likely to invest in firm training. Similarly, large firms are more likely to engage in worker training. By contrast, foreign firms are found to be less likely to invest in training. A possible reason is that multinational firms are more likely to maintain their training

Table 9.4 The Heckman Two-Step Estimates of Bivariate Selection Model

Heckman Two-step:	*1st Step*		*2nd Step*	
Regressand:	*Training Indicator*		*Log Training Expenses*	
One-period lag of log TFP2 $\left(TFP2_{ijt}^{OP}\right)$	-0.549***	(-25.69)	-2.157***	(-18.57)
One-period lag of industry output tariffs	0.016***	(3.27)	0.056***	(2.96)
One-period lag of export indicator	0.110***	(15.92)	0.388***	(12.50)
One-period lag of SOEs indicator	0.236***	(13.74)	1.283***	(18.97)
One-period lag of foreign ownership indicator	-0.193***	(-25.05)	-0.754***	(-17.49)
One-period lag of log firm size	0.203***	(68.49)	1.028***	(29.55)
One-period lag of firm tenure	-0.012***	(-11.05)	-0.045***	(-10.45)
Inverse mills ratio			-0.991***	(-4.12)
Year-specific fixed effects	Yes		Yes	
3-digit industry-specific fixed effects	Yes		Yes	
Observations	228,288		228,288	

Notes: Robust *t*-values corrected for clustering at the two-digit industry level in parentheses. *, **, *** indicate significance at or below the 10%, 5%, and 1% level, respectively. The sample selection model is presented in Equations (participation) and (11) in the text. The regressand in the first-step is firm's training dummy whereas that in the second step is firm's log training expenses. The augmented Olley-Pakes TFP2 is adopted as a measure of firm productivity. Firm tenure is used as an exclusion variable that appeared in the first step but not the second step. The three-digit Chinese industry-specific fixed effects and year-specific fixed effects are also included in the estimations.

Alternative Table 9.4 The Heckman Two-Step Estimates of Bivariate Selection Model

Heckman Two-step:	*1st Step*		*2nd Step*	
Regressand:	*Training Indicator*		*Log Training per-capita*	
One-period lag of log TFP2 $\left(TFP2_{ijt}^{OP}\right)$	−0.549***	(−25.69)	−0.835***	(−14.12)
One-period lag of industry output tariffs	0.016***	(3.27)	0.022***	(2.21)
One-period lag of export indicator	0.110***	(15.92)	0.120***	(7.52)
One-period lag of SOEs indicator	0.236***	(13.74)	0.426***	(12.24)
One-period lag of foreign ownership indicator	−0.193***	(−25.05)	−0.285***	(−12.87)
One-period lag of log firm size	0.203***	(68.49)	0.135***	(7.68)
One-period lag of firm tenure	−0.012***	(−11.05)	−0.017***	(−7.64)
Inverse mills ratio			−1.253***	(−10.14)
Year-specific fixed effects	Yes		Yes	
3-digit Industry-specific fixed effects	Yes		Yes	
Observations	228,288		228,288	

Notes: Robust *t*-values corrected for clustering at the two-digit industry level in parentheses. *, **, *** indicate significance at or below the 10%, 5%, and 1% level, respectively. The sample selection model is presented in Equations (participation) and (11) in the text. The regressand in the first-step is firm's training dummy whereas that in the second step is firm's log training expenses. The augmented Olley-Pakes TFP2 is adopted as a measure of firm productivity. Firm tenure is used as an exclusion variable that appeared in the first step but not the second step. The three-digit Chinese industry-specific fixed effects and year-specific fixed effects are also included in the estimations.

investment in their foreign headquarters and have not high training expenses in foreign affiliates. Finally, older firms are found to have lower training expenses. Once the inverse mills ratio obtained in the first-step Probit estimates with three-digit industry-level fixed effects are calculated, we are ready to estimate the second-step of the bivariate selection model by including the inverse mills ratio as an additional regressor. All the coefficients have identical signs to their counterparts in the first stage and are highly significant at the conventional statistical level.

9.4.3 Different measures of TFP

To further check whether our main findings are sensitive to the measure of firm TFP and the empirical specifications, Columns (1) and (2) of Table 9.5 use the Levinsohn and Petrin (2003) TFP as the regressand while Columns (3) and (4) use the value-added TFP. After controlling for the firm's self-selection to training and both firm-specific and year-specific fixed effects, estimates in Column (1) ascertain that the effect of training on firm productivity is positive and significant. Exporters are found be more productive and SOEs less productive.

Previous works have recognized that processing firms are less productive (Dai et al., 2016), since they are usually pure exporters that sell all their

Table 9.5 Further CRC Estimates using Different TFP Measures

Regressand: Firm TFP	*TFP (Levinsohn-Petrin)*		*TFPOP(Value-Added)*	
	(1)	*(2)*	*(3)*	*(4)*
Log firm fitted training	0.028***	0.028***	0.013***	0.015***
	(7.00)	(6.85)	(3.11)	(3.46)
Industry output tariffs	-0.002	-0.001	-0.001	-0.001
	(-0.57)	(-0.52)	(-0.19)	(-0.25)
Export indicator	0.083***	0.086***	0.050***	0.052***
	(8.02)	(8.23)	(4.49)	(4.64)
Foreign indicator	0.040	0.049	-0.011	-0.005
	(1.29)	(1.55)	(-0.33)	(-0.13)
SOE indicator	-0.069***	-0.069***	-0.098***	-0.097***
	(-2.72)	(-2.70)	(-3.44)	(-3.41)
Industry external tariffs	0.000	0.000	0.002***	0.002***
	(0.09)	(0.14)	(3.35)	(3.23)
Pure exporters dropped	No	Yes	No	Yes
Firm-specific fixed effects	Yes	Yes	Yes	Yes
Year-specific fixed effects	Yes	Yes	Yes	Yes
Observations	126,757	125,614	151,063	148,894
R-squared	0.05	0.05	0.09	0.09

Notes: T-values in parentheses. *, **, *** indicate significance at or below the 10%, 5%, and 1% level, respectively. All regressions include firm-level fixed effects and year fixed effects. Pure exporters are dropped in Columns (2) and (4).

products abroad. To make sure that our results are not driven by processing firms, we drop all pure exporters in Column (2) and still find similar results as in Column (1).

Thus far, our productivity measure is gross output function TFP. It is interesting to see whether our results are robust when measured by value-added TFP. Estimates in the last two columns of Table 9.6 thus pick up this task by using the value-added Olley and Pakes TFP. The value-added TFP is measured by using value-added as the output of the production function and estimating output elasticity with respect to capital and labor, respectively. Estimates in Column (3) include pure exporters whereas those in Column (4) drop pure exporters from the sample. It turns out that the results are insensitive to using value-added TFP as the regressand.

9.4.4 Further robustness checks

It is widely recognized that today China has been engaged to a great extent in the global supply chain. In previous estimates we abstracted away firms' input tariffs from the regressions, possibly because imported intermediate inputs for processing trade are already duty-free (Yu, 2015). Still, non-processing firms bear some amount of input tariffs. One solution is to adopt firm-level input tariffs as constructed in Yu (2015). However, such an approach is at the expense of losing large number of observations, since the construction of firm-specific input tariffs requires a merged dataset between firm-level production data (used to estimate TFP) and production-level trade data (used to calculate firm-specific input tariffs). As input tariffs reduction is not the key variable in the present paper, we abstract it away allow it to be captured in the error term.

Instead, we consider another interesting case. A firm's imported intermediate goods are not necessarily used as intermediate inputs; it is possible for firms to import capital goods, which could, in turn, boost firm productivity from channels other than firm training. To rule out this case, we drop industries that include mostly intermediate inputs. According to description of the Broad Economic Classification (BEC) and its concordance with China's industrial classification, industries like machinery (code 36 and 37) belong to capital goods. Hence, we drop two industries in Column (1) of Table 9.6. It turns out that higher firm training still leads to higher firm productivity. Column (2) drops pure exporters and yields similar results. Thus, our findings remain robust even after dropping capital goods.

Our last exercise is to drop industries that are exposed to various non-tariff barriers such as import quotas, as our main objective is to check whether trade liberalization boosts firm productivity through the channel of firm training. Since exports of textile and garments are restricted by the multi-fiber agreement, which lasted for a decade from 1994 to 2004 (Khandelwal et al., 2013), we drop textile and garment from the estimations in Column (3) with the Olley-Pakes TFP as the regressand and Column (4) with the Levinsohn-Petrin TFP as the

Table 9.6 Further Robust Estimates

Specifications	*No Capital-goods*		*No Quota-imposed*	
Regressand: Firm TFP	TFP^{OP}	TFP^{OP}	TFP^{OP}	TFP^{LP}
	(1)	*(2)*	*(3)*	*(4)*
Log firm fitted training	0.007***	0.007***	0.007***	0.018***
	(5.41)	(5.28)	(5.77)	(4.37)
Industry output tariffs	-0.008***	-0.008***	-0.007***	-0.012***
	(-8.63)	(-8.75)	(-5.30)	(-2.84)
Export indicator	0.008**	0.008**	0.010***	0.065***
	(2.27)	(2.36)	(2.99)	(6.07)
Foreign indicator	0.000	0.002	0.008	0.054*
	(0.03)	(0.24)	(0.74)	(1.65)
SOE indicator	-0.001	-0.001	-0.002	-0.068***
	(-0.11)	(-0.09)	(-0.24)	(-2.58)
Log firm size	-0.027***	-0.027***	-0.025***	0.204***
	(-10.91)	(-10.97)	(-10.30)	(26.67)
Industry external tariffs	-0.001***	-0.001***	-0.001***	-0.000
	(-3.72)	(-4.01)	(-4.49)	(-0.15)
Pure exporters dropped	No	Yes	Yes	Yes
Firm-specific fixed effects	Yes	Yes	Yes	Yes
Year-specific fixed effects	Yes	Yes	Yes	Yes
Observations	135,377	133,324	135,596	113,132
R-squared	0.02	0.02	0.01	0.07

Notes: *T*-values in parentheses. *, **, *** indicate significance at or below the 10%, 5%, and 1% level, respectively.

regressand. Once again, both estimates suggest that output trade liberalization boosts firms' productivity. More importantly, output trade liberalization affects a firm's probability of investing in worker training, which, in turn, boosts firm productivity.

9.5 Concluding remarks

In this paper we found that trade liberalization increases firms' training investment, which in turn boosts firms' productivity and increases their exports. We are thus able to identify a new mechanism through which trade liberalization affects firm productivity. Our paper has strong policy implications, as well as academic contributions. The competitiveness of Chinese firms is shrinking due, in large part, to increasing labor costs in recent years. To overcome this kind of a challenge, the government in China is working hard to facilitate the macro-environment for firm R&D. Meanwhile, the government helps firms in labor-intensive industries invest in lower labor-cost African countries (see Tian and Yu, 2014 for detailed discussions). Our empirical findings in this paper suggest that, in addition to the on-the-job training provided by firms themselves, China's government may provide more training by having more technical schools and initiating more training programs to increase worker productivity and, hence, boost firm productivity.

9.6 Acknowledgements

We thank the editor, the referee, Chin Hee Hahn, Archanun Kohpaiboon, Dionisius A. Narjoko, Ju Hyun Pyun, Shujiro Urata, and other workshop participants in the microdata and productivity workshops held by the Economic Research Institute for ASEAN and East Asia (ERIA). However, all errors are ours.

Notes

1 For example, the UK and Italian governments thought that, one of the key factors behind the loss of competitiveness of their firms in the global economy was the lack of training compared with other countries like Germany and Japan. Thus, they initiated large training programs in their countries.

2 Aggregated data on the industrial sector in the annual *China's Statistical Yearbook* by the Natural Bureau of Statistics are compiled from this dataset.

3 For example, information on some family-based firms, which usually have no formal accounting system in place, is based on a unit of 1 RMB, whereas the official requirement is a unit of 1,000 RMB.

4 For example, observations are dropped if any of the following are true: (1) liquid assets are greater than total assets; (2) total fixed assets are greater than total assets; (3) the net value of fixed assets is greater than total assets; (4) the firm's identification number is missing; or (5) an invalid established time exists (e.g., the opening month is later than December or earlier than January).

5 By separating firms into pure exporter (i.e., firms that export all of their products), non-pure exporters (i.e., those that, at most, export some products), and non-exporters (i.e., firms that do not export any products), we see that exporters spend

more on worker training than non-exporters. Simultaneously, non-pure exporters have higher worker training expenses than pure exporters. Such results are not reported in the text but available upon request.

6 The data are from WTO webpage http://tariffdata.wto.org/ReportersAndProducts.aspx. Note that TRAINS data generally suffer from missing values problems, particularly regarding the tariffs imposed by other countries for Chinese exports. The product-destination-year combinations that have missing tariffs are hence dropped.

7 Specifically, foreign-invested enterprises (FIEs) include the following firms: foreign-invested joint-stock corporations (code: 310), foreign-invested joint venture enterprises (320), fully FIEs (330), foreign-invested limited corporations (340), Hong Kong/Macao/Taiwan (henceforth, H/M/T) joint-stock corporations (210), H/M/T joint venture enterprises (220), fully H/M/T-invested enterprises (230), and H/M/T-invested limited corporations (240). Appendix Table 5A presents the transitional probability for such foreign firms.

8 By the official definition reported in the *China City Statistical Yearbook* (2006), SOEs include firms such as domestic SOEs (code: 110), state-owned joint venture enterprises (141), and state-owned and collective joint venture enterprises (143), but exclude state-owned limited corporations (151). Appendix Table 5B presents the transitional probability for all SOEs.

9 Olley and Pakes (1996) showed that the investment demand function is monotonically increasing in the productivity shockx_{jt}, by making some mild assumptions about the firm's production technology.

10 Note that here the non-linear least squares approach is adopted to estimate (2-step) since it requires the estimated coefficients of the log-capital in the first and second term to be identical (Pavcnik, 2002).

References

Acemoglu, Daron and Jörn-Steffen Pischke (1998), "The Structure of Wages and Investment in General Training," *Journal of Political Economy* 107(3), pp. 539–72.

Almeida, Rita and Pedro Carneiro (2009), "The Return to Firm Investments in Human Capital," *Labour Economics* 16(1), pp. 97–106.

Amiti, Mary and Jozef Konings (2007), "Trade Liberalization, Intermediate Inputs, and Productivity: Evidence from Indonesia," *American Economic Review* 97(5), pp. 1611–38.

Aw, Bee Yan, Mark J. Roberts, and Daniel Yi Xu (2011), "R&D Investment, Exporting, and Productivity Dynamics," *American Economic Review* 101(4), pp. 1312–44.

Baldwin, Richard E. (1992), "Measurable Dynamic Gains from Trade," *Journal of Political Economy* 100(1), pp. 162–74.

Bernard, Andrew and Brad Jensen (2004), "Why Some Firms Export," *Review of Economics and Statistics* 86(2), pp. 561–69.

Black, Sandra and Lisa Lynch (2001), "How to Compete: The Impact of Workplace Practices and Information Technology on Productivity," *Review of Economics and Statistics* 83(3), pp. 434–45.

Blundell, Richard, Lorraine Dearden, and Costas Meghir (1996), *The Determinants of Work-Related Training in Britain*, Institute for Fiscal Studies, London.

Blundell, Richard, Dearden Lorraine, Costas Meghir, and Barbara Sianesi (1999), "Human Capital Investment: The Returns from Education and Training to the Individual, the Firm and the Economy," *Fiscal Studies* 20(1), pp. 1–23.

Brandt, Loren, Johannes van Biesebroeck, and Yifan Zhang (2012), "Creative Accounting or Creative Destruction? Firm-Level Productivity Growth in Chinese Manufacturing," *Journal of Development Economics* 97(2), pp. 339–51.

Cai, Fan (2010), "Demographic Transition, Demographic Dividend, and Lewis Turning Point in China," *China Economic Journal* 3(2), pp. 107–19.

Cameron, Colin and Pravin Trivedi (2005), *Microeconometrics: Methods and Applications*, Cambridge University Press.

Conti, Gabriella (2005), "Training, Productivity and Wages in Italy," *Labour Economics* 12(4), pp. 557–76.

Dai, Mi, Madura Maitra, and Miaojie Yu (2016), "Unexceptional Exporter Performance in China? Role of Processing Trade," *Journal of Development Economics* 121, pp. 177–89.

Deardorff, Alan (2000), "Policy Implications of Trade and Wage Debates," *Review of International Economics* 8, pp. 478–96.

Dearden, L., Reed, H., Van Reenen, J. 2006. "The Impact of Training on Productivity and Wages: Evidence from British Panel Data," *Oxford Bulletin of Economics and Statistics* 68(4), pp. 397–421.

Feenstra, Robert, and Gordon H. Hanson (2005), "Ownership and Control in Outsourcing to China: Estimating the Property-Rights Theory of the Firm," *The Quarterly Journal of Economics* 120(2), pp. 729–761.

Feenstra, Robert, Zhiyuan Li, and Miaojie Yu (2014), "Exports and Credit Constraints under Incomplete Information: Theory and Applications to China," *Review of Economics and Statistics* 96(4), pp. 729–44.

Gorlitz, Katja, and Joel Stiebale (2011), "The Impact of Product Market Competition on Employers' Training Investments. Evidence from German Establishment Panel Data," *De Economist* 159(1), pp. 1–23.

Helpman, Elhanan, Oleg Itskhoki, and Stephen Redding (2010), "Inequality and Unemployment in a Global Economy," *Econometrica* 78, pp. 1239–83.

Hsieh, Chang-Tai, and Peter Klenow (2009), "Misallocation and Manufacturing TFP in China and India," *Quarterly Journal of Economic*s 124(4), pp. 1403–48.

Khandelwal, Amit K., Peter K. Schott, and Shang-Jin Wei. 2013. "Trade Liberalization and Embedded Institutional Reform: Evidence from Chinese Exporters," American Economic Review 103(6), pp. 2169–95.

Keller, Wolfgang, and Stephen Yeaple (2009), "Multinational Enterprises, International Trade, and Productivity Growth: Firm-Level Evidence from the United States," *Review of Economics and Statistics* 91(4), pp. 821–31.

Lai, Tat-kei and Travis Ng (2014), "The Impact of Product Market Competition on Training Provision: Evidence from Canada," *Canadian Journal of Economics* 47, pp. 856–88.

Levinsohn, James and Amil Petrin (2003), "Estimating Production Functions Using Inputs to Control for Unobservable," *Review of Economic Studies* 70(2), pp. 317–41.

Li, H-C. (2009), Import Competition and Company Training: Evidence from the US Microdata on Individuals, Working Paper, University of Southern California.

Lileeva, Alla and Daniel Trefelr (2010), "Improved Access to Foreign Markets Raises Plant-Level Productivity…for Some Plants," *Quarterly Journal of Economics* 125(3), pp. 1051–95.

Long, Ngo Van, Raymond Riezman, and Antoine Soubeyran (2007), "Trade, Wage Gap, and Specific Human Capital Accumulation," *Review of International Economics* 15, pp. 75–92.

Melitz, Marc (2003), "The Impact of Trade on Intra-industry Reallocations and Aggregate Industry Productivity," *Econometrica* 71(6), pp. 1695–725.

Melitz, Marc and Daniel Trefler (2012), "Gains from Trade When Firms Matter," *Journal of Economic Perspectives* 26(2), pp. 91–118.

OECD (1993), "Enterprise Tenure, Labour Turnover and Skill Training," in OECD Employment Outlook, Chapter 4. Paris.

Olley, Steven and Ariel Pakes (1996), "The Dynamics of Productivity in the Telecommunications Equipment Industry," *Econometrica* 64(6), pp. 1263–97.

Qiu D. Larry and Miaojie Yu (2013), "Multiproduct Firms, Export Product Scope, and Trade Liberalization: The Role of Managerial Efficiency," Working Paper, Hong Kong Institute for Monetary Research.

Tian, Wei and Yu, Miaojie, Measuring the Impact of Trade Protection on Industrial Production Size, *Review of Development Economics*,Vol. 18, Issue 2, pp. 231–253, 2014,

Topalova, Petia and Amit Khandelwal (2011), "Trade Liberalization and Firm Productivity: The Case of India," *Review of Economics and Statistics* 93(3), pp. 995–1009.

Yu, Miaojie (2015), "Processing Trade, Firm Productivity, and Tariff Reductions: Evidence from Chinese Firms," *Economic Journal* 125(585), pp. 943–88.

Yu, Miaojie and Wei Tian (2012), "China's Processing Trade: A Firm-Level Analysis," in Huw McMay and Ligang Song (eds.), *Rebalancing and Sustaining Growth in China*, Australian National University E-press, pp. 111–48.

Appendix A
Measuring *Ex-ante* TFP (TFP2)

This section draws heavily from Qiu and Yu (2013) to discuss how we construct and measure TFP using two different approaches: *ex-post* TFP (TFP1) and *ex-ante* TFP (TFP2) inspired by Feenstra et al. (2014).

We extend the Olley and Pakes (1996) approach to fit with China's reality in the following ways. Firstly, given that the measure of TFP requires real terms of firms' inputs (labor and capital) and outputs, we adopt different price deflators for inputs and outputs from Brandt et al. (2012), in which the output deflators are constructed using "reference price" information from *China's Statistical Yearbooks* and input deflators are constructed based on output deflators and China's national input-output table (2002).

Secondly, we take China's WTO accession in 2001 into account, since such a positive demand shock would push Chinese firms to expand their economic scales, which, in turn, can exaggerate the simultaneous bias of their measured TFP. Thirdly, it is essential to construct a real investment variable when using the Olley and Pakes (1996) approach. As usual, we adopt the perpetual inventory method to investigate the law of motion for real capital and real investment. Different from assigning an arbitrary number for the depreciation ratio, we use the firm's exact real depreciation, provided by the Chinese firm-level dataset.

Finally, we also consider the firm's processing behavior in the TFP realization by constructing a processing export indicator (one denotes processing export and zero otherwise). The idea is that processing firms may use different technology than non-processing firms (Feenstra and Hanson, 2005).

Thus, a firm's investment function is $V_{it} = g_1(x_{it}, \ln K_{it}, EX_{it}, PE_{it}, WTO_t)$ where EX_{it} (PE_{it}) is the export (processing export) indicator to measure whether firm i exports (engages in processing exports) in year t, and WTO_t is an indicator that equals one if the WTO agreement has occurred after 2001 and zero before that. Therefore, inverting the investment function with respect to its first argument, we obtain:[9]

$$x_{it} = g_1^{-1}(V_{it}, \ln K_{it}, EX_{it}, PE_{it}, WTO_t).$$

Given the gross production function

$$\ln Y_{it} = \alpha_k \ln K_{it} + \alpha_l \ln L_{it} + \alpha_m \ln M_{it} + x_{it} + \varepsilon_{it}$$

and defining the function $g_2(\cdot)$ as $\alpha_k \ln K_{jt} + g_1^{-1}(V_{it}, \ln K_{it}, EX_{it}, PE_{it}, WTO_t)$, the estimation of the labor (materials) coefficients $\alpha_l\ (\alpha_m)$ is obtained as:

$$\ln Y_{it} = \alpha_l \ln L_{it} + \alpha_m \ln M_{it} + g_2(V_{it}, \ln K_{it}, EX_{it}, PE_{it}, WTO_t) + \varepsilon_{it}.$$

The next step is to obtain an unbiased estimated coefficient of α_k. Olley and Pakes (1996) use the following specification:

$$\begin{aligned} \ln Y_{it} - \hat{\alpha}_l \ln L_{it} - \hat{\alpha}_m \ln M_{it} &= \alpha_k \ln K_{it} + E(x_{it} \mid x_{it-1}, pr_{it}) \\ &\quad + \left[x_{it} - E(x_{it} \mid x_{it-1}, pr_{it})\right] + \varepsilon_{it}, \end{aligned}$$

where the estimated values of the labor coefficient and materials coefficient are used on the left. The expectation of productivity appearing in (two-step) is modeled as a fourth-order polynomial function of lagged productivity, which can be obtained as $\left(g_{2i,t-1} - \alpha_k \ln K_{i,t-1}\right)$ and also the predicted probability of the firm's survival into the year t, pr_{it}, based on year $t-1$ information. The predicted probability is obtained from Probit estimation.[10] The term $\left[x_{it} - E(x_{it} \mid x_{it-1}, pr_{it})\right]$ is the productivity shock for surviving firms, but does not affect the investment or exit choice, so it is treated as an error.

Once the coefficient of capital $\hat{\alpha}_k$ is estimated in Equation (2-step), it is ready to obtain the standard *ex-post* TFP:

$$TFP1_{it} \equiv x_{it} = \ln Y_{it} - \hat{\alpha}_k \ln K_{it} - \hat{\alpha}_l \ln L_{it} - \hat{\alpha}_m \ln M_{it}.$$

In this way, TFP1 includes both true production productivity and managerial efficiency. By contrast, the *ex-ante* productivity (TFP2), which only captures true production productivity, is given by

$$TFP2_{it} = g_1^{-1}(V_{it}, \ln K_{it}, EX_{it}, PE_{it}, WTO_t).$$

Appendix Table 9.A1 reports the estimated coefficients of labor, capital, materials, TFP1 and TFP2.

Table 9.A1 Total Factor Productivity of Chinese Firms (2000–2007)

CIC	*Labor*	*Capital*	*Materials*	*Variance in*	
				TFP1	*TFP2*
13	0.077	0.060	0.814	0.322	0.148
14	0.055	0.071	0.857	0.300	0.172
15	0.094	0.113	0.799	0.381	0.235
16	0.020	0.270	0.783	0.631	0.479
17	0.066	0.044	0.868	0.218	0.103
18	0.110	0.039	0.798	0.310	0.093

CIC	*Labor*	*Capital*	*Materials*	*Variance in*	
19	0.084	0.041	0.857	0.276	0.098
20	0.099	0.071	0.841	0.300	0.167
21	0.103	0.055	0.814	0.218	0.119
22	0.063	0.053	0.867	0.234	0.127
23	0.065	0.068	0.815	0.215	0.210
24	0.091	0.039	0.823	0.223	0.113
25	0.014	0.069	0.865	0.324	0.327
26	0.063	0.058	0.820	0.318	0.175
27	0.062	0.064	0.790	0.360	0.219
28	0.040	0.060	0.889	0.313	0.169
29	0.087	0.081	0.769	0.333	0.186
30	0.069	0.046	0.836	0.288	0.180
31	0.046	0.059	0.844	0.287	0.145
32	0.061	0.029	0.891	0.249	0.116
33	0.080	0.079	0.850	0.278	0.322
34	0.062	0.037	0.841	0.311	0.093
35	0.061	0.055	0.837	0.247	0.188
36	0.053	0.049	0.841	0.326	0.123
37	0.063	0.045	0.835	0.283	0.160
39	0.077	0.066	0.836	0.303	0.135
40	0.109	0.075	0.806	0.358	0.194
41	0.049	0.054	0.806	0.386	0.208
42	0.091	0.039	0.857	0.271	0.092

Notes: We do not report standard errors for each coefficient to save space, though they are available upon request. The logarithm of firm productivity for Chinese firms (TFP1 and TFP2) is estimated by industry by the augmented Olley-Pakes approach introduced in the text. Coefficients of labor, capital, and materials are calculated at the sectorial average whereas TFP1 and TFP2 is measured at firm-level using firm-level sales, capital, materials, and labor, respectively. The last three columns report the sectorial mean of log TFP1, log TFP2, and log of worker training, respectively.

10 Trade protection and firm productivity

Evidence from Thai manufacturing

Juthathip Jongwanich and Archanun Kohpaiboon

10.1 Issues

While, globally, the volume of tariffs in general has gone down substantially over the past two decades after the establishment of World Trade Organization (WTO) in 1995, much remains to be done in developing countries. Exceptions in liberalization schedules (i.e., tariff peaks) are often found. In particular, efforts concerning tariff liberalization are often lopsided, emphasizing tariff cuts on raw materials and intermediates, whereas tariffs on outputs remain untouched. This is reflected by a mounting tariff structure wherein rates escalate from raw materials to finished products. This leads to nominal protection underestimating actual/effective protection levels. It is done with the hope that maintaining such cross-border measures will give firms more time to improve their international competitiveness and survive in an increasingly intense competitive environment.

Until the 1990s such a hope received little empirical support. The analysis was based on the statistical relationship between economic growth and aggregate trade openness across countries using a standard growth-regression analysis.[1] Such a relationship is unable to provide a better understanding of the mechanism dictating how trade openness affects firms' productivity. As argued in Levine and Renelt (1992) and Sala-i-Martin (1997), cross-country econometric analyses are tenuous at best.

From the late 1990s, there was a proliferation in the availability of plant-level data in many countries, allowing researchers to revisit and mitigate the above shortcomings. Where the effect of trade policy on firms' performance is concerned, there are at least two aspects of relevance in the policy circles of developing countries. The first is related to a self-selection hypothesis wherein firms entering export markets are already more productive.[2] The key inference for further studies from such a self-selection hypothesis is that the nature of trade policy and firms' market orientation must be treated as two separate explanatory variables within the analysis. While both could be on par in terms of their important influence on productivity, they remain two different entities. The former relates to the policy environment, whereas the latter concerns firms' decision-making processes.

The second aspect concerns examining the possible different favorable effects of input and output tariff reductions on firms' productivity. Relevant studies include Amiti and Konings (2007), who used an Indonesian dataset; and Goldberg et al. (2010) and Topalova and Khandelwal (2011), both of which employed Indian datasets and found that the favorable effect of the former is much larger than that of the latter. By contrast, Yu (2015) used Chinese plant-level data and revealed more considerable effects of output tariff reduction. The difference in their findings perhaps suggests that how tariff reductions affect firms' productivity potentially varies from country to country, leaving a need for further in-depth country-specific analysis.

Against this backdrop, this paper aims to examine the determinants of firm productivity with particular emphasis on the effects of trade policy. Our proposed study has at least three contributions to make to the existing literature. Firstly, we carefully delineate the possible effects between trade (export and import) and trade policy (e.g., cross-border protection) on productivity. Secondly, we examine whether the effects of trade policy vary across types of firm by introducing an interaction term between firm specific and trade-policy variables. Two firm-specific factors are emphasized in this paper, market orientation (whether firms participate in the global market) and input sourcing (whether firms import raw materials or intermediates from abroad). Thirdly, the effects of output and input tariffs are re-examined, as opposed to cases using effective rate of protection (ERP) (both input and output tariffs combined). Whether the effect of output is actually different than that of input remains an open question with immense policy implications. In developing countries, the impact of policy preference is lopsided, emphasizing input tariff reduction, but expressing reluctancy for tariff cuts on outputs.

The case of Thailand is chosen in order to investigate this issue, as trade policy reform remains a challenging issue for policymakers in the country. In particular, the effort to streamline the range of tariff rates to three rates only (0%–1% for raw materials, 5% for intermediates, and 10% for finished products) is, at best, far from complete. Almost one-fifth of tariff lines remain subject to a 20% tariff rate or more. By design, the tariff structure follows a cascading pattern, so that nominal protection tends to underestimate an effective one. Hence, effective protection seems to vary across industries. This allows us to test the effect of protection on firms' rates of productivity.

The paper's structure is as follows; the next section presents our analytical framework (Section 10.2). In Section 10.3, trade policy challenges are discussed, together with a brief statistical analysis of certain characteristics of Thai manufacturing firms. The research model is discussed in the following section (Section 10.4), followed by details of our econometric procedures and results (Sections 10.5 and 10.6). The conclusion and policy inferences are presented in the final section.

10.2 Analytical framework

The gains arising from trade in terms of output growth/productivity have been studied for several decades. Research initiatives began with the standard neoclassical trade model, Ricardian comparative advantage model and/or

Heckcsher-Ohlin-based comparative advantage paradigms. In this model, gains from trade are derived from resource reallocation from sectors in which the country has a comparative disadvantage to those in which it holds a comparative advantage. This reallocation leads to productivity improvement at the aggregate level, despite the fact that individual firms' productivity remains unchanged. The country's comparative advantage is driven by either technology, resource endowment, or both. Hence, trade liberalization tends to generate a favorable impact on productivity.

In the 1980s, amid the introduction of the monopolistic competition theory of international trade, Krugman (1979) and Helpman and Krugman (1985) highlighted the fact that the origins of gains from trade had shifted more to intra-industry trade. Different from the Ricardian model, this theory stressed that not all firms would benefit from the productivity gains arising from trade liberalization. For some firms, liberalization increases sales and expands the scale of production scale. This leads to a riding down of the cost curve so that productivity improvement is observed. In the meantime, some firms potentially exit. Nonetheless, in this model, the analysis is based on a representative (homogenous) firm. Hence, the selection (i.e., some gain and the others lose) takes place on a purely random basis. This cannot explain satisfactorily why in a given industry only some firms export, not all (Greenaway and Kneller 2007).

Pioneered in Melitz (2003), the assumption of representative firms is relaxed, with the research focus being on firm heterogeneity. Even within a narrowly defined industry, some firms are much larger in size, more productive, and more profitable than others (Melitz and Trefler 2012). International trade drives better-performing firms to expand their products into larger markets, while resources are reallocated from less productive firms into productive ones. This, therefore, leads to productivity improvement, despite the fact that individual firms' productivity remains unchanged.[3]

As plant/firm-level panel data has become increasingly available in many countries, researchers have revisited the trade liberalization-productivity nexus, under the firm heterogeneity framework. Using a micro dataset, a new hypothesis is formulated, related to the impacts of trade liberalization on firms' performance. The positive relationship discovered is explained by two competing theses. One is the self-selection thesis wherein firms entering export markets are already more productive than non-exporters. As a result, any positive relationship would not be directly related to trade liberalization. The key inference here is that the nature of trade policy and firms' market orientation are different and must be treated as two separate explanatory variables in any analysis. The former refers to policy environment, whereas the latter concerns a firm's decision-making process.[4]

The second premise concerns the learning-by-exporting thesis wherein firms participating in foreign markets are more likely to experience productivity gains when compared to non-exporters. The former are able to receive new information about technological progress, product designs, and quality of goods arising from their foreign exposure (Grossman and Helpman 1991; Aw and Hwang

1995; Bernard and Wagner 1997).[5] Given the learning-by-exporting thesis, trade liberalization could further improve firms' productivity. Lowering output tariffs can increase productivity by inducing tougher competition. This results in the reallocation (selection) effect wherein the more competitive firms experience gains in their market share, while less competitive organizations are forced to exit (Trefler 2004; Lileeva and Trefler 2010). For firms producing multiple products, tougher competition potentially drives them to streamline their operations in order to remain globally competitive (Amiti and Konings 2007). This might induce firms to introduce advanced production technology and/or R&D investment in order to enhance their competitiveness (Fernandes 2007; Bustos 2011). Similarly, cutting input tariffs prompts firms to use cheaper imported inputs and benefit from the technology embodied within them, thereby stimulating their productivity. They also benefit from the variety and quality effects inherent in imported inputs (Halpern, Koren, and Szeidl 2015).

Recently, a number of researchers have taken another step by examining the possibility that altering either input or output tariffs can have different effects on firms' productivity. The results remain mixed. For example, Amiti and Konings (2007), using an Indonesian dataset, and Goldberg et al. (2010) and Topalova and Khandelwal (2011), both using Indian datasets, found that the favorable effect of input tariffs is much larger than that of output tariffs. By contrast, Yu (2015) found a contradictory result using Chinese plant-level data. The different effects found in these empirical research projects point to the important role of country-specific factors. For example, in Yu (2015) the special treatment afforded to imported inputs for export-oriented firms constitutes an explanation making the effect of output tariff reduction greater than that of input tariff reduction. In addition, firms might respond to changes in trade policy environments differently. All in all, findings point to the need for in-depth country-level analyses in order to be able to find definitive generalizations from such theses.

Interestingly, the main mechanism through which input and output tariff reductions affect productivity in these studies is price elasticity. When an input tariff is lowered, firms tend to import more foreign inputs. Similarly, a lower output tariff induces more imported goods. Irrefutably, this could potentially enhance firms' productivity. Nonetheless, such a conclusion exists under the assumption that the effect of (input, output, or both) tariff reduction on productivity takes place in a frictionless manner. This seems a restrictive assumption. As argued in a number of case studies[6], and in East Asian literature in particular, the productivity improvement process involves a prolonged, circuitous evolution of learning and mastery. Such a process takes time and requires a concerted investment of effort and resources to result in productivity gains. In these circumstances, therefore, competitive pressure influenced by trade policy is needed to force firms to commit to such a long developmental and transformational process.

The influence of trade policy on competitive pressure was reflected in the well-developed concept known as ERP pioneered by Corden (1966) and Balassa

(1965). Under ERP, it does not matter whether any effective protection granted comes from either lowering input tariffs, raising output tariffs, or both. This raises two important implications for the empirical research. The first concerns whether decomposing input and output tariffs is justified. This represents an empirical question to be addressed. The second issue involves the possibly ambiguous effect of input tariffs. In line with the ERP concept, solely lowering an input tariff while leaving an output tariff unchanged, would, in turn, lead to an increase in the ERP granted to firms. This could limit competitive pressures and lower any incentives for firms to commit resources to productivity improvement processes. Hence, the net effect on productivity of input tariff cuts would be ambiguous.

10.3 Trade policy and firm productivity in Thai manufacturing

In Thailand, tariffs represent a core tool in conducting trade policy. Non-tariff measures have been used occasionally in a narrow range of products, mainly in certain sensitive agricultural products, such as soybean, palm seed, silk, and milk. Like other developing countries, the high tariff levels associated with an escalating tariff structure were used to promote industrialization between the 1960s and the mid-1980s. From 1983 to 1995, tariff levels remained virtually unchanged with few exceptions, whereas efforts to promote Thailand as an export platform for multinationals were undertaken through the introduction of various tariff exemption schemes (Kohpaiboon 2006; Jongwanich and Kohpaiboon 2007).

As part of its commitments under the WTO, a comprehensive plan for tariff reduction and rationalization was proposed in 1990 and implemented in 1995 and 1997. Maximum tariff levels were reduced from 100% to 30%. Tariffs were significantly lowered on some 4,000 items, at the six-digit Harmonized System (HS) level, or 75% of total tariff lines. By the end of the 1990s, the number of tariff bands was reduced from 39 to 6 (0%, 1%, 5%, 10%, 20%, and 30%). Nonetheless, there were numerous exceptions where tariff rates exceeded 30%. Tariff restructuring has received a renewed emphasis as an essential part of the overall economic reform strategy aimed at strengthening efficiency and competitiveness (WTO 1999). The Thai government introduced tariff cuts, commencing in June 2003 (implemented in October 2003), followed by a four-year period of tariff reduction from 2004 to 2008. In 2010, there were around 900 items involved in the tariff-reduction process, covering a wide range of manufacturing intermediates, such as rubber and articles thereof (HS40), glass and glassware (HS70), knitted fabrics (HS60), other base metals (HS81), woven fabrics (HS58), articles of stone (HS68), man-made staple fiber (HS55), wadding yarns (HS56), cotton (HS52), and miscellaneous vegetable preparations (HS21) (Jongwanich and Kohpaiboon 2007).

Table 10.1 presents the average of most-favored-nation tariffs of Thailand and selected Asian economies in 2010. It is clear that the average Thai tariff rate was relatively high as compared to other middle-income countries in the region. The weighted average was lower than the unweighted, implying that tariffs imposed on certain products are redundant. Generally, agricultural products are subject to higher tariffs than manufacturing products.

Table 10.2 illustrates the distribution of tariff lines in Thailand over the past two decades. Clearly this distribution changed as a result of the comprehensive tariff reforms of the mid-1990s. During the pre-1997 period, more than a quarter of the total of HS6 tariff lines had tariff rates of more than 20% (Table 10.2). After 1997, there was a dramatic shift of tariff lines to lower brackets. For example, more than 75% of tariff lines are in the 0%–10% bracket, followed by 6.3%

Table 10.1 Weighted Average of Most-Favored-Nation Tariff Rate of Selected Countries during 2010–2012

Country (Year)	*Unweighted*	*Weighted*	*Agricultural Products*	*Nonagricultural Products*
Thailand (2011)	8.7	5.0	9.0	4.9
Vietnam (2010)	9.8	12.2	24.4	10.7
Singapore (2011)	0.0	0.0	0.0	0.0
Philippines (2011)	6.2	12.2	23.2	10.4
Myanmar (2011)	5.6	6.6	12.6	4.9
Malaysia (2012)	5.3	6.7	8.7	6.5
Indonesia (2012)	6.6	9.8	1.8	11.1
Laos (2008)	9.7	13.6	19.3	12.6
Brunei (2011)	2.5	1.7	0.0	2.6
Cambodia (2012)	10.9	12.0	14.7	11.1
Australia (2011)	2.8	3.8	1.6	3.9
New Zealand (2011)	2.0	2.7	1.9	2.8
China (2010)	9.9	8.6	21.5	7.4
India (2012)	13.3	9.4	48.6	7.7
Japan (2011)	3.0	2.1	7.0	1.3
Korea (2011)	11.2	9.6	34.1	5.6

Source: Author's calculation using most-favored-nation tariff rates from the World Trade Organization.

Table 10.2 Share of Four-Digit Harmonized System Categories of Applied Tariff Rates in Thailand, 1989–2008 (%)

Tariff Bands	*1989*	*1995*	*2002*	*2003*	*2004–2008*
0	2.5	2.6	5.6	5.7	6.0
0.1–5	14.4	17.3	33.3	37.7	48.8
5.1–10	14.2	17.6	14.1	14.2	14.8
10.1–15	12.7	3.2	3.9	4.5	3.6
15.1–20	15.4	16.4	21.4	17.9	8.4
20.1–30	15.8	16.0	13.8	14.3	12.7
30–100	25.0	26.8	7.8	5.8	5.7

Source: Data for 1989 and 1995 is from WTO (1990) and WTO (1995), respectively. Data for 2002–2008 is from authors' compilation from official documents provided by the Ministry of Finance.

and 11.9% in the 10%–20% and 20%–30% brackets, respectively. The share of the more than 30% classification dropped sharply to around 15% in 2010.

Relatively high tariff levels together with a cascading tariff structure tend to alter relative prices in favor of producing goods for the domestic market, instead of targeting exports. This seems to be in contradiction with the export orientation of Thailand, reflected by the increasing share of exports to GDP over the past two decades. A possible explanation involves the presence of effective tariff-exemption schemes in Thailand. In this setting, domestic firms can be export oriented and apply available tariff-exemption schemes in order to mitigate any adverse effects of input tariffs on their international competitiveness. In Thailand, imports subject to all tariff-exemption schemes accounted for 45% of total imports in 2012 (Kohpaiboon and Jongwanich 2014).

Table 10.3 reveals statistical indicators denoting how firms engage in globalization, that is, export-sale ratios and ratios of raw material imports to total materials used, both measured in percentages. They are reported in terms of average, maximum, and minimum rates. Results are classified into five categories across ERP figures. Patterns observed in Table 10.3 tend to be in line with the theoretical postulations of the firm heterogeneity literature. Engaging in exports incurs fixed and sunk costs. Therefore, in a given industry, regardless of the ERP figure, only some firms export. There is a vast difference between the maximum and minimum values in all ERP categories. Secondly, in theory, industries subjected to high and positive ERP tend to sell their products locally in order to reap the economic rents induced by protection. This pattern, to a certain extent, is found in Table 10.3. The mean value of the export-sale ratio of firms located in industries with around zero and negative ERP is higher than those experiencing positive ERP. Interestingly, such a pattern is not clearly

Table 10.3 Market Orientation and Raw Material Sourcing Behavior of Thai Manufacturing Firms in 2011

	Mean	*Max.*	*Min.*
Export-sale ratios (% of total sales):			
Highly negative ERP (< –10%)	9.1	88.8	0.0
Moderately negative ERP (–2%–10%)	8.3	85.5	0.0
Around zero ERP (–2%–2%)	9.0	81.3	0.0
Moderate positive ERP (2%–10%)	7.1	79.6	0.0
Highly positive ERP (> 10%)	8.8	85.9	0.0
Raw material imports (% of total raw materials used):			
Highly negative ERP (< – 10%)	8.6	90.3	0.0
Moderately negative ERP (–2%–10%)	6.8	81.3	0.0
Around zero ERP (–2%–2%)	9.5	87.9	0.0
Moderate positive ERP (2%–10%)	8.6	86.4	0.0
Highly positive ERP (> 10%)	9.3	83.6	0.3

Source: Authors' compilation from the 2011 industrial census.
Note: ERP = effective rate of protection.

observed when considering the raw material import criterion. The mean value of the percentage of raw material imports to total used goods swings up and down across ERP categories. Industries subject to around zero ERP exhibit the highest raw material import ratios, followed by those in highly positive ERP conditions. Firms in highly negative ERP and moderate positive ERP environments have the same figure of raw material import ratios. This unclear pattern is likely due to the fact that the extent to which domestic and imported raw materials are substituted varies across industries rather than due to any protection-related considerations.

10.4 The model

The model used here starts with the trans-log production function of the firm. The plant's value added is a function of two primary inputs (i.e., labor and capital), their squared terms, and their interaction patterns. Labor is further disaggregated into production and non-production workers to capture their difference in contributing to firm productivity. Blue-collar workers are regarded as the former and white-collar the latter. Over and above these considerations, a set of firm- and industry-specifics as well as trade-policy variables are included as controlling variables, as expressed in equation (1):

$$\begin{aligned}\ln VA_{ij} = &\beta_0 + \beta_1 \ln K_{ij} + \beta_2 \left(\ln K_{ij}\right)^2 + \beta_3 \ln PL_{ij} + \beta_4 \ln NL_{ij} + \beta_5 \left(\ln PL_{ij}\right)^2 \\ &+ \beta_6 \left(\ln NL_{ij}\right)^2 + \beta_7 \ln PL_{ij} * \ln K_{ij} + \beta_8 \ln NL_{ij} * \ln K_{ij} + \gamma_1 FS_{ij} \\ &+ \gamma_2 IS_j + \gamma_3 tradepolicy_j + \varepsilon_{ij} \qquad (1)\end{aligned}$$

where VA_{ij}: value added of firm i in industry j,
K_{ij}: capital used by firm i in industry j,
PL_{ij}: production workers employed by firm i in industry j,
NL_{ij}: non-production workers employed by firm i in industry j,
FS_{ij}: a set of firm-specific characteristics of firm i in industry j,
IS_j: a set of industry-specific characteristics of industry j, and
$tradepolicy_j$: the nature of trade policy of industry j.

There are four firm-specific constituents of firm i in industry $j\left(FS_{ij}\right)$. The first two constituents of firm i in industry j concern market orientation, measured by two proxies. One involves the export-sale ratio $\left(mkt_{ij}\right)$ introduced in the model. Firms whose output is intended for export tend to be alert to any productivity improvement opportunities and eventually enhance their productivity. Hence, the coefficient associated with mkt_{ij} is expected to be positive. The second aspect of market orientation is the extent to which imported raw materials are used as a percentage of total raw materials $\left(rawm_{ij}\right)$. Firms which import raw materials benefit from the technology embodied in such materials, thus improving their productivity. The coefficient associated with $rawm_{ij}$ is also expected to be positive.

The other three that comprise FS_{ij} are ownership (own_{ij}), R&D investment (RD_{ij}), and (FS_{ij}) promoted status by Thailand's Board of Investment (BOI_{ij}). Firm ownership is introduced into the model due to the consensus in foreign direct investment (FDI) literature (e.g., Caves 2007) that foreign firms are generally more productive than indigenous counterparts. So, own_{ij} is expected to be positive and is measured by the firms' foreign equity (%) share. As measured here by the firm's research, planning, and development expenditure to total sales, RD_{ij} positively affects firms' productivity, so the associated coefficient is expected to be positive. The variable BOI_{ij} is a zero-one binary dummy variable, which is equal to one when a firm is Thailand's Board of Investment (BOI) promoted and zero otherwise. This is intended to control for the possible effect of BOI tariff-exemption schemes on the relationship between productivity and input tariffs.

Three industry-specific factors are introduced in the model. The first concerns the extent to which an industry engages in global production networks. This is important for many economies in East Asia, such as Thailand, which have been long integrated into the global production network of multinationals (Athukorala and Kohpaiboon 2015). Ideally, details at the firm level (e.g., whether firms are actually engaged in MNEs' production sharing, whether they import tailor-made raw materials for specific customers, etc.) are needed. Unfortunately, such details at the firm level are not available within the Thai dataset. To overcome the unavailability of perfect measures of global production sharing, two alternative proxies at the industry level are used in this study. The first two proxies involve shares of parts and component in total imports $(GPN1_j)$ and total trade $(GPN2_j)$, respectively, as reflected in Equations (2) and (3):

$$GPN1_j = \frac{\text{P\&C Imports}_j}{\text{Total Imports}_j}, \tag{2}$$

$$GPN2_j = \frac{\text{P\&C trade (import+export)}_j}{\text{Total Trade}_j}. \tag{3}$$

The higher the share, the more important the global production sharing involved is to the industry. The parts list is the result of a careful disaggregation of trade data based on Revision 3 of the Standard International Trade Classification (SITC Rev. 3) extracted from the United Nations trade data reporting system (UN Comtrade Database). It is important to note that the Comtrade Database does not provide for the construction of data series covering the entire range of fragmentation-based trade. The parts list used here is from that developed in Athukorala and Kohpaiboon (2009).[7] To convert SITC to International Standard Industry Classification (ISIC), standard concordance is applied.

The second industry-specific variable concerns producer concentration (CR_j). Industries with high barriers to entry are likely to be concentrated and are often capital and/or skills intensive. This could make firms less responsive to any technological improvement, so it negatively affects productivity (negative sign). On the other hand, as argued in the well-known creative destruction thesis by Schumpeter, a highly concentrated industry would give firms greater incentive to innovate. If so, the coefficient associated with producer concentration could be positive. Producer concentration is measured by the sum of the sales share of the top-four firms in total.

The variable $tradepolicy_j$ is introduced to examine the study's main hypothesis. Two alternatives of trade policy are used in this study. The first is effective rate of protection (ERP_j) measured according to Equation (4). As argued in previous studies, input and output tariff cuts could have different effects on productivity, so they are introduced together as alternative measures of trade policy.

$$ERP_j = \frac{t_j - \sum_{k=1}^{n} a_{kj} t_k}{1 - \sum_{k=1}^{n} a_{kj}}, \tag{4}$$

where t_j: tariff on outputs on industry j,
t_k: tariff on inputs k, and
a_{kj}: a value share of inputs k used in finished products on industry j.

To examine whether the effect of trade policy varies across firms, an interaction term between firms' specific and the trade-policy variable is introduced. That is, $ERP_j * mkt_{ij}$ and $ERP_j * rawn_{ij}$ are activated. The former implies that once protection is given to an industry, the effects potentially vary according to the extent to which firms export their products to world markets. Similarly, in the latter case, the effect of protection on firms' productivity could depend on how much such firms are integrated globally through importing raw materials and intermediates. In addition, the interaction term between ERP and ownership $(ERP_j * own_{ij})$ is introduced in view of the fact that foreign firms might behave differently in different trade policy environments (known as Bhagwati's hypothesis).[8] Trade liberalization could provide an incentive for foreign firms to behave productively. By contrast, the rent-seeking behavior of foreign firms is more likely under trade restriction. This could hinder overall productivity improvement.

When input and output tariffs, represented by $inputtariff_j$ and $outputtariff_j$, are separately introduced, interactions are incorporated according to Equation (5):

$$\begin{aligned} &ERP_j + ERP_j * \mathrm{mkt}_{ij} + ERP_j * rawm_{ij}; \\ &\left(t_j - \sum_{k=1}^{n} a_{kj} t_k\right) + \left(t_j - \sum_{k=1}^{n} a_{kj} t_k\right) * \mathrm{mkt}_{ij} + \left(t_j - \sum_{k=1}^{n} a_{kj} t_k\right) * rawm_{ij}, \\ &outputtariff_j - inputtariff_j + outputtariff_j * \mathrm{mkt}_{ij} - inputtariff_j * \mathrm{mkt}_{ij} \\ &\quad + outputtariff_j * rawm_{ij} - inputtariff_j * rawm_{ij} \end{aligned} \tag{5}$$

where $outputtariff_j$: tariff on outputs of industry $j\left(t_j\right)$, and
$inputtariff_j$: the weighted average of input tariff from $k = 1, \ldots, n$, $\left(\sum_{k=1}^{n} a_{kj} t_k\right)$.

Note that to mitigate for any possible endogeneity problem from these industry-specific factors, they are all in lag. All in all, the empirical model to be estimated is as follows:

$$\begin{aligned}\ln VA_{ij} &= \beta_0 + \beta_1 \ln K_{ij} + \beta_2 \left(\ln K_{ij}\right)^2 + \beta_3 \ln PL_{ij} + \beta_4 \ln NL_{ij} + \beta_5 \left(\ln PL_{ij}\right)^2 \\ &+ \beta_6 \left(\ln NL_{ij}\right)^2 + \beta_7 \ln PL_{ij} * \ln K_{ij} + \beta_8 \ln NL_{ij} * \ln K_{ij} + \gamma_1 own_{ij} \\ &+ \gamma_2 RD_{ij} + \gamma_3 rawm_{ij} + \gamma_4 mkt_{ij} + \gamma_5 BOI_{ij} + \lambda_1 CR_{j,t-j} + \lambda_2 GPN_{j,t-j} \\ &+ \lambda_4 tradepolicy_{j,t-1} + \phi_1 tradepolicy_{j,t-1} * mkt_{ij} \\ &+ \phi_2 tradepolicy_{j,t-1} * rawm_{ij} + \varepsilon_{ij} \end{aligned} \tag{6}$$

where $\ln VA_{ij}$: value added of firm i in industry j (in natural log);
$\ln K_{ij}$: capital used by firm i in industry j (in natural log);
PL_{ij}: productive workers employed by firm i in industry j;
NL_{ij}: non-productive workers employed by firm i in industry j;
$tradepolicy_{j,t-1}$: lag variable of trade policy, measured alternatively by:

1 effective rate of protection $\left(ERP_j\right)$ and
2 $outputtariff_j$ $\left(t_j\right)$ and $inputtariff_j$ $\left(\sum_{k=1}^{n} a_{kj} t_k\right)$;

mkt_{ij}: market orientation of firm i of industry j, measured by the percentage of exports to total sales;

$rawm_{ij}$: input sourcing of firm i of industry j, measured by the percentage of imported raw materials and intermediates to total inputs;

own_{ij}: ownership of firm i of industry j, measured by the share of foreign owners in total capital;

RD_{ij}: the share of R&D expenditure as a percentage of the total sales of firm i of industry j;

BOI_{ij}: a binary dummy variable, which is equal to one when firm i of industry j is BOI promoted, and zero otherwise;

$CR_{j,t-j}$: producer concentration ratio of industry j at time t–j, that is, $CR_{j,2006}$ is used; and

$GPN_{j,t-1}$: the degree of industry involvement in the global production networks of industry j at time t–1, measured by two alternatives:

1 $GPN1_{j,t-1}$: the share of parts and component imports to total imports at the four-digit ISIC level and
2 $GPN2_{j,t-1}$: the share of parts and components trade (exports + imports) to total trade at the four-digit ISIC level.

10.5 Dataset and cleaning procedure

The dataset best suited for our current purposes would comprise long-panel data derived from establishments in Thai manufacturing, covering the period both before and after major trade-reform measurements. Unfortunately, such a dataset is not available in Thailand. So far, Thailand has had three industrial censuses, 1996, 2006, and 2011, all of which are cross-sectional in nature. These three censuses are not able to be formulated for use as a panel dataset as the identification numbers (ID Nos.) used in each census are assigned differently. In particular, a given ID No. of two different censuses does not necessarily denote the same firm.

The latest census (2011) contains 98,482 observations. Of this, 71,387 observations refer to self-employed workers (zero record of paid workers) or micro enterprises (entailing less than or equal to 10 workers). Given the current research focus, we exclude self-employed and micro-enterprise figures. Hence, the remaining observations number 27,095. As occurred in the censuses of 1996 and 2006, there are many duplicate samples, in which at least two observations report the same values for most of the variables. To identify duplicated observations, we employ the criterion wherein if samples report identical values of seven key variables, they are treated as duplicated samples. The seven key variables include total workers, female workers, initial fixed assets, ending fixed assets, registered capital, sales value, and input values. Following this criterion, 4,418 duplicated samples had to be removed. The remaining observations comprise 22,677 cases.

Next, we decided to discount observations reporting unrealistic values of key variables. They include negative value-added, low value-added (less than 10,000 baht), and low fixed assets (less than 10,000 baht). Finally, eight industries that either serve minority niches in the domestic market (e.g., processing of nuclear fuel, manufacture of weapons and ammunition, etc.), in the service sector (e.g., building and repair of ships, manufacture of aircraft and spacecraft, and recycling), or are explicitly preserved for local enterprises (e.g., manufacture of ovens, furnaces, and furnace burners, manufacture of coke oven products, etc.) were excluded. All in all, 13,593 observations remain. Please see the summarization and correlation of variables in Tables 10.4 and 10.5 for a more definitive picture.

Table 10.4 Data Summary

Variables	*Mean*	*Std. Dev.*	*Min.*	*Max.*
VA_{ij}	15.88	2.40	9.21	25.26
PL_{ij}	0.99	1.39	0.00	8.88
NL_{ij}	3.67	1.13	0.00	9.50
K_{ij}	15.84	2.32	9.21	26.32
own_{ij}	4.19	17.21	0.00	100.00

(*Continued*)

Variables	Mean	Std. Dev.	Min.	Max.
mkt_{ij}	7.430	21.90	0.00	100.00
$rawm_{ij}$	6.27	18.53	0.00	100.00
RD_{ij}	-11.87	6.85	-13.82	20.51
BOI_{ij}	0.07	0.253	0.00	1.00
ERP_j	0.05	0.17	-0.58	0.60
$cr4_{j,t-j}$	0.45	0.09	0.32	0.65
$GPN1_{j,t-j}$	0.04	0.12	0.00	1.00
$GPN2_{j,t-j}$	0.03	0.11	0.00	1.00

Source: Authors' calculation.
Note: All variables are in logarithms, with the exception of ownership (own_{ij}), market-oriented (mkt_{ij}), imported raw materials ($rawm_{ij}$), trade policy (ERP_j), concentration ratios ($CR_{j,t-1}$), and production networks ($GPN1_{\ j,t-1}$, $GPN2_{\ j,t-1}$).

10.6 Results

Initially the equations are estimated using the ordinary least squares (OLS) method, while paying attention to the possible presence of heterogeneity and outliers. Due to the nature of cross-sectional data, it is likely that outliers could impact on and mislead the estimated parameters and, therefore, careful treatment of outliers is needed. Cook's distance is used to identify suspected outliers. The intra-class correlation or the clustered data, based on industry level, is tested (Table 10.6) and the results show a low level of correlation (0.267).

Tables 10.7 and 10.8 present estimation results wherein trade policy is measured by ERP and the tariffs of output and inputs separately introduced, respectively. Column A in both tables is based on $GPN1_{j,t-1}$, whereas Column B is based on $GPN2_{j,t-1}$. The overall results from both tables are largely similar. The estimation results are not sensitive to choice of global production networks. Hence, the following result interpretation will be discussed, based on these two tables. The coefficients corresponding to the interaction terms between non-production workers and capital, as well as the squared terms of two types of workers, are statistically significant, suggesting the trans-log production function fits well with the data, as opposed to the more restrictive Cobb-Douglas measure. The statistical difference of coefficients associated with production and non-production workers supports the hypothesis that quality of labor matters in determining firm productivity. The higher the incidence of white-collar workers employed by firms, the higher their productivity, all other things remaining constant.

In both tables, the coefficients corresponding to own_{ij}, mkt_{ij}, and $rawm_{ij}$ turn out to be positive and significantly different from zero at the 1% level. This finding is in line with previous studies, in that foreign firms tend to be more productive than their indigenous counterparts, all things being equal. Meanwhile, firms, either domestic or foreign, engaging in international business

Table 10.5 Correlation Matrix of Variables Used in the Regression Analysis

Variables	VA_{ij}	PL_{ij}	NL_{ij}	K_{ij}	own_{ij}	mkt_{ij}	$rawm_{ij}$	RD_{ij}	ERP_j	$outputtariff_j$	$inputtariff_j$	$cr4_{j,t-j}$	$GPN1_{j,t-1}$	$GPN2_{j,t-1}$
VA_{ij}	1.00													
$PLij$	0.61	1.00												
NL_{ij}	0.54	0.46	1.00											
K_{ij}	0.81	0.57	0.49	1.00										
own_{ij}	0.23	0.22	0.23	0.21	1.00									
mkt_{ij}	0.29	0.33	0.24	0.25	0.37	1.00								
$rawm_{ij}$	0.25	0.22	0.23	0.23	0.34	0.36	1.00							
RD_{ij}	0.23	0.20	0.19	0.21	0.05	0.11	0.11	1.00						
ERP_j	−0.01	0.003	0.01	−0.01	0.08	0.02	0.05	−0.02	1.00					
$outputtariff_j$	0.08	0.06	0.07	0.08	0.07	0.09	0.04	0.02	0.73	1.00				
$inputtariff_j$	0.14	0.10	0.10	0.12	0.04	0.06	0.00	0.03	−0.19	0.32	1.00			
$cr4_{j,t-j}$	0.02	−0.01	0.01	0.06	−0.004	0.02	0.02	−0.02	0.06	0.04	−0.05	1.00		
$GPN1_{j,t-1}$	0.14	0.12	0.10	0.10	0.11	0.08	0.07	0.03	0.14	0.17	0.24	0.13	1.00	
$GPN2_{j,t-j}$	0.13	0.13	0.09	0.10	0.11	0.05	0.08	0.03	0.20	0.21	0.24	0.14	0.92	1.00

Source: Authors' calculation.

Table 10.6 Intragroup Correlation (No. of obs. = 13,593; R^2 = 0.26)

Source	*SS*	*df*	*MS*	*F*	*Prob. > F*
Between ISIC_obs.	22,120.752	60	368.679	80.13	0.000
Within ISIC_obs.	62,257.048	13,532	4.601		
Total	84,377.800	13,592	6.21		
Intra-class correlation	Asym. S. E.	95% Conf. interval	Estimated S. D. of ISIC Obs. effect	Estimated S. D. within ISIC Obs.	Estimated reliability of ISIC Obs. mean (evaluated at n = 217.59)
0.267	0.056	0.16–0.37	1.29	2.14	0.98

Source: Authors' estimates.

Table 10.7 Productivity Determinants Based on Effective Rate of Protection and the 2011 Census

Variables	*Column A*		*Column B*	
	Coefficient	t-*statistics*	*Coefficient*	t-*statistics*
Intercept	2.02**	3.91	1.96**	3.80
PL_{ij}	0.41**	3.53	0.41**	3.52
NL_{ij}	2.27**	23.9	2.27**	23.89
K_{ij}	0.82**	12.25	0.83**	12.33
$PL_{ij} \times K_{ij}$	0.00	0.04	0.00	0.05
$NL_{ij} \times K_{ij}$	−0.12**	−20.48	−0.12**	−20.44
PL_{ij}^2	0.003	0.3	0.003	0.31
NL_{ij}^2	0.04**	6.29	0.04**	6.16
K_{ij}^2	−0.004*	−1.29	−0.004*	−1.37
BOI_{ij}	0.10*	2.04	0.11**	2.14
own_{ij}	0.003**	3.47	0.003**	3.55
mkt_{ij}	0.002**	3.49	0.002**	3.67
$rawm_{ij}$	0.002**	2.85	0.002**	2.76
RD_{ij}	0.01**	8.03	0.01**	8.06
$ERP_{j,\,t-j}$	−0.29**	−3.8	−0.29**	−3.74
$ERP_{j,\,t-j} \times mkt_{ij}$	−0.01*	−1.97	−0.01**	−2.12
$ERP_{j,\,t-j} \times rawm_{ij}$	0.003	0.85	0.004	0.90
$cr4_{j,\,t-j}$	−0.35**	−3.02	−0.32**	−2.76
$GPN1_{j,\,t-1}$	0.63	6.88		
$GPN2_{j,\,t-1}$			0.54	5.02
No. of obs.	13,593		13,593	
Adjusted R^2	0.73		0.73	
F-statistic	1,717 (p-value=0.00)		1,711 (p-value=0.00)	

Source: Authors' estimate.

Note: An increase in effective rate of protection (ERP) reflects a higher level of trade protection. ** and * represent statistical significance at the 1% and 5% level, respectively.

Table 10.8 Productivity Determinants Based on Effective Rate of Protection Decomposition and the 2011 Census

Variables	*Column A*		*Column B*	
	Coefficient	t-*statistics*	*Coefficient*	t-*statistics*
Intercept	2.01**	3.89	1.96**	3.79
PL_{ij}	0.42**	3.55	0.42**	3.55
NL_{ij}	2.26**	23.79	2.26**	23.79
K_{ij}	0.81**	11.94	0.81**	11.98
$PL_{ij} \times K_{ij}$	−0.0003	−0.03	−0.0002	−0.02
$NL_{ij} \times K_{ij}$	−0.12**	−20.40	−0.12**	−20.37
PL_{ij}^2	0.004	0.40	0.004	0.41
NL_{ij}^2	0.04**	6.32	0.04*	6.21
K_{ij}^2	−0.003	−1.09	−0.003	−1.13
BOI_{ij}	0.10**	2.06	0.11*	2.14
own_{ij}	0.003**	3.50	0.003**	3.59
mkt_{ij}	0.004**	2.33	0.004**	2.41
$rawm_{ij}$	0.006**	4.08	0.01**	4
RD_{ij}	0.01**	8.12	0.01**	8.15
$outputtariff_j$	−0.27	−1.01	−0.27	−0.99
$inputtariff_j$	3.02**	4.90	3.25**	5.3
$outputtariff_j \times mkt_{ij}$	−0.02*	−2.09	−0.02*	−2.25
$inputtariff_j \times mkt_{ij}$	−0.01	−0.27	−0.01	−0.23
$outputtariff_j \times rawm_{ij}$	−0.004	−0.30	−0.003	−0.25
$inputtariff_j \times rawm_{ij}$	−0.09**	−2.81	−0.09**	−2.78
$cr4_{j,\,t\text{-}j}$	−0.32**	−2.74	−0.28**	−2.45
$GPN1_{j,\,t-1}$	0.54**	5.71		
$GPN2_{j,\,t-1}$			0.42**	3.83
No. of obs.	13,593		13,593	
Adjusted R^2	0.73		0.73	
F-statistic	1,503.3(p-value=0.00)		1,500 (p-value=0.00)	

Source: Authors' estimates.
** and * represent statistical significance at the 1% and 5% level, respectively.

dealings (either exporting their products, importing raw materials, or both), tend to be more productive than those strictly engaged in local markets. Similarly, the positive sign of RD_{ij} suggests firms spending more on R&D tend to have higher value-added incorporated, ceteris paribus. The positive and statistically significant coefficient associated with BOI_{ij} is likely to reflect the positive effect of BOI privileges on firms' value added, including that of BOI tariff-exemption schemes.

With respect to industry-specific factors, our study found negative statistical significance of $CR_{j,2006}$ at the 1% level. Such a negative sign suggests that industries that are highly concentrated or that entail high barriers to entry tend to include firms that are less responsive to any technological improvement. Both $GPN1_{j,t-1}$ and $GPN2_{j,t-1}$ are positive and significant at 1%, confirming the robustness of the fact that participating in global production networks potentially results in higher productivity improvements among firms. This finding is consistent with Kohpaiboon and Jongwanich (2014), who revealed that participation in the global production network of Thai firms is beyond simple assembly and wage premiums in the industries engaged in the network being statistically found.

Regarding the effects of trade policy, the coefficient corresponding to ERP_j turns out to be negative and significant statistically (Table 10.7). All other things being equal, firms under higher cross-border protection have lower productivity. In other words, protection can hinder the process of productivity improvement. This finding reconfirms the conclusions in previous studies in favor of trade liberalization. Interestingly, the negative effect of ERP_j on productivity is higher for exporting firms, as suggested by the statistical significance of the interaction term between ERP_j and mkt_{ij}.

Table 10.8 presents estimate results when ERP_j is deconstructed into output and input tariffs. The coefficient associated with $outputtariff_j$ attains the theoretically expected sign, but is not statistically significant. The coefficient corresponding to the interaction term between $outputtariff_j$ and mkt_{ij} is negative and statistically significant. That is, negative effects would occur only with exporting firms. There is no significant effect on non-exporting firms.

This finding seems intuitive for a country like Thailand. In such circumstances, where output is subject to higher tariff rates than input and various tariff-exemption schemes are available, firms choose either to export or sell domestically. It would be costly for a firm to sell in both domestic and foreign markets simultaneously as they must deal with administrative complications, such as how much to sell locally, how to refund the portion of input tariff paid, as well as any cumbersome technicalities tariff-exemption schemes might entail. This is especially true for small and medium-sized firms. The histogram showing the export-sales ratios of exporting firms presented in Figure 10.1 confirms such behavior. In particular, firms selling in both domestic and foreign markets (i.e., their export-sales ratio is between 25% and 80%) account for less than 30% of the total sample. The majority of these firms export either more than 80% of their products, or less than 20%.

While export-oriented firms pay less attention to any protection granted to the domestic market, such protection certainly does matter for domestic-oriented organizations to remain in business. Keeping domestic-oriented firms in business inflates wages to a certain extent, as they compete with export-oriented to attract the local workforce. Inflated wages would have an uneven and negative effect on these two groups of firms. The adverse effect tends to be greater on exporting firms as their output price is driven by worldwide forces. All other things being equal, inflated wages could not be passed onto output price, thereby squeezing markups. On the other hand, domestic-oriented firms would be in a better position to pass inflated wages onto output prices to a certain extent due to the presence of their trade protection. A reduction in output tariffs could generate a tougher competitive environment in the domestic market. Less productive firms, which are likely to be purely domestic-oriented, would potentially be forced out of business. For exporting firms, such a reduction would not have any direct effect as they sell at world-price levels. Instead, the reduction in output tariffs would lower pressure on domestic wages and lead to a situation wherein some

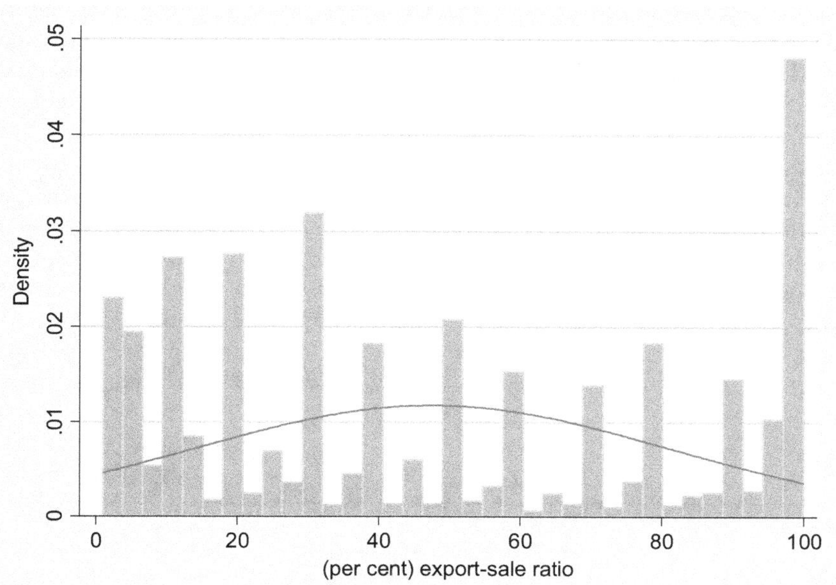

Figure 10.1 Histogram of Export-Sales Ratios of Exporting Thai Manufacturing Firms in 2011.

Source: Authors' calculation using the database discussed in the text.

Note: Exporting firms are defined as firms whose export value is greater than zero. The line is normal density plot.

workers relocate from less productive and more domestically oriented firms to more productive and export-oriented operations (i.e., resource reallocation).

The positive and statistical significance of $inputtariff_j$ is in line with findings in Table 10.8, that is, a negative effect of protection on productivity was revealed, as discussed above.[9] This suggests that for a given level of output tariff, lowering input tariffs would simply increase the protection effectively granted to output producers. Note that the net effect of input tariff reduction on productivity remains ambiguous, as the interaction term between $inputtariff_j$ and $rawm_{ij}$ turns out to be negative and statistically significant. When firms rely substantially on imported raw materials (defined as imported raw materials accounting for more than 33.6% of their total raw material expenses), input tariff reduction could have a net positive effect on productivity, all other things being equal. The positive effects derived from technology being embodied tends to overshadow the negative effects from increased effective protection. Operations relying less on imported raw materials are less likely to benefit from embedded technology and, consequently, any net effects they experience would be negative.[10] One finding we reveal that is different from Amiti and Konings (2007) concerns highlighting the role of country-specific factors, such as economic development and the extent to which firms are engaged in the global economy, in explaining the relationship between tariffs and productivity. The analysis in Amiti and Konings (2007) covers the period of 1991 and 2001 where input tariffs in Indonesia remained substantially high. By contrast, our analysis involves 2006 where major tariff reform undertaken in the late 1990s had focused on input tariff cuts.

Another interesting finding is that the interaction term between ownership and trade policy (both ERP_j and the disaggregated function) is statistically insignificant (Table 10.9). This potentially reflects the dominant role of export-oriented and efficiency-seeking FDI, which is motivated by strengthening global competitiveness. These foreign firms tend to be eligible for tariff-exemption schemes, so their behavior would not be altered by being granted protection.

As a robustness check, the empirical model (Equation 6) is re-estimated, using the previous 2006 industrial census. Tables 10.10–10.12 correspond to

Table 10.9 Productivity Determinants Based on Effective Rate of Protection Decomposition, Interaction with Ownership, and the 2011 Census

Variables	*Column A*		*Column B*	
	Coefficient	t-*statistics*	*Coefficient*	t-*statistics*
Intercept	2.01**	3.88	1.95**	3.78
PL_{ij}	0.42**	3.57	0.42**	3.57
NL_{ij}	2.26**	23.83	2.27**	23.84
K_{ij}	0.81**	11.96	0.81**	12
$PL_{ij} \times K_{ij}$	−0.0005	−0.05	−0.0004	−0.04
$NL_{ij} \times K_{ij}$	−0.12**	−20.43	−0.12**	−20.4
PL_{ij}^2	0.0046	0.42	0.005	0.43
NL_{ij}^2	0.042**	6.30	0.04**	6.19
K_{ij}^2	−0.003	−1.09	−0.003	−1.14
BOI_{ij}	0.10*	2.02	0.11*	2.1
own_{ij}	0.001	0.29	0.0005	0.23
$own_{ij} \times outputtariff_j$	−0.01	−0.51	−0.01	−0.5
$own_{ij} \times inputtariff_j$	0.05*	1.51	0.06*	1.61
mkt_{ij}	0.004**	2.58	0.004**	2.69
$rawm_{ij}$	0.01**	4.27	0.01**	4.22
RD_{ij}	0.01**	8.15	0.01**	8.18
$outputtariff_j$	−0.27	−1.01	−0.27	−0.99
$inputtariff_j$	2.98**	4.83	3.21**	5.22
$outputtariff_j \times mkt_{ij}$	−0.02*	−1.94	−0.02*	−2.11
$inputtariff_j \times mkt_{ij}$	−0.02	−0.63	−0.02	−0.63
$outputtariff_j \times rawm_{ij}$	−0.003	−0.23	−0.003	−0.18
$inputtariff_j \times rawm_{ij}$	−0.10**	−3.07	−0.10**	−3.07
$cr4_{j,\,t\text{-}j}$	−0.32**	−2.79	−0.29**	−2.51
$GPN1_{j,\,t-j}$	0.53**	5.65		
$GPN2_{j,\,t-j}$			0.42**	3.78
No. of obs.	13,593		13,593	
Adjusted R^2	0.73		0.73	
F-statistic	1,389.6 (p-value=0.00)		1,387.0(p-value=0.00)	

Source: Authors' estimate.

** and * represent statistical significance at the 1% and 5% level, respectively.

Tables 10.7–10.9, respectively, but use the 2006 census. To a certain extent, the results are in line with findings in the more recent census, with a few exceptions of statistical insignificance concerning some coefficients. The main finding of Tables 10.10–10.12 supports the crucial role of trade liberalization in productivity improvement. Despite being smaller in magnitude, the coefficient associated with ERP is negative and statistically significant (Table 10.10). The difference lies in the fact that the coefficient corresponding to the interaction term $ERP_j \times mkt_{ij}$ in Table 10.10 is not statistically significant. However, it is when the 2011 census is applied. Another difference is that all the interaction terms with input and output tariffs turn out to be statistically insignificant, although their corresponding coefficients attain their theoretical expected sign. The divergence in these results between 2006 and 2011 industrial censuses are potentially due to the differences in labor market conditions. As mentioned above, the channel through which lowering output tariffs affects the productivity of exporting firms is via competing workforces. The extent to which the labor market is tightening is significantly different between these two periods.

Table 10.10 Productivity Determinants Based on Effective Rate of Protection and the 2006 Census

Variables	*Column A*		*Column B*	
	Coefficient	t-*statistics*	*Coefficient*	t-*statistics*
Intercept	5.88**	18.48	5.85**	18.38
PL_{ij}	1.77**	29.88	1.77**	29.93
NL_{ij}	1.69**	34.57	1.69**	34.6
K_{ij}	0.04	0.84	0.04	0.9
$PL_{ij} \times K_{ij}$	–0.10**	–23.94	–0.10**	–23.97
$NL_{ij} \times K_{ij}$	–0.10**	–31.52	–0.10**	–31.54
PL_{ij}^2	0.05**	14.09	0.05**	14.12
NL_{ij}^2	0.07**	18.4	0.07**	18.43
K_{ij}^2	0.03**	15.27	0.03**	15.23
BOI_{ij}	0.27**	8.08	0.27**	8.11
own_{ij}	0.003**	5.62	0.003**	5.83
mkt_{ij}	0.002**	–3.17	–0.002**	–2.96
$rawm_{ij}$	0.004**	6.96	0.004**	6.93
RD_{ij}	0.01**	9.73	0.01**	9.67
$ERP_{j,\,t-j}$	–0.15*	–2.23	–0.15**	–2.27
$ERP_{j,\,t-j} \times mkt_{ij}$	0.001	0.71	0.001	0.53
$ERP_{j,\,t-j} \times rawm_{ij}$	–0.003	–0.95	–0.003	–0.88
$cr4_{j,\,t-j}$	0.20**	2.88	0.21**	3.07
$GPN1_{j,\,t-j}$	0.53**	6.34		
$GPN2_{j,\,t-j}$			0.44**	4.19
No. of obs.	15,564		15,564	
Adjusted R^2	0.76		0.76	
F-statistic	2,768.5 (*p*-value=0.00)		2,776.0 (*p*-value=0.00)	

Source: Authors' estimates.

Note: An increase in effective rate of protection (ERP) reflects a higher level of trade protection. ** and * represent statistical significance at the 1% and 5% level, respectively.

Table 10.11 Productivity Determinants Based on Effective Rate of Protection Decomposition and the 2006 Census

Variables	*Column A*		*Column B*	
	Coefficient	t-*statistics*	*Coefficient*	t-*statistics*
Intercept	5.94**	18.64	5.91**	18.55
PL_{ij}	1.76**	29.75	1.77**	29.78
NL_{ij}	1.69**	34.47	1.69**	34.51
K_{ij}	0.02	0.32	0.02	0.34
$PL_{ij} \times K_{ij}$	−0.10**	−23.85	−0.10**	−23.87
$NL_{ij} \times K_{ij}$	−0.10**	−31.43	−0.10**	−31.45
PL_{ij}^2	0.05**	14.08	0.05**	14.12
NL_{ij}^2	0.07**	18.3	0.07**	18.31
K_{ij}^2	0.03**	15.53	0.03**	15.51
BOI_{ij}	0.27**	8.11	0.27**	8.13
own_{ij}	0.003**	5.63	0.003**	5.83
mkt_{ij}	0.001	0.1	0.0003	0.26
$rawm_{ij}$	0.01**	4.22	0.01**	4.05
RD_{ij}	0.01**	9.55	0.01**	9.48
$outputtariff_j$	−0.28	−1.18	−0.29	−1.19
$inputtariff_j$	3.35**	5.55	3.58**	5.96
$outputtariff_j \times mkt_{ij}$	0.001	0.17	−0.0002	−0.03
$inputtariff_j \times mkt_{ij}$	−0.04*	−1.99	−0.04**	−2.01
$outputtariff_j \times rawm_{ij}$	−0.01	−0.67	−0.01	−0.58
$inputtariff_j \times rawm_{ij}$	−0.03*	−1.23	−0.03	−1.09
$cr4_{j,\,t\text{-}j}$	0.24**	3.42	0.26**	3.67
$GPN1_{j,\,t-1}$	0.43**	5.08		
$GPN2_{j,\,t-1}$			0.31**	2.89
No. of obs.	15,564		15,564	
Adjusted R^2	0.76		0.76	
F-statistic	2,415.2 (p-value=0.00)		2,421.7 (p-value=0.00)	

Source: Authors' estimates.
** and * represent statistical significance at the 1% and 5% level, respectively.

Table 10.12 Productivity Determinants Based on Effective Rate of Protection Decomposition, Interaction with Ownership, and the 2006 Census

Variables	*Column A*		*Column B*	
	Coefficient	t-*statistics*	*Coefficient*	t-*statistics*
Intercept	5.95**	18.65	5.92**	18.56
PL_{ij}	1.76**	29.74	1.77**	29.78
NL_{ij}	1.69**	34.47	1.69**	34.51
K_{ij}	0.01	0.29	0.02	0.32
$PL_{ij} \times K_{ij}$	−0.10**	−23.83	−0.10**	−23.85
$NL_{ij} \times K_{ij}$	−0.10**	−31.41	−0.10**	−31.44
PL_{ij}^2	0.05**	14.04	0.05**	14.08
NL_{ij}^2	0.07**	18.23	0.07**	18.25
K_{ij}^2	0.03**	15.54	0.03**	15.51
BOI_{ij}	0.28**	8.13	0.28**	8.14
own_{ij}	0.004**	2.46	0.003**	2.38
$own_{ij} \times outputtariff_j$	0.01	0.71	0.01	0.66
$own_{ij} \times inputtariff_j$	−0.03	−0.99	−0.02	−0.79

Variables	*Column A*		*Column B*	
	Coefficient	*t-statistics*	*Coefficient*	*t-statistics*
mkt_{ij}	0.004	−0.01	0.0002	0.18
$rawm_{ij}$	0.01**	4.19	0.005**	4.05
RD_{ij}	0.01**	9.51	0.01**	9.45
$outputtariff_j$	−0.29	−1.19	−0.29	−1.19
$inputtariff_j$	3.36**	5.57	3.59**	5.97
$outputtariff_j \times mkt_{ij}$	0.0003	0.00	−0.0014	−0.18
$inputtariff_j \times mkt_{ij}$	−0.03*	−1.7	−0.03*	−1.77
$outputtariff_j \times rawm_{ij}$	−0.01	−0.79	−0.01	−0.69
$inputtariff_j \times rawm_{ij}$	−0.02	−1.03	−0.02	−0.94
$cr4_{j,\ t\text{-}j}$	0.24**	3.39	0.26**	3.65
$GPN1_{j,\ t-j}$	0.44**	5.09		
$GPN2_{j,\ t-j}$			0.31**	2.87
No. of obs.	15,564		15,564	
Adjusted R^2	0.76		0.76	
F-statistic	2,224.4 (*p*-value=0.00)		2,230.2 (*p*-value=0.00)	

Source: Authors' estimates.
** and * represent statistical significance at the 1% and 5% level, respectively.

10.7 Conclusion and policy recommendations

The paper examined the effect of trade protection on firm productivity, using the Thai manufacturing sector as a case study. In our analysis, trade policy and global participation are treated as two different variables. Our key finding is that foreign firms tend to be more productive than indigenous, all other things remaining constant. Firms, either domestic or foreign, engaging in global market participation tended to be more productive than those strictly operating in local markets. As expected, firms spending more on R&D are inclined to have higher productivity. Participating in global production networks could result in higher rates when considering a firm's productivity improvement.

While controlling for firms' global participation, defined as the export-sales ratio, and the extent to which raw materials are imported, our study highlights the important role of trade policy. Trade liberalization, measured by lowering the ERP, could potentially encourage firms to commit to productivity improvement activities. When ERP is decomposed, the effects of input and output tariffs on productivity are different, in line with the findings from previous studies.

However, this study differs from previous research projects in finding an ambiguous effect of lowering input tariffs on productivity, as there are two distinct effects running opposite to each other. Lowering input tariffs potentially allows firms to access higher quality foreign inputs and benefit from the learning effects from the foreign technology embedded in such inputs and the increased variety they represent, all of which lead to improvements in their productivity. What is novel in this study, on the other hand, is the emphasis on the fact that lowering input tariffs could also lead to an increase in the effective rate of protection granted to the finished products of firms. This could discourage them from being active in productivity improvement activities and, thus, hamper their productivity. This represents a highly pertinent consideration for policymakers in developing countries whose trade policy reform process is lopsided. Their policymakers put great effort into lowering input tariffs, while being reluctant to alter output tariffs. Such a lopsided reform process is risky. The policy lessons learnt by many Latin American/African economies during the 1950s–1970s in their pursuit of import substitution industrialization strategies (i.e., maintaining high tariffs on output to nurture domestic firms, but lowering input tariffs) represent pertinent reference cases in this context. Focusing solely on lowering input tariffs, while leaving output tariffs untouched, may well obstruct overall productivity improvement significantly.

Two policy inferences can be made from our research. Firstly, our study supports global integration (e.g., exporting products, importing raw materials) as it potentially promotes productivity enhancement. With respect to policymaking, what matters is the prevailing policy environment. Conditions must be conducive for firms to enthusiastically engage with globalization. Such an environment represents the second priority concerning channels that will potentially reap benefits. Some might prefer to enter into a joint venture with a leading foreign firm, while the others may derive benefits from the advance technology embodied in imported machinery and/or raw materials. Secondly, our findings raise policy awareness issues regarding solely overemphasizing input tariffs when performing trade policy reform. Input and output tariffs are able to work differently in promoting firms' productivity. Where the trade policy reform process is concerned, both input and output tariffs must be taken into consideration together. This ensures that the economic incentives between selling in domestic and foreign markets are neutralized and that trade is actually liberalized. Otherwise, this could potentially act as a barrier to productivity improvement.

10.8 Acknowledgements

The authors would like to thank the journal's anonymous referee for the valuable comments. We also benefited from suggestions and comments from Professor S. Urata, Dr. K. Hayakawa, Associate Professor C. Hahn, Dr. C. Lee, Associate Professor S. Thangavelu, and other participants in the Economic Research Institute for ASEAN and East Asia (ERIA) Microdata Project Workshop held on February 10–11, 2015 in Bali.

Notes

1 One noteworthy consideration is that there was another group that examined the effects of trade liberalization/restriction on productivity through case studies. Two influential works include the Bhagwati-Krueger project for the NBER in the 1970s and the Papageorgious-Michalely-Choksi study for the World Bank in the 1980s. While there were policy insights suggested, their case studies include only a handful of countries and their analytical tools varied significantly from one case to the other. This makes caution a prerequisite when any generalization from the findings is made.

2 See the literature review in López (2005).
3 Later works such as Melitz and Ottaviano (2008) or Bernard, Redding, and Schott (2011) propose different mechanisms of the selection effect. The former focuses on the fact that liberalization increases demand elasticity and lower markups. This forces unproductive firms to exit. In the latter, the selection effect takes place between ex ante endowment-driven comparative advantage and disadvantage industries.
4 Interestingly, Yu (2015) makes uses of uniquely rich information utilizing transaction-level custom data and constructs input and output tariffs at the firm level. In particular, they employ weighted averages of input and output tariffs at the industry, using actual firms' import and export transaction records as weights.
5 See a possible explanation of self-selection, for example, sunk costs, imported technology, and increased R&D in Bernard and Jensen (2004), and López (2005).
6 For example, Kessing (1983); Westphal, Rhee, and Pursell (1979, 1984); Aw and Batra (1998); Wortzel and Wortzel (1981); Hobday (1995); Pietrobelli (1998); Pack and Saggi (1997); and Nelson and Pack (1999).
7 The use of lists of parts in the Board Economics Classification (BEC) 42 and 53 is a point of departure. Note that the parts in BEC211 are not included as they are primary products, which are usually classified as traditional, rather than fragmented intermediates. The additional lists of parts are included based on firm interviews reported in Kohpaiboon (2010). Data on trade in parts are separately listed under the commodity classes of machinery and transport equipment (SITC7) and miscellaneous manufacturing (SITC8). This was based on firm interviews elaborated in Kohpaiboon (2010). The list of parts and components is available on request.
8 See the discussion in Kohpaiboon (2006).
9 Considering ERP formula expressed in Equation (6) above, the negative coefficient associated with ERP will result in negative and positive coefficients on output and input tariffs, respectively.
10 Note that the cutting point found in this study seems high as opposed to the average figure of 6% when all firms are included. In fact, the firms which rely substantially on imported raw materials are exporting firms. The corresponding average in these exporting firms is 24.2%, so that the cutting point is reasonable.

References

Amiti, Mary, and Jozef Konings. 2007. "Trade Liberalization, Intermediate Inputs, and Productivity: Evidence from Indonesia." *American Economic Review* 97, no. 5: 1611–38.

Athukorala, Prema-chandra, and Archanun Kohpaiboon. 2009. "Intra-Regional Trade in East Asia: The Decoupling Fallacy, Crisis, and Policy Challenges." ADBI Working Paper no. 177. Tokyo: Asian Development Bank Institute.

———. 2015. "Global Production Sharing, Trade Patterns, and Industrialization in Southeast Asia." Chapter 7 in *Routledge Handbook of Southeast Asian Economics*, edited by Ian Coxhead. New York: Routledge, 139–161.

Aw, Bee Yan, and Geeta Batra. 1998. "Technological Capability and Firm Efficiency in Taiwan (China)." *World Bank Economic Review* 12, no. 1: 59–79.

Aw, Bee Yan, and Amy R. Hwang. 1995. "Productivity and the Export Market: A Firm-Level Analysis." *Journal of Development Economics* 47, no. 2: 313–32.

Balassa, Bela. 1965. "Tariff Protection in Industrial Countries: An Evaluation." *Journal of Political Economy* 73, no. 6: 573–94.

Bernard, Andrew B., and J. Bradford Jensen. 2004. "Why Some Firms Export." *Review of Economics and Statistics* 86, no. 2: 561–69.

Bernard, Andrew B., Stephen J. Redding, and Peter K. Schott. 2011. "Multiproduct Firms and Trade Liberalization." *Quarterly Journal of Economics* 126, no. 3: 1271–318.

Bernard, Andrew B., and Joachim Wagner. 1997. "Exports and Success in German Manufacturing." *Review of World Economics* 133, no. 1: 134–57.

Bustos, Paula. 2011. "Trade Liberalization, Exports, and Technology Upgrading: Evidence on the Impact of MERCOSUR on Argentinean Firms." *American Economic Review* 101, no. 1: 304–40.

Corden, Warner Max. 1966. "The Structure of a Tariff System and the Effective Protective Rate." *Journal of Political Economy* 74, no. 3: 221–37.

Caves, R. 2007. *Multinational Enterprise and Economic Analysis* (3rd edn). Cambridge, MA: Cambridge University Press.

Fernandes, Ana M. 2007. "Trade Policy, Trade Volumes and Plant-Level Productivity in Colombian Manufacturing Industries." *Journal of International Economics* 71, no. 1: 52–71.

Goldberg, Pinelopi, Amit K. Khandelwal, Nina Pavcnik, and Petia Topalova 2010, "Multiproduct Firms and Product Turnover in the Developing World: Evidence from India." *Review of Economics and Statistics* 92(4): 1042–49.

Greenaway, David, and Richard Kneller. 2007. "Firm Heterogeneity, Exporting and Foreign Direct Investment." *Economic Journal* 117, no. 517: F134–F161.

Grossman, Gene M., and Elhanan Helpman. 1991. *Innovation and Growth in the Global Economy*. Cambridge, MA: MIT Press.

Halpern László, Miklós Koren, and Adam Szeidl. 2015. "Imported Inputs and Productivity." *American Economic Review* 105(2): 3660–703.

Helpman, Elhanan, and Paul R. Krugman. 1985. *Market Structure and Foreign Trade: Increasing Returns, Imperfect Competition, and the International Economy*. Cambridge, MA: MIT Press.

Hobday, Mike. 1995. "East Asian Latecomer Firms: Learning the Technology of Electronics." *World Development* 23, no. 7: 1171–93.

Jongwanich, Juthatip, and Archanun Kohpaiboon. 2007. "Determinants of Protection in Thai Manufacturing." *Economic Papers* 26, no. 3: 276–94.

Kessing, Donald B. 1983. "Linking Up to Distant Markets: South to North Exports of Manufactured Consumer Goods." *American Economic Review* 73, no. 2: 338–42.

Kohpaiboon, Archanun. 2006. *Multinational Enterprises and Industrial Transformation: Evidence from Thailand*. Cheltenham: Edward Elgar.

———. 2010. *Product Fragmentation Phenomenon, Production Networks of Multinationals and Implication on Thai Manufacturing* [in Thai]. Bangkok: Misterkopy.

Kohpaiboon, Archanun, and Juthathip Jongwanich. 2014. "Global Production Sharing and Wage Premiums: Evidence from the Thai Manufacturing Sector." *Asian Development Review* 31, no. 2: 141–64.

Krugman, Paul R. 1979. "Increasing Returns, Monopolistic Competition, and International Trade." *Journal of International Economics* 9, no. 4: 469–79.

Levine, Ross, and David Renelt. 1992. "A Sensitivity Analysis of Cross-Country Growth Regressions." *American Economic Review* 82, no. 4: 942–63.

Lileeva, Alla, and Daniel Trefler. 2010. "Improved Access to Foreign Markets Raises Plant-Level Productivity ... For Some Plants." *Quarterly Journal of Economics* 125, no. 3: 1051–99.

López, Ricardo A. 2005. "Trade and Growth: Reconciling the Macroeconomic and Microeconomic Evidence." *Journal of Economic Surveys* 19, no. 4: 623–48.

Melitz, Marc J. 2003. "The Impact of Trade on Intra-Industry Reallocations and Aggregate Industry Productivity." *Econometrica* 71, no. 6: 1695–725.

Melitz, Marc J., and Giancarlo I. P. Ottaviano. 2008. "Market Size, Trade, and Productivity." *Review of Economic Studies* 75, no. 1: 295–316.

Melitz, Marc J., and Daniel Trefler. 2012. "Gains from Trade When Firms Matter." *Journal of Economic Perspectives* 26, no. 2: 91–118.

Nelson, Richard R., and Howard Pack. 1999. "The Asian Miracle and Modern Growth Theory." *Economic Journal* 109, no. 457: 416–36.

Pack, Howard, and Kamal Saggi. 1997. "Inflows of Foreign Technology and Indigenous Technological Development." *Review of Development Economics* 1, no. 1: 81–98.

Pietrobelli, Carlo. 1998. *Industry Competitiveness and Technological Capabilities in Chile: A New Tiger from Latin America?* Basingstoke: Macmillan; New York: St. Martin's Press.

Sala-i-Martin, Xavier X. 1997. "I Just Ran Two Million Regressions." *American Economic Review* 87, no. 2: 178–83.

Topalova, Petia, and Amit Khandelwal. 2011. "Trade Liberalization and Firm Productivity: The Case of India." *Review of Economics and Statistics* 93, no. 3: 995–1009.

Trefler, Daniel. 2004. "The Long and Short of the Canada-U.S. Free Trade Agreement." *American Economic Review* 94, no. 4: 870–95.

Westphal, Larry E., Yung W. Rhee, and Garry Pursell. 1979. "Foreign Influences on Korean Industrial Development." *Oxford Bulletin of Economics and Statistics* 41, no. 4: 359–88.

———. 1984. "Sources of Technological Capability in South Korea." In *Technological Capability in the Third World*, edited by Martin Fransman and Kenneth King. London: Macmillan, 279–300.

World Trade Organization (WTO). 1990. *Trade Policy Review: Thailand*. Geneva: WTO.

World Trade Organization (WTO). 1995. *Trade Policy Review: Thailand*. Geneva: WTO.

World Trade Organization (WTO). 1999. *Trade Policy Review: Thailand*. Geneva: WTO.

Wortzel, Lawrence H., and Heidi Vernon Wortzel. 1981. "Export Marketing Strategies for NIC and LDC-Based Firms." *Columbia Journal of World Business* 16, no. 1: 51–60.

Yu, Miaojie. 2015. "Processing Trade, Tariff Reductions and Firm Productivity: Evidence from Chinese Firms." *Economic Journal* 125, no. 585: 943–88.

11 Overseas expansion and domestic business restructuring in Japanese firms

Keiko Ito and Kenta Ikeuchi

11.1 Introduction

The expansion of overseas production by multinational enterprises (MNEs) is expected to have various impacts on their domestic activities. To date, a number of researchers have investigated the impacts of overseas expansion on domestic employment and production, exports and imports, productivity, and so on, using either firm-, plant-, or industry-level data.

The majority of such studies have not found a strong negative relationship between overseas expansion and domestic activities such as employment and production within MNEs.[1] Rather, many studies confirm that MNEs tend to be more productive and that their overseas expansion contributes to their productivity growth. Although the mechanism of MNEs' productivity growth has not yet been understood sufficiently, restructuring or reshuffling business activities within MNEs is likely to be a source of their productivity growth. On the one hand, the changes in skill compositions within an MNE can produce productivity growth, as confirmed by many papers such as Head and Ries (2002); Hijzen, Görg, and Hine (2005); and Becker, Ekholm, and Muendler (2013), who identify a link between offshoring and labor demand shifts toward high-skilled workers. More recently, a growing number of papers have focused on labor demand shifts away from manual low-wage task workers toward non-routine high-wage task workers. For example, Oldenski (2012) showed that US MNEs are more likely to offshore more routine tasks, whereas less routine tasks are performed in their headquarters.

On the other hand, related to the skill composition changes, domestic activities are likely to be reshuffled within an MNE and some domestic establishments would be forced to change their line of business drastically if an MNE shifts a part of their domestic operation to a foreign country. Some establishments may even be shut down, while other domestic establishments may be able to improve their productivity, either by expanding their operations or by shifting their activities to more technologically advanced ones. Such restructuring within an MNE is likely to contribute to overall productivity improvement at the firm level.

In fact, several recent studies suggest that MNEs tend to be more active in resource reallocation across establishments within a firm. For example, Kneller et al. (2012), using firm plant-linked data for Japanese manufacturing firms, found that plants belonging to multi-plant MNEs are the most likely to be shut, followed by multi-plant non-MNE firms and then single-plant MNEs. Kodama and Inui (2015) also find that multi-establishment MNEs show a high job-reallocation rate, that is, the sum of the job creation rate and job destruction rate, suggesting that MNEs have greater flexibility in adjusting to changing market conditions. Furthermore, using British firm plant-linked data, Simpson (2012) found that firms investing in low-wage economies tend to close down plants in low-skill industries at home.

The findings of these studies suggest that MNEs actively reallocate resources across establishments within the firm, while overall firm-level employment is not necessarily reduced in response to overseas expansion. Rather, they are more likely to improve overall productivity as a result of efficient resource reallocation within the firm.[2]

Numerous previous studies have examined why MNEs relocate low-skill labor intensive processes to low-wage developing countries and are expected to shift their activities at home toward less labor intensive and/or high-skill labor intensive processes. More recently, however, an increasing number of studies have added another dimension to this issue: tradability of tasks. Grossman and Rossi-Hansberg (2008) claim that offshoring is costly if the tasks required for processes at an offshore location are not easily moved offshore even though workers can be hired more cheaply abroad. The literature has shown that firms are more likely to offshore routine tasks and keep non-routine tasks in their headquarters (Oldenski 2014). Routine tasks can be broken down into clear steps and procedures and communicated to someone located overseas. Non-routine tasks, however, involve decision making and problem solving that often require face-to-face communication within a team and are more difficult to communicate to overseas affiliates. Taking the tradability of tasks into account, recent studies such as Ebenstein et al. (2014); Goos, Manning, and Salomons (2014); and Keller and Utar (2016) argue that offshoring or import competition from low-wage countries leads to job polarization mainly by pushing workers from initially abundant mid-level routine jobs in manufacturing toward both high-wage non-routine and low-wage manual jobs.[3] Oldenski (2014), taking both comparative advantages and task tradability into account, also showed that offshoring by US firms has contributed to relative gains for the most high-skilled workers performing non-routine tasks and relative losses for middle-skilled workers performing routine tasks.[4]

Moreover, as the servitization of manufacturing firms, in other words, the phenomenon where activities of manufacturing firms are shifted toward more non-manufacturing services activities, has been observed often in developed countries, MNEs' domestic activities may shift toward activities using non-tradable service jobs intensively. Therefore, the bottom line of these arguments is that globalization affects not only the relative demand for low-skill and high-skill workers within manufacturing activities, but also the relative demand for workers in tradable task sectors and in non-tradable task sectors including both manufacturing and services activities.

Such changes in labor demand are expected to lead to within-firm reallocation of resources, that is, domestic business restructuring by MNEs, and to industry composition changes within a firm depending on the skill type of each industry. Therefore, in this paper, we examine: (1) what type of establishments are closed or newly established, and (2) what type of establishments increase or reduce their employment, when an MNE expands its overseas operation. Although our paper is closely related to Simpson (2012), a novelty of our study is that it investigates the impact of overseas business expansion on domestic business restructuring within the firm, taking task tradability (or task "offshorability") into account. We assume that routine tasks are more tradable (or offshorable) tasks in the sense that such tasks can be easily displaced by computers and relocated overseas. Therefore, when the cost of investment abroad decreases, firms are expected to relocate routine-task labor-intensive activities abroad and keep non-routine-task labor-intensive activities within their home country, if the MNE's home country has a comparative advantage in non-routine occupations. Moreover, we examine not only establishment closures but also new establishment entries and employment growth in continuing establishments within an MNE, which is an aspect that most previous studies have ignored.

The remainder of this study is organized as follows. Section 11.2 describes the data and presents some descriptive statistics. Section 11.3 explains the empirical framework we use in this study. Section 11.4 presents the empirical results. Finally, Section 11.5 presents the conclusion and future research questions.

11.2 Data and descriptive statistics

11.2.1 Firm establishment-matched data

The main dataset used in this study is an establishment-level panel dataset constructed from the Establishment and Enterprise Census (for years 2001 and 2006) and the Economic Census (for years 2009 and 2012) for Japan. The censuses are provided by the Ministry of Internal Affairs and Communications and cover all establishments in all industries (and only incorporated establishments in the case of agriculture, forestry, and fishery industries) in Japan. Although the censuses, except for 2012, do not contain detailed firm-level financial information, other information for each establishment such as the number of workers, the business activities at the three-digit JSIC (Japan Standard Industry Classification) industry level (approximately 480 industries), and location is available.[5] Moreover, firm ID code is attached to each establishment and we can identify which establishment belongs to which firm. For each establishment, we can identify whether it is a single-establishment firm, a branch establishment of a firm, or the headquarters establishment of a firm. For each firm, information on whether it owns domestic or foreign subsidiaries is available. We mainly use this information to identify whether a firm is multinational.[6] We should note that in the censuses, branch establishments and subsidiaries are clearly distinguished. Although a substantial number of firms own branch establishments in foreign countries, we define MNEs as firms with at least one foreign subsidiary. Therefore, firms with foreign branches but without foreign subsidiaries are defined as non-MNEs.

Unfortunately, information on the location (country or region) of foreign subsidiaries is not available in the censuses. Although many previous studies suggest that investment or offshoring to low-income countries has a different impact on domestic economies from that to high-income countries, we cannot examine potentially different effects by destination because of data constraints. However, in the case of Japanese MNEs, more than 80% of MNEs have subsidiaries in Asian countries, according to the Basic Survey of Japanese Business Structure and Activities conducted by the Ministry of Economy, Trade and Industry. Probably reflecting the geographical proximity to Asian low-wage countries relative to American or European countries, the majority of Japanese MNEs set up their subsidiaries in an Asian country first, and then expand to other regions. Therefore, it would be safe to assume that they are very likely to have a subsidiary in an Asian country.

We construct the establishment-level panel dataset for the years 2001, 2006, 2009, and 2012. Moreover, we link the firm-level information such as employment size, firm industry, and domestic or foreign subsidiaries with the establishment-level data.

For exits of establishments and/or firms, we identify them by noting if an establishment or a firm existed in the census for a certain year but disappeared in the next census. For entry of establishments and/or firms, we identify them by using the information on the start-up year.

11.2.2 Data on skill-mix by industry

Using this dataset, we investigate how firms restructure their domestic business activities when they become multinational, whether such behavior of firms with overseas subsidiaries differs from that of firms without overseas subsidiaries, and whether firms with overseas subsidiaries are more likely to concentrate on higher-skill non-routine activities domestically. More specifically, we investigate what types of establishments with respect to skills are closed or newly established when multinational firms restructure their domestic activities.

In order to measure the skill level of each establishment, following previous studies such as Costinot, Oldenski, and Rauch (2011) and Oldenski (2012), we utilize the Occupational Information Network (O*NET).[7] We use the importance of "making decisions and solving problems" as our index of how routine a task is. Similar to Oldenski (2012), who argues for the existence of a strict connection between job autonomy and routine intensity, we consider a routine-intensive task as a task with little autonomy for the individual at work. Following Costinot, Oldenski, and Rauch (2011), we measure routineness at the three-digit sector level, by combing task-level data for each occupation with sector-level data from the Japanese Population Census. Because detailed task-level data equivalent to the O*NET are not available in Japan, we use the task information for each

US occupation and match the US occupations with the Japanese occupations.[8] More specifically, we construct our "routine" task intensity measure at the sector level in the following way.

First, we match the information on tasks for each US occupation included in the June 2007 version of O*NET[9] with each Japanese occupation, using the concordance table between the 2010 US Standard Occupational Classification (SOC) codes and Japan's 2005 occupation classification codes constructed by Tomiura, Wakasugi, and Zhu (2015).[10] Then, we measure the routineness $\mu(t)$ of an occupation t as:

$$\mu(t) = 1 - P(t)/100,$$

where $P(t) \in [0, 100]$ measures the importance of making decisions and solving problems of an occupation, t, according to O*NET but matched with the Japanese occupation classifications. We define a sector as a three-digit industry in the JSIC Revision 11. We use the share of workers in each occupation for each industry, which is calculated from the 2005 Population Census data, and construct the JSIC three-digit level routine-task measure:

$$\mu^s = \sum_{t=1}^{T} b^s(t)\mu(t),$$

where μ^s is our proxy for routineness at sector s, and $b^s(t)$ is the share of employment of each occupation, t, in sector s. Thus, we construct the three-digit sector-level routine-task measure as a weighted average of occupation-level routine-task measures. Our measure is a sector-specific but time-invariant measure, assuming that the task contents do not change substantially within a sector during the period of our analysis, 2001–2012. Although we may construct a time-variant task measure, we believe that it is likely to be endogenous to establishment share changes across industries. Therefore, we use the time-invariant task measure in our analysis.

Moreover, as mentioned above, we measure the routine-task measure for each establishment using the three-digit industry-level information because of data constraints. That is, we assume that the routine-task measure is the same for all the establishments belonging to the same three-digit industry. Appendix Table 11.A1 shows the list of the 50 industries with the highest routine-task measure and the 50 industries with the lowest routine-task measure. In addition, we should note that we use the task information for each US occupation, assuming that the task contents for each occupation in Japan are the same as those in the United States. Looking at the routine-task index constructed from the OECD's Programme for the International Assessment of Adult Competencies (PIAAC) database,[11] the correlation coefficient between the Japanese and US routine-task index by occupation is over 0.6 and the Spearman rank correlation between them is also over 0.6.[12] Although the task contents for each occupation may not be exactly the same in the both countries, the correlation is high and we use the US task measure as a proxy for the Japanese task measure.

We also checked the correlation between our routine-task intensity measure and the share of unskilled workers based on the education attainment for workers in each industry. That is, we calculate the share of workers who graduated from junior college or had higher education for each industry, using the data taken from the 2000 Population Census in Japan. Then, we measure the share of unskilled workers in each industry as the residual from one: 1 – (share of workers who graduated from junior college or had higher education). The correlation coefficient for our routine-task measure and the unskilled worker share is 0.23 (statistically significant at the 1% level). The Spearman rank correlation is 0.21 and also statistically significant. The positive correlation between the two measures indicates that non-routine-task intensity positively correlates with unskilled worker share in terms of education attainment. However, the magnitude of the correlation coefficient also indicates that these two measures are not very highly correlated and that they reflect somewhat different skill characteristics. Although closer investigation of the differences across various skill intensity measures is required in our future research, we use the Costinot, Oldenski, and Rauch-type, routine-task intensity for this study.[13]

11.2.3 Descriptive statistics

Table 11.1 summarizes the number of establishments by firm ownership type and by firm-level industry. We focus on establishments belonging to private firms. More specifically, our dataset includes establishments for which the legal organization is: (1) a joint-stock company, (2) a limited or unlimited partnership, (3) a limited liability company, or (4) a mutual insurance company. We exclude branch establishments whose headquarters are located in foreign countries, because firm-level information is not available in the Japanese census for these establishments. We also exclude establishments for which employment is zero or missing. As a result, in 2006, approximately 2.6 million privately owned establishments in Japan remained in our dataset. Furthermore, we exclude establishments of firms that disappeared in the next census (the 2009 Economic Census). These firms are likely to have exited and were shut down sometime between 2006 and 2009. That is, we focus on establishments of firms that continued operating until the next census year and consequently have approximately 1.9 million such privately owned establishments in 2006 as summarized in Table 11.1. As mentioned above, we define Japanese MNEs as firms that have at least one foreign subsidiary while we define foreign MNEs as firms with a parent company in a foreign country. As shown in Table 11.1, reflecting the fact that MNEs tend to be large firms, most of the establishments of Japanese MNEs are part of a firm with more than one establishment (multi-establishment firm). Although the number of establishments of Japanese MNEs is only 4% of the total number of establishments (= 78,896/(1,817,023 + 78,896 + 6,652)), the corresponding

Table 11.1 Number of Establishments by Firm Industry and by Ownership Type in 2006

		Domestic Firms			Japanese MNEs			Foreign MNEs		
	Industry code	Total No. of Establishments	Share of establishments owned by		Total No. of Establishments	Share of establishments owned by		Total No. of Establishments	Share of establishments owned by	
Headquarters' Industry			Single-Establishment firms (%)	Multi-Establishment firms (%)		Single-Establishment firms (%)	Multi-Establishment firms (%)		Single-Establishment firms (%)	Multi-Establishment firms (%)
Primary	A, B, C, D	12,714	79.3	20.7	113	11.5	88.5	12	25.0	75.0
Construction	E	276,329	80.5	19.5	5,009	0.7	99.3	21	28.6	71.4
Manufacturing	F	281,880	67.3	32.7	23,403	3.4	96.6	1,291	8.7	91.3
Utility	G	1,524	19.4	80.6	1,007	0.2	99.8	—	—	—
Telecommunication	H	33,444	56.4	43.6	1,852	6.6	93.4	331	44.1	55.9
Transportation services	I	65,415	47.5	52.5	4,072	2.9	97.1	212	18.4	81.6
Wholesale & retail trade	J	610,081	49.5	50.5	20,385	2.1	97.9	3,029	17.9	82.1
Finance & insurance	K	31,663	39.6	60.4	9,813	0.4	99.6	854	6.6	93.4
Real estate	L	99,355	79.9	20.1	867	7.6	92.4	22	59.1	40.9
Restaurants & accommodation	M	110,822	52.8	47.2	4,972	0.2	99.8	196	10.2	89.8
Medical services & social welfare	N	17,519	61.4	38.6	67	9.0	91.0	7	28.6	71.4
Education	O	21,017	35.4	64.6	1,152	0.4	99.6	12	41.7	58.3
Miscellaneous services	P, Q	255,260	57.7	42.3	6,184	2.1	97.9	664	26.5	73.5
Total		1,817,023	60.0	40.0	78,896	2.2	97.8	6,652	16.9	83.1

Note: MNE = multinational enterprise.

share becomes nearly 10% (= 78,896 * 0.978/(1,817,023 * 0.40 + 78,896 * 0.978 + 6,652 * 0.831)) when we focus on multi-establishment firms.

As shown in Table 11.1, nearly 98% of Japanese MNEs' establishments are part of a multi-establishment firm. Given this fact and because we focus on within-firm business restructuring, we restrict our sample for the following analyses to the establishments belonging to multi-establishment firms.

Table 11.2 shows the descriptive statistics for the establishments used in our analysis: establishments belonging to multi-establishment firms. The figures in the table, except the number of observations, are averaged over the years 2001, 2006, and 2009. In fact, the 2012 census does not have information on whether a firm has at least one foreign affiliate, and we cannot identify multinationals as of 2012. Therefore, we show the average value of the statistics for the three years. To calculate exit and entry rates during the period from 2009 to 2012, however, we also use the data taken from the 2012 census, where we classified a firm's multinational status using the data for year 2009.[14]

In Table 11.2, we show the statistics for the establishments belonging to manufacturing and non-manufacturing firms, separately. Various characteristics are shown for establishments owned by three different types of firms: domestic only, Japanese-owned multinationals, and foreign-owned multinationals. First, the proportion of establishments that exit or enter in the period between two censuses is much higher for Japanese-MNE and foreign-MNE establishments than for establishments owned by domestic firms. We should note that we exclude single-establishment firms and focus on establishments belonging to multi-establishment firms that continued operating for the period between the two censuses. Even focusing on multi-establishment firms, domestic firms show lower exit and/or entry rates than Japanese and foreign MNEs, implying that MNEs are more likely to be active in shutting down and/or opening establishments. In addition, establishments owned by domestic

Table 11.2 Establishment Characteristics by Ownership Type (2001–2012)

	Manufacturing Firms			*Non-manufacturing Firms (Excluding Primary and Public Services)*		
	Domestic Firms	*Japanese MNEs*	*Foreign MNEs*	*Domestic Firms*	*Japanese MNEs*	*Foreign MNEs*
Number of observations	318,528	73,704	5,027	2,160,655	191,080	18,582
Exit (%)	15.7	19.5	21.9	18.5	22.9	25.3
Entry (%)	16.8	20.1	24.2	21.7	27.2	26.9
Employment per establishment	30.8	110.8	71.9	19.5	38.4	43.0
Multi_same 3-digit industry (%)	49.4	24.9	23.8	73.3	74.7	77.7
Multi_manufacturing (%)	11.3	10.3	4.0	1.6	1.8	1.5
Multi_nonmanufacturing (%)	37.2	62.7	70.4	24. 0	22.2	19.9
Average routine-task index	0.36	0.38	0.39	0.35	0.34	0.36

Note: MNE = multinational enterprise.

firms are on average much smaller in terms of employment size than those owned by multinationals.

We construct three indicators of multi-establishment firms: *Multi_same 3-digit industry*, *Multi_manufacturing*, and *Multi_nonmanufacturing*. *Multi_same 3-digit industry* is a dummy variable that equals one for establishments that are part of a firm with other establishments (a multi-establishment firm) and for which the three-digit industry is the same as the firm-level industry. *Multi_manufacturing* is a dummy variable that equals one for establishments that are part of a multi-establishment firm and for which the three-digit industry is not the same as the firm-level industry but is a manufacturing industry. *Multi_nonmanufacturing* is a dummy variable that equals one for establishments that are part of a multi-establishment firm and for which the three-digit industry is not the same as the firm-level industry but is a non-manufacturing industry. In the case of manufacturing firms, the share of *Multi_nonmanufacturing* is much higher for Japanese and foreign MNEs than for domestic firms, suggesting that manufacturing MNEs have many non-manufacturing establishments within the firm although their main business activity is manufacturing. The figures show that more than half (over 60%) of the establishments of manufacturing MNEs conduct non-manufacturing business activities, which is consistent with the growing importance of the servitization of manufacturing firms in developed countries (e.g., Crozet and Milet 2017; Bernard, Smeets, and Warzynski 2017). On the other hand, in the case of non-manufacturing firms, the majority of establishments within a firm belong to the same industry as the firm-level industry, suggesting that business activities are less diversified within a non-manufacturing firm.

As for average task measures, establishments owned by MNEs tend to have a slightly higher routine-task index on average than those owned by domestic multi-establishment firms in the case of manufacturing firms. However, in the case of non-manufacturing firms, establishments owned by Japanese MNEs tend to have a slightly lower routine-task index than those owned by domestic multi-establishment firms. By only looking at the average routine-task index, the differences in task intensities between domestic firms' establishments and MNEs' establishments are less clear. We will examine the relationship between routine-task intensity and establishments' dynamics in more detail by estimating empirical models in the following sections.

In Table 11.3, we examine the share of foreign-owned establishments by firm industry and its evolution over time. Columns (1)–(3) show the share of Japanese MNEs at the firm level: the number of Japanese multinational firms divided by the total number of firms, while Columns (4)–(6) show the corresponding share at the establishment level: the number of establishments owned by Japanese multinational firms divided by the total number of establishments. Looking at the firm-level shares, industries such as manufacturing, telecommunication, and finance and insurance tend to show a higher share of multinationals. Moreover, the shares tend to decrease from 2006 to 2009 while they tend to increase from

Table 11.3 Share of Multinational Enterprises by Firm Industry: Multi-establishment Firms Only

		Firm-Level Share (%)			*Establishment-Level Share (%)*		
Headquarters' Industry	*Industry Code*	*Share of MNEs in Total Number of Multi-establishment Firms*			*Share of MNEs in Total Number of Establishments of Multi-establishment Firms*		
		2001	*2006*	*2009*	*2001*	*2006*	*2009*
		(1)	*(2)*	*(3)*	*(4)*	*(5)*	*(6)*
Primary	A, B, C, D	1.4	1.9	1.0	3.2	3.4	3.4
Construction	E	0.7	0.8	0.6	7.3	8.4	8.8
Manufacturing	F	6.4	9.1	7.3	16.3	20.4	20.6
Utility	G	1.6	6.0	5.0	9.5	39.0	44.7
Telecommunication	H	3.1	5.1	4.7	9.0	14.0	10.1
Transportation services	I	1.5	2.0	1.6	15.2	10.9	8.2
Wholesale & retail trade	J	1.5	2.1	1.7	4.5	6.8	7.9
Finance & Insurance	K	5.9	5.1	4.0	40.8	35.2	46.9
Real estate	L	1.5	1.0	0.6	5.2	3.2	4.8
Restaurants & accommodation	M	0.4	0.5	0.4	5.7	10.1	11.7
Medical services & social welfare	N	0.4	0.5	0.2	0.3	0.9	1.2
Education	O	0.7	0.9	0.6	5.0	8.6	7.1
Miscellaneous services	P, Q	0.9	1.2	0.9	3.8	5.7	5.5
Total		2.2	3.1	2.4	8.6	10.2	10.9

Note: MNE = multinational enterprise.

2001 to 2006 in many industries, which might reflect the trend in the growth of the world economy.

The establishment-level shares in Columns (4)–(6) show a more or less similar trend, but the magnitude of the shares are much larger than the firm-level shares, reflecting the fact that multinationals tend to be larger and have more establishments within a firm than non-multinational firms. Moreover, the establishment-level MNE shares did not decrease substantially from 2006 to 2009 in many industries, although the firm-level corresponding shares decreased in many industries during the period. This finding may imply that MNEs have increased their presence in the overall Japanese economy in recent years not by extensive margin changes but by intensive margin changes. That is, although the number of new MNEs may be stagnant, existing MNEs may have increased the number of establishments within their firm. However, the decrease in the share of MNEs for the period 2006–2009 could be a short-run impact of the drastic economic downturn after the 2008 financial crisis.

11.3 Estimation approach

11.3.1 Baseline specifications

Following the research frameworks in Kneller et al. (2012) and Simpson (2012), the starting point of our empirical analysis is to examine the determinants of the exit of establishments, taking routine-task intensity of establishments into account. Then, we will also examine the routine-task intensity of new establishments.

Simpson (2012) assumes that foreign countries are more abundant in low-skill labor with lower wages than the home country and that the wages of high-skill workers at home are no higher than the wages of high-skill workers in foreign countries. Then, she shows that a reduction in the fixed cost of investment in a relatively low-skill-abundant country results in the substitution of domestic production for overseas production in low-skill-intensive industries but not in high-skill-intensive industries. Therefore, the likelihood of plant closure resulting from outward FDI will decrease with the high-skill intensity of the industry. On the other hand, for firms that switch production overseas, expand output, and increase profits, their remaining activities at home will increase output and the likelihood of survival.

Although we follow the empirical model of Simpson (2012), our theoretical motivation follows Acemoglu and Autor (2011) and Oldenski (2014). In the model of Acemoglu and Autor (2011), workers are classified as low-, medium-, or high-skilled, and each skill level has a comparative advantage in the performance of a subset of production tasks. Tasks are indexed such that high-skilled workers have a comparative advantage in the higher numbered tasks. They assume that although workers of any skill level can perform any task, only one skill level in which workers have a comparative advantage will actually be used in the production of that task in equilibrium. If a set of tasks that had previously been performed by middle-skilled workers were offshored, the range of tasks performed by these workers would be reduced. However, the ranges of tasks performed by high-skilled workers (non-routine tasks) and by low-skilled workers (manual tasks) are less likely to be affected.

Therefore, taking task "offshorability" into account, we expect that firms that expand overseas activities are more likely to shut down establishments in medium-skill-intensive industries than establishments in high or low skill-intensive industries. We use the routine-task intensity measure explained above to characterize both skill levels and task tradability for each industry. Following Simpson (2012), we estimate a linear probability model of establishment death:

$$\begin{aligned} Exit_{it+s} = {} & \alpha + X_{it}\beta + \gamma MNE_{ft} + \delta MNE_{ft} * Relative\ RTI_{it} + \mu Relative\ RTI_{it} \\ & + \varphi SIZE_{ft} + Ind_j + T_t + R_r + F_f + \varepsilon_{it}, \end{aligned} \tag{1}$$

where i indicates establishment, f firm, j establishment's industry, t year, and r establishment's prefecture. The variable $Exit_{it+s}$ is a dummy variable that equals one if establishment i exits during the period from t and $t + s$: s denotes the number of years until the next census. X_{it} is a vector of establishment characteristics and includes age and establishment size (measured as log employment). We also include a dummy variable, *Same three-digit industry*, that equals one for establishments for which the three-digit industry is the same as the firm-level industry. The variable MNE_{ft} is a firm-level variable that equals one if firm f, which owns establishment i, has one or more subsidiaries in foreign countries, and zero, otherwise. The variable *Relative* RTI_i is the routine-task index for establishment i relative to the average routine-task index for firm f. The routine-task index is defined at the three-digit industry level as explained in the previous section, but we take the deviation from the simple average of the routine-task index for all the establishments belonging to a firm. As described above, the routine-task index is the same for all the establishments belonging to the same three-digit industry and is not a time variant index. However, by taking the deviation from the firm-level average, our relative RTI measure becomes establishment-specific and time variant. The higher the relative RTI value is, the more routine-task intensive the establishment within the firm is. Assuming that routine tasks are relatively low- or medium-skill tasks and are more easily moved offshore than non-routine tasks, we expect that MNEs are more likely to shut down establishments in more routine-task intensive industries at home when they expand overseas activities. Therefore, we expect a positive value for δ. The variable $SIZE_{ft}$ is the log of employment at the firm level, which is included to control for the firm size, and Ind_j are establishment i's industry dummies that control for industry-level offshoring or import competition and industry-specific technological changes, and so on. We also include year dummies, T_t, establishment i's region (defined as one of the 47 prefectures in Japan) dummies, R_r, and firm f's dummies F_f, and are in order to control for year-, region-, and firm-specific shocks or characteristics, respectively. In the estimations, the standard errors are clustered at the firm level. As mentioned above, we restrict our sample to establishments of firms that continue operating until the next census year in order to avoid possible biases arising from firm exits. Moreover, we restrict our sample to establishments that are part of a multi-establishment firm, because the decision for firm exits and for closure of one of the establishments owned by a firm should be considered separately.

In addition to the exit analysis, we also examine whether new establishments of MNEs have different characteristics from those of domestic firms. More specifically, our main interest is whether MNEs are more likely to shift their business activities toward less routine-task intensive activities. In order to examine whether new establishments of MNEs are less routine-task intensive than those of other domestic firms, we estimate the following model:

$$Relative\ RTI_{it+s} = \alpha + X_{ft}\beta + \gamma MNE_{ft} + Ind_k + T_t + R_r + F_f + \varepsilon_{it}, \quad (2)$$

where *Relative* RTI_{it+s} is the routine-task index for establishment i which was newly established between years t and $t + s$, and it is relative to the average routine-task index for firm f as of year $t + s$. The vector of firm characteristics,

X_{ft}, includes firm age, size (measured as log employment), and the number of domestic establishments firm f owns. The variable MNE_{ft} is a firm-level variable that equals one if firm f, which owns establishment i, has one or more subsidiaries in foreign countries. Firm f's industry dummies, Ind_k, control for firm industry-specific effects. The variables T_t, R_r, and F_f are year, new establishment i's region (prefecture), and firm dummies, respectively. We estimate Equation (2) using OLS, clustering standard errors at the firm level. We restrict our sample to establishments of firms that continued operating during the period between two censuses in order to avoid possible biases arising from firm entries. We also restrict our sample to establishments that are part of a multi-establishment firm, because the decision for a new firm's entry and for adding of new establishments by an incumbent firm should be considered separately.

Furthermore, we examine the determinants of employment growth for the continuing establishments. We estimate the following model and see whether the establishments of MNEs in routine-task intensive industries increase their employment more than establishments of other types.

$$\Delta \ln EMP_{it+s} = \alpha + X_{it}\beta + \gamma MNE_{ft} + \delta MNE_{ft} \times Relative\ RTI_{it} + \mu Relative\ RTI_{it} + \varphi SIZE_{ft} + Ind_j + T_t + R_r + F_f + \varepsilon_{it}, \tag{3}$$

where $\Delta \ln EMP_{it+s}$ is the growth rate of employment for establishment i from year t to $t + s$. The other variables are defined in the same way as those in Equation (1) above. However, in order to control for within-firm resource reallocation effects, we include a dummy variable that equals one if firm f, which owns the continuing establishment, shut down at least one other establishment i during the period from year t to $t + s$. We restrict our sample to establishments that continue operating during the period between the two censuses and to establishments that are part of a multi-establishment firm. We estimate Equation (3) using OLS, clustering standard errors at the firm level.

11.3.2 Empirical issues

The decision to invest in a foreign country is potentially endogenous, because decisions to invest abroad and to shut down establishments at home (or restructure domestic business activities) are possibly made simultaneously. Moreover, a firm may invest abroad in order to survive in the domestic market. Therefore, we control for the time-invariant firm-specific effects in the above specifications in order to take into account the possibility that unobserved firm-characteristics are related to both the decisions to invest abroad and restructure domestic activities.

In order to address the potential endogeneity issue more rigorously, however, we estimate the probability of a firm owning a subsidiary abroad as an instrument. This type of approach is used in Simpson (2012) and Bandick (2016), etc., and this approach generates estimates comparable to Heckman's (1978) well-known endogeneity bias-corrected OLS estimator. In order to generate a firm's predicted probability to invest abroad, we estimate the following model using the linear probability model approach:

$$\Pr\left(MNE_{ft}=1\right)=\Phi\left(X_{ft},\ Ind_j,\ T_t,\ R_r,\ F_f,\ USDIA_{jt-2}\right), \tag{4}$$

where X_{ft} is a vector of relevant firm-specific characteristics in year t, which may affect the firm's probability to invest in foreign countries in year t. Ind_j, T_t, R_r, and F_f control for time-invariant fixed industry, year, prefecture, and firm effects, respectively. The estimation is conducted using firm-level data, not establishment-level data, and we control for firm-level industry fixed effects and prefecture fixed effects of the location of a firm's headquarter. Given firm-level data availability and assuming that a firm's decision to invest abroad is influenced by its productivity and the degree of its exposure to foreign markets, we include the following firm-level variables in the vector X_{ft}. We include log employment, number of domestic branch establishments owned by a firm, and number of foreign branch establishments owned by a firm, which are proxies for firm size and productivity. The number of three-digit industries that a firm is engaged in is also included as another proxy for its productivity, assuming that the more diversified firms should have higher productivity by exercising economies of scope. As proxies for the degree of a firm's exposure to foreign markets, we include ownership share of foreign shareholders and the ratio of employment at foreign branch establishments to total employment of the firm. We also control for firm age and the routine-task index for a firm.[15]

As for the exogenous explanatory variable included in the FDI decision equation, we include the two-year lagged ratio of workers employed by overseas affiliates of US MNEs to the total employment in the United States at the industry level. The ratio is calculated using the number of employed workers taken from the US Current Employment Statistics compiled by Bureau of Labor Statistics and the number of employees at foreign affiliates of US Multinational firms taken from the US Direct Investment Abroad, Activities of US Multinational Enterprises (MNEs), compiled by the US Bureau of Economic Analysis. Because it is not straightforward to find a strictly exogenous variable at the firm level, we use the industry-level foreign worker share for the US MNEs as an exogenous variable that explains Japanese firms' propensity to become multinational.

We estimate Equation (4) using the linear probability model and calculate the probability to invest abroad for each firm.[16] Then, using the estimated probability as an instrument for the MNE dummy variable, we estimate instrumental variables (IV) regressions for Equations (1), (2), and (3).

For further robustness checks, we split our sample into establishments owned by manufacturing firms and those owned by non-manufacturing firms and conduct separate estimations, taking into account the possibility that the domestic business restructuring of manufacturing firms is different from that of non-manufacturing firms because of the structural, technological, and demographic changes of developed economies. We define manufacturing firms as firms whose firm-level industry is classified as one of the manufacturing industries.

11.4 Estimation results

11.4.1 Exit of establishments

Table 11.4 shows the estimation results for Equation (1). Larger establishments are less likely to exit, which is consistent with most previous studies on firm exits. Although older establishments are less likely to exit, they are more likely to exit in the case of establishments owned by manufacturing firms (Columns 2 and 5). Establishments in the same industry as the firm's industry are less likely to exit. The coefficient of the *MNE* variable is positive and significant in the case of the IV regressions (Columns 4–6), suggesting that the probability of establishment exits increases when a firm becomes multinational. However, the coefficient of the *MNE* variable is not significant for the OLS regressions (Columns 1–3). The variable *Relative RTI* tends to have a positive coefficient and the estimated coefficient is statistically significant for all the cases except the cases of manufacturing firms (Columns 2 and 5). As for the coefficient of the interaction term of *MNE* and relative *RTI*, it is positive and significant in the case of the IV regression for non-manufacturing firms (Column 6), while the OLS estimations show somewhat different results. According to these results, more routine-task intensive establishments are more likely to exit and the likelihood of exit is even higher when the firm becomes multinational. This is the case particularly for non-manufacturing firms. This result is consistent with our prediction that routine-task intensive establishments are more likely to be shut down when a firm becomes multinational.

11.4.2 Type of new establishments

Table 11.5 shows the estimation results for Equation (2). The *MNE* variable tends to have a negative coefficient in all the cases, and the estimated coefficient is statistically significant in the case of the IV regression for non-manufacturing firms (Column 6). The negative coefficient suggests that newly added establishments tend to be less routine-task intensive compared with other establishments belonging to the same firm when a firm becomes multinational as expected. However, such results are not statistically significant in most cases.

As for the other explanatory variables, the number of establishments owned by a firm tends to have a positive coefficient and the estimated coefficient is statistically significant in Columns 4 and 5. This suggests that firms that already have many establishments tend to open less routine-task intensive establishments.

11.4.3 Employment growth rate of continuing establishments

Table 11.6 shows the estimation results for Equation (3). The coefficient of the MNE variable is positive and statistically significant in all the cases, suggesting that establishments owned by MNEs tend to have a higher employment growth rate than those owned by non-MNEs. Moreover, the coefficient of the

Table 11.4 Exit of Establishments and Overseas Expansion of MNEs: Multi-establishment Firms Only (Dependent Variable: Exit [Dummy variable])

	(1)	*(2)*	*(3)*	*(4)*	*(5)*	*(6)*
	All Firms	*Manufacturing Firms*	*Non-manufacturing Firms*	*All Firms*	*Manufacturing Firms*	*Non-manufacturing Firms*
	OLS	*OLS*	*OLS*	*IV*	*IV*	*IV*
Establishment Age	-0.00029***	0.00024***	-0.00035***	-0.00028***	0.00025***	-0.00034***
	[0.00004]	[0.00008]	[0.00005]	[0.00003]	[0.00007]	[0.00003]
Establishment size (log)	-0.07180***	-0.07431***	-0.07198***	-0.07232***	-0.07427***	-0.07261***
	[0.00078]	[0.00103]	[0.00091]	[0.00033]	[0.00087]	[0.00037]
Multi_same 3-digit industry	-0.04069***	-0.03388***	-0.04686***	-0.04033***	-0.03408***	-0.04705***
	[0.00197]	[0.00279]	[0.00246]	[0.00080]	[0.00270]	[0.00093]
Relative RTI	0.08595***	0.01683	0.11674***	0.09270***	0.04311	0.11835***
	[0.01648]	[0.03856]	[0.01989]	[0.01327]	[0.03734]	[0.01541]
MNE	-0.00335	-0.01028	0.00242	0.09269***	0.16608***	0.13993***
	[0.01106]	[0.00858]	[0.01506]	[0.00966]	[0.03623]	[0.01240]
*MNE * Relative RTI*	-0.08078*	-0.10564***	0.02372	-0.01718	-0.10264	0.19230***
	[0.04552]	[0.04073]	[0.07461]	[0.05116]	[0.08536]	[0.07350]
Firm size (log)	0.04016***	0.04935***	0.04001***	0.03683***	0.03577***	0.03703***
	[0.00139]	[0.00258]	[0.00165]	[0.00065]	[0.00338]	[0.00070]
Constant	0.23631***	0.18111***	0.23365***			
	[0.01742]	[0.03998]	[0.02797]			
Industry effect (three digit)	Yes	Yes	Yes	Yes	Yes	Yes
Firm effect	Yes	Yes	Yes	Yes	Yes	Yes
Region effect (prefecture)	Yes	Yes	Yes	Yes	Yes	Yes
Year effect	Yes	Yes	Yes	Yes	Yes	Yes
No. of establishments	2,297,666	302,460	1,987,861	2,176,251	289,586	1,872,594
R^2	0.048	0.071	0.045	0.047	0.064	0.042
No. of firms	283,845	56,874	245,109	226,993	44,097	194,263
Underidentification test				13752.8	1508.8	8478.6
(p-value)				0.000	0.000	0.000
Weak identification test				7485.9	701.5	4716.6

Note: Standard errors (in brackets) are clustered at the firm level. *** $p < 0.01$; ** $p < 0.05$; * $p < 0.10$.

Table 11.5 Routine-Task Index for New Establishments: Multi-establishment Firms Only (Dependent Variable: New Establishment's Relative RTI)

	(1)	(2)	(3)	(4)	(5)	(6)
	All Firms	*Manufacturing Firms*	*Non-manufacturing Firms*	*All Firms*	*Manufacturing Firms*	*Non-manufacturing Firms*
	OLS	*OLS*	*OLS*	*IV*	*IV*	*IV*
Firm age	-0.00001	-0.00008	-0.00002	-0.00001	-0.00008*	-0.00002
	[0.00003]	[0.00006]	[0.00003]	[0.00001]	[0.00004]	[0.00001]
Firm size (log)	-0.00017	0.00008	-0.00040	-0.00016	0.00009	-0.00033**
	[0.00045]	[0.00091]	[0.00051]	[0.00013]	[0.00119]	[0.00013]
No. of establishments	0.00035	0.00028	0.00050	0.00044***	0.00026	0.00063***
	[0.00030]	[0.00136]	[0.00032]	[0.00010]	[0.00062]	[0.00010]
MNE	-0.00159	-0.00050	-0.00278	-0.00335	-0.00037	-0.00791***
	[0.00181]	[0.00183]	[0.00229]	[0.00239]	[0.01351]	[0.00280]
Constant	-0.02257**	-0.01100	-0.00723			
	[0.01055]	[0.00695]	[0.01085]			
Industry effect (three digit)	Yes	Yes	Yes	Yes	Yes	Yes
Firm effect	Yes	Yes	Yes	Yes	Yes	Yes
Region effect (prefecture)	Yes	Yes	Yes	Yes	Yes	Yes
Year effect	Yes	Yes	Yes	Yes	Yes	Yes
No. of establishments	605,209	67,840	535,685	519,583	52,726	460,909
R^2	0.018	0.028	0.014	0.016	0.028	0.012
No. of firms	138,638	25,005	118,035	64,045	9,930	54,238
Underidentification test				11615.4	416.5	9083.4
(p-value)				0.000	0.000	0.000
Weak identification test				11906.9	418.7	9283.8

Note: Standard errors (in brackets) are clustered at the firm level. *** $p < 0.01$; ** $p < 0.05$; * $p < 0.10$.

Table 11.6 Employment Growth Rate for Continuing Establishments: Multi-establishment Firms Only (Dependent Variable: Employment Growth Rate [Continuing Establishments])

	(1)	*(2)*	*(3)*	*(4)*	*(5)*	*(6)*
	All Firms	*Manufacturing Firms*	*Non-manufacturing Firms*	*All Firms*	*Manufacturing Firms*	*Non-manufacturing Firms*
	OLS	*OLS*	*OLS*	*IV*	*IV*	*IV*
Establishment age	0.00090***	0.00026**	0.00100***	0.00092***	0.00028**	0.00103***
	[0.00007]	[0.00012]	[0.00008]	[0.00005]	[0.00012]	[0.00005]
Establishment size (log)	−0.20421***	−0.13419***	−0.22037***	−0.20628***	−0.13422***	−0.22364***
	[0.00337]	[0.00219]	[0.00406]	[0.00082]	[0.00192]	[0.00092]
Multi_same three-digit industry	0.07419***	0.04976***	0.07152***	0.07735***	0.04985***	0.07468***
	[0.00292]	[0.00509]	[0.00340]	[0.00144]	[0.00509]	[0.00167]
Relative RTI	−0.06543*	−0.25326***	0.00945	−0.02068	−0.19995***	0.04831*
	[0.03354]	[0.06577]	[0.04309]	[0.02453]	[0.06666]	[0.02871]
MNE	0.08090***	0.05899***	0.06926**	0.22411***	0.25618***	0.15227***
	[0.02133]	[0.00930]	[0.02820]	[0.01588]	[0.06403]	[0.01924]
*MNE * Relative RTI*	−0.14105**	−0.08673	−0.02876	−0.38144***	−0.20476	−0.28561*
	[0.06460]	[0.07121]	[0.10137]	[0.10314]	[0.16783]	[0.14836]
Firm size (log)	−0.10618***	−0.13081***	−0.13047***	−0.10804***	−0.14627***	−0.12831***
	[0.00411]	[0.00599]	[0.00519]	[0.00135]	[0.00676]	[0.00151]
Exiting establishment dummy	0.06660***	0.06128***	0.07085***	0.06627***	0.06165***	0.07019***
	[0.00296]	[0.00517]	[0.00346]	[0.00166]	[0.00429]	[0.00185]
Constant	0.85702***	0.80896***	0.93254***			
	[0.04002]	[0.08890]	[0.05917]			
Industry effect (three digit)	Yes	Yes	Yes	Yes	Yes	Yes
Firm effect	Yes	Yes	Yes	Yes	Yes	Yes
Region effect (prefecture)	Yes	Yes	Yes	Yes	Yes	Yes
Year effect	Yes	Yes	Yes	Yes	Yes	Yes
Number of establishments	1,838,572	246,071	1,586,214	1,705,593	229,773	1,461,160
R squared	0.112	0.078	0.125	0.111	0.074	0.125
Number of firms	272,808	54,448	235,307	197,705	38,226	168,011
Underidentification test				10651.7	1180.6	6714.9
(*p*-value)				0.000	0.000	0.000
Weak identification test				5954.1	557.6	3883.2

Note: Standard errors (in brackets) are clustered at the firm level. *** $p < 0.01$; ** $p < 0.05$; * $p < 0.10$.

Table 11.7 Regular Worker Employment Growth Rate for Continuing Establishments: Multi-establishment Firms Only (Dependent Variable: Regular Worker Employment Growth Rate [Continuing Establishments])

	(1)	*(2)*	*(3)*	*(4)*	*(5)*	*(6)*
	All Firms	*Manufacturing Firms*	*Non-manufacturing Firms*	*All Firms*	*Manufacturing Firms*	*Non-manufacturing Firms*
	OLS	*OLS*	*OLS*	*IV*	*IV*	*IV*
Establishment age	−0.00045***	−0.00082***	−0.00036***	−0.00044***	−0.00082***	−0.00034***
	[0.00008]	[0.00012]	[0.00009]	[0.00005]	[0.00012]	[0.00006]
Establishment size (log)	−0.11436***	−0.09135***	−0.12073***	−0.11610***	−0.09154***	−0.12311***
	[0.00333]	[0.00210]	[0.00404]	[0.00078]	[0.00188]	[0.00087]
Multi_same three-digit industry	0.03766***	0.02476***	0.03465***	0.03966***	0.02538***	0.03702***
	[0.00227]	[0.00516]	[0.00269]	[0.00149]	[0.00521]	[0.00173]
Relative RTI	−0.01352	−0.17974***	0.00836	0.02743	−0.12297*	0.04184
	[0.02871]	[0.06661]	[0.03566]	[0.02627]	[0.07064]	[0.03069]
MNE	0.05110***	0.05546***	0.04624**	0.08749***	0.13343**	0.04972***
	[0.01601]	[0.00908]	[0.02220]	[0.01547]	[0.06115]	[0.01892]
*MNE * Relative RTI*	−0.06293	−0.10684	0.06449	−0.33588***	−0.32210*	−0.22793
	[0.05135]	[0.06538]	[0.07858]	[0.10350]	[0.16778]	[0.14947]
Firm size (log)	−0.05584***	−0.09576***	−0.06542***	−0.05572***	−0.10191***	−0.06369***
	[0.00230]	[0.00555]	[0.00292]	[0.00133]	[0.00679]	[0.00146]
Exiting establishment dummy	0.03633***	0.04049***	0.03883***	0.03587***	0.04057***	0.03818***
	[0.00252]	[0.00511]	[0.00294]	[0.00173]	[0.00444]	[0.00196]
Constant	0.44577***	0.57054***	0.44833***			
	[0.03639]	[0.09473]	[0.05036]			
Industry effect (three digit)	Yes	Yes	Yes	Yes	Yes	Yes
Firm effect	Yes	Yes	Yes	Yes	Yes	Yes
Region effect (prefecture)	Yes	Yes	Yes	Yes	Yes	Yes
Year effect	Yes	Yes	Yes	Yes	Yes	Yes
No. of establishments	1,566,132	222,561	1,338,176	1,435,737	206,179	1,215,996
R^2	0.042	0.040	0.045	0.042	0.039	0.045
No. of firms	244,921	50,644	209,366	170,054	34,329	142,606
Underidentification test				9686.9	1133.4	5965.9
(p-value)				0.000	0.000	0.000
Weak identification test				5839.5	531.9	3865.6

Note: Standard errors (in brackets) are clustered at the firm level. *** $p < 0.01$; ** $p < 0.05$; * $p < 0.10$.

interaction term of MNE and relative RTI is negative and significant in Columns 1, 4, and 5, implying that less routine-task intensive establishments within an MNE increase their employment more than other establishments. The coefficient of relative RTI is negative and statistically significant in the cases of all firms and manufacturing firms (Columns 1, 2, and 5) while it is positive and statistically significant in the case of non-manufacturing firms (Column 6). These results suggest that more routine-task intensive establishments tend to have a lower employment growth rate in the case of manufacturing firms while they tend to have a higher employment growth rate in the case of non-manufacturing firms.

The coefficient of exiting establishment dummy is positive and significant in all cases. In fact, plant workers are often relocated to other plants within the same firm when one of the plants is shut down. We include a dummy variable that equals one if a firm has shut down at least one other establishment, in order to take account of worker relocations because of exits of other establishments owned by a firm. The result may imply that a firm is likely to relocate their workers to other continuing establishments within the firm when it shuts down one or more establishments.

We also estimate the same equation using the employment growth rate for only regular workers as the dependent variable, instead of the total employment growth rate including non-regular workers. The estimation results are shown in Table 11.7. The results in Table 11.7 are very similar to those in Table 11.6. However, the coefficient of relative RTI is now insignificant in Column 6. Therefore, when non-regular workers are excluded, the employment growth rate of routine-task intensive establishments owned by non-manufacturing firms is not significantly higher than other establishments, suggesting that the employment growth for routine-task intensive establishments owned by non-manufacturing firms can be explained largely by the increase in non-regular workers. The coefficient of the interaction term of MNE and relative RTI remains negative in most cases and significant in Columns 4 and 5, while it is insignificant in Columns 1 and 6. The coefficient of the stand-alone MNE term remains positive and significant, suggesting that the employment growth rate is higher for continuing establishments when the firm becomes an MNE even though non-regular workers are excluded. Moreover, when the firm becomes an MNE, less routine-task intensive establishments tend to increase their employment more than more routine-task intensive establishments.

11.5 Conclusions

In this paper, we examined the effects of the expansion of overseas activities on the restructuring of domestic activities within MNEs by utilizing the large-scale firm establishment-linked data constructed from the Establishment and Enterprise Census (for years 2001 and 2006) and the Economic Census (for years 2009 and 2012) in Japan. More specifically, focusing on the routine-task intensity of establishments, we examined (1) what types of establishments are closed or newly established, and (2) what types of establishments increase or reduce their employment when an MNE expands its overseas operations.

When the cost of investment abroad decreases, firms are expected to relocate labor-intensive, particularly tradable-task labor-intensive, activities abroad. We measured the skill level of each establishment by mainly using the routine-task intensity measure constructed in the same manner as Costinot, Oldenski, and Rauch (2011) and the occupation compositions for each industry taken from the 2005 Population Census in Japan.

We found that more routine-task intensive establishments were more likely to exit when a firm becomes multinational, which is consistent with our expectation. This was the case particularly for non-manufacturing firms. In the case of continuing establishments, we found that less routine-task intensive establishments were more likely to increase or less likely to reduce employment, when a firm becomes multinational. Moreover, newly entered establishments tend to be less routine-task intensive compared with other establishments within an MNE, although the results are somewhat weak.

Our results show that firms investing abroad accelerate establishment closures in routine-task intensive industries and that employment growth rate is higher for MNEs' continuing establishments in routine-task intensive industries than for non-MNEs' continuing establishments. Therefore, overseas expansion accelerates domestic business restructuring within an MNE and shifts domestic activities toward less routine-task intensive ones. Such changes within an MNE may lead to economy-wide industrial composition changes in employment.

Our results suggest that routine-task workers are more likely to lose their workplaces and to be forced to change their place of work or their job than other types of workers. From a policy perspective, it is important to ensure a non-disruptive and smooth job transfer particularly for routine-task workers.

Finally, we did not take geographical dimensions into account in this study. However, a natural extension would be to examine how different are the impacts of MNEs' overseas expansion on domestic establishments located in urban areas compared with those located in rural areas. If endowments of labor with certain skill levels are associated with various regional characteristics such as per capita income and social infrastructure including schools and transportation networks, domestic business restructuring by MNEs may have asymmetric effects across regions. We believe that further research on this issue will provide important empirical evidence with which to develop appropriate policy schemes for the human capital development and social infrastructure upgrading in response to changes in industrial structure driven by internationalization of business activities.

11.6 Acknowledgements

This research was conducted as part of research projects for the Economic Research Institute for ASEAN and East Asia (ERIA) and the National Institute for Science and Technology Policy (NISTEP). This work was supported by the Japan Society for the Promotion of Science (JSPS KAKENHI Grant Number

15K03456). The opinions expressed and arguments employed in this paper are the sole responsibility of the authors and do not necessarily reflect those of ERIA, NISTEP, or any institution with which the authors are affiliated.

Notes

1 Although the evidence overall is rather mixed, more recent studies tend to show that overseas operations and home operations are complementary (e.g., Desai, Foley, and Hines 2009). Harrison and McMillan (2011) do not find a strong negative relationship between overseas activities and home employment, although the effect of overseas activities on employment at home differs depending on the tasks performed at home and abroad in the case of US-based multinationals. Similarly, for Japan, Yamashita and Fukao (2010), using a matched dataset of parent firms and their overseas affiliates, found no evidence that the expansion of overseas operations reduces MNEs' home employment.

2 Giroud and Mueller (2015) also find that within-firm resource reallocation increases aggregate firm-wide productivity, although they do not focus on MNEs but rather on US plants that received a positive productivity shock such as the introduction of new airline routes.

3 Autor and Dorn (2013) find that rising employment and wages in service occupations account for a substantial share of aggregate polarization of the US employment and earnings distributions.

4 Keller and Yeaple (2013), focusing on the difficulty of communicating knowledge from one person to another, show that more knowledge-intensive production processes are less likely to be moved to distant locations. Their finding also suggests that MNEs tend to keep their non-routine task processes at home or in regions closer to their home country.

5 For the 2012 Economic Census, more detailed information on business activities such as sales of goods produced and sales of supporting service activities at the establishment level is available.

6 The number of domestic or foreign subsidiaries for each firm is available only for the 2006 and 2009 censuses. Therefore, we do not use this information and mainly use a binary indicator as to whether a firm owns at least one foreign subsidiary or not.

7 This is the US Department of Labor's successor to the Dictionary of Occupational Titles (DOT) (US Department of Labor 1977), which is used to construct task measures from previous studies such as Autor and Dorn (2013). We use the information taken from the O*NET, not the DOT, because the job task information described in the DOT is that of year 1977. Taking into account the fact that tasks have changed substantially even within the same occupation in recent decades, we use more recent job-task information taken from the O*NET.

8 Although the Japan Institute for Labour Policy and Training started a similar service to O*NET, called "Career Matrix (CMX)," in 2006, the CMX website was closed in 2011 and the data are no longer available because this service was abandoned as a result of the Japanese government's budget screening process. If we can obtain the data underlying the CMX in the future, we would like to check the robustness of our results using the Japanese task-occupation matched data.

9 We use the 0–100 score that O*NET reports to measure the importance of each task in each occupation. These scores are constructed from surveys of individuals in those occupations and are normalized to a 0–100 scale by analysts at the Department of Labor. Lindsay Oldenski kindly provided us with the 0–100 scale index and we utilized her data.

10 Although the original task importance measures provided by Oldenski were available for over 500 US occupations, the occupation-level task importance measures are

aggregated to the 172 Japanese occupations. When more than one US occupation matches with one Japanese occupation, we took an average value of the importance score for the US occupations.

11 See, for example, Marcolin, Miroudot, and Squicciarini (2016).

12 Luca Marcolin kindly provided us with the routine-task index at the three-digit occupation level for Japan and the United States.

13 Simpson (2012) mainly uses the share of workers with qualifications (basically measured by education level). We could also have used the wage rank of occupation data compiled by Goos, Manning, and Salomons (2009) in order to construct a measure of skill intensity for each industry.

14 More specifically, to calculate the entry and exit rates, we count the number of exited establishments and new establishments for the three periods: 2001–2006, 2006–2009, and 2009–2012. A firm's multinational status is identified using the information of the initial year of each period, 2001, 2006, and 2009.

15 The routine-task index for a firm is the routine-task index for the firm's headquarter industry.

16 The OLS estimation results for the determinants of investing abroad are shown in Appendix Table 11.A2.

References

Acemoglu, Daron, and David H. Autor. 2011. "Skills, Tasks and Technologies: Implications for Employment and Earnings." In *Handbook of Labor Economics*, vol. 4B, edited by David Card and Orley Ashenfelter, Chapter 12, pp. 1043–1171. Amsterdam: North Holland.

Autor, David H., and David Dorn. 2013. "The Growth of Low-Skill Service Jobs and the Polarization of the US Labor Market." *American Economic Review* 103, no. 5: 1553–97.

Bandick, Roger. 2016. "Offshoring, Plant Survival and Employment Growth." *World Economy* 39, no. 5: 597–620.

Becker, Sascha O., Karolina Ekholm, and Marc-Andreas Muendler. 2013. "Offshoring and the Onshore Composition of Tasks and Skills." *Journal of International Economics* 90, no. 1: 91–106.

Bernard, Andrew B., Valerie Smeets, and Frederic Warzynski. 2017. "Rethinking Deindustrialization." *Economic Policy* 32, no. 89: 5–38.

Costinot, Arnaud, Lindsay Oldenski, and James Rauch. 2011. "Adaptation and the Boundary of Multinational Firms." *Review of Economics and Statistics* 93, no. 1: 298–308.

Crozet, Matthieu, and Emmanuel Milet. 2017. "Should Everybody be in Services? The Effect of Servitization on Manufacturing Performance," Journal of Economics and Management Strategy 26, no. 3: 820–841.

Desai, Mihir A., C. Fritz Foley, and James R. Hines. 2009. "Domestic Effects of the Foreign Activities of US Multinationals." *American Economic Journal: Economic Policy* 1, no. 1: 181–203.

Ebenstein, Avraham, Ann Harrison, Margaret McMillan, and Shannon Phillips. 2014. "Estimating the Impact of Trade and Offshoring on American Workers Using the Current Population Surveys." *Review of Economics and Statistics* 96, no. 4: 581–95.

Giroud, Xavier, and Holger M. Mueller. 2015. "Capital and Labor Reallocation within Firms." *Journal of Finance* 70, no. 4: 1767–804.

Goos, Maarten, Alan Manning, and Anna Salomons. 2009. "Job Polarization in Europe." *American Economic Review* 99, no. 2: 58–63.

———. 2014. "Explaining Job Polarization: Routine-Biased Technological Change and Offshoring." *American Economic Review* 104, no. 8: 2509–26.

Grossman, Gene M., and Esteban Rossi-Hansberg. 2008. "Trading Tasks: A Simple Theory of Offshoring." *American Economic Review* 98, no. 5: 1978–97.

Harrison, Ann, and Margaret McMillan. 2011. "Offshoring Jobs? Multinationals and U.S. Manufacturing Employment." *Review of Economics and Statistics* 93, no. 3: 857–75.

Head, Keith, and John Ries. 2002. "Offshore Production and Skill Upgrading by Japanese Manufacturing Firms." *Journal of International Economics* 58, no. 1: 81–105.

Heckman, James J. 1978. "Dummy Endogenous Variables in a Simultaneous Equation System." *Econometrica* 46, no. 4: 931–59.

Hijzen, Alexander, Holger Görg, and Robert C. Hine. 2005. "International Outsourcing and the Skill Structure of Labor Demand in the United Kingdom." *Economic Journal* 115, no. 506: 860–78.

Keller, Wolfgang, and Hâle Utar. 2016. "International Trade and Job Polarization: Evidence at the Worker-Level." NBER Working Paper no. 22315. Cambridge, MA: National Bureau of Economic Research.

Keller, Wolfgang, and Stephen Ross Yeaple. 2013. "The Gravity of Knowledge." *American Economic Review* 103, no 4: 1414–44.

Kneller, Richard, Danny McGowan, Tomohiko Inui, and Toshiyuki Matsuura. 2012. "Closure within Multi-Plant Firms: Evidence from Japan." *Review of World Economics* 148, no. 4: 647–68.

Kodama, Naomi, and Tomohiko Inui. 2015. "The Impact of Globalization on Establishment-Level Employment Dynamics in Japan." *Asian Economic Papers* 14, no. 2: 41–65.

Marcolin, Luca, Sébastien Miroudot, and Mariagrazia Squicciarini. 2016. "Routine Jobs, Employment and Technological Innovation in Global Value Chains." OECD Science, Technology and Industry Working Papers no. 2016/01. Paris: OECD Publishing.

Oldenski, Lindsay. 2012. "Export versus FDI and the Communication of Complex Information." *Journal of International Economics* 87, no. 2: 312–22.

———. 2014. "Offshoring and the Polarization of the U.S. Labor Market." *ILR Review* 67, Suppl.: 734–61.

Simpson, Helene. 2012. "Investment Abroad and Labour Adjustment at Home: Evidence from UK Multinational Firms." *Canadian Journal of Economics* 45, no. 2: 698–731.

Tomiura, Eiichi, Ryuhei Wakasugi, and Lianming Zhu. 2015. "A Concordance between US and Japanese Classifications of Occupations for Empirical Analyses of Tasks in Japan." KIER Discussion Paper no. 923. Kyoto: Kyoto Institute of Economic Research, Kyoto University.

US Department of Labor. 1977. *Dictionary of Occupational Titles.* 4th ed. Washington, DC: US Government Printing Office.

Yamashita, Nobuyuki, and Kyoji Fukao. 2010. "Expansion Abroad and Jobs at Home: Evidence from Japanese Multinational Enterprises." *Japan and the World Economy* 22, no. 2: 88–97.

Appendix

Table 11.A1 Task Measures by Industry (Top 50 Industries for each Task Measure)

Rank	*High Routine-Task Intensity*			*Low Routine-Task Intensity*		
	Index	*Industry Code and Name*		*Index*	*Industry Code and Name*	
1	0.73	213	Cut stock and findings for boots and shoes	0.01	822	Barbershops
2	0.73	214	Leather footwear	0.01	823	Hair-dressing and beauty salon
3	0.62	832	Domestic services	0.02	999	Industries unable to classify
4	0.59	201	Tires and inner tubes	0.07	693	Automobile parking
5	0.59	202	Rubber and plastic footwear and its findings	0.07	75G	Offender rehabilitation services
6	0.55	116	Dyed and finished textiles	0.07	75H	Home care help services
7	0.54	371	Transmission of correspondence	0.07	75J	Miscellaneous social insurance, social welfare and care services
8	0.54	781	Postal services	0.08	84H	"Mah-jong" clubs
9	0.54	782	Contracted postal services	0.08	84J	"Pachinko" parlors
10	0.54	221	Glass and its products	0.08	84K	Game centers
11	0.51	833	Garment sewing services and repairs	0.08	84L	Miscellaneous amusement and recreation facilities
12	0.51	873	Paper hangers	0.09	773	Supplementary tutorial schools
13	0.51	879	Miscellaneous repair services	0.09	761	Elementary schools
14	0.49	225	Clay refractories	0.09	762	Lower secondary schools
15	0.49	226	Carbon and graphite products	0.09	763	Upper secondary schools, secondary schools
16	0.49	227	Abrasive products	0.09	764	Institution of higher education

Rank	*High Routine-Task Intensity*			*Low Routine-Task Intensity*		
	Index	*Industry Code and Name*		*Index*	*Industry Code and Name*	
17	0.49	228	Aggregate and stone products	0.09	765	Special education schools
18	0.49	229	Miscellaneous ceramic, stone and clay products	0.09	766	Kindergartens
19	0.47	143	Sliding doors and screens	0.09	75C	Special nursing home for the elderly
20	0.46	203	Rubber belts and hoses and mechanical rubber goods products	0.09	75D	Care and health services facilities for the aged
21	0.46	209	Miscellaneous rubber products	0.09	75E	Fee charging home for the aged
22	0.46	011	Crop farming	0.09	75F	Miscellaneous welfare services for the aged and care services
23	0.46	012	Livestock farming	0.10	75A	Day nursery
24	0.45	121	Textile outer garments and shirts, including bonded fabrics and lace, except Japanese style	0.10	75B	Miscellaneous child welfare services
25	0.45	122	Knitted garments and shirts	0.10	829	Miscellaneous laundry, beauty and bath services
26	0.45	123	Underwear	0.13	921	Shintoism
27	0.45	124	Japanese style apparel and "tabi"-sock	0.13	922	Buddhism
28	0.45	125	Other textile apparel and accessories	0.13	923	Christianity
29	0.45	129	Miscellaneous fabricated textile products	0.13	929	Miscellaneous religions
30	0.45	861	Automobile maintenance services	0.13	582	Retail trade (bicycles)
31	0.45	522	Chemicals and related products	0.13	77F	Music instructions
32	0.45	098	Animal and vegetable oils and fats	0.13	77G	Calligraphy instructions
33	0.45	533	Electrical machinery, equipment and supplies	0.13	77H	Flower, tea ceremony instructions
34	0.44	106	Prepared animal foods and organic fertilizers	0.13	77J	Abacus instructions
35	0.44	222	Cement and its products	0.13	77K	Foreign language instructions

Table 11.A2 Determinants of Multinational Enterprises (Dependent Variable: MNE Dummy)

	(1)
US FDI	0.01498***
	[0.00267]
RTI	-0.02057*
	[0.01134]
Firm age	-0.00006**
	[0.00003]
Firm size (log)	0.01830***
	[0.00060]
Foreign ownership share	-0.00002
	[0.00012]
No. of domestic establishments	0.00571***
	[0.00106]
No. of overseas branch establishments	0.20246***
	[0.00658]
Share of workers employed in overseas branches	0.00275***
	[0.00030]
No. of active industries (three digit)	0.00481***
	[0.00058]
Constant	-0.06551***
	[0.02510]
Industry effect (three digit)	Yes
Firm effect	Yes
Region effect (prefecture)	Yes
Year effect	Yes
No. of observations	589,357
R^2	0.122
No. of firms	270,496

Notes: 1. RTI = routine-tax index. 2. Standard errors (in brackets) are clustered at the firm level. *** $p < 0.01$; ** $p < 0.05$; * $p < 0.10$.

12 The impacts of import tariff reduction on income growth and distribution in urban China*

Mi Dai and Yifan Zhang

12.1 Introduction

The relationship between globalisation and income inequality in China has received considerable attention among economists and policymakers (e.g., Wei and Wu, 2001). On one hand, China's integration into the world economy has accelerated since it entered the World Trade Organization (WTO) in December 2001. China aggressively cut tariff rates to meet its WTO obligations.[1] As a result, the weighted average tariff rate went down from 15% in 2001 to 4% in 2007. This was accompanied by a sharp reduction in the share of imports regulated by non-tariff barriers through licences and import quotas (Branstetter and Lardy, 2008). On the other hand, China has also experienced explosive economic growth since the WTO entry. Consequently, household income has grown rapidly. Nominal individual income in urban areas increased nearly 80% between 2002 and 2007 (Table 12.1). Meanwhile, China's poverty rate decreased drastically, but the distribution of poverty reduction was uneven across different regions. Despite tremendous success in income growth and poverty reduction, China has transformed itself from an egalitarian country before the reform into one of the most unequal countries in the world. According to a recent influential study (Xie and Zhou, 2014), China's Gini coefficient had risen to 0.55 in 2012, among the world's highest.

To better understand the profound impacts of trade liberalisation (particularly China's entry into the WTO) on household income, this paper examines the effect of import tariff reductions on urban income growth and income distribution. We focus on import tariff reductions for two reasons. First, tariff reductions provide accurate measures of trade liberalisation. Second, compared to actual imports, tariff reduction is a policy variable under the discretion of the government.

We take advantage of a comprehensive individual-level survey dataset and industrial firm survey dataset. Our identification strategy relies on the heterogeneity of tariff cuts across industries and city-level variation of initial industry composition. Since industrial composition is predetermined, it is possible to interpret the correlation between income growth and inequality and trade exposure as a causal relationship. To deal with the endogeneity of tariffs, we use the initial year tariff rate as an instrument for the tariff reduction in later period.

Table 12.1 Summary Statistics

	2002	*2003*	*2004*	*2005*	*2006*	*2007*
Individual Income						
Total income	10.480	11.148	12.897	14.275	16.028	18.671
	(3.620)	(3.888)	(4.635)	(5.164)	(5.702)	(6.107)
Wage income	10.011	10.646	12.348	13.668	15.312	17.861
	(3.422)	(3.719)	(4.477)	(4.968)	(5.417)	(5.794)
Operational income	0.015	0.019	0.015	0.032	0.026	0.109
	(0.024)	(0.043)	(0.036)	(0.075)	(0.055)	(0.150)
Transfer income	0.387	0.388	0.421	0.446	0.504	0.514
	(0.443)	(0.339)	(0.340)	(0.346)	(0.399)	(0.415)
Property income	0.069	0.095	0.113	0.130	0.186	0.187
	(0.074)	(0.121)	(0.133)	(0.167)	(0.253)	(0.286)
City-Level Variables						
Mean log dev. of income	0.244	0.256	0.256	0.259	0.255	0.251
	(0.046)	(0.053)	(0.051)	(0.050)	(0.047)	(0.046)
S.d. of log income	0.749	0.786	0.778	0.787	0.769	0.750
	(0.172)	(0.189)	(0.170)	(0.180)	(0.160)	(0.163)
Gini coefficient	0.341	0.358	0.357	0.362	0.357	0.349
	(0.060)	(0.070)	(0.067)	(0.066)	(0.062)	(0.060)
Theil index	0.228	0.253	0.251	0.256	0.247	0.228
	(0.080)	(0.104)	(0.093)	(0.091)	(0.084)	(0.078)
Return to schooling	0.062	0.058	0.059	0.063	0.065	0.066
	(0.035)	(0.031)	(0.033)	(0.033)	(0.032)	(0.031)
Share skilled	0.306	0.314	0.328	0.354	0.371	0.390
	(0.088)	(0.084)	(0.084)	(0.085)	(0.086)	(0.093)
Share unemployed	0.084	0.088	0.085	0.087	0.078	0.057
	(0.055)	(0.055)	(0.055)	(0.054)	(0.048)	(0.040)
Share manufacturing	0.261	0.237	0.229	0.215	0.212	0.206
	(0.132)	(0.124)	(0.117)	(0.110)	(0.112)	(0.105)
Number of cities	189	194	192	193	192	191

Source: Authors' computation.
Note: Standard deviation in parentheses.

Our estimation suggests that cities with larger tariff reductions after WTO entry were associated with lower manufacturing income growth. The main channel of the tariff reduction effect is through wage income and property income. We find no evidence that tariff reductions affected unemployment. In addition, when we instrument tariff cut with the initial tariff, we find that tariff liberalisation actually reduced within-city income inequality.

Our findings should be interpreted with caution for two reasons. First, globalisation has many dimensions, including imports, exports, foreign direct investment (FDI), etc. Our paper focuses only on one particular aspect – import tariff reduction. We do not address the issues of general globalisation or WTO effects. Second, our study captures only the relative effect of tariff liberalisation on cities with more or less exposure to trade. We do not answer the question of whether tariff reductions decreased urban income growth or inequality. Rather, we focus on whether certain cities with greater tariff reductions are affected more than other cities with smaller tariff reductions.

Our study is related to a large literature on trade and growth. For a long time, economists have found only a weak causal link between these two. Some authors demonstrate that open economies tend to grow faster than closed ones. (e.g., Sachs and Warner, 1995; Frankel and Romer, 1999). Others are sceptical about the methodology and conclusions of these studies (e.g., Rodrik and Rodriguez, 2001). Even if we understand how trade liberalisation promotes growth, it is not clear whether it can produce beneficial results across all households and individuals. If the benefit is unequally distributed, the effects of trade liberalisation on income growth will lead to greater (smaller) income inequality depending on whether the income of the poor grows by less (more) than the average (Deaton, 2005). Goldberg and Pavcnik (2007a) surveyed the literature on trade liberalisation and inequality. They found the results inconclusive. The debate remains unsolved despite a large number of studies on this topic.

Recent empirical literature on trade and growth has shifted away from cross-country studies to within-country studies and focuses more on income growth using household survey data. Cross-country studies typically find no relationship between trade liberalisation and income growth. Within-country studies have an advantage that significantly increase sample size and allow regions comparable in main aspects. Major empirical studies on tariff reduction have examined topics such as return on education, income inequality, poverty, and migration. These include Goldberg and Pavcnik (2007b) on Colombia, Topolova (2007, 2010) on India, Kovak (2013), and Carneiro and Kovak (2015) on Brazil. Generally, the evidence on the effects of trade liberalisation is mixed across countries. For example, Kovak (2013) finds a strong negative impact of trade liberalisation on wage income in Brazil. In contrast, Goldberg and Pavcnik (2007b) find no significant impact of trade liberalisation on poverty in Colombia. For India, Topolova (2010) argues that trade liberalisation increased poverty only in rural areas.

In the case of China, Han et al. (2012) find that globalisation increased urban wage inequality through the mechanism of higher returns on education. A major difference between their seminal paper and our study is that they measure globalisation by dividing six provinces in their sample into 'high' and 'low' globalisation exposure regions. They rely on exports and FDI to measure globalisation exposure. In our paper, we use HS six-digit import tariff reductions as a measure for trade liberalisation. In another paper, Brandt, Van Biesebroeck, Wang and Zhang (2017) study the impact of China's tariff reduction on manufacturing firms after the WTO entry. They find that tariff cuts increase firm productivity but reduce price and mark-up, probably due to more intense competition from imports.

Methodologically, our paper is also related to emerging literature on the regional impacts of trade liberalisation. These include Kovak (2013), Carneiro and Kovak (2015), Topolova (2007, 2010), Hasan et al. (2007), Edmonds et al. (2010), and McLaren and Hakobyan (2012). These studies examine the effects of trade liberalisation on labour market outcomes at the sub-national level. They measure trade policy at the regional level as a weighted average of industry-level trade policy, with weights reflecting the initial industrial composition of the region. In this paper, we adopt this local labour market approach and apply the methodology to Chinese data.

The remainder of the paper is organised as follows: Section 12.2 outlines our empirical strategy, Section 12.3 describes the data, Section 12.4 reports estimation results, and Section 12.5 is the conclusion.

12.2 Empirical methodology

In our study, we take advantage of China's geographic diversity on how urban households are affected by tariff cuts. Excluding Hong Kong, Macau, and Taiwan, China has 31 provincial-level regions, which are further divided into about 340 prefecture-level cities. These cities differed in their industrial composition before China entered the WTO. Our identification strategy uses this within-China city-level heterogeneity in exposure to tariff protection. Following Topalova (2007, 2010), we define a city's tariff reduction between 2001 and 2006 as the weighted average of the tariff cut in all industries of the city. We use the industry's employment share in 2001, the WTO entry year, as the weights when constructing this measure. In other words, we calculate the weighted average tariff of city j in year t as follows:

$$Tariff_{jt} = \frac{\sum_i employment_{ij,2001} * Tariff_{it}}{Total\ Employment_{jt}} \quad (1)$$

Then the log difference of tariff rates between 2001 and 2006 for city j becomes

$$\Delta \ln(Tariff)_j = \ln(Tariff_{j,2006}) - \ln(Tariff_{j,2001}) \quad (2)$$

To study the impact of trade reform on income growth and distribution, we estimate various forms of the following model:

$$\Delta Z_j = \alpha + \beta \Delta \ln(Tariff)_j + \gamma X + \{FE\} + \varepsilon_j, \quad (3)$$

where Z is a local labour market outcome variable such as individual income, unemployment rate, or inequality measures. X is a vector of city-level control variables, including initial year share of skilled labour, initial year share of manufacturing employment in total employment, and initial year unemployment rate. We also include provincial fixed effect in the regressions.

One concern of our empirical approach is the migration between cities resulting from tariff liberalisation. If there were large-scale migration across cities in response to tariff reductions, our analysis comparing cities over time would not give the full estimate of the impact. However, even after many years reforming the household registration (*hukou*) system, internal migration in China is still constrained by government policy. Zhu and Tombe (2015) show that high migration costs still significantly limit internal migration in China. Therefore, our analysis can still properly address the questions of the impact of tariff liberalisation on income growth and inequality.

Another concern is the endogeneity of tariff reduction. Grossman and Helpman (2002) show that tariff liberalisation is often an outcome of the political economy process. We take the following measures to deal with the endogeneity of tariff reduction:

First, our measure of tariff change alleviates reverse causality since our city-specific employment weights are based on initial year industrial employment composition. Our measure is not affected by the change in employment in later years that may be the result of tariff changes.

Second, we lag all independent variables by one year. While we study labour market outcomes between 2002 and 2007, the tariff change variable is calculated with 2001 and 2006 data, and the initial city0level control variables use 2001 data.

Third, over the sample period, there was very little policy discretion in the extent of trade liberalisation in each industry. Figure 12.1 plots the change in city-level tariffs on the vertical axis against the initial level (2001) of protection on the horizontal axis. We find that the relationship between tariff reduction

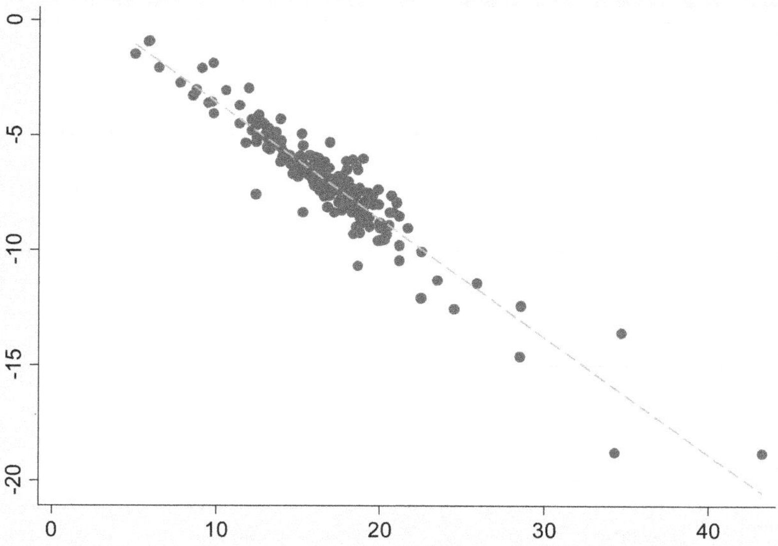

Figure 12.1 Initial Tariff and Tariff Reduction.
Source: Authors' computation.

between 2001 and 2006 and initial tariff in 2001 is almost one-to-one. Those industries with initial high tariff levels experienced a greater reduction in tariffs. Regardless of the initial level of tariff, post-WTO-entry tariffs converged to a uniform level of protection in 2006. As a robustness check, to deal with possible endogeneity concerns, we take advantage of the uniform tariff cut in the WTO agreement and use the initial tariff (in 2001) as an instrumental variable for tariff reduction over 2001–2006.[2]

12.3 Data

12.3.1 Urban household survey and industrial firm survey

Our empirical work exploits several comprehensive datasets. The Chinese Urban Household Survey (UHS) is conducted annually by the National Bureau of Statistics (NBS). Using sampling techniques and the daily accounting method, NBS collects data from non-agricultural households in all prefecture-level cities of all 31 provinces. It records household information about income and consumption expenditure, demographic characteristics, work and employment, accommodation, and other family-related matters (Ge and Yang, 2014). We have access to 18 provinces of the UHS data for 2002–2007. Among these are the coastal provinces of Beijing, Liaoning, Shanghai, Jiangsu, Zhejiang, Shandong, and Guangdong, and the inland provinces of Shanxi, Heilongjiang, Anhui, Jiangxi, Henan, Hubei, Chongqing, Sichuan, Yunnan, Gansu, and Xinjiang. In 2007, our UHS sample covered 131,000 individuals in 191 cities. Since household samples for UHS were drawn from a large sampling frame of households having an urban *hukou*, migrant workers were not included. The UHS gives education information for all individuals. Here our definition of skilled labour includes all workers with education level of senior high school or above.

The UHS data does not provide detailed industry information of the individuals. As a result, we do not have an individual-level tariff exposure measure. Instead, we rely on the city-level measure. Since we need detailed information for city industrial employment composition, we use the 2001 NBS annual survey of above-scale industrial firms for this purpose. It covers all state-owned firms and all non-state firms above with sales revenue of 5 million yuan.

Table 12.1 summarises our urban household survey data. The UHS classifies individual income in four categories:

1. Wage income: salaries and other labour compensation
2. Operational income: income from household business
3. Property income: income from the ownership of properties such as interests, rents, and dividends
4. Transfer income: income from government transfer payments.

Table 12.1 shows that total income increased substantially from 10,480 yuan in 2002 to 18,671 yuan in 2007. Throughout the sample period, the share of wage income in total income stayed relatively constant at around 95%.

Regarding the city-level variables, among all four inequality measures that we will discuss soon, income inequality increased gradually from 2002 to 2005, then declined slightly between 2005 and 2007. Return to schooling dropped first in 2003 but increased slowly afterwards. The share of unemployed workers and share of manufacturing in total employment decreased significantly between 2002 and 2007.

12.3.2 Tariff, non-tariff barriers, and FDI policy

Tariff data at the six-digit HS level for 2001–2006 come from Chinese Customs. Since the NBS uses its own industry classification of industrial firm data, we create a concordance table to merge the six-digit HS code with the four-digit Chinese industry classification (CIC) code. City-level tariffs are computed as the weighted average of tariffs of all industries, using the employment share of 2001 as weights. Average tariff across all cities declined from 16.4% in 2001 to 9.7% in 2007. We divide all cities into three groups based on the size of the tariff cut between 2001 and 2007. Figure 12.2 shows the evolution of average tariff rate in 2001–2007 by these three city groups. Appendix Table 12.A1 presents the tariff cut of the two-digit industries (from largest to smallest). It seems that heavy industries such as steel, non-ferrous metals, and petroleum had the largest tariff cut. Appendix Table 12.A2 lists five cities with the largest tariff cuts and five cities with the smallest. No clear geographic patterns cut across cities.

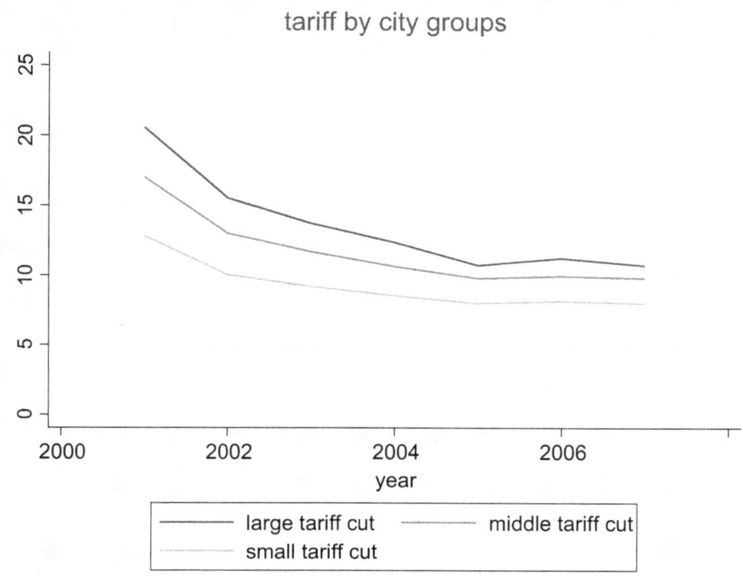

Figure 12.2 Tariff Reduction by City Groups 2001–2007.

Source: Authors' computation.

Note: We divide all cities into three groups with equal number of cities based on the size of tariff cut: large, medium, and small tariff cuts.

In addition to tariff reductions, China also substantially reduced non-tariff barriers. One potential confounding factor in our analysis is the relaxation of import licence control. We assembled information on licensing imports at the HS eight-digit level, drawing on annual circulars of the Ministry of Foreign Trade and Economic Cooperation and the Ministry of Commerce. We calculate the share of HS8 products under import licence control for each 4-digit CIC industry, and then calculate city-level import licence control as employment weighted average of the share across all four-digit CIC manufacturing industries.[3] The average city-level measure of import licences declined by 6.5 percentage points in 2001–2006.

Another major form of liberalisation accompanying the WTO entry is FDI liberalisation policies. Although China started to liberalise FDI before its WTO accession, FDI was still restricted in a wide range of industries in both the manufacturing and service sectors. The restrictions took various forms, such as higher initial capital requirements, less favourable tax treatments, more complicated business registry and approval procedures, and, in the case of joint ventures, requirement of majority shareholding by a Chinese party. These restrictions were largely removed right after China's WTO accession. Our data on FDI restrictions is from the Catalogue for the Guidance of Foreign Investment Industries issued by the Ministry of Commerce of China. The catalogue is a major source of reference for the government in approving foreign investment projects. It lists the industries in which FDI to China is 'encouraged', 'restricted', or 'prohibited'. Unlisted industries are 'allowed'. Investments are completely banned in 'prohibited' industries and subject to various forms of restrictions in 'restricted' industries. The catalogue is amended every three to five years. For our sample period, we use the list issued in 1997, 2002, and 2004.

We construct city-level FDI restriction measures. First, based on the industry descriptions listed in the catalogue, we map them to CIC 4-digit. We categorise a CIC industry as subject to FDI restrictions if it is either restricted or prohibited. We then further map 4-digit CIC to the 1-digit industry classification in the UHS data and calculate the share of 4-digit CIC industries that are restricted within each 1-digit industry. Finally, we construct city-level FDI restriction as the employment weighted average of the share across all 1-digit industries, where the 1-digit employment data is obtained from the UHS.[4] Note that the restricted industries cover the manufacturing and service sectors, so our city-level FDI restriction measure captures FDI liberalisation in both manufacturing and services. The average city-level FDI restriction declined by 2 percentage points during 2001–2006.

12.4 Estimation results

12.4.1 Income growth

Figure 12.3 plots the change of *ln(income)* against the change of *ln(tariff)* at the city level. We observe a clear positive relationship between tariff change and

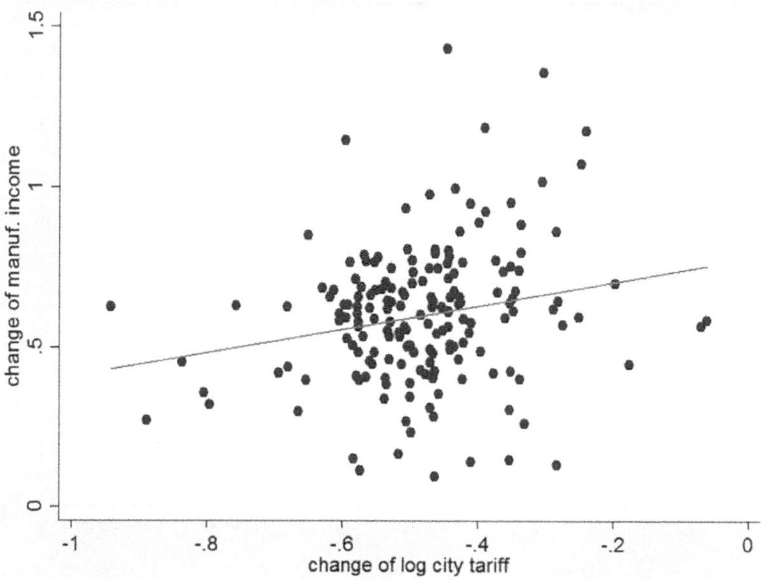

Figure 12.3 City-Level Manufacturing Income Growth and Tariff Change.
Source: Authors' computation.

income growth, which implies that tariff reduction (or negative tariff change) led to lower income growth at the city level. Table 12.2 presents the estimation results of Equation (3) with the dependent variable of log difference in city average individual income between 2002 and 2007. Panels A, B, and C show the regression results for all workers, manufacturing workers, and non-manufacturing workers, respectively. Although our tariff data mainly cover manufacturing goods, tariff cuts may also affect non-manufacturing industries through economic linkages. Throughout the paper, we report robust standard errors in parentheses.

Column (1) of Table 12.2 shows the regression results without provincial fixed effects and city-level control variables. We add these controls in Columns (2) and (3). Controlling provincial fixed effects is important as the R-Sq. jumps from 0.013 to 0.326. In Column (1), we find positive coefficient for tariff change. However, such an effect is statistically significant only for manufacturing workers. The results are similar in Columns (2) and (3), although the size of the effect is smaller. The tariff cut effect estimated in Table 12.2 is also quantitatively significant. If we use the estimates of Column (3) for manufacturing workers, a tariff cut of 7 percentage points (i.e., the average tariff cut across all cities) is associated with 0.07*0.299 = 0.021 or a 2.1 percentage points decrease of income growth in 2002–2007.

Table 12.2 Income Regressions (Total Income Per Worker)

	(1)	*(2)*	*(3)*
Panel A: All Workers			
dlog(tariff)	0.114	0.078	0.071
	(0.078)	(0.093)	(0.092)
Province FE	No	Yes	Yes
City-level controls	No	No	Yes
Observations	177	177	177
R-squared	0.013	0.326	0.460
Panel B: Manufacturing Workers			
dlog(tariff)	0.368***	0.308*	0.299*
	(0.129)	(0.160)	(0.153)
Province FE	No	Yes	Yes
City-level controls	No	No	Yes
Observations	176	176	176
R-squared	0.047	0.179	0.221
Panel C: Non-manufacturing Workers			
dlog(tariff)	0.076	0.063	0.067
	(0.088)	(0.095)	(0.090)
Province FE	No	Yes	Yes
City-Level controls	No	No	Yes
Observations	177	177	177
R-squared	0.005	0.305	0.369

Source: Authors' computation.
Note: Robust standard errors in parentheses. *** p<0.01, ** p<0.05, * p<0.1.

To understand how a tariff change affects different sources of urban income, in the new regressions we replace the total income with the four components of income as dependent variables. In Table 12.3, we only report the estimation results with provincial fixed effects and city-level initial characteristics. Consistent with Table 12.2, tariff changes only affect manufacturing workers. But only wage income and property income are statistically significant. We find no evidence that income from household, business, or government transfer payment is affected by trade reform.

Although long difference models are less sensitive to measurement errors, they are less efficient than panel data models. As a robustness check, instead of a long difference model, we also estimate a city fixed effect model by utilising every year's data in our sample period. Table 12.4 presents the regression results with city fixed effects, year fixed effects, and city characteristics. We find that trade liberalisation affects only manufacturing workers and only through wage and property income.

China's tariff liberalisation was accompanied by the reduction of non-trade barriers (NTBs) and a relaxation of FDI policy at the same time. To further check the robustness of our results, as control variables we include in the regressions the share of products under import licences and the share of the FDI 'restricted/prohibited' industries. The calculation of these two variables is discussed in greater detail in Section 3.2. We report the regression results in

Table 12.5. Column (1) includes only the change of NTBs and Column (2) includes only the change of FDI policy. We can see that the tariff change variable remains positive and statistically significant for manufacturing workers. The results vary little if we include both NTBs and FDI variables in Column (3). In fact, these two new control variables are never statistically significant across all specifications.

To deal with the endogeneity problem, using initial tariff as an instrumental variable (IV) for tariff change, we estimate the baseline model and report the IV regression results in Table 12.6. In Panel A, when manufacturing workers and non-manufacturing workers are grouped together, we observe a negative and statistically significant impact of tariff reduction on wage income and property income. Further inspection of Panels B and C reveals that tariff reductions only affected manufacturing workers. Although our IV estimation results are qualitatively similar to those reported in Table 12.3, the coefficients of the tariff change variable are generally larger.

Our finding that tariff reductions reduce the growth of manufacturing workers' wage income at the city level should not be surprising. Brandt et al. (2015) show that Chinese manufacturing firms cut their prices in response to the import

Table 12.3 Income Regressions (By Income Source)

	(1)	*(3)*	*(4)*	*(5)*
Dependent Variable	*Wage Income*	*Operational Income*	*Property Income*	*Transfer Income*
Panel A: All Workers				
dlog(tariff)	0.102	1.276	0.784	-0.237
	(0.0885)	(1.896)	(1.290)	(0.780)
Province FE	Yes	Yes	Yes	Yes
City-level controls	Yes	Yes	Yes	Yes
Observations	177	177	177	177
R-squared	0.490	0.200	0.190	0.174
Panel B: Manufacturing Workers				
dlog(tariff)	0.399***	-1.730	3.150**	-1.834
	(0.148)	(1.744)	(1.394)	(2.321)
Province FE	Yes	Yes	Yes	Yes
City-level controls	Yes	Yes	Yes	Yes
Observations	176	176	176	176
R-squared	0.231	0.189	0.173	0.073
Panel C: Non-manufacturing Workers				
dlog(tariff)	0.0522	2.268	1.297	0.420
	(0.0860)	(1.712)	(1.375)	(0.789)
Province FE	Yes	Yes	Yes	Yes
City-level controls	Yes	Yes	Yes	Yes
Observations	177	177	177	177
R-squared	0.398	0.133	0.193	0.081

Source: Authors' computation.

Note: Robust standard errors in parentheses. *** $p < 0.01$, ** $p < 0.05$, * $p < 0.1$.

Table 12.4 Income Regressions (City Fixed Effects)

	(1)	*(2)*	*(3)*	*(4)*
Dep. Var.	*Wage Income*	*Operational Income*	*Property Income*	*Transfer Income*
Panel A: All Workers				
log(tariff)_t–1	0.101	0.384	1.078	-0.113
	(0.065)	(1.228)	(0.770)	(0.520)
City FE	Yes	Yes	Yes	Yes
Year FE	Yes	Yes	Yes	Yes
City-level controls	Yes	Yes	Yes	Yes
Observations	1,129	1,129	1,129	1,129
R-squared	0.957	0.501	0.713	0.730
Panel B: Manufacturing Workers				
log(tariff)_t–1	0.336***	0.906	3.135***	–1.176
	(0.128)	(0.938)	(1.101)	(1.491)
City FE	Yes	Yes	Yes	Yes
Year FE	Yes	Yes	Yes	Yes
City-level controls	Yes	Yes	Yes	Yes
Observations	1,126	1,126	1,126	1,126
R-squared	0.874	0.381	0.621	0.635
Panel C: Non-manufacturing Workers				
log(tariff)_t–1	0.053	0.510	1.292	–0.232
	(0.071)	(1.223)	(0.821)	(0.505)
City FE	Yes	Yes	Yes	Yes
Year FE	Yes	Yes	Yes	Yes
City-level controls	Yes	Yes	Yes	Yes
Observations	1,129	1,129	1,129	1,129
R-squared	0.950	0.486	0.680	0.711

Source: Authors' computation.
Note: Robust standard errors in parentheses. *** $p < 0.01$, ** $p < 0.05$, * $p < 0.1$.

tariff reduction after China's WTO entry. Import competition resulting from reduced tariffs could adversely affect wages of manufacturing firms.

Next, we study the impact of tariff reductions on income growth of skilled and unskilled workers. We would like to investigate the heterogeneous effect based on skill because it could contribute to income inequality. In Columns (1) and (2) of Table 12.7, we regress the income growth of skilled and unskilled workers on tariff change and other control variables using OLS estimation. The IV estimation results are reported in Columns (3) and (4). It seems that tariff reductions affect both skilled and unskilled workers, but such an effect is statistically significant only with the IV estimation in Panel A for the full sample – all workers.

Table 12.5 Income Regressions Robustness Check (Total Income per Worker)

	(1)	(2)	(3)
Panel A: All Workers			
dlog(tariff)	0.058	0.068	0.055
	(0.096)	(0.092)	(0.096)
dshare_licence	0.133		0.132
	(0.165)		(0.165)
dFDIrestriction		−0.199	−0.194
		(0.395)	(0.398)
Province FE	Yes	Yes	Yes
City-level controls	Yes	Yes	Yes
Observations	177	177	177
R-squared	0.462	0.461	0.463
Panel B: Manufacturing Workers			
dlog(tariff)	0.285*	0.298*	0.284*
	(0.151)	(0.155)	(0.152)
dshare_licence	0.193		0.188
	(0.283)		(0.287)
dFDIrestriction		−0.314	−0.295
		(0.862)	(0.867)
Province FE	Yes	Yes	Yes
City-level controls	Yes	Yes	Yes
Observations	176	176	176
R-squared	0.223	0.222	0.224
Panel C: Non-Manufacturing Workers			
dlog(tariff)	0.064	0.067	0.064
	(0.092)	(0.091)	(0.092)
dshare_licence	0.046		0.047
	(0.189)		(0.189)
dFDIrestriction		0.030	0.038
		(0.427)	(0.428)
Province FE	Yes	Yes	Yes
City-level controls	Yes	Yes	Yes
Observations	177	177	177
R-squared	0.369	0.369	0.369

Source: Authors' computation.
Note: Robust standard errors in parentheses. *** $p < 0.01$, ** $p < 0.05$, * $p < 0.1$.

Did the tariff reduction decrease manufacturing employment? Did it increase the unemployment rate? To answer these questions, we investigate the effect of tariff changes on employment and unemployment at the city level. The first two columns of Table 12.8 show that tariff reductions tend to decrease manufacturing's share of total employment. The coefficient of tariff change becomes statistically significant at the 10% level when we include provincial fixed effects. This result may imply a substitution effect of manufacturing and

Table 12.6 IV Estimation of Income

	(1)	*(2)*	*(3)*	*(4)*
Dep. Var.	*Wage Income*	*Operational Income*	*Property Income*	*Transfer Income*
Panel A: All Workers				
dlog(tariff)	0.231*	1.921	3.610*	−0.437
	(0.136)	(2.744)	(1.844)	(1.219)
Province FE	Yes	Yes	Yes	Yes
City level controls	Yes	Yes	Yes	Yes
Observations	177	177	177	177
R-squared	0.480	0.199	0.162	0.174
Panel B: Manufacturing Workers				
dlog(tariff)	0.612**	−0.846	4.365*	−4.202
	(0.260)	(2.764)	(2.550)	(3.294)
Province FE	Yes	Yes	Yes	Yes
City-level controls	Yes	Yes	Yes	Yes
Observations	176	176	176	176
R-squared	0.221	0.188	0.170	0.059
Panel C: Non-manufacturing Workers				
dlog(tariff)	0.128	4.258	2.412	0.837
	(0.132)	(2.623)	(1.910)	(1.232)
Province FE	Yes	Yes	Yes	Yes
City level controls	Yes	Yes	Yes	Yes
Observations	177	177	177	177
R-squared	0.394	0.125	0.189	0.080

Source: Authors' computation.
Note: Robust standard errors in parentheses. *** $p < 0.01$, ** $p < 0.05$, * $p < 0.1$.

Table 12.7 Income Regressions Skilled vs. Unskilled Workers

	(1)	*(2)*	*(3)*	*(4)*
	OLS	*OLS*	*IV*	*IV*
Dep. Var.	*Skilled Income*	*Unskilled Income*	*Skilled Income*	*Unskilled Income*
Panel A: All Workers				
dlog(tariff)	0.142	0.062	0.280*	0.295*
	(0.102)	(0.107)	(0.146)	(0.154)
Province FE	Yes	Yes	Yes	Yes
City-level controls	Yes	Yes	Yes	Yes
Observations	177	177	177	177
R-squared	0.266	0.491	0.256	0.469

	(1)	(2)	(3)	(4)
	OLS	*OLS*	*IV*	*IV*
Dep. Var.	*Skilled Income*	*Unskilled Income*	*Skilled Income*	*Unskilled Income*
Panel B: Manufacturing Workers				
dlog(tariff)	0.458	0.289	0.331	0.530*
	(0.281)	(0.191)	(0.429)	(0.277)
Province FE	Yes	Yes	Yes	Yes
City-level controls	Yes	Yes	Yes	Yes
Observations	160	175	160	175
R-squared	0.178	0.275	0.177	0.265
Panel C: Non-manufacturing Workers				
dlog(tariff)	0.138	-0.004	0.314**	0.144
	(0.106)	(0.108)	(0.146)	(0.157)
Province FE	Yes	Yes	Yes	Yes
City-level controls	Yes	Yes	Yes	Yes
Observations	177	177	177	177
R-squared	0.273	0.405	0.258	0.396

Source: Authors' computation.
Note: Robust standard errors in parentheses. *** $p < 0.01$, ** $p < 0.05$, * $p < 0.1$.

Table 12.8 Manufacturing Employment Share and Unemployment Rate

	(1)	(2)	(3)	(4)
Dep. Var.	*Manufacturing Labour Share*	*Manufacturing Labour Share*	*Unemployment Rate*	*Unemployment Rate*
dlog(tariff)	0.050	0.097*	−0.010	−0.042
	(0.034)	(0.051)	(0.033)	(0.041)
Province FE	No	Yes	No	Yes
Observations	177	177	177	177
R-squared	0.007	0.162	0.001	0.118

Source: Authors' computation.
Note: Robust standard errors in parentheses. *** $p < 0.01$, ** $p < 0.05$, * $p <0.1$.

non-manufacturing jobs. Note that we cannot study total employment since our sample is a random one and the sample size reflects only the survey design, not total employment.

The last two columns of Table 12.8 report the estimation results of the unemployment rate. Tariff reductions seem to increase the unemployment rate, but the effect is not statistically significant. One caveat is that we observe unemployed workers in the data, but we do not know their industry of employment before they were unemployed. Therefore, we can only study the total unemployment rate. We do not know whether the impact of tariff reductions on the manufacturing unemployment rate will be statistically significant.

12.4.2 Income inequality

In the literature, there are many measures of income inequality within a region. The most popular are probably the Gini coefficient and the Theil index. In studies on poverty and consumption inequality, some economists (e.g., Topalova, 2007) propose alternative measures such as mean log deviation of consumption and standard deviation of log consumption. Since our focus is income inequality rather than consumption inequality, we also calculate the mean log deviation of income and standard deviation of log income.

We compute all four measures for income inequality at the city level. It turns out that these four inequality measures are highly correlated. Tables 12.9 and 12.10 present the OLS estimation and IV estimation results of inequality regressions. Panels A, B, and C study the inequality measures for all workers, manufacturing workers only, and non-manufacturing workers only, respectively. From Table 12.9, with OLS results we find no evidence that a tariff change affects income inequality at the city level. Among manufacturing workers, a tariff change bears a positive sign but is only marginally significant for the Theil index. However, when we estimate the same equations with the IV, the results are very

Table 12.9 Income Inequality Regressions (OLS)

	(1)	*(2)*	*(3)*	*(4)*
Dep. Var.	*Gini Coefficient*	*Theil Index*	*Mean Deviation*	*S.D. of Logs*
Panel A: All Workers				
dlog(tariff)	−0.018	−0.025	−0.008	−0.046
	(0.031)	(0.041)	(0.023)	(0.144)
Province FE	Yes	Yes	Yes	Yes
City-level controls	Yes	Yes	Yes	Yes
Observations	177	177	177	177
R-squared	0.493	0.558	0.474	0.364
Panel B: Manufacturing Workers				
dlog(tariff)	0.099	0.149*	0.071	0.235
	(0.074)	(0.090)	(0.059)	(0.169)
Province FE	Yes	Yes	Yes	Yes
City-level controls	Yes	Yes	Yes	Yes
Observations	153	153	153	153
R-squared	0.166	0.149	0.165	0.204
Panel C: Non-manufacturing Workers				
dlog(tariff)	−0.014	−0.016	−0.006	−0.087
	(0.034)	(0.041)	(0.026)	(0.086)
Province FE	Yes	Yes	Yes	Yes
City-level controls	Yes	Yes	Yes	Yes
Observations	177	177	177	177
R-squared	0.164	0.151	0.162	0.129

Source: Authors' computation.
Note: Robust standard errors in parentheses. *** $p < 0.01$, ** $p < 0.05$, * $p < 0.1$.

different (Table 12.10). The tariff change is statistically significant at the 10% or 5% level for the Gini coefficient, Theil index, and mean deviation of log income. Its positive sign also indicates that tariff cuts tend to reduce income inequality at the city level.

There is not much theoretical guidance on why tariff liberalisations reduce income inequality. As we have shown earlier, income growth is lower for those cities with larger tariff cuts. Perhaps tariff reductions affect high-income people more than low-income ones. Or those cities with a greater share of high-wage industries are more affected by tariff reductions. Unfortunately, we cannot directly test these mechanisms with our data.

Did tariff reductions decrease return to schooling? This is important because in the existing literature, rising return to schooling is often cited as a main source of income inequality. We adopt a two-stage approach to answer this question. In the first stage, we run the following Mincer-type regressions for each city in 2002 and 2007 and obtain an estimate of β_2:

$$\ln(wage) = \beta_0 + \beta_1 female\_dummy + \beta_2 Schooling + \beta_3 Experience + \beta_4 Experience^2 + u \tag{4}$$

Table 12.10 Income Inequality Regressions (IV)

	(1)	*(2)*	*(3)*	*(4)*
Dep. Var.	*Gini Coefficient*	*Theil Index*	*Mean Deviation*	*S.D. of Logs*
Panel A: All Workers				
dlog(tariff)	0.048	0.092	0.025	0.017
	(0.053)	(0.070)	(0.040)	(0.197)
Province FE	Yes	Yes	Yes	Yes
City-level controls	Yes	Yes	Yes	Yes
Observations	177	177	177	177
R-squared	0.481	0.537	0.468	0.363
Panel B: Manufacturing Workers				
dlog(tariff)	0.185**	0.259**	0.128*	0.371
	(0.0908)	(0.120)	(0.0704)	(0.243)
Province FE	Yes	Yes	Yes	Yes
City-level controls	Yes	Yes	Yes	Yes
Observations	153	153	153	153
R-squared	0.154	0.137	0.156	0.199
Panel C: Non-manufacturing Workers				
dlog(tariff)	0.019	0.064	0.005	−0.018
	(0.056)	(0.062)	(0.043)	(0.148)
Province FE	Yes	Yes	Yes	Yes
City-level controls	Yes	Yes	Yes	Yes
Observations	177	177	177	177
R-squared	0.160	0.128	0.161	0.126

Source: Authors' computation.
Note: Robust standard errors in parentheses. *** $p < 0.01$, ** $p < 0.05$, * $p < 0.1$.

Table 12.11 Return to Schooling Regressions

	OLS	*IV*
	(1)	*(2)*
Panel A: All Workers		
dlog(tariff)	−0.026	−0.046
	(0.024)	(0.086)
Province FE	Yes	Yes
City-level controls	Yes	Yes
Observations	177	177
R-squared	0.123	0.121
Panel B: Manufacturing Workers		
dlog(tariff)	−0.023	0.147
	(0.295)	(0.516)
Province FE	Yes	Yes
City-level controls	Yes	Yes
Observations	172	172
R-squared	0.099	0.094
Panel C: Non-Manufacturing Workers		
dlog(tariff)	−0.054	−0.108
	(0.052)	(0.067)
Province FE	Yes	Yes
City-level controls	Yes	Yes
Observations	177	177
R-squared	0.132	0.121

Source: Authors' computation.
Note: Bootsrapped standard errors in parentheses. *** $p < 0.01$, ** $p < 0.05$, * $p < 0.1$.

In the second stage, we use the change of $\hat{\beta}_2$ between 2002 and 2007 as a dependent variable in Equation (3). Table 12.11 shows the estimation results of both OLS and IV regressions. Bootstrapped standard errors are reported in the parentheses. In Panels B and C, return to schooling is estimated using only manufacturing and non-manufacturing workers. In all regressions, we find no statistically significant relationship between city-level tariff reductions and change in return to schooling.

12.5 Conclusions and policy implications

In this paper, we examined the impact of import tariff reduction on the growth and distribution of urban household income due to China's entry into the WTO. We took advantage of industry variations in tariff cuts and regional variations in initial industry employment compositions. To deal with the endogeneity of tariff reductions, we also used initial year tariff as an IV for tariff cuts. Our findings suggest that cities with larger tariff reductions after WTO entry experienced slower income growth for manufacturing workers. We find no such effect for non-manufacturing workers. Tariff reductions affected the growth of wage income and property income, but not operation income and transfer income. Our results on income growth are robust under different estimation methods (OLS and IV) and different specifications (including non-trade barriers and FDI policy variables). We also calculated different measures of income inequality at the city level. Our IV estimation results indicated that tariff reductions actually helped reduce income inequality.

The results in this paper have important policy implications. Developing countries often pursue trade openness as an engine for faster economic growth and higher living standards. Although it is mostly believed that in the long run open policies contribute to economic development, in the short to medium run, the process towards openness – trade liberalisation – may negatively affect certain parts of the economy. Our estimation results show that in China, manufacturing workers in cities that are exposed to larger tariff reductions experienced slower income growth. We stress that these results do not make any conclusions on the impact of trade liberalisation on aggregate income growth. Rather, they suggest that trade liberalisation has heterogeneous effects across regions and sectors. In China, the adjustment costs of liberalisation fall onto the manufacturing sector and regions where industries are more exposed to tariff reductions. Based on this finding, it is the government's responsibility to help those individuals affected by trade reforms.

On the other hand, reducing China's disturbingly high level of income inequality is one of the most difficult but critical challenges facing the government. The income distribution reforms initiated by the Xi Jinping administration have shown a strong desire to make fundamental changes to the structure of China's income distribution. Background factors of these reforms include the political need to achieve a 'comprehensive well-off society' by 2020. Our study argues that, contrary to popular belief, there is evidence that tariff reductions actually lowered city-level income inequality after the WTO entry. Therefore, trade reforms should not be regarded as a major driver of the rising income inequality in China.

Notes

* This report was prepared for the ERIA Microdata project 2016.

1 In fact, China experienced significant tariff reductions in the 1990s, perhaps in preparation for the WTO entry.

2 Using initial tariff as instrument for tariff cuts is common in the literature. See Amiti and Konings (2007) and Kovak (2013).

3 Like the construction of city-level tariffs, the employment data are obtained from the Annual Survey of Industrial Firms. We use the 2001 employment share as weights to avoid endogeneity.

4 We use 2002 data to alleviate the endogeneity problem.

References

Amiti, M., and J. Konings (2007), 'Trade Liberalization, Intermediate Inputs, and Productivity: Evidence from Indonesia', *American Economic Review* 97(5): 1611–38.

Brandt, L., J. Van Biesebroeck, L. Wang and Y. Zhang (2017), 'WTO Accession and Performance of Chinese Manufacturing Firms,' *American Economic Review* 107(9): 2784–2820.

Branstetter, L., and N. Lardy (2008), 'China's Embrace of Globalization', in L. Brandt and T.G. Rawski (eds.), *China's Economic Transition: Origins, Mechanisms, and Consequences*. New York: Cambridge University Press: 633–682.

Carneiro, R.D., and B.K. Kovak (2015), 'Trade Liberalization and the Skill Premium: A Local Labor Markets Approach', *American Economic Review* 105(5): 551–57.

Deaton, A. (2005), 'Measuring Poverty in a Growing World (or Measuring Growth in a Poor World)', *Review of Economics and Statistics* 87(1): 1–19.

Edmonds, E.V., N. Pavcnik, and P. Topalova (2010), 'Trade Adjustment and Human Capital Investments: Evidence from Indian Tariff Reform', *American Economic Journal: Applied Economics* 2(4): 42–75.

Frankel, J., and D. Romer (1999), 'Does Trade Cause Growth?', *American Economic Review* 89(3): 379–99.

Ge, S., and D. Yang (2014), 'Changes in China's Wage Structure', *Journal of European Economic Association* 12(2): 330–36.

Goldberg, P., and N. Pavcnik (2007a), 'Distributional Effects of Globalization in Developing Countries', *Journal of Economic Literature* 45(1): 39–82.

Goldberg, P., and N. Pavcnik (2007b), 'The Effects of the Colombian Trade Liberalization on Urban Poverty', in A. Harrison (ed.), *Globalization and Poverty*. Cambridge, MA: National Bureau of Economic Research: 241–90.

Grossman, G., and E. Helpman (2002), *Interest Groups and Trade Policy*. Princeton, NJ: Princeton University Press.

Han, J., R. Liu, and J. Zhang (2012), 'Globalization and Wage Inequality from Urban China', *Journal of International Economics* 87(2): 288–97.

Hasan, R., D. Mitra, and B.P. Ural (2006), 'Trade Liberalization, Labor-Market Institutions, and Poverty Reduction: Evidence from Indian States', *India Policy Forum* 7: 71–122.

Kovak, B. (2013), 'Regional Effects of Trade Reform: What is the Correct Measure of Liberalization?', *American Economic Review* 103(5): 1960–76.

McLaren, J., and S. Hakobyan (2010), 'Looking for Local Labor Market Effects of NAFTA', *NBER Working Paper* No. 16535, Cambridge: NBER.

McLaren, J. and S. Hakobyan (2012),

Rodrik, D., and F. Rodriguez (2001), 'Trade Policy and Economic Growth: A Skeptic's Guide to the Cross-National Evidence', in B. Bernanke and K.S. Rogoff (eds.), *Macroeconomics Annual* 2000. Cambridge, MA: MIT Press: 261–388.

Sachs J., and A. Warner (1995), 'Economic Reform and Process of Global Integration', *Brookings Papers on Economic Activity* 26(1): 1–118.

Topalova, P. (2007), 'Trade Liberalization, Poverty and Inequality: Evidence from Indian Districts', in Ann Harrison (ed.), *Globalization and Poverty*. Cambridge, MA: NBER: 291–336.

Topalova, P. (2010), 'Factor Mobility and Regional Impacts of Trade Liberalization: Evidence on Poverty from India', *American Economic Journal: Applied Economics* 2(4): 1–41.

Wei, Shang-Jin, and Y. Wu (2001), 'Globalization and Inequality: Evidence from Within China', *NBER Working Paper* No. 8611, Cambridge: NBER.

Xie, Y., and X. Zhou (2014), 'Income Inequality in Today's China', *PNAS* 111(19): 6928–33.

Zhu, X., and T. Tombe (2015), 'Trade, Migration and Productivity: A Quantitative Analysis of China', *University of Toronto Working Paper* No. 542.

Appendix

Table 12.A1 Tariff Cut by 2-Digit Industry

CIC Code	*Industry Name*	*Tariff 2001*	*Tariff 2006*	*Change of Tariff*
15	Manufacture of beverages	42.71	23.34	-19.36
21	Manufacture of furniture	20.50	1.52	-18.97
16	Manufacture of tobacco	46.34	31.54	-14.80
13	Processing of food	28.26	16.52	-11.73
14	Manufacture of foods	26.53	16.57	-9.97
28	Manufacture of chemical fibres	14.09	4.27	-9.81
17	Manufacture of textile	20.77	11.34	-9.44
40	Computers & other electronic equipment	14.69	5.95	-8.74
37	Manufacture of transport equipment	19.44	11.02	-8.42
36	Manufacture of special purpose machinery	13.69	5.48	-8.21
30	Manufacture of plastics	17.46	10.26	-7.20
42	Manufacture of artwork	20.40	13.45	-6.95
22	Manufacture of paper and paper products	12.54	5.67	-6.86
24	Manufacture of articles for culture, education, and sport activities	19.41	12.67	-6.74
20	Processing of timber, manufacture of wood, bamboo, rattan, palm and straw products	11.43	4.70	-6.73
18	Manufacture of textile wearing apparel, footwear, & caps	24.01	17.56	-6.46
41	Manufacture of measuring instruments & machinery for cultural activity & office work	13.27	7.08	-6.19
39	Manufacture of electrical machinery and equipment	17.04	11.38	-5.66
23	Printing, reproduction of recording media	9.90	4.36	-5.54
19	Manufacture of leather, fur, feather, & related products	20.04	14.89	-5.15
35	Manufacture of general purpose machinery	13.42	8.50	-4.92
27	Manufacture of medicines	9.72	5.23	-4.49
29	Manufacture of rubber	17.63	13.78	-3.85
31	Manufacture of non-metallic mineral products	15.23	11.41	-3.81
26	Manufacture of raw chemical materials and chemical products	11.68	8.47	-3.21
34	Manufacture of metal products	13.39	10.88	-2.51
32	Smelting and pressing of ferrous metals	4.88	3.46	-1.42
33	Smelting and pressing of non-ferrous metals	4.48	3.21	-1.27
25	Processing of petroleum, coking, processing of nuclear fuel	5.34	4.36	-0.99

Table 12.A2 Cities with the Largest and Smallest Tariff Cuts

City	*Province*	*Tariff 2001*	*Tariff 2006*	*Change of Tariff*	*Major Industry*	*Major Industry Share*
5 cities with largest cut						
Lin Cang	Yunan	43.27	24.46	−18.82	Processing of food	0.55
Shiyan	Hubei	34.30	15.54	−18.76	Manufacture of transport equipment	0.73
Shuang Ya Shan	Heilongjiang	28.52	13.92	−14.60	Processing of food	0.35
Baoshan	Yunan	34.72	21.14	−13.58	Processing of food	0.42
Hegang	Heilongjiang	24.51	11.96	−12.54	Manufacture of non-metallic mineral products	0.15
5 cities with smallest cut						
Tongling	Anhui	6.50	4.44	−2.06	Smelting and pressing of non-ferrous metals	0.36
Changzhi	Shanxi	9.80	7.93	−1.88	Smelting and pressing of ferrous metals	0.31
Panzhihua	Sichuan	5.04	3.56	−1.48	Smelting and pressing of ferrous metals	0.91
Jinchang	Gansu	5.84	4.91	−0.93	Smelting and pressing of non-ferrous metals	0.79
Yingtan	Jiangxi	5.94	5.03	−0.91	Smelting and pressing of non-ferrous metals	0.71

Source: Authors' computation.

13 Overseas production expansion and domestic transaction networks

Kazunobu Hayakawa and Toshiyuki Matsuura

13.1 Introduction

The internationalisation of firms significantly influences the economy through supply chain linkages. Once firms start to invest and expand their production abroad, they may reorganise their sales and procurement strategy in the home country. The expansion of overseas production by multinational enterprises (MNEs) definitely affects the performance of domestic suppliers. However, the impact of foreign direct investment (FDI) on domestic suppliers can be positive or negative. For example, some suppliers may follow the firms and start to invest abroad to maintain a transactional relationship with them. Others, especially small and medium-sized suppliers with financial constraints, may have difficulty in following suit, and, thus, may lose the transactional relationship. Also, some suppliers, especially key component suppliers, may benefit from the expansion of customers' overseas production. If MNEs' overseas affiliates procure the key parts and components from domestic suppliers, the transactional relationship between the MNEs and domestic suppliers may be strengthened; it may also increase the demand for the products of domestic suppliers. These changes in first-tier suppliers further affect business activities with second-tier suppliers. Through such input-output linkages, the internationalisation of some firms affects the whole economy.

In this study, we empirically examine how firms' FDI affects their suppliers' business activities or performance. Specifically, we first explore the difference of firm characteristics between MNEs' suppliers and other firms and then examine whether customers' FDI strengthens or suspends their transaction ties with domestic suppliers. Second, we examine how much the expansion of MNEs' overseas production affects the employment growth of suppliers. Furthermore, we examine how these effects are different between first- and second-tier suppliers. This analysis will contribute to uncovering how firms' FDI affects the economy through supply chains.

To this end, we use a unique firm-level survey in Japan that contains information on the inter-firm transaction network matched with FDI data. Specifically, the information on inter-firm transaction network, i.e., firms' customers and suppliers, is derived from Tokyo Shoko Research (TSR) data, while that on

Japanese FDI, i.e., overseas affiliates owned by Japanese firms, is from *Overseas Japanese Companies Data* published by Toyo Keizai (TKZ). Using these data in 2006 and 2011, we examine the effects of firms' FDI on suppliers' business activities. One important feature of our dataset is that it covers not only listed firms but also small- and medium-sized enterprises (SMEs). The inclusion of such firms is crucial for our analysis, because we investigate the effects on both direct and indirect suppliers, the latter of which are likely SMEs.

This study is related to three strands of studies. First, many investigate the impact of FDI on corporate performance. In regard to the effect on productivity, while Navaretti et al. (2010) in their study on Italy and France and Hijzen et al. (2011) in their study on France demonstrated that horizontal FDI (HFDI) improves domestic productivity. Hayakawa et al. (2013) in their study on Japan found positively significant effects on productivity in the case of vertical FDI (VFDI). Navaretti et al. (2010) found positive impacts on sales and employment through both HFDI and VFDI. Hijzen et al. (2011) and Hayakawa et al. (2013) used French and Japanese firm-level data, respectively, and found that both HFDI and VFDI by French and Japanese firms increase domestic employment. In contrast, Debaere et al. (2010), in their study on Korea, reported not finding any positive impact on employment through either FDI type. While these studies focus on the effects of firms' FDI on their own performance, we investigate those of firms' FDI on their suppliers' performance.

The second strand of studies looks at the impact of FDI on their suppliers' behaviour. Yamashita et al. (2013) and Nakajima and Ito (2014) investigated the extent to which the FDI of transaction partners affects suppliers' decision to invest abroad and in which location. Both studies found strongly positive and significant impact on suppliers' FDI decision. Javorcik and Spatareanu (2009) examined whether the transactions with foreign-owned companies (FOCs) improve the productivity of indigenous suppliers using Czech firm-level data. In the literature on development economics, many studies examine whether there is a technological spill-over from the FOCs to indigenous firms. Javorcik and Spatareanu (2009) utilises firm-level information on transaction ties with the FOCs and distinguish the self-selection and learning as a source of superior performance of the suppliers of the FOCs. They found that even if the selection effect is considered, there is a positive spill-over effect from the FOCs to indigenous firms. Ito and Tanaka (2013), whose study is most closely related to ours, investigated the effect of the expansion of MNEs' overseas production on suppliers' employment. They found that such overseas production positively impacts suppliers' employment. Since their dataset was restricted to firms with more than 50 employees, the suppliers in their study were relatively good firms that provided key components to MNEs, i.e., they were the MNEs' first-tier suppliers. Furthermore, they did not consider the selection bias stemming from the fact that the good firms are more likely to be MNEs suppliers. In contrast to their study, as mentioned above, our dataset covers even small firms and enables us to differentiate first- and second-tier suppliers.

The third stream of research that our study is also related to is the growing literature on the domestic production network. For example, Bernard et al. (2019) developed a two-sided heterogeneous network model in terms of productivity and distance. They examined the impact of the extension of high-speed train (*shinkansen*) on domestic transaction networks. Furusawa et al. (2015) investigated theoretically and empirically how the import decision by transaction partners affects their reorganisation of the domestic production network.[1] Furusawa et al. considered heterogeneity of the degree of relationship specificity as well as efficiency and distance, and found that offshoring induces supplier churning and improves firms' productivity. Our analysis will contribute by adding further evidence on the reorganisation of production networks, with differentiating impacts on the first- and second-tier suppliers.[2]

The rest of this paper is organised as follows. The next section explains the data issues and presents an overview of the data. Section 13.3 discusses our empirical framework and Section 13.4 reports the estimation results. Section 13.5 is the conclusion and provides some policy implications.

13.2 Data issues and data overview

In our empirical analysis, we apply data on transaction among firms in Japan. This section introduces our data sources and briefly presents an overview of our dataset.

13.2.1 Data source and construction procedure

Our primary data sources are the firm-level survey extracted from the TSR data and Japanese FDI data from *Overseas Japanese Companies Data* published by TKZ in 2006 and 2011. The TSR data comprises three databases. The first is the TSR company information database, which contains firm-level basic information, such as the name of firms, their location, industry classification, sales, the number of employees, and profit. The second is TSR's company linkage database, which includes the inter-firm linkage among firms located in Japan and enables us to identify suppliers and customers among firms in the TSR data. Although this database provides a maximum of 24 suppliers and customers for each individual firm, we complement it with the information reported by their transaction partners.[3] The third is the TSR establishment database, which provides geographic information on plants owned by firms in the TSR company information database. We obtain the address information of MNEs' plants. Most MNEs have multiple plants in Japan.

One feature of the TSR data is its coverage. It covers not only listed firms but also SMEs. According to Bernard et al. (2019), compared with census data, the TSR data underrepresent firms with four or less employees. However, the distribution of firms with five or more employees in the TSR sample is close to the full population from census data. On the flip side, since the TSR data do not contain variables such as intermediate input and capital stock, it is impossible to calculate total factor productivity. In addition, we do not have any information on the volume of transaction.

The TKZ data are from the firm-level survey for Japanese firms that own foreign affiliates with more than 20% capital share. Although the TKZ data are not a government survey, it is one of the data sources used most frequently to analyse Japanese FDI (see Head et al., 1995; Belderbos and Carree, 2002). The data focus on a survey of about 5,000 listed and non-listed enterprises, and include their overseas affiliate data on location, investment year, investment type (new establishment, capital investment, and acquisition), amount of capital, total number of employees, number of employees from Japan, earnings, business content, purpose of investment, and funding relationship.

The data construction procedure is as follows: First, we extract manufacturing firms from the 2006 and 2011 editions of the TSR company information database. We focus on firms that reported their financial information in both 2006 and in 2011.[4] Second, we match this dataset with the TKZ database and identify firms that owned manufacturing affiliates abroad as of 2006 or that started investing abroad from 2006 to 2011. We call the former group of firms 'incumbent MNEs' and the latter firms 'new MNEs'. Third, focusing on intermediate goods producers, we define the direct and indirect suppliers to MNEs. The intermediate goods producers are manufacturing firms in the intermediate goods industries identified based on the 2005 version of Input–Output table compiled by the Ministry of Internal Affairs and Communications.[5] We define direct/indirect suppliers as follows: Among non-MNEs, if at least one of their customers is an MNE, it is regarded as a direct supplier. Among firms that are neither MNEs nor direct suppliers, if at least one of their customers is a direct supplier of an MNE, it is regarded as an indirect supplier to MNEs.

We obtain firm-level variables (e.g., sales, the number of employees, plants, and customers) from the above-matched dataset. We also construct the distance between customer firm and supplier firm, which is calculated by great-circle distance calculator using information on the latitude and longitude of firm location. This is obtained from the CSV address-matching service provided by the Center for Spatial Information Science, University of Tokyo. In this computation, we identify each firm's headquarters location. However, large-sized firms, especially MNEs, are likely to have multiple plants in their home country. Therefore, only when computing distance with MNEs, we complement plant location information from the TSR establishment database as mentioned above. Specifically, we calculate distance from MNEs to their suppliers, referring to the MNEs' nearest plants to the suppliers. In our analysis of the labour demand function, we use the average distance to all customers for each supplier firm.

13.2.2 Data overview

This subsection presents the data overview based on 2006 and 2011 data. Table 13.1 presents the number of firms in our dataset – 1,778 incumbent MNEs and 133 new MNEs. As for the number of suppliers, the number of direct and

Table 13.1 The Number of Firms According to Firm Types

	# of firms	*share*
Incumbent MNEs	1,778	1.7%
New MNEs	133	0.1%
Direct supplier	31,810	29.9%
to incumbent MNEs	31,243	29.3%
to new MNEs	567	0.5%
Indirect suppliers	17,648	16.6%
to incumbent MNEs	17450	16.4%
to new MNEs	198	0.2%
Other firms	55,097	51.8%
Total	106,466	100.0%

Source: Authors' computation.
Notes: In this table, we use mutually exclusive definition of suppliers; for example, while the direct suppliers to incumbent MNEs are non-MNEs supplying to incumbent MNEs, the direct suppliers to new MNEs are non-MNEs supplying to new MNEs but not to incumbent MNEs.

indirect suppliers to the MNEs are 31,810 and 17,648, respectively. One may argue that the number of observations for indirect suppliers looks small, compared with that of direct suppliers. Actually, there are 38,892 firms whose customers are direct suppliers of MNEs in our sample. However, since 21,244 out of 38,892 firms are also categorised as direct suppliers, we regard the rest of firms as indirect suppliers (i.e., 17,648 firms). In other words, the sample in this table for indirect suppliers comprises those firms that transact with the direct suppliers of MNEs but do not transact directly with MNEs themselves.[6]

Table 13.2 shows firm characteristics, i.e., the number of employees, suppliers, and customers; average distances from/to their suppliers and customers; and growth rates of employment by type of firms. Obviously, MNEs are larger in terms of the number of employees and transact with many suppliers and customers compared to non-MNEs. It is worth mentioning that MNEs have a higher employment growth ratio. In particular, the employment growth ratio of new MNEs is positive while that of all other groups is negative. These results are consistent with previous studies, as discussed in Section 13.1.

In terms of the characteristics of MNE suppliers, the number of employees and transaction partners also differs between the direct and indirect suppliers. The latter have fewer employees and transaction partners than the former. While the average distance from the suppliers is shorter for MNEs than for direct and indirect suppliers, MNEs are farther from customer firms than direct and indirect suppliers. This may imply that MNEs tend to co-locate with their suppliers and sell their products to distant customers. Growth rates of employment also differ according to type of firm. Compared with MNEs, direct and indirect suppliers have a smaller growth rate in terms of employment. 'Other firms' are smaller in terms of the number of employment, customers, and suppliers and they have the lowest growth rates of employment.

Table 13.2 Average Firm Characteristics According to Firm Types

	Number of Employees	*Distance to Suppliers*	*Distance to Customers*	*Number of Suppliers*	*Number of Customers*	*Growth of Employment*
Firm status						
Incumbent MNEs	989.93	141.46	223.83	98.61	92.25	−0.009
New MNEs	379.44	158.41	198.63	33.92	46.29	0.120
Direct supplier (incumbent MNEs)	67.01	179.76	198.74	7.35	8.70	−0.040
Direct supplier (new MNEs)	36.87	170.45	167.78	6.06	7.05	−0.040
Indirect suppliers (incumbent MNEs)	36.97	185.59	216.73	5.26	6.76	−0.049
Indirect suppliers (new MNEs)	32.90	131.97	193.00	4.95	6.31	−0.094
Other firms	24.59	221.88	238.81	4.03	5.24	−0.085
Total	62.79	195.73	217.72	7.45	8.65	−0.063

Source: Authors' computation.

One may be concerned that these results are subject to differences in the industry or the regional composition of firms. To address this issue, we regress each variable on industry and prefecture dummies and calculate the direct and indirect supplier premium following Bernard and Jensen (1999; Table 13.3). There are significant differences in terms of the number of employment and the number of customers among supplier status. Direct suppliers of incumbent MNEs are 65%–80% larger compared with 'other firms'. As for employment growth rate, only direct and indirect suppliers of incumbent MNEs have significantly higher growth rate. These results may reflect the fact that only good firms can be direct or indirect suppliers. As discussed in Javorcik and Spatareanu (2009), if suppliers of MNEs are requested to have better products or timely delivery, firms with higher ex-ante productivity self-select into being suppliers. We discuss this issue again in Section 13.3.

In Table 13.3, we also explore the differences in the supplier premium by industry. If MNEs are electric or automobile assemblers and their direct or indirect suppliers are parts and components manufacturers, these suppliers might be relatively small firms. However, if the direct or indirect suppliers are chemical products or primary metal products manufacturers, these suppliers may not always be small firms. To explore the differences among industries, we split our sample into three groups: labour-intensive industries, capital-intensive material-producing industries (capital-intensive material), and capital-intensive machinery industries (capital-intensive machinery).[7] While there is a similar pattern for the number of employment and customers, employment growth is basically positive but significant only in case of machinery manufacturers.

Next, we investigate whether suppliers' transaction ties with MNEs are more likely to be suspended or not. We define MNEs or supplier status based on the

Table 13.3 The Supplier Premium

	(1)	(2)	(3)	(4)
Variables	*Manufacturing*	*Labour Intensive*	*Capital-Intensive Material*	*Capital-Intensive Machinery*
log (employee)				
Direct supplier (incumbent MNEs)	0.835***	0.798***	0.807***	0.812***
Direct supplier (new MNEs)	0.413***	0.389***	0.453***	0.405***
Indirect suppliers (incumbent MNEs)	0.266***	0.333***	0.335***	0.178***
Indirect suppliers (new MNEs)	0.178**	0.138	0.236**	0.218
log (# of customers)				
Direct supplier (incumbent MNEs)	0.652***	0.651***	0.650***	0.585***
Direct supplier (new MNEs)	0.438***	0.494***	0.488***	0.342***
Indirect suppliers (incumbent MNEs)	0.318***	0.385***	0.385***	0.203***
Indirect suppliers (new MNEs)	0.243***	0.289***	0.288***	0.137
Emp growth				
Direct supplier (incumbent MNEs)	0.020***	0.003	0.004	0.030***
Direct supplier (new MNEs)	0.016	0.032	0.052	-0.001
Indirect suppliers (incumbent MNEs)	0.016***	0.016**	0.011	0.020***
Indirect suppliers (new MNEs)	-0.002	0.004	0.019	-0.017

Source: Authors' computation.

Notes: Figures are the coefficients of the supplier dummy variable in the regression models with industry and prefecture fixed effects. *, **, and *** indicate statistical significance at 10%, 5%, and 1%, respectively.

transaction relationship in 2006. However, one may be concerned whether this is stable or not. To this end, we calculate the survival rate of transaction tie between 2006 and 2011 among our sample firms.[8] Panel (a) in Table 13.4 presents the survival rate by firm size. The overall annual average survival rate is around 96%. The survival rate of transaction ties for suppliers with 300 or more employees is slightly lower than that for smaller suppliers, implying that larger firms more actively reorganise transactional relationships. Panel (b) in Table 13.4 summarises the differences in the survival rate according to MNE status. Obviously, the survival rate of transaction ties with incumbent MNEs is lower than that with non-MNEs. As confirmed in Tables 13.2 and 13.3, incumbent MNEs are relatively large firms and have more customers than other firms. Therefore, these results may simply reflect the fact that firms with more customers are more likely to reorganise transactional relationships. However, the survival rate with new MNEs is slightly higher than that with non-MNEs, although new MNEs have

Table 13.4 Survival Ratio of Transaction Ties

Panel (a) Supplier Size in Terms of the Number of Employees

	Continue	*New*	*Stop*	*Total*	*Survival Ratio*
-299	181,322	88,144	45,095	314,561	96.0%
300–	40,760	18,931	10,937	70,628	95.8%
Total	222,082	107,075	56,032	385,189	96.0%

Panel (b) MNE Status

	Continue	*New*	*Stop*	*Total*	*Survival Ratio*
Non-MNEs	188,990	92,083	47,103	328,176	96.0%
Incumbent MNEs	31,831	14,314	8,642	54,787	95.7%
New MNEs	1,370	795	336	2,501	96.1%
Total	222,191	107,192	56,081	385,464	96.0%

Panel (c) Co-location with transaction partners

	Continue	*New*	*Stop*	*Total*	*Survival ratio*
Other prefecture	129 12	70,501	35,729	235,442	95.7%
Same prefecture	92,979	36,691	20,352	150,022	96.4%
Total	222,191	107,192	56,081	385,464	96.0%

Source: Authors' computation.

more customers than non-MNEs. Finally, we check whether transactional relationships with distant customers are more vulnerable or stable. Panel (c) in Table 13.4 divides our samples depending on the location of customers – whether they locate in the same prefecture or not. We find that the survival rate for transactional relationships with neighbouring customers is more stable than that with distant customers.

Table 13.4 may reflect various industry or firm characteristics. Before going into the formal econometric analysis, we estimate the following probit model:

$$\Pr\left(Stop_{ij}=1\right)=\Phi\left(\mathbf{X}_i\alpha+\mathbf{Y}_j\beta+\mathbf{Z}_{ij}\gamma\right)$$

The dependent variable, *Stop*, is the dummy variable that takes the value 1 if the transaction tie between supplier i and customer j was broken off between 2006 and 2011. Basically, we examine explanatory variables measured as of 2006. The vector $\mathbf{X}_i$ consists of variables for supplier's characteristics. We include (a log of) the number of employees, multi-plant firm dummy variable, agglomeration of firms, and (a log of) the number of customers. The vector $\mathbf{Y}_j$ is composed of customers' characteristics, such as customers' size in terms of (a log of) the number of employees. As our main variables, we include four dummy variables on customers' FDI status. 'Incumbent MNEs' and 'New MNEs' are dummy variables that take the value one if a customer is an incumbent MNE and a new MNE, respectively. 'DS to incumbent MNEs' and 'DS to new MNEs' are dummy variables that take the value one if a customer is not an MNE but a supplier to an incumbent MNE and to a new MNE, respectively (i.e., direct suppliers [DS] to MNEs). These variables are constructed using the information on customers' FDI status in both 2006 and 2011. Finally, $\mathbf{Z}_{ij}$ is a vector of the variables that captures the relationship between supplier i and customer j. Specifically, we examine the geographical distance between those two firms.

The estimation results are presented in Table 13.5. To highlight the impact of transactions with MNEs, we restrict our sample firms only to direct suppliers,

Table 13.5 Estimation Results of Probit Model: Excluding MNEs (Marginal Effects)

	(1)	*(2)*	*(3)*	*(4)*
Industry	*All Manufacturing*	*Labour Intensive*	*Capital Intensive Material*	*Capital Intensive Machinery*
Supplier characteristics log (employee)	-0.003***	-0.003**	0.004*	-0.005***
	(0.001)	(0.001)	(0.002)	(0.001)
log (# of plants)	-0.001	0.004	-0.009*	-0.002
	(0.002)	(0.003)	(0.005)	(0.003)
log (# of customers)	0.009***	0.010**	-0.028***	0.022***
	(0.003)	(0.005)	(0.009)	(0.005)
Agglomeration	0.003***	0.005***	0.002	0.003*
	(0.001)	(0.002)	(0.003)	(0.002)
Customer characteristics log (Employee)	0.010***	0.013***	0.012***	0.008***
	(0.001)	(0.001)	(0.001)	(0.001)
log (# of plants)	0.003	0.005	0.003	0.000
	(0.002)	(0.004)	(0.006)	(0.003)
log (# of customers)	-0.007***	-0.006*	-0.000	-0.012***
	(0.003)	(0.004)	(0.007)	(0.004)
Incumbent MNEs	-0.091***	-0.084***	-0.086***	-0.095***
	(0.003)	(0.005)	(0.008)	(0.004)
New MNEs	-0.118***	-0.123***	-0.082*	-0.122***
	(0.017)	(0.030)	(0.049)	(0.023)
DS to incumbent MNEs	-0.060***	-0.057***	-0.063***	-0.065***
	(0.003)	(0.006)	(0.010)	(0.005)
DS to new MNEs	-0.011	-0.019	0.171***	-0.074**
	(0.022)	(0.037)	(0.051)	(0.033)
Bilateral characteristics log (Distance)	0.012***	0.01 l***	0.009***	0.013***
	(0.001)	(0.001)	(0.001)	(0.001)
Number of observations	192,193	77,913	27,978	86,302
logLL	-93161	-38278	-12911	-41818
PseudoR2	0.0153	0.0143	0.0157	0.0191

Source: Authors' computation.

Notes: A dependent variable is the dummy variable that takes the value one if transaction tie was broken off between 2006 and 2011. Figures in parentheses are robust standard errors. *, **, and *** indicate statistical significance at 10%, 5%, and 1%, respectively. Industry and prefecture fixed effects are included.

indirect suppliers, and other firms. The result shows that the incumbent and new MNE dummy variables have negatively significant coefficients, indicating that transaction ties with MNEs are less likely to be suspended. In other words, on average, direct suppliers tend to maintain transaction tie with MNEs compared with other firms. In the case of transaction ties between direct suppliers and indirect suppliers, only the coefficient for direct suppliers to incumbent MNEs is negative and significant. This result may indicate that the effects of FDI on indirect suppliers are limited.

One may be interested in whether transaction relationships differ from industry to industry. In the literature on international trade, for example, product-level analysis has shown that differentiated goods or parts and components in machinery industry tend to be traded for a long time, and transaction ties in that industry are less likely to be suspended (Besedes and Prusa, 2006a, 2006b; Obashi, 2010). Thus, the stability of transition ties will vary by industry. To examine this difference, we split our sample into three groups, as in Table 13.3. The results are shown in Columns (2), (3), and (4) in Table 13.5 and do not change much compared with our baseline results although the coefficient for DS to New MNEs is positively significant in material industries.

13.3 Methodology

This paper examines the impact of being a direct or indirect supplier on employment growth. As mentioned, better firms possibly self-select into being direct and indirect suppliers. To address the selection bias, this study adopts matching techniques, particularly the propensity score-matching method of Rosenbaum and Rubin (1983). The instrument variable method is an alternative technique but it is sometimes difficult to find convincing instruments. On the other hand, under some assumptions, the matching method enables us to estimate counterfactuals that cannot be directly observed. Furthermore, the matching method is a kind of non-parametric analysis and has the advantage of not needing to specify the functional form of outcomes and disturbances (Friedlander et al., 1997).

Specifically, we first estimate the probit model to obtain the propensity score of being direct or indirect suppliers. A dependent variable is the dummy variable that takes a value of one if a firm is categorised as a direct or indirect supplier. As for independent variables, we include the logged number of employees, the logged number of customers, and the multi-plant firm dummy and their squares. We also control two agglomeration measures. One is the agglomeration of firms in the same four-digit level industry category and in the same prefecture. The other is the agglomeration of MNEs or the direct suppliers in the same two-digit level industry category and the same prefecture. While the former is a proxy for the extent of local competition, the latter is proximity to MNEs or direct suppliers. Second, a counterfactual firm is selected as follows:

$$\left|P_i - P_j\right| = \min_{k \in \{l|D_l = 0\}} \{P_i - P_k\}$$

where P_i is the predicted probability of being the direct and indirect suppliers. We used the one-to-one nearest-neighbour matching (NNM) technique in our baseline estimation. Then, we calculate the average treatment effect as follows:

$$\alpha_{ATT} = \frac{1}{n}\sum_{i \in I}\left[y_{i,t}^{1} - y_{j,t}^{0}\right]$$

where y^1 is the actual employment growth ratio of direct or indirect suppliers (treatment) and y^0 is the counterfactual firm's employment growth rate (control).

Third, as a robustness check, the employment impact was carried out by adding industry-level control variables. Following the conventional labour demand function estimation, we include demand sizes on their products and factor prices as additional control variables. Therefore, we specify our equation as follows:

$$\Delta \ln L_i = D_i\alpha + \mathrm{y}_s\beta + \varepsilon_i$$

The dependent variable is a log-difference of firm *i*'s employment from 2006 to 2011. *Di* indicates the dummy variable for direct or indirect suppliers while sector *s* specific elements are included in a vector of y. Sector *s* is the one to which firm *i* belongs. We capture the role of demand on firms' products by the following variables. First, we introduce log-differences of three sector-level variables during 2005–2010, including output prices, import prices, and total output values. We also introduce the interaction term of import prices with the import penetration ratio to consider the exposure to import competition. To control for factor prices, we also introduce a log-difference of province-level wages between 2005 and 2010, in addition to two-digit level industry fixed effect.

13.4 Estimation result

This section presents our estimation results. First, we estimate the probit model to obtain the propensity score of being direct or indirect suppliers of MNEs. The estimation results are presented in Table 13.6.[9] While Column (1) indicates the result for the probit model for being direct suppliers, the one for indirect suppliers is shown in Column (2). As for being direct suppliers, the number of employment and multi-plant dummy variables and the number of customers are all significant positive coefficients, suggesting that larger firms are more likely to be direct suppliers. In contrast, in Column (2), only the number of customers has a significant coefficient, implying that size does not matter in being indirect suppliers. The agglomeration of firms in the same four-digit level industry has a negative coefficient whereas the coefficients of the agglomeration of MNEs or the direct suppliers are positive and significant. The former set of results implies that firms facing fierce competition are less likely to be suppliers. The latter indicates that the proximity to MNEs or direct suppliers are important determinants for being suppliers.

Table 13.6 Estimation Results of Probit Model: Excluding MNEs, Estimation by Industry

	(1)	(2)
Variables	*Direct Suppliers*	*Indirect Suppliers*
log (employee)	0.258***	0.018
	(0.014)	(0.017)
log (employee)^2	-0.009***	0.003
	(0.002)	(0.003)
Multi-plant firm	0.073***	0.001
	(0.011)	(0.015)
log (# of customers)	1.554***	0.549***
	(0.038)	(0.048)
log (# of customers)^2	-0.447***	-0.108***
	(0.016)	(0.021)
Agglomeration	-0.056***	-0.053***
	(0.004)	(0.005)
Agglomeration of MNEs	0.004***	
	(0.000)	
Agglomeration of direct suppliers		0.001**
		(0.000)
Observations	96,086	64,323
Industry FE	Yes	Yes
Pseudo R2	0.169	0.155
log likelihood	-50685	-31901
Prob(chi2)	0.000	0.000

Source: Authors' computation.

Notes: A dependent variable is the dummy variable that takes the value one if transaction tie is broken off between 2006 and 2011. Figures in parentheses are robust standard errors. **, and *** indicate statistical significance at 5% and 1%, respectively. Industry and prefecture fixed effects are included.

Using the propensity score of being suppliers, we find counterfactuals, as discussed in Section 13.3. We assign matched pairs within two-digit level industries. To ensure the validity of the estimation of the propensity score and the matching based on the estimated propensity score, we statistically tested the condition of the balancing property as follows:

$$D \perp X \mid P(D=1 \mid X).$$

This means that, for a given propensity score, treatment observations are randomly chosen. As a result, the treatment and the control are identical on average. To check whether the balancing property is satisfied, we implement the test of balancing property proposed by Becker and Ichino (2002). Table 13.7 presents the results of t-test statistics comparing variables for firm characteristics. We find no statistically significant differences between the treatments and the controls.

Next, we examine the effect of being direct or indirect suppliers. Panel (a) of Table 13.8 presents the results of propensity score matching for direct suppliers. In addition to the one-to-one NNM method, we use 5-NNM and radius-matching methods. Looking at our baseline result, the one by the one-to-one

Table 13.7 The Test of Balancing Property

Direct Supplier					
Variable	*Treated*	*Control*	*%bias*	t	*Prob>t*
log (employee)	2.896	2.893	0.20	0.04	0.968
log (employee)^2	9.702	9.647	0.80	0.16	0.874
Multi-plant firm	0.251	0.225	6.30	1.28	0.199
log (# of customers)	1.172	1.168	1.00	0.21	0.835
log (# of customers) ^{2}	1.555	1.555	0.10	0.01	0.99
Indirect Supplier					
Variable	*Treated*	*Control*	*%bias*	t	*Prob>t*
log (Employee)	2.614	2.548	5.90	0.93	0.354
log (Employee)^2	8.029	7.642	6.40	0.97	0.33
Multi-plant firm	0.203	0.182	5.30	0.82	0.412
log (# of customers)	1.072	1.055	4.00	0.62	0.536
log (# of customers) ^{2}	1.345	1.302	3.80	0.6	0.548

Source: Authors' computation.

Table 13.8 Estimation Results for Propensity Score Matching

Panel (a) Employment Growth Ratio of Being the Direct Suppliers						
Method	*Treated*	*Controls*	*Difference*	*Std. Err.*	T-*stat*	p-*value*
Unmatched	-0.0397	-0.0756	0.0359	0.0032	11.3029	0.0000
NNM	-0.0391	-0.0633	0.0243	0.0036	6.7738	0.0000
NNM-3-digit	-0.0418	-0.0630	0.0212	0.0039	5.4795	0.0000
NS	-0.0398	-0.0681	0.0283	0.0027	10.3282	0.0000
Radius	-0.0397	-0.0666	0.0268	0.0025	10.5686	0.0000
Panel (b) Employment Growth Ratio of Being the Indirect Suppliers						
Method	*Treated*	*Controls*	*Difference*	*Std. Err.*	T-*stat*	p-*value*
Unmatched	-0.0487	-0.0860	0.0373	0.0042	8.8766	0.0000
NNM	-0.0492	-0.0770	0.0278	0.0051	5.4807	0.0000
NNM-3-digit	-0.0530	-0.0797	0.0267	0.0055	4.8974	0.0000
NS	-0.0492	-0.0766	0.0273	0.0037	7.3143	0.0000
Radius	-0.0492	-0.0767	0.0275	0.0034	7.9748	0.0000

Source: Authors' computation.
NNM = Nearest Neighbour Matching.

NNM method, while the difference of employment growth ratio between treatment and unmatched control is 3.59%, the difference in matched pair is 2.43%. This implies that a simple comparison between treatment and unmatched control suffers from selection bias. Since the differences in the matched pair is statistically significant, MNEs have a positive impact on domestic suppliers.

As mentioned in Table 13.2, MNEs have a higher employment growth ratio compared to other firms. This result suggests positive spill-over effects between MNEs and their suppliers. In the third row of panel (a) of Table 13.8, we assign matched pairs within three-digit level industries instead of within two-digit level industries. The result does not change so much. The fourth and fifth rows of panel (a) of Table 13.8 present the results using 5-NNM (N5) and radius matching. These results are slightly higher than our baseline results but not so different from NNM.

We examine the employment growth rate of indirect suppliers in panel (b) of Table 13.8. Similar to the results for direct suppliers, the differences of employment growth rate in the matched pair are smaller than those in the unmatched pair. Still, the treatments are statistically higher employment growth rate than the controls, suggesting MNEs positively impact both indirect and direct suppliers. We also confirm that regardless of the matching methodology, the employment growth rates for the treatments are higher than those for the controls. The differences of employment growth ratio in matched pairs range from 2.67% to 2.78%. These figures are almost equivalent to treatment effect for direct suppliers.

Table 13.9 includes additional control variables, restricting our sample to the treatments and the matched controls from NNM. In Columns (1) and (4), we include the industry-level or regional-level control variables. While the size of industry demand and average wage are not significant, higher input prices significantly raise employment growth rates. For direct suppliers, the significantly negative coefficient for import prices is not consistent with our expectation. Although industries with a higher import penetration ratio have higher import price elasticity of labour demand, considering that the average import penetration is around 0.159, the average elasticity ($-0.017 = -0.057+0.267*0.159$) gets close to zero. As for indirect suppliers, while the coefficient of the import penetration ratio is not significant, that for interaction term of the import penetration and import price is positive. This implies that in industries with a higher import penetration ratio, a decline in import prices reduces the employment growth ratio. These results suggest that import competition significantly affects the employment growth ratio for small firms such as indirect suppliers or their matched controls. Although the coefficients of 'Treated' slightly differ from those in Table 13.8 both for the direct and indirect suppliers, there is a significant positive impact of being direct or indirect suppliers. These results do not change when we control industry or prefecture fixed effect as in Columns (2), (3), (5), and (6).

Table 13.10 includes the interaction term of 'Treated dummy' with several dummy variables. To focus on the differences among industries, Columns (2) and (5) include the interaction terms of industry dummies. However, the coefficient of interaction terms is not significant. Also, in Columns (3) and (6), we examine the interaction terms with the new MNEs dummy. However, the results show no significant differences of impact on employment growth between incumbent MNEs and new MNEs.

Table 13.9 Controlling Additional Variables: Industry and Regional Variables

	(1)	(2)	(3)	(4)	(5)	(6)
	Impact of Being the Direct Suppliers			*Impact of Being the Indirect Suppliers*		
Treated (DS or IDS)	0.022***	0.016***	0.017***	0.028***	0.032***	0.032***
	(0.004)	(0.004)	(0.004)	(0.005)	(0.006)	(0.006)
D. log (outputs)	0.001			0.004		
	(0.005)			(0.007)		
D. log (input price)	0.157***			0.102***		
	(0.024)			(0.034)		
D. log (wage)	-0.076	-0.013		-0.073	-0.017	
	(0.091)	(0.092)		(0.126)	(0.128)	
D. log (import price)	-0.057***			-0.046		
	(0.020)			(0.028)		
* Import penetration	0.267***			0.207**		
	(0.064)			(0.095)		
Observations	52,622	52,932	52,932	26,765	27,010	27,010
R-squared	0.002	0.027	0.031	0.002	0.036	0.041
Industry FE	No	Yes	Yes	No	Yes	Yes
Pref FE	No	No	Yes	No	No	Yes

Source: Authors' computation.
Notes: *, **, and *** indicate statistical significance at 10%, 5%, and 1%, respectively.

Table 13.10 Controlling Additional Variables: Differences in Industries and New MNEs

	(1)	(2)	(3)	(4)	(5)	(6)
	Impact of Being the Direct Suppliers			*Impact of Being the Indirect Suppliers*		
Treated (DS)	0.017***	0.033**	0.016***	0.032***	0.030***	0.033***
	(0.004)	(0.013)	(0.004)	(0.006)	(0.008)	(0.006)
Treated*CI-Material		0.006			-0.008	
		(0.006)			(0.021)	
Treated*CI-Machinery		0.013			0.007	
		(0.009)			(0.012)	
Treated*New FDI			0.001			-0.009
			(0.012)			(0.012)
Observations	52,932	52,932	52,932	27,010	27,010	27,01 0
R-squared	0.031	0.027	0.027	0.041	0.036	0.036
Industry FE	Yes	Yes	Yes	Yes	Yes	Yes
Pref FE	Yes	Yes	Yes	Yes	Yes	Yes

Source: Authors' computation.
Notes: Column (1) and (4) come from Column (3) and (6) in Table 13.9. *, **, and *** indicate statistical significance at 10%, 5%, and 1%, respectively.

13.5 Conclusion

The outward FDI of firms has induced anxiety about the hollowing out of domestic industries. Against this backdrop, many microdata studies have investigated the 'effects' of outward FDI and have shown non-negative effects on domestic performance in at least FDI firms. On the other hand, this chapter examined the effects on the performance of transaction partners of FDI firms, i.e., whether the non-negative effects in FDI firms spread to direct and indirect suppliers through supply chain linkages. Specifically, we first explored whether customers' FDI results in strengthening or suspending their transaction ties with domestic direct and indirect suppliers. Second, we examined how much the expansion of MNEs' overseas production affects the corporate performance of the MNEs' direct and indirect suppliers.

Our results can be summarised as follows. There is no evidence that customers' FDI is more likely to suspend their domestic transactions. Rather, the transaction ties of direct suppliers with MNEs are more persistent than those with other firms. Although such an effect becomes weak for transactions between direct and indirect suppliers, we did not find, at least, a negative effect. Furthermore, customers' FDI has a significant and positive impact on performance (i.e., employment growth) in both direct and indirect suppliers. In short, firms' investing abroad improves not only their performance but also that of their domestic direct and indirect transaction partners. These results lend strong support for policy to further encourage firms to invest abroad.

Notes

1 Our study differs from Furusawa et al. (2015) in the sense that we focus on the impact of the expansion of MNEs' overseas production. Besides, we also focus on the impact on the corporate performance of their suppliers.

2 Furthermore, in terms of examining the duration of transactions, our paper is related to the literature that has examined the mechanisms for the survival of international transactions (e.g., Besedes and Prusa, 2006a, 2006b; Nitsch, 2009; Obashi, 2010; Gorg et al., 2012; Esteve-Perez et al., 2013; Gullstrand and Persson, 2015). These studies find, for example, that international transactions will likely survive when they are related to exports by more productive firms, countries with larger GDPs, or geographically closer countries.

3 For example, although Toyota purchases parts and components from hundreds of suppliers, it can report only 24 suppliers. However, by looking at parts and components firms reporting Toyota as a primary customer, we can make up the list of Toyota's suppliers.

4 This means that we restrict our sample firms only to those that existed in both 2006 and 2011. Exiting rate of firms is around 3%.

5 We calculate the ratio of intermediate demand to total output by sector using the Input–Output table. Then we define sectors with the ratio greater than 75% as intermediate goods industries.

6 One may be interested in whether FDI to developing countries, such as East Asian countries, has a different impact or not. Among 1,778 incumbent MNEs, 1,673 firms have affiliates in East Asian countries. As for new MNEs, 119 out of 133 firms have invested in East Asia. Thus, our results are mostly driven by FDI towards East Asian countries.

7 'Labour-intensive' industry includes food, textile, wood, paper and paper products, non-metallic mineral products, and other manufacturing. 'Capital-intensive material' consists of chemical, oil, and coal products; and primary metal manufacturing industries. 'Capital-intensive machinery' comprises metal products, machinery, electric machinery, and transport equipment.

8 The TSR dataset captures new transaction ties from 2006 to 2011. The total number of transactions substantially increased from 3.6 million to 4.5 million, which is an unrealistically high growth rate. Furusawa et al. (2015) suggest that the potential reason for this increase might be measurement error. Therefore, they exclude firms that enter or exit during the sample period and use balanced panel dataset.

9 Summary statistics are presented in Table 13.A1.

References

Becker, S.O., and A. Ichino (2002), 'Estimation of Average Treatment Effects Based on Propensity Scores', *The Stata Journal* 2(4): 358–77.

Belderbos, R., and M. Carree (2002), 'The Location of Japanese Investments in China: Agglomeration Effects, Keiretsu, and Firm Heterogeneity', *Journal of the Japanese and International Economies* 16: 194–211.

Bernard, A.B., and B. Jensen (1999), 'Exceptional Exporter Performance: Cause, Effect, or Both?', *Journal of International Economics* 47: 1–25.

Bernard, A.B., A. Moxnes, and Y. Saito (2019), 'Production Network, Geography and Firm Performance', Journal of Political Economy, 127(2), 639–688.

Besedes, T., and T. Prusa (2006a), 'Ins, Outs, and the Duration of Trade', *Canadian Journal of Economics* 39(1): 266–95.

Besedes, T., and T. Prusa (2006b), 'Production Differentiation and Duration of US Import Trade', *Journal of International Economics* 70(2): 339–58.

Debaere, P., H. Lee, and J. Lee (2010), 'It Matters Where You Go: Outward Foreign Direct Investment and Multinational Employment Growth at Home', *Journal of Development Economics* 91(2): 301–309.

Esteve-Perez, S., F. Requena-Silvente, and V.J. Pallardo-Lopez (2013), 'The Duration of Firm-Destination Export Relationships: Evidence from Spain', 1997–2006, *Economic Inquiry* 51(1): 159–80.

Friedlander, D., D.H. Greenberg, and P.K. Robins (1997), 'Evaluating Government Training Programs for the Economically Disadvantaged', *Journal of Economic Literature* 35 (4):1809–55.

Furusawa, T., K. Ito, T. Inui, and H. Tan (2015), 'Offshoring, Relationship-Specificity, and Domestic Production Networks', *RIETI Discussion Paper* 15-E-122.

Gorg, H., R. Kneller, and B. Murakozy (2012), 'What Makes a Successful Export? Evidence from Firm-product-level Data', *Canadian Journal of Economics* 45(4): 1332–68.

Gullstrand, J., and M. Persson (2015), 'How to Combine High Sunk Costs of Exporting and Low Export Survival', *Review of World Economics* 151(1): 23–51.

Hayakawa, K., T. Matsuura, K. Motohashi, and A. Obashi (2013), 'Two-dimensional Analysis of the Impact of Outward FDI on Performance at Home: Evidence from Japanese Manufacturing Firms'. *Japan and the World Economy* 27: 25–33.

Head, K., J. Ries, and D. Swenson (1995), 'Agglomeration Benefits and Location Choice: Evidence from Japanese Manufacturing Investments in the United States', *Journal of International Economics* 38: 223–47.

Hijzen, A., S. Jean, and T. Mayer (2011), 'The Effects at Home of Initiating Production Abroad: Evidence from Matched French Firms', *Review of World Economics* 147(3): 457–83.

Ito, K., and A. Tanaka (2013), 'The Impact of Multinationals' Overseas Expansion on Employment at Suppliers at Home: New Evidence from Firm-level Transaction Relationship Data for Japan', *REITI Discussion Paper* 15-E-122.

Javorcik, B.S., and M. Spatareanu (2009), 'Tough Love: Do Czech Suppliers Learn from their Relationships with Multinationals?', *Scandinavian Journal of Economics* 111(4): 811–33.

Nakajima, K., and R. Ito (2014), 'Impact of Supply Chain Network Structure on FDI: Theory and Evidence', *RIETI Discussion Paper* 14-E-27.

Navaretti, B., Castellani, D., and Disdier, A.C. (2010), How Does Investing in Cheap Labor Countries Affect Performance at Home? France and Italy, *Oxford Economic Papers* 62(2): 234–60.

Nitsch, V. (2009) 'Die Another Day: Duration in German Import Trade', *Review of World Economics* 145(1): 133–54.

Obashi, A. (2010), 'Stability of Production Network in East Asia: Duration and Survival of Trade', *Japan and the World Economy* 22(1): 21–30.

Rosenbaum, P.R., and D.B. Rubin (1983), 'The Central Role of the Propensity Score in Observational Studies for Causal Effects', *Biometrika* 70 (1): 41–55.

Yamashita, N., T. Matsuura, and K. Nakajima (2014), 'Agglomeration Effects of Inter-firm Backward and Forward Linkages: Evidence from Japanese Manufacturing Investment in China', *Journal of the Japanese and International Economy* 34: 24–41.

Appendix

Table 13.A1 Summary Statistics for Probit Model

	N	*Mean*	*S.D.*	*p10*	*p90*
DS dummy	95945	0.330	0.470	0.000	1.000
log (employee)	95945	2.873	1.237	1.386	4.500
log $(\text{employee})^2$	95945	9.785	8.030	1.922	20.248
Multi-plant firm	95945	0.227	0.419	0.000	1.000
log (# of customers)	95945	0.994	0.431	0.445	1.546
log $(\#\text{ of customers})^2$	95945	1.174	1.039	0.198	2.389
Agglomeration	95945	3.262	1.379	1.386	4.970
Agglomeration of MNEs	95945	9.301	16.778	0.000	26.000
Stats	*N*	*Mean*	*S.D.*	*p10*	*p90*
IDS dummy	64251	0.274	0.446	0.000	1.000
log (employee)	64251	2.656	1.179	1.099	4.174
log $(\text{employee})^2$	64251	8.445	7.190	1.207	17.426
Multi-plant firm	64251	0.193	0.395	0.000	1.000
log (# of customers)	64251	0.929	0.420	0.423	1.472
log $(\#\text{ of customers})^2$	64251	1.039	0.984	0.179	2.168
Agglomeration	64251	3.244	1.370	1.386	4.970
Agglomeration of direct suppliers	64251	8.075	15.745	0.000	23.000

Source: Authors' computation.

14 The exchange rate and exporting

Evidence from the Indonesian manufacturing sector

Chandra Tri Putra and Dionisius Narjoko

14.1 Background

Factors affecting export performance, or export participation, have long been the attention of researchers, acknowledging the significance of exporting in advancing the industrialisation of countries. Not only does it provide foreign revenue for a country from the macro perspective but it also motivates productivity improvement and innovation at the micro/firm and industry levels. Discussion to date, however, has skewed toward addressing the supply-side factors of exporting. Little attention has been given to demand-side factors or macroeconomic variables that affect a country's export performance. This paper addresses this topic, examining the impact of the exchange rate on export performance using firm- and product-destination-level data for Indonesian manufacturing firms over the period 2008–2012.

The exchange rate is critical for exporting, essentially for two reasons. First, it affects the expected profitability of exported products and, hence, not only the overall export value of a firm but the distribution of the firm's exported product portfolio. In a recent study, Chatterjee et al. (2013) provided a model for this, focusing on the impact of the level of the exchange rate. Second, exchange rate volatility affects the risk valuation of exporting, which in turn may affect a firm's decision of whether or not to respond to export demand. While in general, the direction of the exchange rate level is clear, it is not so for volatility. More recent works suggest that it depends on several other factors, such as the availability of measures for hedging or the extent of credit constraints in the firm or industry.

The lack of empirical evidence on the impact of volatility is one motivation for this paper. Another motivation is to add evidence for the exploration of the impact of the exchange rate using micro-level data at the firm and product levels. This chapter examines the impact on performance to cover the value, scope, and choices of a firm's exported products. The investigation, therefore, covers not only the impact on the scale but also on the dynamics of exporting within firms.

This chapter is organised as follows. Section 14.2 briefly reviews the literature on the impact of the exchange rate on exports. Section 14.3 outlines the methodology, including some descriptions of the data and variables used. Section 14.4 presents and discusses the estimation results, and Section 14.5 is the conclusion.

14.2 Analytical Framework

The choice of export destination could be affected by the exchange rate between the destination and origin countries. This is despite US dollar-invoicing practices being typical in exporting activities because most exported products are, in the end, consumed or used for production inputs in an importing country and valued using the local currency. This study, therefore, considers the exchange rate between the origin and destination country, either its level or volatility, as one of the potential determinants of the export destination.

Chatterjee et al. (2013) developed a model to explain how a multiproduct firm adjusts the price, product scope, and distribution of sales across the products (or the product mix) amongst exported products of the firm. The model addresses the impact of the level of the exchange rate. It postulates that since a firm produces a number of exported products, an exchange rate devaluation will increase the price of products closer to the firm's core competence more than that of products far from it. The quantity impact follows, with a weaker impact on products closer to the firm's core competence and a stronger impact on products far from the firm's core competence.

Consistent with this, an exchange rate devaluation increases the scope of products being exported. Exchange rate depreciation increases the profitability of all goods produced by the exporter, and, because of this, products that initially were not chosen as exported products now become profitable for export and hence are inserted in the list of products eligible for export. Thus, the scope of exported products could be expanded in the event of an exchange rate devaluation.

An exchange rate devaluation provides an incentive for a firm/exporter to increase sales of products that are far from its core competence. This is because there is a varying impact on the price and quantity of the mix of products being exported. The model postulates that the price effect (i.e., increase in price) is concentrated in products closer to the firm's core competence, which means the quantity impact is minimal for these products. This is in contrast to products far away from the firm's core competence; the increase is the lowest and, therefore, the quantity impact is the highest for the group of exported products that are far from the firm's core competence. The distribution of exporting sales, therefore, is changed because of the exchange rate devaluation, becoming more skewed towards the non-core products.

As for the impact of exchange rate volatility on exporting, an earlier analytical framework predicts a negative relationship; that is, higher volatility reduces the extent of exporting. This comes directly through the higher uncertainty and additional costs faced by exporters, who are assumed to be risk-averse agents (e.g., Ethier 1973; Cote 1994).[1] In this framework, hedging is assumed either not possible or very costly.

Evidence on the impact of the volatility, however, is mixed. A survey by McKenzie (1999) concluded that the impact may depend on market specifics, while studies done by Greenaway and Kneller (2007) and Byrne et al. (2008) identified that the impact is either significant but very small or insignificant. The impact is also suggested to depend on the level of financial development in the country of export origin. An insignificant or small effect was found by Broda and Romalis (2011), who focused on examining the volatility in rich countries with developed financial markets. In contrast, a substantial negative effect was found by Grier and Smallwood (2007) in the case of developing countries.

The non-negative relationship between exchange rate volatility and export, explored by more recent theoretical and empirical works, is possible if exporters can protect themselves from the negative effect by swiftly adjusting to the sudden change in the exchange rate or by hedging (Chit et al. 2010). In other words, non-negativity is possible if there are factors that are able to mitigate the negative impact of volatility.

De Grouwe (1988) showed that the impact is ambiguous when q firm exports all of its output, depending on the net effect between the substitution and income effects arising as a response to the increase in volatility. The substitution effect decreases export activities to less risky ones, while the income effect will draw resources into the export sector when the expected utility of export revenues is reduced as a result of the higher exchange rate risk imposed by higher exchange rate volatility (Chit et al. 2010: 242). Thus, if the income effect is greater than the substitution effect, the (overall) impact of the volatility on exporting is positive.

Consistent with this is the model developed by Broll and Eckwert (1999), which demonstrates the flexibility to choose by a firm with a large domestic market. In the model, the firm can easily reallocate its share of sales between the domestic and foreign markets in an environment with a volatile exchange rate. Adding to the analysis on the ability to adjust, De Grauwe (1994) showed that a firm could actually benefit from exchange rate volatility if it could – presumably quickly – adjust output in response to the change in price.

Hedging becomes important in mitigating the negative effect of exchange rate volatility because it reduces the extent of uncertainty for the potential earnings of exporters. Room for hedging is provided by the size and maturity of the financial market in the country of export origin. Countries with well-developed financial markets – exposed to substantial numbers of measures for hedging – should allow exporters (in those countries) to hedge against the exchange rate risk, hence reducing the negative impact of the volatility on exporting (Hericourt and Poncet, 2013). While this mechanism seems to be straightforward, evidence of it has not really been established in the literature.[2]

The importance of financial markets in the analysis implies that the impact of the volatility may depend on whether firms/exporters are financially constrained. The argument for this hypothesis can be derived from another mechanism, relying more on the idea that exchange rate volatility may be another source of sunk costs for exporting (Greenaway and Kneller, 2007). Here, an exporter may invest more in exporting in the event of a real depreciation, using the gains from the depreciation; but once this investment is made, it cannot be recovered, making it irreversible. In this case, if the exporter is financially constrained, the risk exposed by the irreversibility, from the volatility, is higher and may cause it not to engage in exporting even if there are real opportunities. A well-developed financial market means the extent of the credit constraint faced by the exporter is relaxed, which means it is 'shielded' by the risk imposed by the irreversibility.

14.3 Methodology

14.3.1 Data

The data used for the estimations combine the annual data of medium and large establishments in the Indonesian manufacturing sector from the statistical agency (*Badan Pusat Statistik*, BPS) with firm-product-destination-year-level data of export transactions from Indonesian Customs. The merging of the two datasets is made possible using the unique firm ID available in both datasets. The period for the merged dataset is from 2008 to 2012.

The firm-level dataset has been used by many researchers since the 1990s and is known to be reliable. It covers firms with 20 or more employees and includes rich information at the firm level, including the value of shipments (both domestic and export shipments), ownership (foreign, domestic, and government) information, employment, and costs, etc. The survey asks about the sales destination of the firm (whether it sells to domestic or exporting markets, or both). The Customs data consists of the export value and volume from a specific firm in a specific product and to a specific destination. The product codes for the Customs data are in ten-digit HS 2012.

In addition, this study also uses several macroeconomic variables (GDP, GDP per capita, exchange rate, and tariff) from several sources. GDP, GDP per capita, and annual exchange rates are extracted from WDI World Bank. Meanwhile, the daily exchange rates used for volatility measurement come from IMF. Lastly, the tariff rates are extracted from the UNCTAD-TRAINS (accessed via WITS World Bank).

14.3.2 Empirical Models

This study conducts an econometric estimation testing of the impact of the variables representing the export destination market, defined above on export performance. Before doing so, it is important for the study to provide some insights on the impact from some descriptive statistics. The descriptive analysis is conducted by examining the distribution of the performance variables for major exporting countries and/or industries (by two- or three-digit ISIC classifications). The descriptive analysis tries to pick up whether there are some non-random patterns in the distribution. It also provides several basic facts about the average exporting performance of firms with a focus on the export destination.

The importance of the export destination market on export performance variables is estimated using the following general functional form, with *i, j, k, c,* and *t* denoting the firm, product, export destination, and time, respectively.

$$\ln\left(X_{ijct}\right) = f\left(RER10_{ict}, NERV_{ict}, \ln\left(GDP_{ict}\right), \ln\left(GDPPC_{ict}\right), tariff_{ikct}, \boldsymbol{Z}_{it}\right) \quad (1)$$

Both the subscript *j* and *k* denote the product, but they represent the product at different HS-code levels; that is, *j* represents it at the ten-digit level, while *k* represents it at the six-digit level. Equation (1) is estimated by a fixed-effect panel estimation method using several fixed effects, which are year fixed effects and the interaction of firm, product, and destination fixed effects.

X_{ijct} is defined as the export value of product j (in constant 2010 US dollars) sold by firm i to destination country c at time t.[3] $RER10_{ict}$ is the bilateral real exchange rate of country c (which is the export destination of firm i) with respect to Indonesia, indexed using 2010 as the base year in order to normalise the different value of the RER across countries.[4] Formally, it is

$$RER_{c,IDN} = \frac{NER_{c,IDN} CPI_{IDN}}{CPI_c} \quad (2)$$

where $NER_{c,IDN}$ is the nominal exchange rates of one Indonesian rupiah in the currency of country c. $\frac{CPI_{IDN}}{CPI_c}$ is the relative price between Indonesia and country c, proxied by the consumer price index (*CPI*). *RER*10 is the normalised index of *RER* using 2010 as the base year (*RER*10 = 100 in year 2010). Higher *RER*10 indicates real appreciation, while lower *RER*10 indicates real depreciation of rupiah against the currency of country c.

Meanwhile, $NERV_{ict}$ is a measure of exchange rate volatility for country c's currency against rupiah at time t which comes from the annual standard deviation of the daily exchange rate movements.

$$NERV_{c,IDN,t} = \sqrt{\frac{\sum_{d=1}^{D_{ct}} \left(\Delta\ln\left(NER_{c,IDN,d}\right) - \overline{\Delta\ln\left(NER_{c,IDN,d}\right)}\right)^2}{D_{ct} - 1}} \quad (3)$$

Where $\Delta\ln\left(NER_{c,IDN,d}\right) = \ln\left(NER_{c,IDN,d}\right) - \ln\left(NER_{c,IDN,d-1}\right)$. d represents the day of observation and D_{ct} is the number of days of observation for country c at year t. $\overline{\Delta\ln\left(NER_{c,IDN,d}\right)}$ denotes the average of $\Delta\ln\left(NER_{c,IDN,d}\right)$ at year t. With this construction, higher *NERV* means more volatile exchange rate, and *vice versa*.

Equation (1) includes GDP_{ict}, $GDPPC_{ict}$ (GDP per capita), and $tariff_{ikct}$ to control for market size, consumer tastes and preferences, and export barriers in the destination country c, respectively. GDP_{ict} is measured in its real value at the 2010 USD constant price, while $GDPPC_{ict}$ is measured by dividing GDP_{ict} by the mid-year population of country c. $tariff_{ikct}$ represents the tariff for product k sold by firm i to country c at time t. This study uses the simple average of effectively applied tariff rate in each six-digit of various versions of HS code (which is then concorded to HS 2012). The applied tariff rate is preferred instead of the MFN (Most Favoured Nation) because it tends to reflect the rate set by free trade agreements.

In addition, the equation also includes a set of control variables drawn from firm characteristics ($\boldsymbol{Z}_{it}$). Variables included in the set are size, age, labour productivity (in real terms), ownership (foreign and domestic), capital intensity, skill intensity, and imported input intensity. Capital intensity (*capine*) and skill intensity (*skill*) are calculated as the following.

$$capine_{it} = \frac{enexp_{it}}{WPI_{it}\, pw_{it}} \tag{4}$$

$$skill_{it} = \frac{nw_{it}}{size_{it}} \times 100 \tag{5}$$

The proxy for capital intensity is derived from the energy expenditures (*enexp*), including expenditure on fuel and electricity, divided by the wholesale price index (*WPI*) and number of production workers (*pw*). The argument for this proxy is that a more capital-intensive firm uses energy more intensively compared to the less capital-intensive firms. The proxy for skill intensity is derived from the share of non-production workers (*nw*) in the firm. This share is often used to represent the ratio of skilled against unskilled workers.

Equation (1) examines the importance of export destination factors using information derived from firm, product, and destination country variation. While indeed very useful, it may mask the importance of the 'gravity' theoretical argument for international trade, where the macroeconomic variables are the key variables derived by theory. This study thus re-estimates Equation (1) in the firm-country-year dimension, and for this, the data on exports and tariffs for each product are then aggregated to the country level.

$$\ln(X_{ict}) = f\left(RER10_{ict}, NERV_{ict}, \ln(GDP_{ict}), \ln(GDPPC_{ict}), tariff_{ict}, \boldsymbol{Z}_{it}\right) \tag{6}$$

Where $tariff_{ict}$ is derived from the simple average of $tariff_{ikct}$. To estimate Equation (6), we use year effects as well as the interaction of firm and destination country fixed effects.

As noted, this study is also interested in checking the impact of the exchange rate on the scope and concentration of exported products at the firm-destination-year level. This is done by replacing X_{ict} in (6) with product scope (NJ_{ict}) and product concentration (HHI_{ict}). Product scope is measured by counting the total number of products exported to each country destination c by firm i at time t. This is similar for the product concentration, which measures the concentration of a product portfolio (a basket of products) exported to each country destination c by firm i. This study uses the Herfindahl index to measure the product concentration.

14.4 Estimation Results

Tables 14.1 and 14.2 present the results of the estimations of Equations (1) and (6), respectively.[5] The results reported in the table are based on fixed-effect panel-data estimations using interactive fixed effects, that is, the interaction between firm, product, and destination country fixed effects for Equation (1), and the interaction between firm and destination country fixed effects for Equation (6). In addition to the interactive fixed effects, estimations for each of the equations include year fixed effects in them to control for overtime changes within the period of the observations. The estimations use robust standard errors to correct for potential heteroscedasticity.

The experiment finds a quite high collinearity between $\ln(GDP)$ and $\ln(GDPPC)$. Therefore, it introduces these two variables separately. The

Table 14.1 Determinants of Export Value (firm-product-country-year dimension)

Variables	*Dependent variable: $ln(X_{ijct})$*					
	(1)	*(2)*	*(3)*	*(4)*	*(5)*	*(6)*
$\ln(GDP_{ict})$	0.832***	0.739***	0.555***			
	(0.142)	(0.162)	(0.173)			
$\ln(GDPPC_{ict})$				0.985***	0.923***	0.771***
				(0.148)	(0.167)	(0.175)
$RER10_{ict}$	-1.39e-05		-0.00372***	-1.57e-05		-0.00360***
	(1.46e-05)		(0.00123)	(1.47e-05)		(0.00120)
$NERV_{ict}$		-19.92***	-17.09***		-18.85***	-16.19***
		(5.169)	(5.220)		(5.171)	(5.221)
$tariff_{ikct}$	-0.00513***	-0.00399**	-0.00360*	-0.00487***	-0.00374**	-0.00340*
	(0.00185)	(0.00188)	(0.00189)	(0.00184)	(0.00188)	(0.00188)
Year-effects	Yes	Yes	Yes	Yes	Yes	Yes
FE: firm × product × destination country	Yes	Yes	Yes	Yes	Yes	Yes
Firm-level controls	Yes	Yes	Yes	Yes	Yes	Yes
Observations	109,411	94,054	93,965	109,411	94,054	93,965
R-squared	0.854	0.854	0.854	0.854	0.854	0.854
Adj. R2	0.783	0.784	0.784	0.783	0.784	0.784

Source: Authors' calculation.

Note: Robust standard errors in parentheses, *** $p < 0.01$, ** $p < 0.05$, *<0.1.

Firm-level control: In *capine* (capital intensity, measured by energy intensity), In (*RLP*) (labour productivity), In (*size*) (number of labour), *Owndom* (private–domestic share of ownership), *ownf* (foreign share of ownership), skill (skill intensity), *impin* (import intensity), and In (*age*) (relative age, since 2000).

experiment finds that *RER*10 statistically performs better if it is specified to enter the equation together with *NERV*, although *NERV* is actually a more robust and consistent variable than *RER*10 if it enters the equations separately.

Consider first the results reported in Table 14.1 [for Equation (1)]. The exchange rate is found to affect export values. The estimated parameters of both real exchange rate and exchange rate volatility are negative and statistically significant. The importance of the exchange rate, however, does not depend merely on the level, but needs to come together with the (over time) variation of the exchange rate volatility. As shown, the parameter of *RER*10 is only significant when the variable enters the equation jointly with *NERV*; in most cases, the parameter of *RER*10 is not statistically significant if it enters separately.

Thus, consistent with the experience of other countries using similar methods (e.g., Chatterjee et al. 2013), a real depreciation of rupiah (against a destination's currency) leads to an increase in the sales of exported products. This finding indicates that a real exchange rate depreciation of rupiah, in general, lowers the price and further increases the demand of goods exported by Indonesian exporters.

As predicted, volatility also matters. In fact, the results suggest that it is more important than the level; that is, when these two variables enter separately, only the parameter of *NERV* is statistically significant, while the parameter of *RER*10 is not. Thus, for Indonesian manufacturing, the more volatile the exchange rate, the lower the value of the exports. This is similar to the other findings from developing countries, as reviewed earlier.

Analytically, the result reflects two potential situations: (i) there are not many opportunities or mechanisms for hedging that the exporters can use; and (ii) the exporters are financially constrained. All of these are signals of a not fully developed financial market. Similar to other developing countries, the financial markets in Indonesia indeed are not yet at an advanced state; they are still developing. The findings, therefore, provide support to the theory of hedging as an important mechanism for mitigating the negative impact of exchange rate volatility on exports. As for the extent of financial constraint, the study needs to explore the data for this.

It is worth commenting here on the results of the control variables that represent the other market destination factors. Market size in the export destination country is an important determinant. Estimated parameters of GDP are positive and highly statistically significant across all specifications. Not only size, but the tastes and preferences of consumers in the destination country also matter. Estimated parameter of GDP per capita are positive and also highly statistically significant in all specifications. This implies that a higher income level in the destination country leads to a higher value of exports going to that country, suggesting the possibility of higher demand for more sophisticated, or more differentiated, products from consumers in the country.

Tariffs are suggested to reduce the value of exports, accord to the theoretical prediction. The estimated parameters of tariff are all negative. The impacts of tariffs, however, are not strong in affecting the extent of exporting. Some of the estimates are not statistically significant, and when they are, the significance level is marginal only at the 5% to 10% levels.

The discussion above refers to the estimations using data with firm-product-country-year dimension. Let us now turn to the estimation results using the data with firm-country-year dimension and only the interaction of the firm and destination as the fixed effects (Table 14.2). As explained, estimation using the aggregated data dimension is necessary in order to underline the importance of the 'gravity' theoretical argument for international trade, where macroeconomic variables play a key role derived by theory.

The finding for the relationship between the exchange rate and the export value is the same. In fact, it is stronger based on the aggregated data. Compared with the earlier results, the statistical significance of *NERV* parameter substantially improves to become significant at the 1% level in all specifications, including when the variable enters the equation together with *RER*10. Moreover, the magnitude is significantly greater for this variable now. All this suggests there is some important heterogeneity in the impact of the volatility originating from product heterogeneity. In other words, not all products are sensitive to the exchange rate risk. This is important information for policymakers, suggesting they could bear more risk in investing to support the export of some particular products.

The findings on the other variables are also the same. The estimated parameters of GDP and GDP per capita are positive and statistically significant. As for the tariff variable, all estimates exhibit positive signs, which does not agree with the theoretical prediction. This could be because there is not enough variation within the data period used by this study. Thus, the negative relationship on tariffs seems to have only been produced by the specifications with the more detailed/disaggregated data, i.e., with dimension (i, j, c, t) and with interactive firm-product-country fixed effects.

Table 14.3 presents the results of the estimation of Equation (6) with product scope as the dependent variable.[6] The results reported in the table are based on fixed-effect panel-data estimations using the interactive firm and destination country fixed effects. The estimations include year fixed effects in order to control for overtime changes within the data period. The estimations use robust standard errors to correct for potential heteroscedasticity.

Exchange rate volatility seems to matter more than the exchange rate level for the product scope model. Estimated parameters of *RER*10 are often insignificant, even when it is introduced separately as in the previous equation. Meanwhile, estimated parameters of the exchange rate volatility (*NERV*) are robust; they are negative and statistically significant at the 1% confidence level in all experimented specifications. The findings suggest that exporters in the Indonesian manufacturing sector tend to reduce their exported-product scope if there is high uncertainty in the movement of the exchange rate. In other words, the risk imposed by the exchange rate forces exporters to specialise.

It is worth mentioning here that higher GDP per capita tends to increase product scope, as suggested by the positive sign for the estimated parameter of

Table 14.2 Determinants of Export Value (firm-country-year dimension)

Variables	*Dependent variable: ln* (X_{ict})					
	(1)	*(2)*	*(3)*	*(4)*	*(5)*	*(6)*
$\ln(GDP_{ict})$	1.141*** (0.156)	1.031*** (0.178)	0.812*** (0.191)			
$\ln(GDPPC_{ict})$				1.457*** (0.162)	1.338*** (0.184)	1.166*** (0.193)
$RER10_{ict}$	3.67e-06 (1.19e-05)		−0.00442*** (0.00138)	−3.76e-08 (1.19e-05)		−0.00413*** (0.00134)
$NERV_{ict}$		−25.16*** (5.460)	−22.09*** (5.518)		−23.66*** (5.455)	−20.80*** (5.509)
$tariff_{ict}$	0.00151 (0.00183)	0.00227 (0.00182)	0.00251 (0.00182)	0.00174 (0.00181)	0.00247 (0.00181)	0.00267 (0.00181)
Year-effects	Yes	Yes	Yes	Yes	Yes	Yes
FE: firm × destination country	Yes	Yes	Yes	Yes	Yes	Yes
Firm-level control	Yes	Yes	Yes	Yes	Yes	Yes
Observations	59,087	48.785	48.734	59.087	48.785	48.734
R-squared	0.839	0.840	0.841	0.840	0.841	0.841
Adj. R2	0.775	0.778	0.778	0.775	0.778	0.778

Source: Authors' calculation.
Note: Robust standard errors in parentheses, *** p<0.01, ** p<0.05, *<0.1.
Firm-level control: ln(*capine*) (capital intensity, measured by energy intensity), ln(*RLP*) (labour productivity), ln(*size*) (number of labour), *owndom* (private–domestic share of ownership), *ownf* (foreign share of ownership), *skill* (skill intensity), *impin* (import intensity), and ln(*age*) (relative age, since 2000).

Table 14.3 Determinants of Exported Product Scope (firm-country-year dimension)

Variables	*Dependent variable:* $\ln(NJ_{ict})$					
	(1)	*(2)*	*(3)*	*(4)*	*(5)*	*(6)*
$\ln(GDP_{ict})$	0.0321 (0.0515)	0.0265 (0.0585)	0.0196 (0.0635)			
$\ln(GDPPC_{ict})$				0.125** (0.0530)	0.113** (0.0601)	0.0848 (0.0632)
$RER10_{ict}$	4.91e-06 (7.94e-06)		−0.000856* (0.000500)	4.07e-06 (7.94e-06)		−0.000582 (0.000484)
$NERV_{ict}$		−4.263** (1.801)	−3.809** (1.816)		−3.999** (1.802)	−3.734** (1.818)
$tariff_{ict}$	−0.000267 (0.000573)	−0.000409 (0.000585)	−0.000359 (0.000585)	−0.000237 (0.000574)	−0.000392 (0.000586)	0.000361 (0.000586)
Year-effects	Yes	Yes	Yes	Yes	Yes	Yes
FE: firm × destination country	Yes	Yes	Yes	Yes	Yes	Yes
Firm-level control	Yes	Yes	Yes	Yes	Yes	Yes
Observations	59.087	48.785	48.734	59.087	48.785	48.734
R-squared	0.801	0.802	0.803	0.801	0.802	0.803
Adj. R2	0.722	0.725	0.725	0.725	0.725	0.725

Source: Authors' calculation.
Note: Robust standard errors in parentheses, *** $p < 0.01$, ** $p < 0.05$, *<0.1.
Firm-level control: ln(*capine*) (capital intensity, measured by energy intensity), ln(*RLP*) (labour productivity), ln(*size*) (number of labour), *owndom* (private–domestic share of ownership), *ownf* (foreign share of ownership), *skill* (skill intensity), *impin* (import intensity), and ln(*age*) (relative age, since 2000).

ln ($GDPPC$), although the impact is suggested to be only moderate. Product scope thus increases with higher levels of development, reflecting more complex or sophisticated demand for products in more developed countries.

Table 14.4 presents the results of the estimation of Equation (6) with product concentration as the dependent variable. The results reported in the table are based on fixed-effect panel-data estimations using the interactive firm and destination country fixed effects. The estimations include year fixed effects in order to control for over time changes within the data period. The estimations use robust standard errors to correct for potential heteroscedasticity.

The impact of the exchange rate on product concentration within a firm (exporter) is not very clear as the estimated parameters of the exchange rate variables are not stable. The estimated parameters of $RER10$ are generally statistically very significant and positive, but this is not always the case across the experimented specifications, while the estimated parameters of $NERV$ are not significant. Nevertheless, taking the statistically significant results as an indication of the likely impact, the real exchange rate is suggested to be positively related to product concentration within exporters in Indonesian manufacturing during the period of analysis. Thus, a real appreciation

Table 14.4 Determinants of the Exported Product Concentration (firm-country-year dimension)

Variables	*Dependent variable: HHI_{ict}*					
	(1)	*(2)*	*(3)*	*(4)*	*(5)*	*(6)*
$\ln(GDP_{ict})$	0.0714 (0.0501)	0.0746 (0.0554)	0.0618 (0.0599)			
$\ln(GDPPC_{ict})$				0.0213 (0.0530)	0.0292 (0.0578)	0.0111 (0.0610)
$RER10_{ict}$	4.61e-06*** (9.69e-07)		-0.000263 (0.000442)	4.67e-06*** (9.91e-06)		-0.000418 (0.000432)
$NERV_{ict}$		1.192 (2.599)	2.204 (2.639)		2.071 (2.584)	2.478* (2.617)
$tariff_{ict}$	0.000479 (0.000396)	0.000598 (0.000405)	0.000623 (0.000406)	0.000469 (0.000395)	0.000591 (0.000404)	0.000629 (0.000406)
Year-effects	Yes	Yes	Yes	Yes	Yes	Yes
FE: firm x destination country	Yes	Yes	Yes	Yes	Yes	Yes
Firm-level control	Yes	Yes	Yes	Yes	Yes	Yes
Limited sample	$NJ \geq 4$	$NJ \geq 4$	$NJ \geq 4$	$NJ \geq 4$	$NJ \geq 4$	$NJ \geq 4$
Observations	9.403	8.227	8.220	9.403	8.227	8.220
R-squared	0.733	0.737	0.737	0.733	0.737	0.737
Adj. R2	0.616	0.622	0.622	0.616	0.622	0.622

Source: Authors' calculation.

Note: Robust standard errors in parentheses, *** p<0.01, ** p<0.05, *<0.1.

Firm-level control: ln (***capine***) (capital intensity, measured by energy intensity), ln (RLP) (labour productivity) ln (***size***) (number of labour), ***owndom*** (private–domestic share of ownership), ***ownf*** (foreign share of ownership), ***skil*** (skill intensity), ***impin*** (import intensity), and ln (***age***) (relative age, since 2000).

of rupiah against the trading partner's currency encourages exporters to specialise – to concentrate on the export of a few products, presumably the exporters' core-competence.

The result confirms the theoretical prediction, such as that proposed by Chatterjee et al. (2013) for the impact on the level. In this model, an exchange rate depreciation provides an incentive for the firm/exporter to increase the sales of products far from the firm's core competence. Mayer et al. (2014) developed a model of multiproduct firms that highlights how the differences in the market size and geographical features of the export destination affect the within-firm distribution of export sales across destinations (or the exporting product mix). The effect is driven by the extent of competition in the destination market. Tougher competition in the destination market reduces the extent of mark-up across products in a firm's exported product mix and induces the firm to skew its sales towards its best-performing products, which are its core competence products. The model, thus, predicts that the sales of products closer to the firm's core competence increase if there is an increase in the extent of product competition in the export destination market, where one of the sources of tougher competition may come from the real appreciation of the exporters' currency as indicated by the results here.

14.5 Summary and Policy Implications

This chapter examined the impact of the exchange rate on export performance using firm- and product-destination-level data for the Indonesian manufacturing sector over the period 2008–2012. It addressed both the impact of the level and volatility of the exchange rate. The impact of the latter, especially using micro-level data, has been very small in the literature, and this study, therefore, enriches the literature with more evidence on the role of the exchange rate in exporting. The study considers the impact on the value, scope, and composition of exported products. The level of exchange rate affects exporting because it changes the expected profitability of the exported products, while the volatility of the exchange rate is expected to affect exporting through its role in changing the valuation of the risk from exporting.

The estimations suggest that the exchange rate affects the export value for the exports of the Indonesian manufacturing sector over the period of analysis. The results confirm that both the exchange rate level and volatility affect exporting. Thus, a depreciation of the exchange rate leads to an increase in the value of exported products. This shows that exchange rate depreciation lowers the price of goods exported by Indonesian exporters, which fits with the model developed by Chatterjee et al. (2013) and is similar with the findings from the Brazilian manufacturing sector.

The impact of exchange rate volatility is suggested to be as important as the level of the exchange rate. Thus, for Indonesian manufacturing, the more volatile the exchange rate, the lower the value of the exports. This is also similar to other findings from developing countries as reviewed earlier.

The finding on exchange rate volatility reflects two potential situations: (i) there are not many opportunities or mechanisms for hedging that the exporters can use; or (ii) exporters are financially constrained. All of these are signals of an underdeveloped financial market. Similar to other developing countries, financial markets in Indonesia indeed are not yet at an advanced stage; they are still developing. The findings, therefore, provide support to the theory of hedging as an important mechanism for mitigating the negative impact of exchange rate volatility on exporting. A further study is needed to explore whether there is a heterogeneity in the capability of firms, especially based on the firm-specific financial constraints, in dealing with the exchange rate volatility.

As for the impact on product scope, exchange rate volatility seems to matter more than the level. The estimated parameters of the exchange rate level are often are not statistically significant, although the sign when it is significant is as predicted, while the exchange rate volatility is negatively related to product scope and is robust. The finding suggests that exporters in the Indonesian manufacturing sector tend to reduce their exported-product scope if there is high uncertainty in the movement of the exchange rate. In other words, the risk imposed by the exchange rate forces the exporters to specialise.

The impact of the exchange rate on product concentration within a firm (exporter) is not very clear, as the estimates of exchange rate variables are not stable. Nevertheless, the results seem to suggest that the real appreciation of the exporters' currency is positively related to product concentration within exporters in the Indonesian manufacturing sector during the period of analysis.

The real appreciation of the exchange rate thus encourages exporters to specialise; to concentrate on exporting only a few products, presumably their core-competence products. This confirms the theory, especially for the impact on the level (e.g., Chatterjee et al. 2013), as well as another theoretical model (e.g., Mayer et al. 2014) that underlines the importance of product competition in the export market as another factor affecting exported product scope and concentration. That is, tougher competition in a destination market reduces the extent of mark-up across products in a firm's exported product mix and induces the firm to skew its sales toward its best-performing products, which are the firms' core-competence products. The prediction of this model is in line with the one suggested by Chatterjee et al, considering that real appreciation of the exporters' currency may create a tougher competition for these exporters in the destination market.

The findings from this study are useful for policymakers. The most useful perhaps is an understanding that it is not only the level (of the exchange rate) that matters, but also the volatility of it. To date, in many developing countries, policymakers – including central bankers – believe that only the level of the exchange rate matters, which typically results in either maintaining some constant low-level of depreciation over time or keeping the exchange rate at relatively the same level if there is a high pressure for appreciation. This study finds that volatility matters, and it suggests that the impact could even be more important than the level. The impact of the volatility could be quite serious if it is not handled properly; a very volatile exchange rate without a sufficient hedging mechanism could result not only in a decline in exporting but also in unrealised new exports – either to new export destinations or of new exported products. Thus, managing the fluctuation of the exchange rate deserves at least the same attention from policymakers as its level.

Second, the government may use the information about the relationship between the exchange rate and exported product scope or composition should it want to pursue an objective regarding exporting. For example, for Indonesia, based on the results of this study, the government should aim for low exchange rate volatility if it wishes to broaden (diversify) the types of exported products – this is because high volatility encourages firms to specialise their exported products. Third, the finding of a negative impact of exchange rate volatility suggests that it is important for the Indonesian government to develop its financial market. As theory suggests, this will increase the availability of hedging mechanisms that are able to dampen the negative impact of the volatility.

Notes

1 See, for example, Clark (1973), Hooper and Kohlagen (1978), and Kawai and Zilcha (1986) for the other models within this framework.

2 While, again, evidence on this is scarce, macroeconomic literature provides hints to support this hypothesis. Aghion et al. (2009) showed that the negative impact of real exchange rate (RER) volatility (on productivity) decreases with the level of development in the financial market in a country. Benhima (2012) showed that the RER is more detrimental in countries with a high share of foreign currency in their national debt, using data from 76 emerging countries over the period 1995–2004. Benhima's study is more direct in suggesting the importance of credit constraints.

3 We deflated the export value using the US import price index accessed from US Bureau of Labor Statistics. https://www.bls.gov/data/ (accessed 2 November 2020).

4 This is as postulated by Mayer et al. (2014).

5 The basic statistics of the data used for these estimations are provided in Appendix Table 14.A1.

6 The basic statistics for the data used for the estimation of Equations (2) and (3) are provided in Appendix Table 14.A2.

References

Aghion, P., P. Bacchetta, R. Rancière, and K. Rogoff (2009), 'Exchange Rate Volatility and Productivity Growth: The Role of Financial Development', *Journal of Monetary Economics*, 56(4), pp. 494–513.

Benhima, K., (2012), 'Exchange Rate Volatility and Productivity Growth: The Role of Liability Dollarization', *Open Economies Review*, 23(3), pp. 501–29.

Broda, C. and J. Romalis (2011), 'Identifying the Relationship between Trade and Exchange Rate Volatility', in T. Ito and A.K. Rose (eds.), *Commodity Prices and Markets, East Asia Seminar on Economics 20*. Chicago, IL: University of Chicago Press, pp. 79–110.

Broll, U. and B. Eckwert (1999), 'Exchange Rate Volatility and International Trade', *Southern Economic Journal*, 66(1), pp. 178–85.

Byrne, J.P, N. Fiess, and R. MacDonald (2008), 'US Trade and Exchange Rate Volatility: A Real Sectoral Analysis', *Journal of Macroeconomics*, 30(1), pp. 238–59.

Chatterjee, A., R. Dix-Carneiro, and J. Vichyanond (2013), 'Multi-product Firms and Exchange Rate Fluctuations', *American Economic Journal*, 5(2), pp. 77–110.

Chit, M.M., M. Rizov, and D. Willenbockel (2010), 'Exchange Rate Volatility and Exports: New Empirical Evidence from the Emerging East Asian Economies', *The World Economy*, 33(2), pp. 239–63.

Clark, P.B. (1973), 'Uncertainty, Exchange Risk, and the Level of International Trade', *Economic Inquiry*, 11(3), pp. 302–13.

Cote, A. (1994), 'Exchange Rate Volatility and Trade', Bank of Canada Working Paper, No. 94–95, Ottawa: Bank of Canada.

De Grauwe, P. (1988), 'Exchange Rate Volatility and the Slowdown in Growth of International Trade' *IMF Staff Papers*, 35(1), pp. 63–84.

De Grauwe, P. (1994), *The Economics of Monetary Integration*. New York, NY: Oxford University Press.

Ethier, W. (1973), 'International Trade and the Forward Exchange Rate Market', *American Economic Review*, 63(3), pp. 494–503.

Greenaway, D. and R.A. Kneller (2007), 'Firm Heterogeneity, Exporting and Foreign Direct Investment', *Economic Journal*, 117(517), pp. 134–361.

Grier, K.B. and A.D. Smallwood (2007), 'Uncertainty and Export Performance: Evidence from 18 Countries', *Journal of Money, Credit and Banking*, 39(4), pp. 965–79.

Hericourt, J. and S. Poncet (2013), 'Exchange Rate Volatility, Financial Constraints, and Trade: Empirical Evidence from Chinese Firms', *The World Bank Economic Review*, 29(3), pp. 550–78.

Hooper, P. and S.W. Kohlhagen (1978), 'The Effect of Exchange Rate Uncertainty on the Prices and Volume of International Trade', *Journal of International Economics*, 8(4), pp. 483–511.

Kawai, M. and I. Zilcha (1986), 'International Trade with Forward-Futures Markets under Exchange Rate and Price Uncertainty', *Journal of International Economics* 20(1–2), pp. 83–98.

Mayer, T., M.J. Melitz, and G.I. Ottaviano (2014), 'Market Size, Competition, and the Product Mix of Exporters', *American Economic Review*, 104(2), pp. 495–536.

McKenzie, M.D. (1999), 'The Impact of Exchange Rate Volatility on International Trade Flow', *Journal of Economic Surveys*, 13(1), pp. 71–106.

Appendix

Table 14.A1 Summary Statistics for the Export Database [for the Estimation of Equation (1)]

Variable	*Description*	*Unit*	*Obs*	*Mean*	*Std. Dev.*	*Min*	*Max*
X	Export	Constant 2010 US$	209,632	578,671	4,323,316	0.749	4.50E+08
GDP	GDP	Constant 2010 US$	207,691	2.46E+12	4.02E+12	3.18E+07	1.55E+13
GDPPC	GDP per capita	Constant 2010 US$	207,691	27,966	19,597	230	144,246
*RER*10	Real exchange rate (LCU/ IDR)	2010=100	204,842	103.07	292.17	57.81	11,352
NERV	Exchange rate volatility (LCU/IDR)		166,512	0.00853	0.00484	0.00304	0.03162
tariff	Effectively applied tariff	%	173,212	6.04	10.43	0	760
size	Number of workers	Persons	209,635	1,714	4,338	20	32,977
owndom	Private domestic ownership	%	209,628	59.54	46.75	0	100
ownf	Foreign ownership	%	209,635	39.35	46.48	0	100
skill	Skill intensity	%	209,635	17.78	16.60	0	96.0145
impin	Import intensity	%	202,869	31.21	36.97	0	100
age	Firm relative age since 2000	Years	209,635	9.19	3.21	1	13
capine	Capital intensity (energy based)	Constant 2000 thou. IDR	208,305	14,502	151,774	0	1.53E+07
RLP	Labour productivity (output)	Constant 2000 thou. IDR	208,305	317,716	1,647,133	28	1.94E+08

Source: Author's calculation.

Table 14.A2. Summary Statistics for the Product-Scope Database [for the Estimation of Equation (2)]

Variable	*Description*	*Unit*	*Obs*	*Mean*	*Std. Dev.*	*Min*	*Max*
X	Export	Constant 2010 US$	86,270	1,406,142	8,594,857	0.900	5.59E+08
NJ	Number of products (10-digit HS 2012)	Products	86,270	2.43	4.00	1	218
HHI	Product concentration	Index (0,1]	86,270	0.839	0.239	0.060	1
GDP	GDP	Constant 2010 US$	85,314	1.83E+12	3.36E+12	3.18E+07	1.55E+13
GDPPC	GDP per capita	Constant 2010 US$	85,314	25,223	19,737	230	144,246
*RER*10	Real exchange rate (LCU/IDR)	2010=100	83,981	105.58	340.79	57.81	11,352
NERV	Exchange rate volatility (LCU/IDR)		64,474	0.00878	0.00498	0.00304	0.03162
tariff	Effectively applied tariff	%	72,238	5.98	10.89	0	747
size	Number of workers	Persons	86,270	1,070	2,579	20	32,977
owndom	Private domestic ownership	%	86,266	65.40	45.30	0	100
ownf	Foreign ownership	%	86,270	33.30	44.81	0	100
skill	Skill intensity	%	86,270	18.10	16.07	0	96.0145
impin	Import intensity	%	84,213	28.13	35.81	0	100
age	Firm relative age since 2000	Years	86,270	9.15	3.20	1	13
capine	Capital intensity (energy based)	Constant 2000 thou. IDR	85,937	14,915	150,839	0	1.53E+07
RLP	Labour productivity (output)	Constant 2000 thou. IDR	85,937	308,412	1,907,097	28	1.94E+08

Source: Author's calculation.

Index

Note: **Bold** page numbers refer to tables; *italic* page numbers refer to figures and page numbers followed by "n" denote endnotes.